Living on the Edge of the Edge

Letters to a Younger Colleague

Ruth Elizabeth Krall, MSN, Ph.D.

with Lisa Schirch, Ph.D.

FriesenPress

Suite 300 - 990 Fort St
Victoria, BC, V8V 3K2
Canada

www.friesenpress.com

1. Receiving the Gift is written and printed with permission by Dr. Lisa Schirch.

2. Johari Window Diagram Source from The Career Life Institute: https://encrypted-tbn2.gstatic.com/images?q=tbn:ANd9GcSUvstK1tei3dsITlqCLl4P7UZECJakMADVKnWr9P-jQeoGZoC98Q

3. To the Next Generation of Pacifist Theologians is reprinted with the permission of WIPF/Stock and is from and edited collection of articles in the book John Howard Yoder: Radical Theologian (2014) edited by J. Denny Weaver and Earl Zimmerman

4. Toward Mennonite Sexual Integrity is reprinted with the permission of the editor, Paul Schrag, from the Mennonite World Review - from the Mennonite World Review. May 25, 2015.

Appreciation is expressed to Father Thomas P. Doyle, OP
for his willingness to comment upon several of these letters.

ISBN
978-1-5255-0060-2 (Hardcover)
978-1-5255-0061-9 (Paperback)
978-1-5255-0062-6 (eBook)

1. RELIGION, CHRISTIAN THEOLOGY, ETHICS

Distributed to the trade by The Ingram Book Company

These essays include bibliographic references.

- Richard Baker Roshi
- Thomas P. Doyle, OP, JCD, CADC
- Mary Gale Frawley-O'Dea, Ph.D.
- Natalie Goldberg
- Philip Hallie, Ph.D.
- Judith Lewis Herman, M.D.
- Mark D. Jordan, Ph.D.
- Dainin Katagiri Roshi
- William D. Lindsey, Ph.D.
- Robin Meyers, Ph.D.
- Emmett E. Miller, M.D.
- Mark Nepo, Ph.D.
- Henri Nouwen
- Lisa Schirch, Ph.D.
- Bessel van der Kolk, M. D.
- Elie Wiesel
- John Howard Yoder, D. Theol.
- The Johari Window

For information about Dr. Schirch, see
http://www.emu.edu/personnel/people/show/schirchl

For information about Dr. Krall, see
http://www.goshen.edu/news/pressarchive/08-16-04-krall-retires.html

I wish I had had this book in 1979, when I was shunned and shamed by a peace and justice professor because I asked the wrong questions and questioned his methods. It did however demonstrate power, which this collection of letters has helped me to understand at a much deeper level. Again in 1992 when I was working on the documentary about sexual abuse n the church, Ruth's counsel for those involved in walking alongside trauma would have helped, when I came home almost every evening and cried. I was a white man (and continue to be) and I had to choose where I fit in this story. Five years later it would have encouraged me to care for myself as I experienced trauma again as I sat with the stories I was listening to, honoring, and fashioning into forms that fostered larger audiences to be challenged by their assumptions about murder, loss, capital punishment and forgiveness.

I am grateful that I did have Ruth Krall's other writing to accompany me through the project where I tried to visualize the ways the church leaders and theologians failed John Howard Yoder and the depths of what his violence did to generations of women. I appreciate how these letters continue to point out the incongruity of the witness for peace and the violence to women and the risks inherent in a word based theology. Ruth teaches us by revealing her thought life and how she has come to understand the complex issues of power, patriarchy and sexual violence. Like any masterful teacher and mentor she opens up the questions and offers amazing insight, but doesn't close the door as if everything is finished. She invites us to make our own journey, to see our own place in the world and to not take the culturally suggested path. She adds to the complexity by noting how the issues fit together and that we can't just consider one like racism, without noting the connection to sexism, without noting our churches phobia about yet another issue like homosexuality and our own positions of power. (Ruth reminds me of my twelve year old self who asked my mother why there weren't any women pastors in our church when so many of the stories I read in Martyr's Mirror were women. That has never been answered satisfactorily for me.) Ruth also raises the sticky question of when telling/retelling of stories may actually encourage, which is a caution to all of us who shape and tell stories with our art.

This book is one I will share with my students, as I encourage them to speak with their own voice, to be hospitable to those who are not like themselves, to listen carefully, to create collaboratively and to embrace the mystery. This truth-telling collection is challenging, inspiring and healing. Thanks for sharing your voice with the larger community of learners.

Jerry Holsopple, Ph.D. Professor of Visual and Communication Arts, Eastern Mennonite University. Producer of *Beyond the News: Sexual Abuse in 1993.* Author, *7X7 Laments: For an Age of Sexualized Power* (Images by Jerry Holsopple).

Living on the Edge of the Edge is the writing of a faithful follower of the "gospel of peace." Ruth Krall amazes us with honesty in addressing the tragedy of our churches that do violence to persons in the name of peace-making. While primarily addressing her own Anabaptist-Mennonite heritage, her wisdom is for all thoughtful Christians. How is it that Christianity in so many forms shuns the LGBTQ community and yet lets clergy be quietly censured (if at all) for sexual abuse? How is it that families regularly tolerate abusive home situations, yet exclude others who wish to follow Christ from their churches, even their own children? With brilliant scholarship and unflagging clarity, Ruth Krall challenges us all to take the most difficult path of all: continuously examining our own hearts for unacknowledged prejudices, fears, and resistances to the increase of God's commandment of love.

I am reminded of Teresa of Avila's *Vida* (*Life*), her autobiography but also guide book for prayer. Ruth Krall shares much of her life, but also provides a guide book for discussions of sexuality and violence within our churches. She shows us the way forward in the practices of peace, love, and justice for our times.

> Dwight H. Judy, Ph.D., Professor Emeritus of Spiritual Formation, Garrett-Evangelical Theological Seminary. Author of *Embracing God: Praying with Teresa of Avila*; and of *A Quiet Pentecost: Inviting the Spirit into Congregational Life.*

Living on the Edge of the Edge is a classic in the making, which will, I predict, one day be widely used by historians of American Christianity as a lens through which to look carefully at what was going on in American Christianity in the turbulent period in which this book was written.

> William D. Lindsey, MA, PhD; Author of *Shailer Mathews' Lives of Jesus: The Search for a Theological Foundation for the Social Gospel.* Albany, NY: State University of New York Press. His blog, *Bilgrimage,* examines the intersection of religion and culture.

In *Living on the Edge of the Edge: Letters to a Younger Colleague,* Dr. Ruth Krall, in *fortis voce,* puts words to unacknowledged visceral messages and knowings for those of us who experienced the hierarchical and clergy abuses of the 1950's through the current decade. I particularly resonate with Krall pointing out the danger of protecting abusers who are designated heroes in other aspect of life. When this happens, egalitarianism, self-responsibility, inclusivity and self-empowerment are prevented; the abuser hides and abuse proliferates like bacteria. Krall bravely, skillfully, and articulately holds individuals and the system account-able for this body and soul-raping epidemic.

Ellen Swanson, MA, BSN, RN, HNB-BC; author of *Heart, Gut, Head: Creating a Healthier Hierarchy*

For Lisa

One does not have to be a combat soldier, or visit a refugee camp in Syria or the Congo in order to encounter trauma. Trauma happens to us, our friends and families, and our neighbors. Research by the Center for Disease Control and Prevention has shown that one in five Americans was sexually molested as a child; one in four was beaten by a parent to the point of a mark being left on the body; and one in three couples engage in physical violence. A quarter of us grew up with alcoholic relatives, and one in eight witnessed their mother being beaten or hit.

Bessel van der Kolk, M.D.

1 in 5 women and 1 in 71 men in the United States have been raped at some time in their lives; 1 in 2 women and 1 in 5 men have experienced other forms of sexual violence victimization in their lifetime (e.g. made to penetrate someone, sexual coercion, unwanted sexual contact and sexual experiences). Victimization often occurs for the first time before the age of 25 (42% of female victims report being raped before the age of 18 and 37% report being raped between the ages of 18 and 25).

United States: Center for Disease Control and Prevention.

1 in 4 college women report surviving rape or attempted rape at some point in their lifetime. The rate has remained the same since first being reported in the 1980's. 5% of women on college campuses report experienced rape or attempted rape each year. In USA military academies, 5% of the women reports surviving rape each year as do 2.4% of the men.

http://www.oneinfourusa.org/statistics.php

Out of 100 rapes committed: an estimated 5-20 are reported to police; 0.4-5.4 are prosecuted; 0.2-5 result in a conviction; incarceration, 0.2 – 2.8.

National Center on Domestic and Sexual Violence

35% of women worldwide have experienced either intimate partner violence or non-partner violence in their lifetime; 30% of women who have been in an intimate relationship report they have experienced some form of physical or sexual violence from their partner; 38% of murders of women are committed by an intimate partner.

World Health Organization

Table of Contents

Living on the Edge of the Edge

Letters to a Younger Colleague

Preface by Lisa Schirch

Receiving the Gift

Ruth Krall was my professor at Goshen College, a small Mennonite liberal arts college in Indiana, from 1986-1988. I took several courses with her on nonviolence, pacifism, and theology. In her courses I read a wide range of authors, learning to understand feminist theology, liberation theology, Black theology and pacifist theology. The "Ruth Krall Reading List" is legendary. It changes lives. It's a cornerstone for careers; a compass for living ethically. She didn't just lay a foundation for my life's work. She did this for countless other classmates and students for over thirty years of teaching.

In the spring of 2014, I began exchanging emails with a group of male Mennonite authors working on an edited book entitled *John Howard Yoder: Radical Theologian.* Through our email conversations, they invited me to write an *Afterword* to their book, which I entitled "**To the Next Generation of Pacifist Theologians**"[1] Our email exchanges discussed whether a group of all male authors could write a book on Yoder's radical pacifist theology while there was growing recognition of Yoder's widespread sexual violence and harassment of women, particularly Mennonite women leaders and ambitious female students. This email dialogue with the male authors made me see that I owed Ruth a tribute and I needed to reach out to give her my gratitude as an adult some thirty years after sitting in her classes which had provided a conceptual framework for responding to the Yoder tragedy.

As "Yoderians" or followers of John Howard Yoder, my male colleagues wrote the book to support the continued admiration of John Howard Yoder's writings. I wrote the *Afterword* to their book, in part, to provide a different point of view as a woman and as a peacebuilding practitioner: I used the opportunity of writing an *Afterword* to name and cite Ruth Krall's work on John Howard Yoder and the broader issue of sexual abuse in the church. While the male authors followed Yoder's teachings, I followed Ruth Krall's teachings on pacifism.

I recognized that I had a different foundational education than many of my male colleagues. Ruth introduced me to the roots of resistance, liberation, and transformation that nourished the words and concepts in the *Afterword*. Those roots had fed my work all along – and I had wrongly assumed that other colleagues shared those roots. I had been out of touch with Ruth for many years - but the *Afterword* was the spark that compelled me to contact her, thank her profusely for shaping my ethics, theology and social analysis, and ask her to read through the *Afterword* to give permission to the many places where I wanted to cite her jaw-dropping analysis of sexual abuse in the church.[2]

Leaders in the institutional church had fought viciously and persistently against the voices of Yoder's victims and their female allies to uphold his standing in the Mennonite Church and wider Christian circles. Yoder was the most widely known Mennonite in the world; he symbolically represented Mennonites and Mennonite theology. Ruth Krall was denounced, excluded, and discredited for her pioneering work in advocating for the rights of victims of sexual violence; including the victims of John Howard Yoder's extensive sexual violations of women.

While male colleagues defended the reputation of Yoder; none cited Ruth's work. I was in the strange position of advocating for my mentor while they advocated for theirs. Their mentor was world-renowned for his penultimate paradox: Yoder is known for his pacifist theology and his sexual violence. Krall may have affected just as many lives with her transforming impact on students but has been ostracized by male colleagues, many of whom refuse to even cite her written work.

When asked why my male colleagues didn't cite her ground-breaking case study about Yoder's sexual violations, some noted they thought of it as a vendetta, the thoughts of an angry woman. They clearly had not read the book, for it is anything but a vendetta. Others said it wasn't scholarly. Ridiculous! One of the male authors wrote about Yoder's sexual violence without citing any literature, without even being aware that there is an entire literature about sexual violence that Ruth cites in her four volume series of books, *The Elephants in God's Living Room*. In these books Ruth has a conversation with leading authors, and situates her own thoughts in all of her writings within a wider conversation with other scholars on sexual violence in religious contexts. That is the definition of "scholarly."

A generation of male and female Mennonite pacifists is in conflict. Mennonite men tout the powerful and legendary John Howard Yoder. I, and many of her former students, tout Ruth Krall, a Mennonite woman of integrity and passion who doesn't seek the spotlight, but focuses on the alignment of her life's work with her theology; orthopraxis consistent with orthodoxy. Seeking to understand a consistent Mennonite pacifism, we pay attention to her studies in sexual violence as a critical component of Mennonite peace studies.

Ruth E. Krall

Ruth embodies the pacifist ethic of compassion and understanding both for those that do harm that must be stopped and for the victims and survivors of harm. Soon, I saw the pattern, that as a Mennonite woman I was expected to keep quiet about sexual violence. Some of my male colleagues privately affirmed my voice and analysis. And the editor and most of the co-authors of the book for which the *Afterword* was written made the positive step of including the *Afterword*, making space for my analysis – which included many of Ruth's words and her conceptual analysis.

When I was Ruth's undergraduate student in the1980's, I sensed Ruth's work had been unfairly belittled. While the church hierarchy and institutions rejected her conceptual framework and concern for victims of all forms of violence, her students found her teaching provided a more clear and compelling view of pacifism, of Christianity, of spirituality than we found anywhere else.

Now thirty years after I was her student, I now correspond with Ruth frequently on a wide range of issues. As she notes, we both have faced life-threatening illness and in the days before surgery to remove a mass in my breast, it was Ruth and a few women colleagues and friends who gave me the wisdom to see the spiritual resources around me in the natural world for making my way through the crisis.

This book emerges from my own desire to learn more from Ruth – and for her to write things down for future generations. When Ruth informed me she was writing a book based on our correspondence, I remember reading the email over several times. A book? A book for me? For me?

Instead of going to the store to buy Christmas gifts, Mennonite families often make homemade items to share with their loved ones. A carved rocking chair, a knitted sweater, a mixed tape of songs. A gift says something about the giver and the recipient. How much thought did the giver put into the gift? How grateful was the recipient? How could I accept such a gift?

Readers of this book will clearly see that this book is not just a gift to me, one of the thousands of students Ruth taught. This book is a gift to men and women alive today who have much to learn in these pages. It is a gift to future generations, recording the rich and scholarly life of a Mennonite woman whose perspective is much wider than many of her male colleagues as she draws on a variety of religious traditions, psychological scholars, and the natural world of creation, which is the most authentic voice of God.

Ruth's voice and insights in this book make the case for re-thinking our lives. In the tradition of other women writers like Mary Catherine Bateson, who also happens to be my mentor, she writes about her own life as a case study; "an auto-ethnography." In this book, Mennonites, as an ethnic and religious group, are a case study. John Howard Yoder, as a perpetrator of violence, is also a case study of the much broader problem of religiously based sexual violence.

As a Mennonite woman, Ruth notes how the particular experience of Mennonite Anabaptists shapes our work. Anabaptists were martyred for their beliefs in independent thinking and Church-State separation, beginning in the 1500's. She writes, "The fire's flame and the river's water brought about the martyrs' death of men and women, boys and girls with an equality they never had in life.[3] And she notes that "we are descendants of martyrs. We are the voice of our raped ancestors."

Krall reflects on how she learned "...how to disobediently resist a church which saw more sin in lipstick, dancing, and wedding bands than it did in the socially-accepted denial of civil rights to black citizens...; a church which refused to acknowledge sexual violence inside its communal boundaries..." a church which hid the presence of a wide variety of sexual and gender abuse perpetrators under the pious talk of redemptive suffering and community demands for victims to forgive on demand.[4]

Ruth laments, "Orthodoxy has replaced orthopraxis...Word has replaced deed as the theological and sociological marker of belonging."[5] This book is full of profound and novel ways of conceptualizing the challenge of being a human being; particularly a human interested in religion and spirituality. She sums up the challenge like this; "When a religious institution becomes more concerned about status, control, power, theological agreements, sociological unity, authority, behavioral purity, and orthodox words than about embodied love of the neighbor, justice in situations of injustice, spontaneous acts of charity and helpfulness towards the vulnerable, and mutual compassion for each others' humanity in the face of great personal and social differences, it has already crumbled on the inside. What remains is the white-washed face of the tomb where dead religions now rest."[6]

In my world of work, I am an advocate and trainer for the US military and government to identify the relevance of the field of peacebuilding to US foreign policy. US policymakers currently debate whether to negotiate with Iran, or whether there is any alternative way to stop the violence of violent extremists other than through war and punishment. The challenge of engaging with an unacceptable "other" is a theme throughout the book. Ruth advocates for recognizing the humanity in all people, both victims and perpetrators.

Ruth notes Mennonites and other Christians often replicate the very same paradigm of "othering" and "shunning" or refusing to negotiate with and relate to the other.

> "Our collective history as Mennonites should teach us to know better than to shun and exclude others as unacceptable. But it appears to me in the twenty-first century that we have forgotten and idealized the sixteenth-century pain of being shunned, hunted and murdered for differences in thought and praxis. We have forgotten that our faith ancestors once

needed to worship in caves at the end of a long stream which they forded or waded so they could not be traced as they gathered to sing the songs of peace. Now we have become the hunters, the enforcers of purity laws, and the shunning ones. The genetic descendants of the once hated other, now we are the ones who hate. In our individual and collective paranoia and hatred, we force others to find welcoming caves of security and peace far away from our Mennonite Church institutions and our homes."[7]

This book is a divining rod that points us away from a pattern of othering others which drains us of life and pointing toward the way towards a more life-giving way of seeing the integrity of all creation. Ruth gives us stories complemented by key concepts and lists on how offenders can take responsibility; what can be done to support healing for victims; how to care for ourselves as wounded healers. Ruth asks us to focus on how we live our lives, not whether we have the right beliefs or "orthodoxy." What Ruth wants to know about someone is this: "Are they kind? Do they demonstrate compassion for other's suffering? Do they live with integrity? Are they tolerant of diversity...?"[8]

As a woman with her own wounds, Ruth speaks to my own wounds and exhaustion from working at social justice and transformation for three decades, with the attendant compassion fatigue and trauma. Citing Henri Nouwen's *The Wounded Healer,* the prophet Elijah tells a religious seeker to identify the Messiah sitting at Jerusalem's gate as the one who constantly unbinds and re-binds his wounds so that he can continue to heal others. Ruth defines resiliency as "the ability to repeatedly enter, work within, and then leave behind, if only for a few healing time-out minutes, the enchanted forest of violence and trauma."[9]

Ruth notes that failing to heal our own inner sources or motivations to do harm, we have little more to offer the world than ideology. Instead, Ruth asks us to "experiment with our lives by living out a form of spirituality that can ground our peace and social justice activism." [10]

One of the goals, from where I sit, is to achieve this: "in seven generations from now, more women are culturally supported in their actions to fulfill the intellectual and personal promise of their God-given lives."[11] As Mennonite women, we are both on the edge of the edge. Mennonites have 500 years of history of sitting on the edge of the societies where they lived. Mennonite women are sitting on the edge of this edge.

Ruth's generation of Mennonite women made a way for me in my generation. I have more space to operate in because of Ruth's life and work. In my life I too try to make space for the next generation. This book attests to this legacy of women with our elbows out; carving a path, or crafting wings for other women to fly further.

Ruth writes that the pain she felt, ostracized by Mennonite men in her generation is "a hologram of the silence and pain known by every ostracized victim and survivor of the church's many forms of internal violence."[12]

I lament that pain. I join Ruth in saying, "we have begun to unearth a different future for Anabaptist-Mennonite women than the one we inherited from our respective ancestors."[13].

Ruth E. Krall

Living on the Edge of the Edge

Introductory Comments

This series of letter-essays began with an electronic message from Dr. Lisa Schirch, a former student and current colleague, asking me to read and critique an afterword which she had written for a book of essays about the Mennonite ecclesiologist, theologian and ethicist John Howard Yoder.[14] Her questions to me as well as her comments to the book's editor and various chapter authors jump-started me into thinking about how to answer the complex questions raised for me by her electronic message and its attached rough draft of her *Afterword.*[15] For more than two years the two of us have corresponded about a wide variety of professional, personal and Mennonite Church issues. During those months each of us entered the emotional underground of serious, potentially life-threatening physical illness. We began, perhaps as a result of staring death in the face, to talk about our own lives and our own hopes for the current and future Mennonite Church. At some, now distant, point in time, we agreed that perhaps I should transform some of our electronic mail conversations into a book.

In the letters which follow, I seek to re-construct my own personal journey to understanding these complex topics. Each letter, therefore, has two originating sources. The first is the informal back-and-forth electronic correspondence between the two of us. The second is rooted in my own life encounters with these complex issues. As I sorted through our e-mail and began to write, I thought often of Rilke's *Letters to a Young Poet*[16] and William Sloan Coffin's *Letters to a Young Doubter.*[17] One obvious difference is that my collegial correspondent is a mature and accomplished Anabaptist-Mennonite scholar and peace activist in her own voice. So, we are peers in many more ways than were Rilke's young poet or Coffin's young doubter.

As I began to write, I wanted the informality of voice *and* I wanted the influence of her electronic mail to me to be represented in these letters. These essays are, in many ways, therefore, my responses to her correspondence. The nature of our correspondence means that the professional voice and the personal voice are often intermingled because these published letters actually began as informal electronic correspondence. Only as I wrote and then later copy-edited these letter-essay rough drafts, for example, did I add footnotes to help other readers understand the background and context of our conversations with each other.

I have long been committed to the belief that our lived stories and our narrative stories as human beings are the source of our commitments and our work. While there is a place for the abstractions of ethical and philosophical and theological work, intellectually I am more comfortable looking at stories to find their embedded truths and wisdom. This means, I suppose, that I am less interested in absolute proofs for truth and intellectual methodologies for resolving classical antinomies than I am in witnessing and wrestling with the daily struggles of human life as the source of human wisdom.

Thus, these letters represent two generations of Anabaptist-Mennonite pacifist women thinking together and raising questions about the socio-cultural-religious taproots for the often-unchallenged presence of affinity sexual violence and domestic violence inside the boundaries of our shared faith heritage. They involve, at times, our thinking about Mennonite church politics. At other times, in the background, they bear witness to the power of the life force in the face of serious illness. They represent our professional and personal encounters with multiple forms of personal and structural violence and our reflections upon these encounters. They represent our personal commitments to peace-making with justice and with compassion.

As members of two distinct cohort generations, we bring different life histories, cultural histories and unique personal experiences to the work of Mennonite pacifist theory building. I was born during World War Two when most Americans were united in support of the war effort; she was born in the era when the Vietnam War divided American from American. Both of us came of age during the second wave of American feminism and its thorough-going critique of misogyny and patriarchal violence against women. She is married and the mother of maturing children while I am single and have never taken care of a life partner or children on a daily basis.

Because our life experiences to date, our academic careers, and our professional work experiences are different ones, we bring separate vocabularies and personal understandings to this discussion. Yet, as Anabaptist-Mennonite women, we also bring some commonalities of belief and praxis. In addition, at some point in our respective careers we have each worked with members of the United States military establishment. Unlike many or our academic Mennonite colleagues, therefore, we have a certain sympathy for the lives of the actual men and women in uniform who have served or are serving in military combat situations. As each of us thinks about military approaches to international conflicts, therefore, we refuse to demonize the men and women who have served or who are now serving in America's armed forces.

I find no easy way to explain to other Mennonites my decision during the Vietnam War era to wear an MIA bracelet with a man's engraved name as a reminder of his absence from the life he once knew – even as I was simultaneously protesting the war. I did this for five years of my life and do not regret doing it. In a similar manner I find no easy way to explain why I remain a Mennonite and a Jesus path pacifist when intransigent politicized violence seems to beg for military interventions to resolve seemingly intractable and unimaginably violent human conflicts.

This is to say, to speak only for myself, that I have not turned my back on my childhood church's teachings about the Jesus path as one that excludes all deliberate and planned killing and willful harm of other human beings. This is to say, also, that my personal critique of war as a totally inadequate solution to human conflict has become more nuanced as I have grown older. I am willing, therefore, to accept the need in some intransigent war zones for a United Nations Peacekeeping mission. As a very ordinary participant in the nation-state into which I have been born, I am very aware of my complicity in the decisions my nation makes if for no other reason than I pay my annual federal taxes. Yet, I remain a pacifist inside the Anabaptist-Mennonite tradition because I believe this is a path I can walk with integrity. It allows me to express my disbelief in making, dehumanizing, demonizing, vilifying, and killing enemies as a useful solution to human conflict, socio-cultural or religious oppressiveness, corruption, tragedy, and suffering.

In addition, we also bring a common affinity for being present to and learning from the natural world. Observing nature's complex seasonal changes, we learn something about our own lives and their seasonal changes.

Perhaps as one of my undergraduate students, my younger colleague has a better understanding of my own evolving thought in these areas than I do. As an undergraduate young woman she most likely encountered the incomplete sentences and un-examined ideas that exist in every academic classroom. There are some issues which as I matured in my personal and professional life yielded some changing opinions. I try to clarify these changes as we go along. As I said to her in a recent electronic message, *as an old woman, I may, therefore, not be exactly the person you remember from your twenties.*

Life both challenges and changes us as we live it. And while I am simultaneously, therefore, that idealistic mid-life college professor who taught my younger colleague as an undergraduate *and* today's weary retired realist, some of my ideas and beliefs about the world have changed over time. For example, I am no longer as dogmatic about all forms of theological truth as I once was. I no longer base my opposition to warfare, for example, on Biblical, theological and philosophical abstractions. My opposition comes from having visited active war zones and seeing the human tragedies that these killing fields create. As a healer I am opposed to the deliberate creation of human wounds that cannot be healed – even after years of distance from the killing and raping fields. As a feminist woman, I do not believe that helpless women, children, the handicapped, and the aged are collateral damages in violent conflicts – they are real people whose faces could be mine if our life circumstances were changed; they are the direct casualties of war's violence.

Sisterhood is Powerful

As an American woman aging in place, I lived through the opening moments of the feminist critique of sexual violence as an unaddressed problem in American women's lives. I lived through the opening moments of the American feminist women's health movement. I lived through the era in which each feminist author's work was literally passed hand-to-hand as women sought new ways to understand themselves, their culture, systemic oppression, and the patriarchy.

My consciousness-raising group (1972-1976) represented this diversity: a Jewish clinical psychologist; an agnostic social psychologist; a Latina university poetry professor; an engineer; and a basic research bio-chemist. I was the youngest member of this group. I was the only nurse faculty member. I was the only single woman. I was also the least experienced member of the group in my encounters with the messy politics of university tenure. Eventually, as an extension of this group's work, I became a participant in a research project. My social psychologist colleague and her friend, a clinical psychologist, created a research gathering of academic and professional women. A wide variety of women with graduate preparation agreed to meet for ten or twelve consecutive weeks to talk about specific topics: money, domestic violence, sex, salary, children, husbands or lovers, and hiring discrimination inside our various professions, etc. Each week we agreed on the topic for the next week and we agreed to think about our personal and professional lives in light of that topic. Once again I was the youngest individual in these conversations. Once again I was the only nurse.

As unbelievable as this may seem to my friends and colleagues now, I was mostly silent for I felt I had so little life experience to offer to these complex conversations. These were very smart and exceptionally accomplished professional women and I was often intimidated by their personas, their accomplishments, and their positions in the world. I often felt like a socially awkward ten-year-old girl with pigtails who had big hopes for her life but no real knowledge about the large world of culture and intellectual sophistication around her.

Ruth E. Krall

I distinctly remember the afternoon in the early 1970's when I began to understand the realities of culturally-ingrained and society-engineered sexism as it applied to me. I remember the drive home that afternoon as I alternately cried and cursed at what I'd just heard older women tell me about their private and professional lives. For the first time I had heard about private abuse and domestic violence inside "good" families. None of these women were the psychotic patients and their families who usually populated my work world. These were brilliant and often glamorous women who "had made it" and I could not believe the intensity of their pain and the hidden fury of their socially denied and usually silenced anger. As I drove from one of these extended "research" conversations in rush hour traffic, I knew in that moment what sisterhood meant. Whenever I drive by a particular corner in the city of Tucson I recall how heartbroken and enraged I was as I turned north on a side street to head home. In that moment I grew up and claimed my solidarity with all women. My life has never been the same.

I was not altogether naïve as I agreed to be a participating subject in this research project. Already in my twenties I had encountered salary discrimination and it led to me leave the institution which practiced this. Here too I remember the precise board meeting when I learned what a male colleague (with fewer academic credentials and with many fewer people to supervise) was earning. I sat through the rest of that meeting silently enraged but with very few intellectual tools and personal skills in place to understand what was at the root of my much lower salary. Twenty-eight years old, I did not know how to confront the board or the administration with the inherent unfairness and injustice of this situation. But I was not prepared to live with the situation either. So, in essence, I ran. I looked for and found a new job in a public institution which annually published its salary scales for each level of professional it employed. While this system may or may not have been totally transparent about faculty and administrative salaries, at least I had a rough gauge by which to judge the fairness or unfairness of my faculty contract.

Only several years later in this consciousness-raising group in yet another occupational setting and in this somewhat later research process did I come to fully understand gender discrimination. I realized that it affected me as well as every other woman in American society. At the time I was in my very early thirties. It was not that I was a much less worthy or accomplished worker; it was my gender and my gender alone which determined the value of my work in the eyes of my male employers. I was not alone. Women physicians earned less than their male counterparts. Women engineers earned less than their male counterparts. Women chemists earned less than their male counterparts. Inside American colleges and universities, there were far fewer women among the ranks of tenured faculty, and women with advanced degrees were hired, if at all, at lower salaries than men.

This problem remains for American women. We earn, or so the pundits routinely claim, 70 cents to every dollar earned by our male counterparts. Now, an old woman, I comprehend that this issue of salary discrimination is most desperately experienced by the female poor. I agree with Ella Blatt whom I once saw quoted: *What is poverty but a passive form of violence? When a woman does back breaking work for ten hours a day but cannot feed her family with her earnings, society has scorned her labor.* Issues of a guaranteed minimum wage are, therefore, peace and justice issues. The world-wide phenomenon of women's poverty in old age is scandalous in light of this information.

Other pundits tell us that when large numbers of women enter a profession, the social prestige of that profession plummets. It becomes a less desirable occupation or profession for men to enter. Consequently, these same pundits tell us, salary levels for that profession plummet as well.

As more and more women enter the ranks of congressional and gubernatorial elections, this nearly universal cultural devaluation of women entering nontraditional roles has begun to change. At all levels of electoral politics, women are now seen as viable campaigners. Clearly, in the last fifty years, some things about American sexism and the shape or contours of its patriarchy have begun to change. But the cultural fights about reproductive freedom for women are far from over. The cultural fights about women's presence and personal safety in the workplace are far from over. It is my opinion that without equitable salaries, protection form sexual harassment, and accessible, affordable reproductive rights, women are still not freely equal in American society. Without protection from multiple forms of sexual and physical violence in the home, inside educational institutions, and in the workplace, American women, and therefore their children, are not yet free.

While salary discrimination and electoral politics may seem far afield from sexual violence, they are, in my opinion, more trees in the enchanted forest of violence against women and their children. Salary discrimination both supports and reveals men's willingness to dominate women. Refusal of reproductive freedom on religious grounds also reveals a theological and a cultural bias against women's self-determination in areas of their biological sexuality.

In the course of that now-long-ago research project, I became a radicalized secular feminist. I understood gender solidarity to be essential to gaining women's basic rights to be treated fairly. Slowly, I began to understand the ancient cultural roots for women's devalued and exploited place in American life.

In my forties, I then sought out the theological and philosophical roots in Christian dogma and popular culture because I was convinced that these roots were, if not *THE* taproots of male violence against women and children in Western cultures, the necessary rootlets for the sexual violence tree to survive and for the multiple memes of enculturated violence against women and their children to multiply and reproduce.

I began this series of letters in response to our ongoing electronic correspondence about the interfacing connections of sexual violence *and* denominational homophobia. As my colleague and I started this discussion, I hoped that together we might see what we can learn from each other. While our generations separate us in time, I know that my younger colleague carries deep, earned wisdom from inside her own generation. From the hard-earned wisdom of her professional career as a Mennonite pacifist woman who is committed to full inclusion for lesbian, bi-sexual, gay, transgendered, and queer folks, I hope to keep learning from her about this complex relationship of these two forms of embedded sociocultural violence.

Early on I wrote to her:

> *In these letters, therefore, I will roam around in my professional languages in the hopes that you will do the same in your replies. The underlying question, as always these days for me, is simple to ask but complex to answer: what do we know about the violence and violation of our respective worlds that we do not know we know? What have we each learned from our peacemaking work in the world that we do not yet know we know?*
>
> *Your expertise is from the overlapping worlds of diplomacy and militarism. Your academic discipline is conflict mediation and transformation. As part of the work which you do in the world, you have encountered sexual violence as a lived reality in the lives of many international women and children. You understand the connection between militarism and rape. You also have an intuitive understanding of the relation between heterosexism, sexism, and rape.*
>
> *We both have a strong academic interest in anthropological research and scholarship. As I read your published work, I find we have read many of the same authors. As a graduate student I was regularly exposed to the consulting work of American anthropologist Margaret Mead as she visited the university medical school's psychiatry department each quarter. In between her visits we read a wide range of American and European anthropologists and were always in our case study presentations asked about cultural roots of a patient's pathology. You have had the benefit of being the student of Mead's daughter with Gregory Bateson, Mary Catherine Bateson. This interest in the cultural roots and cultural forms of violence presents us, perhaps, with a common language where we can begin.*

Now, nearly eighteen months after we began corresponding, as I begin collating these letters into a publishable form I seek to explain my reasons for doing this book. My professional or academic expertise is from the world of interpersonal affinity violations. As a therapist-clinician and as a feminist thealogian I continue to deepen my personal understanding about the complex reality that in the name of God, family life, or romantic relationships, individuals who know each other attack, batter, assault, and rape each other. The violated ones are usually the less powerful ones in cultural terms - women and their children. We must also, however, recognize and acknowledge the presence of abusive and dominating women.

What can we learn about contemporary male and female relationships as a breeding ground for violence and violation? What is it among so-called equals that creates the power differentials and their concomitant rages between genders? What is the cultural soil that breeds violation? Where, if at all, and how does our concept of God fit in? How do Christian ecclesiology and denominational matters of administrative church polity support the larger culture's violence against women and their children?[18]

Both of us, I gather from our correspondence to date, are also puzzled by the proximity of sexual xenophobia toward sexual minorities, that reality which American poet Adrienne Rich has labeled heterosexism. I am puzzled about why sexual xenophobia occurs so frequently in proximity to sexism, racism, and to domestic violence against women and their children. This is just one of the puzzling elements of the patriarchy's commitment to interpersonal violence I do not pretend to understand. There is no logical and necessary relationship between religious leader rape, racism, sexual orientation xenophobia, sexism, classism, and gender misogyny. But I recognize there is a relationship because of the way American religions treat these issues: inside America's religious soil, their noxious presence keeps arising in proximity to one another. I no longer believe this is coincidental.

Roman Catholic theologian William (Bill) Lindsey, a white, permanently partnered (42 years and counting) and very recently-married Southern gay man, has a blog in which he visits and revisits these topics. I have found his points of view to be intellectually challenging and rewarding. Here is just a small sample of his recent (2014) blog-posts on the interrelationships of these complex and interrelated cultural phenomena[19]

I participated in this cross-generational and cross-discipline correspondence in the hopes that as we corresponded with each other by electronic mail, we might start to uncover and then begin unraveling some of the unresolved paradoxes we each brought with us inside our respective careers into this new century from the old one - now history. As we befriended each other and each other's work, I hoped we would support each other in the work we do.

I have collected these letter-essays into one book in the hopes that these now-redacted letters and essays will trigger similar conversations among other feminist women and their allies. The more of us who seek to understand sexual violence

Ruth E. Krall

and other forms of sexist and heterosexist oppression of women and their children, the more exit paths we can intellectually hack out of the enchanted and toxic forest of gender-based and age-based religious abuse of vulnerable children, adolescents, and adults.

The more we understand the interlocking relationships between the *isms* (sexism, heterosexism, racism, classism, etc.) and affinity violence of all kinds, the more likely we will be able to design effective intervention protocols that may help bring about lasting, permanent, and positive change in how individuals and entire communities choose to encounter each other.

First Letter

Introducing the Johari Window

What We Know and What We Don't Know We Know

Conscious

Public Self (Known to me and others)	**Private Self** (Known to me only)
Hidden Self (Known to others, but not to me)	**Unknown Self** (Not known to me or anyone else)

Public · *Private*

Unconscious

Johari Window diagram [20]

I continue to find an adaptation of the Johari window to be useful in my own thinking about these matters of academic work and collaboration with others. Unassisted by others, we can only push open the windows of our individual awareness a small amount. But collectively, as we interact with each other, we can bring into collective awareness that which has been hidden from us because of our unique personal blinders. There is a synergy in such conversations which cannot be replicated by individual work done in isolation.[21]

In academic collaboration, the goals for both persons are to expand their personal awareness of that which they know but do not know they know *and* to increase the area of awareness that is known to both individuals. A secondary goal is to teach others what they have learned using the scholarship methodologies or apparatus of their respective disciplines in the academic commons. The above diagram illustrates a theoretical model in which all quadrants are equal in value. In real life, however, the quadrants are rarely equal. As individuals work together, awareness regarding aspects of the public self expands and aspects of the hidden self and the unknown self contract as more information and intuitions are uncovered and un-layered in collaborative work. As we work together, therefore, we begin to unearth and understand new aspects of troubling issues. We also begin to unearth information about each participant's skills and limitations in collaborative work. In part this is because each person (and her or his contribution) is unique. In part, it is due to the phenomenon of synergy.

Therefore, the synergy of collective interdisciplinary research and conversation, I believe, also helps us to uncover that which is present but consciously unknown. This is particularly important work as we seek to uncover the individual and cultural roots of violence in its many forms.

Multi-lingual Collaboration

The reality that each person uses a discrete personal and professional language to describe issues being studied and researched is important in creating new, now-shared intuitions and hypotheses to be tested in the greater academic commons. What we know from multi-lingual individuals is that each world language contains a vocabulary which reveals nuances of meaning and that in many instances these nuances of meaning cannot readily be translated verbatim into other world vocabularies without losing these rich nuances of meaning.

This is true, I believe, of professional vocabularies as well. Thus, the more vocabularies which we collectively bring to the table of academic (or activist/advocacy) conversation the more nuanced will be our understanding. It is also true, however, that such interdisciplinary conversations also contain the likelihood of misunderstanding. So, I believe we need to make an effort to clarify specialized vocabularies wherever and whenever we utilize them. In shared collaborative work, it is particularly necessary to avoid code words that contain a universe of meaning to one profession but only contain minimal information to members of another one.

As a nurse, for example, I can speak to a physician about a newly admitted patient's COPD.[22] We will both immediately decode this information in complex ways. But, in talking with an uninformed and newly diagnosed patient and her family, we need to simplify that language into ordinary common speech. This is true as well of the linguistic symbol PTSD.[23] Professional persons who work in the fields of trauma research and treatment will have an elaborate scientific-therapeutic

Ruth E. Krall

vocabulary that can supplement the short-hand abbreviation and immediately guide the treatment regimes of individuals suffering from this traumatic response disorder. However, since this phrase is so commonly seen in popular media, individuals suffering from PTSD may have inadequate information, incorrect information, unreliable information, or almost no information at all. Once again, professionals need to clarify what they are talking about with patients. They need to clarify their patients' pre existing knowledge and ascertain the adequacy of that knowledge for the treatment process. To do this, trauma specialists will usually need to use their common daily language rather than their professional ones.

This is equally true, by the way, when victim advocates use the short-hand phrase PTSD. They may, or may not, understand the clinical nuances of the phrase as they use it to explain a victim's inner experiences of betrayal trauma. For those of us who are advocates, therefore, I believe we need to understand the clinical dimensions and descriptions of PTSD as well as those often unlabeled descriptions of their inner experience given to us by the victimized individuals who live inside the parameters of this condition.

In a recent hospitalization, for example, the admitting physician began talking to me in lay language. I immediately clarified for him that he could use the technical languages of medicine and nursing when talking with me. He immediately switched vocabularies and the complex differential diagnosis which needed to be made before treatment could begin came into view for me. Throughout my hospitalization experience, this information about my professional identity was passed from shift to shift and each new caregiver that entered my life clarified my professional identity before talking with me about clinical issues. Because I was an *insider* I was seen as a member of the doctor-nurse guild and was included in conversations about my care in ways many patients would never be included. These conversations were, therefore, more nuanced than the ordinary and common lay language could accommodate. I was allowed to participate in care decisions in a way that uninformed non-clinicians would not have been allowed to do. I was encouraged to raise anatomical questions and the medical care team responded with computerized images to help me understand. Technicians turned monitors so I could watch their continuous stream of information about my body. Nurses, doctors, and technicians clarified what I saw but didn't understand. They utilized their specialized knowledge and technical vocabularies. If I was confused about what was happening to me, they explained things in lay *and* professional languages so that I could understand what they needed to uncover before beginning to treat my symptoms.

While we often don't think about this level of linguistic complexity when we are working inside our various professional languages, when we move between or among disciplinary languages we are engaging in a form of multi-lingual communication. The more we are aware of this, the more we can move back and forth between our various professional languages and then, when needed, into the common lay language we all share. As we do this we begin to be multi-lingual.

Eventually, over time as we work together, we collectively build our mastery and proficiency with each other's language systems. Once fluency is reached, we can begin to understand and then comprehend cultural nuances and technical nuances inside these very different and unique language systems. It is at this point, I believe, where synergy begins to happen. From within your professional guild, you bring new questions to me and vice verse. It is these new questions, I believe, that hold the power to transform both our conversation and our understanding of complex cultural problems such as sexual violence in its many forms.

This reality is present, for example, at the interface of theology and ethics. The first time I heard the phrase *the priest in Catholic theology is ontologically different than the lay person* as an ideological factor or rootlet in Catholic clergy sexual abuse of the laity, I had to revisit a language to which I'd been exposed in graduate school but one in which I had limited fluency. Now, several years later, I can discuss the so-called ontological difference of Roman Catholic priests from members of the laity with some inner security that I am using the words *ontologically different* in an appropriate manner.

The question of whether gender also affects language and whether men and women have separate linguistic systems and language behaviors has been around for much of the last half of the twentieth-century. I personally assume that women and men share much of their language usage in either ordinary life or professional life. However, I also am aware of cultural differences between men and women in how they manifest language.[24] Verbal and non-verbal aspects of language production do show, therefore, significant gender differences. These differences, then, affect perception. Perception affects interpretation. Interpretation affects behavior.

These same kinds of linguistic issues arise in different minority and ethnic groups which share a common language with the majority. My feminist thealogian friend Nelle Morton used to talk about her perception that in America's deep south black men spoke two languages (white man's white English and black man's black English) while black women spoke four (white man's white English, black man's black English, white woman's white English, and black woman's black English). Each culturally distinct spoken form of English, therefore, contained nuances of meaning which may not have been immediately visible on the surface of any given conversation. When men and women were together, she observed, the masculine form predominated. When white people and black people interacted, the white form predominated. When black men or white men were together in single ethnic and gender groups, they spoke their gendered cultural dialect of English. When black women were alone with each other they spoke a complex mix of their ethnic tongue and their gendered tongue. She further noted that white people in this

Ruth E. Krall

situation, if they were men, spoke only white men's white English and, if they were women, spoke white men's white English and white women's white English. Finally, she noted that where there was easy, repeated and congenial access between the racial or ethnic groups and that access was more or less egalitarian, everyone began to understand and be able to use a much wider variety of linguistic metaphors and images.

In our recent discussion of swearing this issue became quite evident to me. Neither of us learned to swear inside our ethnic Mennonite communities where such verbal behavior was (and is) frowned upon for women. In the years each of us lived outside our ethnic communities, we learned some generational aspects and forms of female swearing. In addition, I am a member of the generation of girls and women who were taught that *ladies don't swear or use vulgar language.* They don't, in your phrase, *have potty mouths.* So, each time I swear, I violate three taboos: the white middle class definition of a lady; the cultural definition of a well-educated professional woman; and the religious definition of a Christian Anabaptist-Mennonite believer. One aspect, I think, of our growing trust in each other is that we can share and discuss these culturally non-acceptable behaviors with each other.

One reason for talking about this at length is your concern about the absence of the female voice in the academy – especially when discussing sexual violence. I've been thinking a lot about this since you wrote. My hypothesis now is this: when we white women enter the religious academy, we are entering the precinct of white male language. For men to feel comfortable with us as colleagues, their implicit and probably unconscious demand is for us to speak their dialect of our guilds' languages. If we don't choose to speak their dialect, they perceive or think we are not equal to them in our skills and knowledge base. We are, I think, presumed to be ignorant or unscholarly. When we use our female dialect; they don't understand us as intelligent. Thus, our "uneducated" and "unwanted" intrusion into their world makes them highly uncomfortable. Their ways of managing this discomfort is to isolate and exclude women. When women insist upon using women's conceptual languages, men automatically assume, therefore, that we have an inferior education and intellectual understanding. Our intellectual work ends up in their trash bins as unworthy and as having nothing to like or to contribute.

All of these transactions, however, go on below conscious levels. One consequence of this in my own professional life is that I double-read and I suspect you do too. We read men's theory and then we read women's theory. We speak, therefore, two theoretical languages: the languages of our discipline in a male dialect and the languages of our disciplines in a female dialect. Because most men, in this situation, are monolingual we women academics spend way too much energy, in my opinion, needing to translate our ideas and intellectual concerns from a female experience and dialect into a male one.

Many dominant academic men, because of this unconscious (or *maybe* conscious) assumption that women and their intellectual contributions are inferior, see the need to read only men's writings. They do not, therefore, need to encounter and to think about women's hypotheses about men's violence and the sexual violation of women and their children. This explains, I think, at least in part your comment about Mennonite academic men's deficient reading.

I am reminded of the Chinese proverb: *Women hold up half the sky.* We need, therefore, to keep insisting that women's concerns about sexual violence are essential to the conversation we all must have in the Anabaptist-Mennonite commons. We must remain insistent about the need to lower the levels of gender-based and age-based violence in the world.

This is analogously the same issue that we face when we want to lower levels of anti-Semitic violence in the world. We must, in that situation, bring together Jewish, Muslim, and Christian scholars and each individual's cultural heritage, language, and contribution must be honored as necessary for complex understanding to emerge.

It is not, therefore, that we must agree. It is not that this concern to pay attention to language issues will automatically end conflict. It is that we must each speak the truth we know and we must each listen as others speak the truth which they know. We must begin to respect each other's life experience and the various linguistic dialects we speak and understand. As we diminish that which is hidden and unknown among the collective us, we bring to bear greater wisdom on the shared problems that confront us. To do this kind of multi-tongues collaboration, we need to learn each other's histories and languages. We need to grapple with our ignorance of each other's perspectives and we must seek together to understand the many cultural icons and myths which sustain violence of all kinds.

I asked my friends and linguist colleagues Rafael and Christine Falcón to read and comment on an early draft of this chapter. They have provided me with the following illustrative example.

> *The example you gave [of Merry Christmas and Feliz Navidad] is perhaps not the strongest for eliciting hard-to-describe nuances, so we tried to think of others. One example we did come up with is "el barrio" and "neighborhood". The article el is significant here since the term barrio is used extensively throughout the Spanish-speaking world as your normal neighborhood or community (example: Barrio Escalante). As we discussed this, we realized that the term el barrio acquires its rich nuances upon becoming that comfortable enclave of an ethnic group within an urban environment. Take for example el barrio puertorriqueño in Humboldt Park in Chicago. Needless to say, the nuances for this neighborhood go far beyond the streets and homes of Barrio Escalante in San José, Costa Rica. ..Enter that urban area under its metallic*

Ruth E. Krall

Puerto Rican [sign] *heralding your arrival to a cultural paradise of smaller-size grocery stores offering everything for your home cooking needs, vegetables and fruits from the tropics, restaurants competing for your PR cuisine desires, food carts offering tasteful PR dishes and desserts, street-side churches with extravagant names, conversations slipping back and forth between English and PR-style Spanish, an occasional drunk taking a nap on the street, etc. An additional point ... is that the term el barrio can engender a nuance of negativity—though...it doesn't have to. [For example], when someone says "I grew up in el barrio," where does that take the listener?*[25]

In thinking about the Falcóns' example about the nuances present in the Spanish words *el barrio* I realize that they further our understanding of the nuances of this conversation in ways I could not. Spanish is Rafael's first language and Spanish is Christine's second language. For years they have collaborated in writing books which bridge these issues and translate them for North American English speakers. In contrast, Spanish is my second language and I learned it as an adult. When I lived in Central America, I traveled extensively in Mexico, Belize, Costa Rica, El Salvador, Nicaragua, and Guatemala. When I was struggling to find an example of linguistic nuance, I headed for a much less nuanced and complex set of words – holiday greetings in English and in Spanish. But as soon as I got their example in my electronic inbox, whole sets of more nuanced meanings fell into place for me. They and I had at lived in the Casa de Goshen in Barrio Escalante in San Jose, Costa Rica. I succeeded them as Goshen College's international program director on location. Thus, Casa de Goshen in Barrio Escalante was my home as it had been theirs the year before my arrival. I can recall in vivid strokes much about that barrio because I walked its streets every day. I shopped in its markets and I rode its public transportation. I can, for example, still taste the hot sweet sugar-coated churros I would buy on the bus at this stop or that stop. The vendors would sweep through the bus while passengers were exiting and loading and, in an exquisitely-timed and culturally-mediated ballet, exit seconds before the driver was ready to move the bus on. Words were never exchanged between the vendors and the drivers but I never saw irritation on either person's part. Each party to this repetitive transaction seemed to know intuitively what was needed for the vendors to gain free access to the bus's hungry passengers on an hourly basis.

I now live in a city that is in close proximity to the Mexican-United States border – a city which has an inner city neighborhood called Barrio Viejo. I live in a city where English and Spanish are both spoken and understood. I live in a city where quick food restaurants have bi-lingual menu boards and where the major interstate highway from Nogales, Mexico to Tucson is marked with speed limits in kilometers rather than in miles.

With the example of *el barrio* a world of nuanced meanings broke open for me as soon as my linguist friends entered the conversation. I can smell the food cart aromas; I can see the church signs; I can hear the music of the salsa and see the swaying hips of dancers, I can identify some of the spices and flavors of food inside el barrio; when they mention the inebriated men one sees, I remember carefully stepping around one very inebriated man "sleeping" on the sidewalk. The Falcóns' example of *el barrio* is a much richer one than the example my first language mind pulled up for me. Their example not only calls up their memories; it calls up mine. It brings their professional and personal expertise as linguists to bear on the questions raised by these paragraphs.

Therefore, as we raise questions for each other to ponder or as we share our own perceptions, the area of shared information grows. Once this information becomes visible to us, then we can begin to codify it into testable hypotheses and abstractions. These theoretical abstractions can then be further refined in the commons of human experience and study. It is inevitable in this process that additional voices will then join the conversation – bringing their own language systems to bear on the questions at hand.

A Brief Linguistic Detour

As academic professors, we both know another reality even if we don't spend much time thinking about it. As generation replaces generation in our classrooms, the daily language the young speak begins to differ greatly from our personal cache of preferred personal and professional languages. This is true whether we are speaking about written term papers, classroom questions, or about cyber-space communications. The first time a student wrote at the bottom of a term paper, *this situation just sucks,* I was glad I was alone in my grading space. I entered a state of mini-annoyance that a student would use such disrespectful language in a formal paper. My first impulse was to roundly scold the student for her unprofessional and inappropriate comment. But the more I thought about how to reply, the more I realized she and I were on the same page. The systemic injustice which she had written about in her paper did, in reality, in her generation's language *suck.* Realizing that academic purity of expression was not the primary issue at hand, I had a long private discussion with myself about what language I probably had used as a twenty-year old – spontaneous language which probably shocked my professors. I don't remember any umbrage being taken with my undergraduate term papers but my teachers also probably shook their heads in concern at my naïveté and failures at creating pious, polite, professional and tediously *old people Mennonite* academic talk.

Because I have a knack for both hearing and understanding American slang as it crosses cultural and generational divides, I must, therefore, watch my vocabulary

Ruth E. Krall

among my own professional peers. *That situation really sucks* and *that situation is totally fucked* are short-hand critiques of systemic oppression that are always at the ready. I was actually glad when I learned what the military-coined acronyms/words, *SNAFU* and *FUBAR,* mean because they are much more polite sounding to use in catawampus situations where no reasonable person can find either justice or sanity.[26] I understand that these words and phrases from my mouth can be and often are highly offensive to others. I don't use them on a daily basis. However, I am no longer offended by them when others use them in my presence. I know they are short-hand for a longer paragraph of often-obfuscating critical speech.

I did not grade down my student's paper for her language. What was more important to me was that in her paper she had captured and properly diagnosed a situation of systemic oppression and was critiquing it in the only language she had available to her in the moment of her rage at what she had learned.

All of which is to say: young people just beginning to understand oppression respond to it at an organic or organismic level; this means that when they trust us to treat them fairly, they often respond with vigorous, un-tamed language. We, their teachers and mentors, need to be able to listen to and not shut down their outrage. We should not seek to turn off their generation's language of outrage because to do so, we might just shut down their generation's emerging sense of compassionate justice and protest.

I am not promoting the use of obscene language. But, I am pointing to a deep awareness that built inside me about the years of classroom distance I had from my own undergraduate years. Each generation is going to do peace work in its own way; in its own voice. We should take care, as their elders, not to stop them in mid-sentence because of some inculcated inner purity code about appropriate peace-speak. We can, and should be, very gentle with them as we seek to teach them what we know and as we seek to free the peace-advocating, idealistic person who already lives within them. We can talk about appropriate language in ways which help them to become more effective as they work with others. But we should never, I have come to believe, seek to stifle their initial outrage at the injustice promulgated by their culture's elders – the so-called wiser people apparently in charge of the universe just as they are coming of age.

Synergy: One + One Equals More Than One
Moving, therefore, like a loom's shuttle between the concrete information which we have from our individual and collective professional and personal lives and the abstractions which help us to refine our knowledge and theory base, any two individuals who begin to talk with each other about a mutual concern have a synergistic effect on each other's thinking and on the field of knowledge being described or examined. The outcome is usually much more than the sum of two numbers.

My participation in our current conversations is grounded, therefore, in the goal of making ourselves and our tenuously conscious information bank visible to (1) ourselves; (2) each other; (3) and the community at large. Only as we bring our unique understandings and concerns to this process of multi-lingual, multi-disciplinary and cross-generational conversations, can we expand our awareness of the socio-cultural-theological subtleties that form the cultural roots and root hairs of any given event of sexual violation.

Roots, Rootlets, and Root Hairs

According to the online dictionary.com, a rootlet is one of a plant's living components that enable a plant to cling to rocks or other supports in order to anchor the plant.[27] These adventitious roots are different from taproots which are strong tapering roots that grow vertically downward and form the center from which all subsidiary rootlets form.[28] They differ, too, from root hairs which gather moisture and nutrients for the plant to use above ground.

In agricultural theory[29] it is well recognized that a plant's root system is the major part of a plant – both in size and in life-supporting functions. A root system usually has a taproot, an adventitious root, rootlets, and root hairs. The root system, therefore, has a lateral dimension in which the rootlets and root hairs spread horizontally while the taproot descends vertically.

A plant's root system, therefore, (1) provides anchorage and support; (2) absorbs nutrients and conducts them to the above ground plant; (3) fosters reproduction by seed production or other means such as shoots and runners.

If we metaphorically think of the various manifestations of sexual violence in our culture as consisting of individual trees in a toxic enchanted forest, then we can see that the socio-cultural-theological roots, rootlets, and root hairs provide support, sustenance, and reproduction resources for these formidable trees. Until we begin to understand the supporting underground and largely invisible root structures for sexual violence, I don't believe we will be able to make progress in the human community towards eradicating this worldwide endemic problem. Until we understand the cultural soil in which these trees grow, we have little or no hope at making a lasting difference that changes the culture of violence to a culture of peace.

Just as the complex and specialized root system of plants sustains their life above ground, so, too do the root systems of violence sustain specific forms of violence in the socio-cultural world of human relationships. Until we understand the relationship between roots below the surface of human understanding and the violence plant we see above ground, we will be unable to begin to eradicate violence from our culture and from our own inner lives.

Ruth E. Krall

Second Letter

The Writer's Voice and Particularity

Introductory Comment

> *As a victim you are amazed that no one will ask you about the crime or the effect that it has on you and your family. You took the defendant's blows, heard his threats, [and] listened to him brag that he'd "beat the rap" or "con the judge." No one ever hears these things. They never give you a chance to tell them.*

A Victim[30]

In your most recent letter, you raised questions about the patriarchy and described the ways patriarchal and misogynous men exclude women's voices from the commons. You note that you are often an only – the only woman included in a group of men who address the peace, justice, and conflict issues that are central to your life's work. This is an issue I have thought about because it has been my life experience also.[31] You note the absence of other women: third-world women; women of color; and women from other world religions in conversations that directly affect all women such as sexual violence against women and their children. I would note, as well, the absence of lesbian and queer women's voices. In the 1970's, for example, it was lesbian women who talked and wrote openly in the commons about domestic abuse, rape, and the sexual violation of women and women's children.[32] Many rape crisis lines, for example, began inside the radical lesbian feminist community. Our debt, as straight women, to this small community of radicalized women is immense. We all too often exclude them – and this is at our own peril as women.

In addition, we often overlook the contributions which traumatically hobbled individuals can make to our understandings of cultural misogyny and exclusion.

As an example of the latter, the victims of clergy sexual violence are usually over-looked in men's theological and ethical writings about peace-making in a violent world. There is apparently no place for the life-taught wisdom of sexually violated women and children in their theological and ethical anti-violence canon.

Reasons for this denial are complex. But I personally believe that the World Health Organization in its Summary Report on World Violence is correct.[33] Violence is not a foreign reality in people's lives. For far too many of us, inside and outside the Christian community, there is the very personal experience of betrayal, violence, and violation in the private sphere. In short, not only others live inside violent relationships: we do too. In addition, many of us inside the private domestic sphere are violence perpetrators.

Too many of us, therefore, are both the victims of violence and the carriers of violence. The WHO Report *Summary* notes and underscores the difficulty of initiating and then carrying through with such a thorough-going cultural transformation. The difficulty in addressing these kinds of needed ideological and behavioral changes, it notes, begins at the individual level.

> *Raising awareness of the fact that violence can be prevented is, however, only the first step in shaping the response to it. Violence is an extremely sensitive topic. Many people have difficulty in confronting it in their professional lives because it raises uncomfortable questions about their personal lives. Talking about violence means touching upon complex matters of morality, ideology and culture. There is, thus, often resistance at official as well as personal levels to open discussion of the topic.*[34]

In short, it is not other people's violence which stops us from working together to stop gender and age-based violence from happening. It is our own. Dominican priest Father Thomas Doyle in a presentation at Goshen College (IN) in October, 2014 talked about one source of resistance in discussing rape inside Christian communities. He said, and I paraphrase, *Christian denominations and their institutional leaders do not know how to talk about rape done by clergymen because rape is scary.*[35] Those of us (and we are usually, but not always, women who are members of a specific faith community where sexual violence has already occurred) who insist that the church must address its own violence, become, therefore, individuals to be disliked, feared and distrusted. Not only is the topic of sexual violence scary and to be avoided. Those of us who insist upon talking about it are also denied a voice and we, too, are also avoided as being scary. In addition to being socially shunned as unfaithful members of the community, we may find our characters maligned as evil.

Liberation theologians have long noted that when individuals from the dominant caste take up citizenship inside of an oppressed group in order to be helpful, they become targets of the dominant group. Dom Helder Camara, the Roman Catholic Archbishop of Recife, Brazil, noted this reality when he remarked, *when I feed the poor, they call me a saint; when I ask why they are poor, they call me a communist.*[36]

You note dominant men's hostility to a woman's perspective on these critical life issues for women. In particular, you note the relative absence of women's voices in the Mennonite Church's on-going academic appraisal of theologian-ethicist-ecclesiologist John Howard Yoder's life and intellectual work.

In these same male-authored academic writings, I have noted the striking absence of concern for hearing about any of Yoder's victims' experiences and perceptions.[37] No one asks victimized women to speak about their personal understanding of the impact of his theology, ecclesiology and missiology on his behavior. Yet, we know that some of the women he victimized have theological, pastoral, and ethical concerns about his theological systems. I think we both know that many of these women victimized by Yoder during the last thirty years of his life are members of the Mennonite and Catholic graduate and undergraduate academy. Many others have divinity degrees from a variety of Christian seminaries. Still others have advanced graduate clinical preparation. The absence of these voices in today's academic debate about the *meaning* of Yoder's theology in the context of his behavior, is striking to me. I am reminded of Philip Hallie's warning about refusing to listen to the voices of the victimized.[38] I do not believe we can have a theologically-adequate and an in-depth ethical discussion of Yoder's life and Yoder's scholarship without these victimized women's voices being visibly present or, at the minimum, their absence being noted, acknowledged, and mourned.

In the Mennonite Church from 1970 until the present moment it has been Mennonite women who have called for the Mennonite Church and its religious academy to hold Yoder accountable to his various, overlapping communities for his behavior. These same women have called into question the church's negligent management of Yoder's behavior. As Stephanie Krehbiel notes, this work of advocate women has been seen and named as gossip, rumor, and innuendo rather than as a contribution to Yoder scholarship.[39] I personally feel that these three words can serve as dismissive remarks because Mennonite bureaucrats knew for more than thirty years that there were substantiated allegations but chose not to publicly validate or vindicate women's information as factual and as truthful. They chose to allow the *inaccurate factual data, rumor-mongering* and *personal vendetta* labels to be attached to the victim-supportive work of Mennonite and Catholic women who chose to speak up rather than doing nothing. Mennonite male administrators of church institutions knew that the women who chose to confront Yoder (and/or the actively negligent church administrators who supervised him) with concerns about his abusive behavior had factual information.[40] It is fact, not gossip, that in the Mennonite Church's and the Mennonite and Roman Catholic academies' historical decisions to shield and protect Yoder, more women were made vulnerable to his harassing acts of victimization.[41] The institutional church's decisions and the religious academy's decision to keep sending Yoder around the world on his lecture and consulting circuits simply added more potential and actual victims to his portfolio of abuse.

In addition, it has been women's voices that have called (and continue to call) the institutional church to repent for its negligence. While there were men's voices in 1992 calling for Bethel College to disinvite Yoder, these men spoke only to Bethel College administrators and the conference planning body.[42] It was victimized women who reached out to each other and continued to urge the church to act denominationally.[43] During mid-decade in the 1990's men and women who publicly attacked Anabaptist-Mennonite women in writing were not confronted (in public writing by other women and men) about the inappropriate nature of their victim-blaming actions. Their hostile comments towards victimized women's advocates and victimized women who were seeking to get the church's attention were allowed to stand unchallenged.[44]

For the most part, then, it has been knowledgeable Anabaptist-Mennonite women who have called for a re-analysis of Yoder's legacy of written work and his interwoven system of ethics, ecclesiology, and theology. It has mostly been concerned church women who have continued to remind Mennonite Church bureaucrats that they must be accountable to the community for their actions in hiding Yoder's behaviors from public awareness. For the most part it has been academic Mennonite women who have confronted the theological silence of the Mennonite Church's academic guilds regarding the need to study Yoder's work in a way that does not deny his lived-life. To my knowledge to date, the earliest academic written comments about Yoder's behavior as a theological or ethical issue are in Mennonite women's doctoral dissertations and master's theses.[45]

The absence of a public male academic voice in support of Yoder's victims has been striking to me. Many men have been and are willing to support women in private; many men in private conversations support women's concerns about Yoder's behavior and the church's behavior. More than a few are willing in private conversations to critique the Mennonite Church's use of power and authority to provide institutional absolution as a pathway to Yoder's restoration to full membership. Few, however, have chosen a public role or a public voice in calling the church to accountability. While there are exceptions to this male silence, these male voices are in the minority.

I noticed, and so did many other women, that the AMBS March 22, 2015 service of confession and lament vis-à-vis the seminary's historical mismanagement of John Howard Yoder's sexual abuses, was largely a female confession and lament. Two women carried the seminary's historical burden of responsibility for confession. It does not appear as if any of the seminary's Yoder era male faculty or male administrators confessed their own personal responsibility for the seminary's lack of action in dealing directly with Yoder's behavior.[46]

I conclude, therefore, that academic Mennonite men, in general, do not see sexual violence as an important peace and justice issue. They most certainly do not risk their careers to support the victims of violence. While there are exceptions to this, they are rare.

It is important to note, therefore, that this absence of a prophetic male voice has not been due to the exclusion of male voices by women. Rather, it has been a self-excluded voice. Men with factual information chose to remain silent as their Mennonite women colleagues' reputations (as honorable scholars with accurate factual information) were shunned and trashed. Outspoken Mennonite women scholars were labeled, avoided, ignored, or isolated as angry or enraged women with a personal vendetta against Yoder or against his church.

Only recently, therefore, have Anabaptist-Mennonite theologians and ethicists publicly entered this discussion about the need for institutional accountability.[47] They do this primarily by short statements that acknowledge that Yoder abused women. Usually, this acknowledgment is followed by a much larger *but* statement. We can condense that *but* into certain recurring phrases: *his church forgave him; he meant no harm; he was just socially awkward; maybe he had Asperger's syndrome; since there was no adultery that included coitus, what he did does not matter in our efforts to understand his theology and* to me the most obscure, troubling, and recurring theme *is that he was developing and experimenting with a revolutionary and ultra-radical Anabaptist theology of sexuality and sexual expression.*[48]

In some of these male-authored articles and blog sites there is an implicit judgment: since some women apparently could successfully say "no" to Yoder's advances or do not seem emotionally, physically, or spiritually scarred by them, the women who were not successful in avoiding his sexual harassment or who were emotionally or spiritually harmed in some way or another are personally responsible for their own victimization at Yoder's hands.[49]

Thus, it has, for the most part, been institutionally entitled white Mennonite, Catholic, and Evangelical men who serve as uncritical apologists for Yoder's work. It is these same men who have tried to keep the door slammed shut on all factually-informed conversations about Yoder's behavior towards his male colleagues' wives and daughters, his women colleagues in the workplace and his women students in the classroom. It has been entitled dominant male individuals inside the Christian evangelical religious academy who have been most hostile to any incisive critique of Yoder's work and life. It has been entitled Mennonite men who chastised, criticized, attacked, and sought to silence – whether openly or passive-aggressively – concerned Mennonite women's voices.

While there is no monolith here (not all knowledgeable Anabaptist-Mennonite men were silent and not all knowledgeable Anabaptist-Mennonite women were outspoken), nevertheless there is a very real gender issue and I am not quite certain I understand its complexity. But issues of misogyny, men's cultural entitlement, and the Mennonite Church's preferential option for Yoder's male academic theological voice are most certainly present.

So, I will end my reply to you with my working analysis of the patriarchal worldview. I reflect, therefore, the scholarship of the second wave of American feminism as it emerged in the 1960's and 1970's.

American Feminist and Womanist Scholarship

Only the victim can speak for the victim.

Elie Wiesel

American feminist and womanist critiques of male scholarship include the idea that an author's personal or social location affects the content of one's scholarship. Therefore, as much as possible, feminist and womanist scholars tend to declare the *who* that one is as well as the *what* which one thinks. They tend to declare their social location in life. This critique is not a demand for prurience, intellectual nakedness, or inappropriate personal revelations. Nor, in its proper forms, is it a manifestation of narcissistic grandiosity.[50] Rather to declare my social location is to acknowledge that as a white, straight, middle-class, well-educated woman living in the United States, there are many realities about being a woman that I have not experienced or do not know and there are multiple life experiences common to many women, such as, for example, giving birth, that I do not share. In addition, as someone who was never raped as an adolescent and never sexually molested as a child, there are very common aspects to a female life experience and socio-personal identity in patriarchal cultures that I only know about second hand.[51]

Consequently, when I bear witness against these violent realities in many women's lives, I must always be aware that my life experiences and my perceptions unconsciously shape my thinking. I, like all other scholars, authors, and teachers (male and female alike) have blinders I do not know I am wearing.

Because of this insistence upon particularity, many feminist and womanist scholars also insist upon making room for the excluded voice or the absent voice. This means paying close attention to all aspects of inclusion. Who is or is not invited to be a part of any given dialogue. Who is or is not, by virtue of some aspect of their personal identity (for example, gender, ethnicity, sexual orientation, national origins, family of origin, skin color, religious background, etc.) deliberately excluded from the conversation. Who is not included just because they are either unknown or overlooked? Who is deliberately excluded because they

Ruth E. Krall

are viewed as an unnecessary, potentially troublesome, politically undesirable, or extraneous participant for the conversation? Who is excluded because their presence might make the dominant majority uncomfortable? Who is excluded to avoid conflict? Whose voice is denied because of politics – the desire to silence that voice in order to perpetuate the status quo?

In the classroom, I used a short-hand formula to teach PJCS students[52] about this issue of exclusion and inclusion. In one discussion or another I would say something like the following. *In whatever kind of peace work you choose to do, teach yourself to be aware of the missing voice, the missing individual. Teach yourself to ask yourself and others, who is missing at this table of conversation. Who needs to be included? How do you identify the missing voice? You look at the participants already included in the conversation and you look to see what group or individual is not represented. For example, if the conversation is about full inclusion for sexual minorities; are there any individuals present who represent sexual minorities? Are you only talking about sexual minorities or are you also talking with members of those minorities? Are you practicing tokenism, for example, seven people representing the sexual majority and one person representing all sexual minorities? If you are working to improve the life status of homeless people, have you talked with homeless people about what they need? Are they included in your task force? Learn to ask yourself if your help is relevant?*

As another example: in Nicaragua and Costa Rica, local service agencies which received used clothing from North America designated for impoverished people would periodically get a box of clothing suitable for Alaska. One of my local friends asked me, *"Don't they look in a box before they ship it to us. We can't use this clothing and we can't afford to ship it back."* The box of warm sweaters, gloves, hats, boots, and coats was consequently thrown away or destroyed. I was told during this conversation that one North American denomination had sent a whole shipping container filled with winter clothing. Somebody, some informed person's voice, somewhere, was missing in the North American conversation about what poor people needed in Central America.

The most important questions are quite simple. Who is needed for the conversation to have integrity, vitality, complexity, and wholeness? Whose presence is urgently needed for the uncovering of truth – either in its abstract philosophical dimensions or in its concrete dimensions such as demographic and incidence data? Whose absence means that factual truth has been obscured, distorted or otherwise compromised?

Convening conversations in conferences, classroom, or in printed media, this issue of inclusion becomes a necessary one to monitor. It becomes an issue of making deliberate interventions when necessary. This does not mean that more inclusive conversations will necessarily be more comfortable ones. It does not guarantee they will be free of conflict and raised voices. But despite that discomfort, efforts at full inclusion are essential to the search for abstract truths and for data-driven factual truths.

Tokenism

It is essential, in this regard to comment upon tokenism.[53] No one individual represents every individual in his or her socio-economic-gender-racial-religious-ethnic-sexual orientation identity. Multiple voices from multiple perspectives are needed. If only one woman is included, perhaps conference organizers should limit themselves to one man. If only one third world person is included in assigned readings about third world realities, perhaps classroom teachers should limit themselves to teaching only one first world person. If only one member of a sexual minority is included, perhaps book editors should limit themselves to only one member of the dominant sexual majority. There does not need to be perfect parity, but there does need to be awareness that tokenism serves the dominant perspective and establishes a preferential option for that perspective's voice. Failing to understand this, the search for truth becomes merely a repetitive search for or, worse yet, a regurgitation of ideological dogma and cultic orthodoxy. When dealing with the messy cultural underpinnings of sexual and gender-based violence, we need to get all relevant voices to the table and we need to do this in a planned and respectful manner.

Having, for example, a conversation about LBGTQ individuals and church membership without listening to and attempting to understand any first-person voices from this marginalized group of individuals means that institutional decisions will be made on the basis of culturally ingrained prejudices; voices and life experiences of the marginalized group will be ignored. Excluding lived-life experiences of LBGTQ individuals means that their personal experiences of their identity and their perspectives on their own life experiences will be denied. Ignored or missing perspectives, therefore, cannot inform the whole. Aspects of factual truth will be distorted.

There is a true story from a Mennonite institution which had recently appointed a token person of color to its governing board. Every time this particular board needed to address issues of racism, they waited until their tokenized-person-of-color-board member was absent from the room and voted without her opinion being asked for or her vote being cast and counted. This individual, one day, in a rest room stall, heard through the wall which separated the men's room from the women's room, one member of this particular church institution board describing the board's strategy for managing complaints about racism *by isolating her.* From that time on, my colleague and friend scheduled her bathroom breaks so that these kinds of secretive votes could not be taken without her presence and

Ruth E. Krall

participation. In essence, once learning that she was institutionally intended to be a token, she refused to be tokenized.

Such an approach of exclusivity rather than inclusivity serves the status quo in which cultural exclusion on the basis of some human difference is codified and rigidified into dogma, doctrine, and orthodoxy. Exclusion serves to reinforce cultural prejudices and stereotypes. In religious settings and in some cultural settings as well, God's name is invoked to maintain the status quo and the use of *HIS* masculine and presumably heterosexual name continues to reinforce intact unjust socio-cultural and religious institutions and helps to maintain or reinforce their boundaries of exclusion.

When people with something important to add to the conversation are deliberately excluded from conversations which deeply involve them, we can conclude that the orthodoxy cavalry has gathered its horses and has circled them continuously around religious institutions and religious academies. This orthodoxy cavalry does this to protect the calcified beliefs and dogma that allow some individuals to be excluded as less than fully human. It does this, I am increasingly convinced, because it is too lazy to search for and enable more complexity.

This is not an honorable way to proceed in any search for factual truth. It has no integrity. It has no accountability. In addition, it cheapens all of God's many names.

Similarly, when the topic is a church's management of a sexual offender whose victims have all been women, to exclude victimized women's voices from relevant ethical, theological, or clinical discussions is absurd. Such a practice raises serious questions about the purposes of such scholarship and such institutional discussions. Are they designed, consciously or unconsciously, to perpetuate male entitlement which in turn perpetuates the problem of male sexual abuse of women into future generations? Are these practices of exclusion meant to continue and foment the current practices of protecting current abusers and their enablers? In an era when internet searches and queries of colleagues can be done in seconds, the excuse that *we just don't know the relevant women's voices* is patently lazy. In addition, it represents poor scholarship.

Complex topics such as sexual violence, therefore, need multiple voices. In particular, deliberately marginalized voices need to be invited to the table as full and equal participants in the conversations.[54] Sexual violence will never be understood as the complex topic it is if the voices of victims, survivors, and informed victim advocates are excluded from the larger, more abstract and philosophical discussion of the causes and manifestations of such violence. Only the survivors of such violence really know the complex interpersonal and intrapersonal terrain of this toxic narrative. No conversation about any social episode of sexual violence and/or the violence of institutional clericalism, therefore, should overlook the personal and public narratives of its survivors.

The most powerful Jewish witnesses to the genocidal atrocities of the Third Reich against Europe's Jewish individuals and communities are, therefore, those individuals who survived the Jewish Shoah. Only they can bear a first-hand witness to the atrocities they witnessed and endured – those atrocities that ended the lives of millions of other European Jews. Witnesses who liberated the extermination camps after the Third Reich's failed efforts at annihilation of every Jewish person alive can also bear direct and first-hand testimony to these genocidal atrocities.

Likewise, the most powerful witnesses to the damages of sexual violation are individuals who have been sexually violated. In an analogous manner, they, too, have the most intimate acquaintance with these multiple forms of violation and personal violence. Those who bear informed witness to the presence of sexual violation in the lives of others can, therefore, also be reliable witnesses to this toxic reality in the middle of the socio-religious commons.

In a similar way, theologies or ethical systems of non-violence also need the voice and witness of those who have been victimized by violence. They need the voice of informed victim advocates and knowledgeable healers. They need the voice of on-location workers for justice and accountability. Too facile an intellectual abstraction; too much insistence that there is only one way to work for peace, justice, and healing; and too dogmatic an approach to the peace-building and healing-restorative work needing to be done in the human commons after acts of violence vitiate the community's collective witness to truth, justice, and the need for human compassion. When the religious community, inside the human commons, *smells like horse manure*, to quote a Mennonite aphorism, the surrounding world is repelled.

While there is a place for theological abstraction in the creation and application of non-violent principles, we must always include space for the particularity of voice that is known as praxis – the lived theology or ethics that emerges from our social engagement with others and eventually circles back on (like the ancient Ouroboros) the abstraction to critique and refine it. This is particularly true when abstract theologies and ideologies are part and parcel of any given culture's socio-theological rationalizations for the perpetuation of violence.

Insisting upon such disclosures as one's social location, therefore, provides a needed corrective to the so-called objective voice of much male scholarship. By seeking to accurately denote one's social location, such a scholarship practice seeks to acknowledge that any one individual's voice is simply that and no more: her or his uniquely personal voice. There is, therefore, no implicit claim for absolute truth. In such a worldview, all intellectual discourse reveals partial truths – filtered through the life experiences and perceptions of the writer as well as through those of the reader.

Such an insistence that the personal and the political merge in every act of scholarship does not only tacitly allow but actively encourages readers of academic scholarship to watch for the usually unseen or unrecognized bias that every human being carries. It provides a place or an opportunity for the corrective voice(s) to emerge. While perhaps absolute truth is never relative, all human knowing of such truth is.

This means that no one individual possesses total and absolute truth. It also means that inside the social collective of the commons there both can and should be disagreements about the community's shared truth. Each individual living inside the commons is capable, therefore, of adding his or her perceptions of truth to the discussion of the whole. Not everyone's perceptions will be equal in their contribution and each person's contributions, therefore, need to be robust enough to stand up to and endure informed critique. This is because no one individual has the complexity of life experiences that are needed in thinking about theological and ethical complexity in matters of violence. And, as Jesus himself reminded us, in our disputations with one another, we are to welcome the child's voice and presence.

There have been times in my life when I have been most informed by those the culture disavows as having any value and any relevant knowledge at all: a blind, old man in a refugee camp in Central America; a developmentally challenged and psychotic mid-life black patient in a state hospital ward; a financially and culturally impoverished withered aging white woman from Appalachia; a severely burned and physically abused seven-year-old boy; and a just-raped young adult woman and her enraged-on-her-behalf boyfriend. These individuals have been my teachers because they knew worlds and life experiences I could only witness by paying attention. They experienced the absence of tranquility, peace, and justice in ways which opened my heart to many different forms of structural violence and social injustice. At some basic level, I think now, they each knew they were on society's discard pile – people having no social power to change the tragic trajectory of their personal lives; people, therefore, of no importance and hence of no value. There is a certain sense, then, that I have not learned and honed my personal convictions – or my theology if you will - about violence in the academic classroom. I learned it first in the lives of those wounded and suffering men and women I met – individuals whose lives were forever altered by the presence of many forms of social abuse and personal violation.

To learn from them, I had to be both fully present and I needed to pay attention. I had to believe that their humanity was complete and equal to mine. I had to be willing to learn from them – to be taught by their share of human wisdom and life experience. This can be the model for doing inclusive theology. We need each other to be fully present and we need everyone to be paying attention. No one's voice can stand for the whole. No one's voice represents absolute truth. No one's voice should attempt to represent and speak for the whole.

A Plea for Integrity[55]

We must take sides. Neutrality helps the oppressor, never the victim. Silence encourages the tormenter, never the tormented.

Elie Wiesel[56]

We can and should aim to demonstrate personal and professional integrity in all forms of scholarship. All readers and writers should be aware, however, that all abstract academic scholarship contains personal bias and partial truths.[57] When we academics and scholars are careful about the social location of any particular voice, the absence of deliberately or negligently excluded voices usually becomes glaringly visible.

It is increasingly clear to me that consumers of academic scholarship are enablers of academic denial when they do not insist upon practices of inclusion and practices of disclosure by authors. Non-inclusive books can be boycotted and publishing companies informed about the theoretical inadequacies of their products. In many clinical conferences it is now a mandated practice for every speaker to disclose any professional or personal identity aspects that might hide conflicts of interests. So a physician lecturing for example on the XY drug to treat the JZ disorder must now disclose his or her financial interests or holdings in the company which produces the drug. In a similar manner many televised drug commercials and advertisements now include a very small-print advisory statement that the "physician" in the advertisement is a paid actor.

This is not about engaging in censorship. It makes no claim that miscreant voices should be silenced. Rather, these paragraphs argue for extending the scope of theological conversations instead of silencing them. Until we all protest the socio-theological exclusion of relevant, therefore needed, voices, these exclusions will continue. These paragraphs about integrity argue for holding each other accountable to high standards of honesty and as much transparency as we are capable of providing each other. They argue for holding administrative officers of the institutional church and its various sub-divisions accountable to the whole for their decision-making processes. Closed-session administrative discussions have, I suppose, some validity in some situations. However, when they are engaged in judging the participation of marginalized people inside the community of faith, this form of executive committee secrecy is unacceptable. Institutions need administrative transparency when they discuss *who belongs and who doesn't belong.* This is particularly true in situations of obvious and not-so-obvious abuses of power. This is also true when some parties attempt to use extortion to influence the outcome of a decision about inclusion or exclusion.[58]

Using Theological Coercion to Conceal or Distort the Truth

The Galileo-Roman Catholic Church disagreement about the heliocentric nature of earth's relationship to its sun in 1615 CE provides me with my permanent working model for academic and religious institution humility in the face of advancing science and cultural change. Using the emergent science and technology of his day, Galileo ran afoul of the Roman Catholic Vatican-based hierarchy and the Inquisition. The church sought to exclude his voice as it did the earlier voice of Copernicus from its theological discussions about the nature of Earth's solar system.

My personal mantra for many years – whenever and wherever I witness the institutional and hierarchical church defensively locking itself into a now-dead worldview and an ideology no longer supported by today's emerging science – is that *Galileo was largely right and his seventeenth century church was totally wrong.*[59] Silencing the voice of knowledgeable and informed dissent serves to guarantee the psychological, intellectual, and spiritual comfort of the elite ruling classes but it does not further the theological, philosophical, or scientific pursuit of truth.

Speaking Our Own Voice

Any given woman, therefore, does not represent womankind in general. As we women come together to protest male violence in its many forms (for example, sexual violence directed against women and children inside the boundaries of our given faith communities) we can seek to make known that which is sensed at deep personal, intuitive, levels but has not yet become part of the shared consciousness of the whole. We can ultimately, I think, speak only in our own voice. We can be respectful in the presence of conflicting voices. Our collective work as feminist, womanist and post-colonial scholars forms a corrective, therefore, to the dominant, highly competitive, controlling male voice of our culture – a voice which accepts and even promulgates the naturalness of personal and social behaviors of male violence against women and their children.

The Need for Factual Truth

Discerning factual truth, however, is a different matter. This truth can be sought, known, and promulgated. In situations of clergy and religious leader sexual abuse, this kind of forthright demographic data-gathering and competent/honorable analysis is essential. To help victimized individuals and entire communities acknowledge the truth of abuse, establishing shared meanings of technical words in the service of complex understanding and shared analysis, correct factual information, truth-filled personal narratives and accurate demographic data are all needed. This assumption about the need for factual truth provided the baseline of twentieth-century feminist scholarship in the areas of anti-rape and anti-domestic violence advocacy work.[60] Early feminist scholarship in these two areas emphasized, therefore, the need for precise and accurate demographic data. During the past five years, I have come to believe that we need better national demographic data about the incidence and prevalence of clergy and religious leader sexual abuse. Until we know the true extent of these forms of abuse, we are handicapped in our efforts to bring about change inside of our respective denominations.

Those of us who are clinicians know that when clients directly and personally encounter the deep factual truth of their story of violation, they can then begin to heal that story by their deliberate, albeit often very painful, work. They can begin a life-long process of learning how to integrate and manage a factually truthful and accurate historical narrative into their ongoing personal life narrative. Truth-telling, by its very nature, participates in the healing of fragmented and dissociated individual lives and fragmented communities.[61]

Institutional Agenda and Issues

Administrators and personnel managers who receive complaints and allegations about sexual harassment and sexual abuse, who hear rumors and gossip about abuse and do not act, are derelict in their duty to investigate all such complaints, to intervene where appropriate, and to inform vulnerable others and the community at large about the situation at hand. By their inept or deliberately malfeasant actions, they perpetuate an absence of truth in the commons. They participate, therefore, in the on-going spiritual violation and wounding of individuals and entire communities.

Victim Advocacy Work

These insights are very important in victim advocacy work. No victim advocate should claim the victim's story as her own. No victim advocate should assume that because she or he has heard 100 stories of abuse, s/he knows the complex and toxic terrain of these multiple vile stories of sexual abuse and violence for every other victimized individual. No victim advocate should lay claim to any specific victim's story in the public sphere without being given express permission to do so. Even then, the victim advocate must make certain that she or he does not transform the victim's story into a commodity of public information, judgment, or persuasion.

In addition, victims should be helped to awareness that while their particular story has many commonalities with other victimized individuals, each person's life trajectory and life decisions will be uniquely their own. There is, therefore, no one guaranteed pathway to healing and self-restoration. In my opinion while there are common markers on the pathway to healing, each individual, after experiences of sexual violation, will need to create a unique and deeply personalized journey back to wholeness and wellness. As they create this journey for themselves, often with professional help, they will add to our knowledge of this journey and these complex many-trail pathways through the enchanted forest of sexual abuse and violence. Body/Self/Soul/community-healing-work is not too strong a vocabulary for what individuals must do to re-create their lives after sexual violence has altered their lives forever.[62] Victims will discover they need to pursue resurrection after the mini-deaths of the self which sexual violence brings. They will need to mourn that which they lost in the violent attacks but, in healing work, they can come to celebrate that which remains and that which is born anew from the ashes of their pre-victimization life.

While those of us who do victim advocacy *and* who think theologically about the roots of violence need the abstractions of theory in doing our sexual violence advocacy work, it is absolutely essential to realize that each individual's encounter with the evils of gender-based discrimination, hostile climate harassment, and overt sexual violation such as rape or sexual molestation of children is uniquely their own.

Each victim's story is both personal and transpersonal – in that the personal story is deeply rooted in the cultural story which surrounds all rape events. Each victim's story carries its own noxious and incendiary power to wound and to destroy. Every victim's story also carries, however, the seeds for healing and wholeness.

The Goals of Victim Advocacy

One goal of victim advocacy is to participate in victim empowerment – assisting the victimized individual to lay claim to her or his own story as an important story; to lay claim to her or his powers of self-other healing as a spiritual birthright. The goal of victim advocacy is healing and personal transformation by means of very common and ordinary social behaviors – which can be practiced by everyone. Victims need to be believed. They need to be acknowledged as truthful story tellers. Their personal encounters with abuse need to be validated and honored. Individuals need to be emotionally and spiritually supported as they sort through the wastelands of their once-upon-a-time violated body, psyche, spirit, memory, and consciousness.

In addition, another goal of victim advocacy is that of education and prevention. It is not enough to heal the wounds of violence. We must seek to transform ourselves and our various cultures so that additional violence is prevented. Our mission as individuals or as representatives of organizations is three-fold: stop the violence from continuing; heal the wounds of its victims and their communities of reference; and prevent future violence from happening. Each of these three tasks will involve different strategies and approaches to the problem of intimate, interpersonal violation and violence.

Women's Work

As women, we are the birth-givers in many different ways. The future flows in our blood lines and in our mitochondrial DNA. One of our tasks as feminist women is to nurture and to protect the young. Encountering sexual violence anywhere in the human chain, as part of this task, we must speak the factual truth which we know *and* we must also share the deep intuitive truths of our female wisdom. To be faithful to our own gender, we need to recognize all forms of sexual abuse as violence. In addition, we must form vital communities of resistance with everyone, male and female, who knows that acts of sexual violence are evil and, in addition, are usually criminal acts as well.

In addition, we Anabaptist-Mennonite women must avoid being seduced by male Mennonite authors and activists who, by their shelves of published books, implicitly make the claim that the terrain of creating authentic twenty-first century Anabaptist-Mennonite theology, ecclesiology, and ethics belong only to denomination-educated men. We must remember that while our male faith ancestors were sometimes book-educated, our female Anabaptist ancestors were not. We must remember, therefore that the vibrantly alive sixteenth-century Anabaptist-Mennonite revolution was fueled by uneducated and illiterate men *and* women, minor nobility, peasants and serfs who experienced a form of spiritual consciousness-raising in which they became worthy participants of a social experiment that sought to repudiate and replace the state's and church's violence with new forms of church *and* state governance. Implicit in that Anabaptist vision was the notion that both male and female adults are equal in God's sight and, as adult believers, both male and female should be baptized upon their uncoerced adult confession of faith. We know that peasants and serfs witnessed to and then baptized other peasants and serfs – often alongside a roadside river or in a forested quiet pool of water. We know as well that in martyrdom, baptized Anabaptist woman and their daughters suffered the same fates as Anabaptist men and their sons. The fire's flame and the river's water brought about the martyrs' deaths of men *and* women, of boys *and* girls with an equality they never had in life.[63]

In our lifetimes, therefore, we can honor the memory of these female faith ancestors by embodying that which they could perhaps not even dream of; the ability to fully participate in the academic enterprise of theology and theory-building as full equals to men. By virtue of all of the women who have gone before us – who desired perhaps the intellectual and social privileges we today enjoy, we have, I believe, an obligation to give back so that we might open wider the door to future generations of women in order that they remain free to make their own life decisions. We need to act today so that in seven generations from now, more women are culturally supported in their actions to fulfill the intellectual and personal promise of their God-given lives.

The Mennonite Church in 2015-2016

In the Mennonite Church of 2015-2016 those of us who advocate for sexual justice as well as those of us who provide a theological analysis of the violence which has already occurred are each working in a variety of venues. We bring a variety of academic and professional backgrounds to our task. We are a group of Anabaptist-Mennonite women who have met each other around the deeply interpenetrated issues of the patriarchy as these are expressed in sexism, racism, heterosexism, sexual abuse, undue nationalism, ethnocentrism, and institutional clericalism.[64] We have met inside the outermost boundaries of our shared Anabaptist-Mennonite Christian tradition. We are the descendants of those women who in the sixteenth century sought a new way of organizing family and community life – a fellowship or communion of social equals. In their era they were penalized harshly for the radicality of their vision. We are, therefore, the descendants of martyrs. We represent this lineage of faith which goes back to the sixteenth century. We are the voice of our raped ancestors – Mennonite women in 19th century and 20th century Russia who later emigrated to the United States, South America, and Canada – their story often alluded to but never spoken about in our denomination's theological commons. We represent our mothers and our grandmothers who were sexually molested in childhood but could never tell anyone. We represent our friends who live inside abusive marriages. We represent today's young American women – raped by boyfriends or family members inside their Anabaptist-Mennonite community of faith. Having a voice, we seek to both empower the voices of others and, where they cannot speak, we seek to acknowledge that absence of voice by our own work on their behalf.

Third Letter

Speaking Truth about Sexual Violence in Christian Churches

Introductory Comments

Our obligation for truth telling in a dispute is to hear all of the pertinent voices before speaking any determination.

Mark D. Jordan[65]

I will begin this letter with a confession. While I have been aware for perhaps twenty-five years of the connection in historical time between the Mennonite Church's cover-up silence about religious leader sexual abuse of the laity and its aggressive denominational denunciations of homosexuality as a purity violation of the church's historical teachings about sexuality, only recently have I begun to think of these two issues as discrete poisonous trees - trees which have inter-twined rootlets in the soil of an enchanted toxic forest. These are trees which grow next to each other in ideologically polluted soil. Inside this enchanted theological forest all kinds of religious abuse can take root and grow.

Only recently, therefore, has the full irony of this Christian dogma and praxis paradox impressed itself on my own consciousness. I have been assisted to think more deliberately and more intently about these issues because of Stephanie Krehbiel's work. She is a young woman scholar with a Mennonite heritage.[66] In addition, Roman Catholic theologian William (Bill) Lindsey has been immensely helpful to my understanding of these complex issues as he uses his blog (Bilgrimage) to explore issues of Christian theology in a Catholic voice, human sexuality, and social justice.[67]

Let me state this paradox as clearly as I know how to do so. Today's (and yesterday's) institutional Christian churches often refuse to accept mutual, consenting, and loving sexual relationships between two same gender adults (refusing them a full participating membership and a spiritual blessing on their relationship) even as the church actively hides, and therefore both enables and implicitly blesses, repeated events and acts of sexual violence and sexual harassment done by its clergy and religious leaders.

In this situation, mutually loving and frequently covenanted same gender relationships which enrich and bless the lives of two individuals (and sometimes their children and extended families as well) are forbidden. In the name of the churches' sexual theologies and purity codes, they cannot be supported. Openly partnered gay men and lesbian women are all too frequently, therefore, force-marched into religious and spiritual exile from their cradle community of faith and family.

On the other hand, inside this toxic religious institution forest, violent sexual relationships which destroy the lives of victims *and* perpetrators can be and often are supported inside institutional covenants of secrecy and lying. They are, therefore, implicitly blessed. The sexual perpetrators of violence are protected and remain a valued part of the community because the community refuses to be accountable to the whole for these individual's episodes of sexual violence and sexual harassment done inside church agencies on the church's institutional watch. Survivors of these assaults are all too frequently left to fend for themselves with little to no experience of community compassion and help.

We have, therefore, the spiritual-religious-theological irony that victims of clergy sexual violence and institutional clericalism, like their same gender compatriots in exile, are also force-marched out of their church. Their life situation is, therefore, remarkably similar to the fate of same gender partnered couples who have sought the institutional church's blessing on their relationship: continuous victimization and revictimization in the name of God and God's people. The institutional human church which in its scriptures is called to the task of healing the wounds of those most victimized and vulnerable becomes, instead, the source of abusive victimization in the names of its gods. The Christian Church, which was in its origins based on welcoming and safe hospitality, becomes contaminated by internal violence.

One can only conclude, therefore, that the institutional church qua institution is either unable or unwilling to deal with the complex realities of human sexual experience as it is actually lived rather than as denominational church leaders say these *should* be. This inability or simple unwillingness to acknowledge that which *already is* causes immense psychological, emotional, and spiritual suffering for those individuals who have, as a result of other's behavior and decisions, been force-marched out of their community.

Ruth E. Krall

This religious-spiritual paradox of refusing to bless that which is freely chosen by loving adults *and* simultaneously choosing to bless that which is violently coerced by sexual predators seems like utter lunacy to me. Perhaps, like Alice in Wonderland, todays (and yesterdays) Christian churches have inadvertently and unwittingly slipped down into a toxic rabbit hole where a crazy-making and perverted spiritual consciousness guides its inhabitants' decisions.

I suspect that this defect in my awareness and my delayed analysis are most likely due to heterosexual privilege. As a woman I have long been aware of the damages done to women by patriarchal and sexist cultural forms.[68],[69] As a heterosexual woman I have not been totally unaware of the heterosexist damages done to gay men and lesbian women by patriarchal and heterosexist cultural forms but I have not studied these in depth. Thus, I do not consider myself to be an expert on these correlational matters. I am a beginner in exploring this toxic religious institution forest with its theologically polluted soil. Nevertheless, it has become apparent to me – given the nature of our recent electronic correspondence – that in a tentative and beginning way these letters need to address these two issues as interpenetrated ones because they have become so clearly associated with each other in institutional-historical-public time.

Becoming aware of this complex paradox, my emotional and spiritual response is simultaneously one of deep grief and profound outrage. I do not want to be complicit in any way with these forced marches into spiritual and emotional exile. I refuse to give my consent. All of my deepest instincts as a healer and as a pastoral thealogian are to bind up and mend the wounds of victimized individuals and communities – not cause or foment them.

Perhaps we should see this letter, then, as an invitation to conversation for all concerned individuals who seek inclusive, welcoming, transparent, and accountable church structures. If we begin to push back the boundaries of that which we don't know and the boundaries of that which we do know but have not yet codified into language as known, perhaps we can begin to untangle the root systems of these two poisonous and toxic trees (the tree of church institution-protected sexual violence acts done by members of its ordained clergy and the tree of sexual orientation xenophobia perpetuated by its institutional leaders).

When sexual orientation xenophobia is defended in the name of religious orthodoxy, then in the name of that orthodoxy the Christian Church seeks to enforce ancient and scientifically outdated sexual purity codes. When it does this, it spiritually and psychologically harms individuals. It also damages the spiritual maturity of entire communities.

Perhaps as we open this conversation, we might be enabled to see each of these two poisonous trees as distinct and long-living memes of toxic violence.[70] Perhaps we might each begin to find new ways of speaking with which to address these issues in the Mennonite commons.

My thinking here is exploratory and tentative. It has more of the nature of an invitation to further conversation than it does about the nature of conclusion and exhortation.

In this letter, therefore, I want to work with the intellectual-theological work of an "out-of-the-closet" gay Roman Catholic theologian, Mark D. Jordan.[71] In his own way Jordan has begun to explore these connections between Christian theology, Christian praxis, and heterosexist privilege from inside his lived-life as a gay Christian man. I recommend his published reflections about speaking truth to you and to other readers of these letters. Anyone, seeking to expand his or her awareness of the interfacing connections between silenced speech and hate speech, will find Jordan's analysis helpful.

In particular I want to work with Jordan's 2003 book, *Telling Truths in Church: Scandal, Flesh, and Christian Speech.* This book collects a series of public lectures which he gave in New England during 2002 – an era when revelations of clergy sexual misconduct and institutional cover-ups by Cardinal Law in the Boston Diocese of the Roman Catholic Church were aggressively uncovered by and reported upon by the SPOTLIGHT journalists from the *Boston Globe.*[72] As an unpredictable byproduct of this historical moment, Jordan was forced by his audiences' anger and their questions to address the sexual abuse issue in his lectures. Even though sexual violence done by Roman Catholic clergy in the context of institutional clericalism was not his assigned topic, during his lectures he was repeatedly asked about the emerging scandal and crisis. Therefore, fragments of his thinking about or theologizing about this complex issue of sexual violence inside the Christian Church remain in this book.

In this letter, therefore, I want to do a close reading of Jordan's first three chapters in which he addresses the issues of hiding secrets and speaking truth. It is important to say as I begin this close reading, therefore, that the focus of his book is not clergy sexual abuse. But I plan to enter conversation with the book's content in order to have such a conversation. These are chapters in which he theoretically and theologically dissects the issue of holding secrets and the rhetorical issues of uncovering these secrets in the service of speaking truth about sexuality and sexual matters.

Telling Truths in Church: Scandal, Flesh and Christian Speech

> *Truth telling is not simple*
>
> Mark D. Jordan[73]

Ruth E. Krall

To reprise and contextualize: Jordan's book of chapter-length essays began life as a series of lectures given in New England – lectures which had been commissioned in 2001 but were actually given in 2002 after the *Boston Globe* began to publish information about the cover-up of sexually abusive priests in the Roman Catholic Boston diocese. Thus, as Jordan notes in his introduction, in actually presenting his lectures, he needed to think about *what kinds of truth needed telling and how best they could be told into a "crisis" if they could be told at all.*[74] Later he notes that *what was new about Boston was that the story was suddenly not just about Boston. It became for some time a scandal about the system of seminary formation and priestly discipline, of official speeches and their anxious silences.*[75] He notes the emergence of hate speech against homosexuality in calls to purge the Roman Catholic priesthood of its gay men. In the cacophony of speech that followed Boston, Jordan reports that he kept wondering how anyone could speak truth in the public commons.[76] Now redacted by Jordan in the years since 2002, this book contains his edited version of those Boston lectures.

He begins to unpack the notion of truth-telling with the comment that *there are different kinds of truth and each requires its own way of speaking.*[77]

- There is the truth which is stored in files, documents, and reports of legal proceedings. He notes that documents are *traces of events* and thus are, or function as, elements of the *official story.* In their role as carriers of official or institutional documentation, they also contain the recorded decisions *not to reveal, to stick by the agreed story.*[78] This kind of record is always, by its very nature, incomplete. Institutional records can get lost or buried in a sea of paper, be deliberately hidden or deliberately destroyed as individuals seek to protect the institution from accountability for its historical actions and non-actions.

- There is the truth of the memories of individuals sexually abused by priests in childhood and adolescence. He notes that trauma *chops itself into memory by chopping up memories.* He further notes that the testimonies of abuse survivors are *probably the truest words we have heard in the scandal. Still, their truth is not a truth of numbered propositions. It is the truth of an unhealed wound.*[79]

- There are institutional truths – the truths of regulations, doctrines, dogma, customs, and theological fictions – that allow the church to operate across time and space. Facing the complexities of institutional existences – for example, the theology and customs of the Roman Catholic priesthood – the question becomes visible: who can tell these truths? *If the most hidden truths in the scandal are truths about clerical institutions, what is the expertise that could begin to tell them?*[80] Noting the absence of Christian theologians – the experts – from the discussions surrounding the scandal in Boston, he comments that Christian theologians have an obligation to take responsibility for speaking these kinds of truth in theological forms.[81] The speech of Christian theology, therefore, is not (and, indeed, cannot be) divorced from all other forms of speaking.[82] Theology ought to be about *sanctifying speech* in the historical context where speech has already been revelatory – including or originating, for example, churchly speech about the sacraments and prayer.[83]

- In concluding this introductory chapter, he notes that speaking about sexuality and sexual desire in any format inside the church *seems to threaten the authority of Christian speaking.* He reiterates his reasons for this series of chapters about truth-speaking in this manner: *I hope you can catch an effort to find a way of speaking theology into institutional "crisis". In part, this will mean figuring out how to talk when so much talking has been distorted by the powerful motives of institutions in conflict.*[84]

Having read Jordan's brief explanatory introduction about the reasons for his book I am left, personally, therefore, with this question: what, therefore, does it mean to have authentic, truthful Christian speech about sexual violence – acts of sexual violation that happen **inside** the Christian community? When accurate information is deliberately obfuscated and kept secret – silenced as it were – how can the Christian community possibly speak truth to perpetrators, to victims, to victim advocates, to the families of perpetrators and victims, and to the community at large? If, as I believe, the healing process demands a foundation in truthful speech, how can individuals and entire communities heal the very personal consequences and the communal wounds caused by this breach of faith, this act of betrayal?

In your essay *Toward Mennonite Sexual Integrity,*[85] you argue that *repressing sexuality by ignoring sexual abuse and scapegoating those with diverse gender identity has made it impossible to place our collective focus on sexual integrity.* You go on to suggest that sexual integrity (*where people respect their own bodies and those of other people*) might provide the denomination with a grounding place to discuss divisive issues of sexuality that have arisen in our common responses to victimization, violence, and violation in a wide variety of forms. I agree with your analysis and am glad the denominational church press has published it.[86]

In his second chapter, Jordan begins to dissect various forms of speech that might be called into play in the search for authentic truth-telling. He begins by noting the ancient nature of the Roman Catholic faith tradition with its historical layers of history and theology. He notes that the Catholic Church is encumbered by its traditions and has developed elaborate institutional patterns or protocols to keep its own secrets hidden. He further notes that when sexual truths cannot be told in church, the church's experiences with various sexual issues must be kept secret if the church is to protect itself.

What happens when the church's sexual sins or its other sexual secrets finally break free into public space and are, therefore, spoken? Challenging the regime

Ruth E. Krall

of silence inside the churchly realms as a pathway to internal reform is not a straightforward path. *Telling scandalous secrets in the churches and the prospect of reform means telling truths about same-sex acts and desire within the churches, out of churchly experience, against well-rehearsed desires for enforcing silence in tense hope for something better.*[87]

In this chapter Jordan notes that the church lies[88] but he refuses to confront that lying in person in this book by deliberately refusing to bear a personal witness to his sexual life as a gay man. Instead, he informs his readers that he wants to move beyond the personal story to examine the concept and practice of telling secrets in the Catholic Church to which he belongs. Quoting Foucault, he notes that Christianity, as a religion, has an obligation to bear witness *against itself.*[89] It is a religion in which confession takes central place – the confession of faith and the confession of sin. *The church is (or ought to be) ours. Bearing witness against it is not an assault on an enemy so much as a testimony within a household.*[90] Even though the church theoretically functions as a new household or family for its members he acerbically comments that it is still a human organization and *not a company of saints in heaven.*[91]

Confronting the paradox of *homoeroticism* and *homophobia* in his church's historical praxis and in its present theologies means engagement with speech as a theoretical and practical issue. An underlying message throughout this book is that we must begin to think about not only the issues of distorted sexuality inside the Christian homeland but also the very speech we initiate and use to think about, to enter, and to explore these cacophonous conversations.

Jordan's personal concern in this book is telling truths about same gender sexual desire inside a Christian frame. I am extrapolating his wisdom to my concerns about telling truths about sexual violence of all kinds inside the boundaries of Christian faith. I do this because of my growing awareness that we cannot begin to understand the Christian Church's nervous, truth-resistant, and always living silence about one of these two issues without understanding the cacophonous, omnipresent, and usually obfuscating speech about the other.

This is not because the two issues are causative of each other. They are not. Phenomenologically there is no rational reason for their merger in ordinary time, ordinary consciousness, and ordinary religious speech inside the Christian community. Same gender sexual desire no more causes the sexual abuse of children, adolescents, and vulnerable adults than does two gender sexual desire.

The issues each sexually mature adult faces about the objects of his or her sexual desire are issues embedded in and somewhat shrouded by our genetic conception and by our social identity as gendered human beings. Because of the complexities of medical and veterinary research, we are now aware that the genetic origins of homosexuality lie in our species' ancient past. We are not the only living species in which same gender sexual desire and behavior are manifested. Our evolutionary history as gendered beings, as sexual beings, therefore, contains genetic tracers which can be identified and studied.

The issue of sexual abuse, on the other hand, is an issue embedded in human choicefulness, therefore, human behavior – not sexual orientation. It is, I have argued elsewhere, an issue of personal violence surrounded by violence-supportive cultural forms – or cultural memes.[92] Without the pre-existing form, it is unlikely that specific events of sexual violence could occur or would occur. But the surrounding cultural forms and the routinized presence or concrete manifestation of sexual violence events in our culture – and in the world's cultures – reinforce each other.

I mention this because we Jews and Christians have a shared textual tradition which teaches each student of scripture that divine providence had a hand – however distant – in our individual creation. In Jewish and Christian theology, it is, therefore, not only the merging of our parents' sperm and egg which created us, but there was a somewhat mysterious divine involvement in God's time with our creation.

In his address to Yahweh, the ancient psalm writer proclaimed: *for you fashioned my inmost being; you knit me together in my mother's womb.*[93] In ways the Christian Church has to date refused to acknowledge in its comprehensive, commonly accepted, pan-denominational theology, our gender *and* our sexual orientation are fashioned by divine consciousness as our humanly conceived bodies mature inside our mother's bodies.

This verse, by the way, does not claim that only male bodies were so miraculously knit together. It does not claim that only heterosexual desire bodies were miraculously created in God's image. Each one of us – each living human being - is created in God's image in some way that human consciousness cannot unravel nor contain. None of us is left behind in God's plan for our human life. Our spirituality and our sexuality are aspects of our creation in God's image.

This is a parenthetical comment which may be irrelevant. But our creation as male and female sexual beings in our maternal lineage begins with the stories and bodies of our grandmothers. A woman's eggs are all in place when she is born. So, the egg which became us not only nested inside our mother's ovaries; it nested in our grandmother's womb as well. Thus, some of our genetic tissue – the very substance of our creation – lodged inside female human flesh long before we were conceived.

In addition, it is clear from the voluminous research of the past four decades that sexual violence is not primarily a sexual violation. It is rather an act of violence that uses the sexual organs to intimidate, dominate, and control the subject of such violence. I believe sexual violence is the weaponry of choice for the ideology and praxis of patriarchal authoritarianism writ large. Thus, sexual intercourse (that intimate act which can bring joy and a deeply satisfying sense of human

connectedness as well as new life) is subverted to that which brings death of potentiality, pain, harm, betrayal, and long-lasting physical, personal, and social consequences in the lives of everyone involved. The human penis – rather than being
used in the service of human connectedness, ecstasy, union, and deep joy – is used
as a weapon of control, domination, and power. It is used to create terror, fear,
rage, despair, and other negative signs of trauma in its victimized human objects.

In your essay *Toward Mennonite Sexual Integrity*,[94] you discuss the damaging issues of closeting. This is a brilliant analogy because it brings together and
addresses the denomination-wide abusive closeting of individuals with a same
gender sexual orientation *and* it addresses the secretive nature of our communal
life when it comes to acts of sexual violence and institutional secrecy. You write:

> *Closets are a monument to consumerism. Like the collection of material
> possessions, sexual abuse and sexual assaults – and even sexual promiscuity
> – require dehumanizing male and female bodes as objects to consume. In too
> many Mennonite homes and congregations, sexual abuse has been passed on
> from generation to generation. Victims accumulate in closets, their voices like
> duct-taped covered boxes.*[95] Noting and reminding all of us you continue:
> *the church can support sexual integrity by acknowledging the humanity of
> male and female victims of sexual violence and giving them space to be agents
> of change and healing.*[96]

The paradox is quite clear: Consenting, long-term same gender or two gender
sexual relationships originate in the desire for human companionship and human
intimacy. Violent sexual acts, on the other hand, originate in the desire for ven-
geance, dominance and control.

As we proceed we must, therefore, stay clear on this. Sexual orientation and the
focus of sexual desire can be and should be differentiated from issues of gender
domination, sexual objectification, and sexual violence. The object of obsessive
or addictive and violent desire is, therefore, not an issue of gendered sexual orientation, gendered sexual desire, or even of gendered self-identification. Rather
than mutuality, the internal driving force of sexual violence is that internal drive
or desire directed towards creating subordination and subservience. The motive
for violent desire is control, dominance, and power-over. It is never intimacy
and accountability.

But churchly discussions in the last century and in the current century have
so conflated the two phenomenons (same gender sexual desire and clergy sexual
abuse of the laity – especially when this abuse involves same gender victims) in
such ideologically dense ways that whenever the scandal of sexual abuse by
Christian clergy surfaces into a public view, the issue of same gender sexual desire
also surfaces into the public consciousness as well. It is as if these two unrelated

experiential phenomenons are Siamese twins: one cannot appear without the other appearing as well.

What is largely ignored in these convoluted discussions is that some and perhaps most clergy sexual violations of small children, adolescents, and vulnerable adults are male-female violations rather than male-male or female-female ones. Because of the single gender nature of the Roman Catholic priesthood, this Christian denomination provides us with an exception to the rule. Most acts of sexual abuse of the laity in Christendom and in other world religions represent, therefore, male-female abuse. To put it bluntly, male clergy abuse female victims.

In my opinion, therefore, we must begin to tease apart the rootlets of these two trees in the enchanted forests of human consciousness, psychic illusion, and cultural distortion: (a) heterosexist privilege and the social violence of discrimination done against same-gendered people in the name of God and b) the affinity violence of sexual abusiveness done by members of the ordained clergy – also sometimes done in the name of God.

Jordan begins his analysis of the church's secrets and initiates his discussion of the issues of truth-telling in the following manner. He notes:

- There must be acknowledgment that we don't know how many sexual secrets the church historically has held; we don't know what kind of secrets; and we don't know the significance of these secrets[97]
- There are secrets hidden behind and within the official teachings of the church – its theology – particularly its theology of sexuality[98]
- There are also secrets about official people (and by implication, their sexuality) in the church's ruling hierarchies [99]
- Finally, there are secrets contained in the church's sprawling set of laws regarding sexuality[100]

Noting the different dynamic for lesbian women in the Catholic Church than for gay men, he writes:

> *Official Catholic silence is pronounced by clerical men and then enforced most melodramatically by them. For that reason, gay men are solicited differently by Roman power than lesbian women. The running subtext of Catholic clerical power is "male" homoeroticism. Perhaps that is why "out" gay men in the Catholic church often seem more timid than "out" lesbians – as if the men were still more muzzled or more complicit in their own muzzling.*[101]

Asking then what kinds of speech can be used for investigation and truth-telling, he notes four rhetorical forms:

Ruth E. Krall

The first is counterargument by the truth-seeker in which he or she resorts to critique and reasoning to counter official church teachings – be these canon law or scriptural exegesis practices. In recent decades, counterargument has been used to document the contradictory history inside the church regarding its teachings about same sex desire. He notes that many official church documents do not invite discussion of these matters but are clearly documents meant to forestall discussion. *Many official documents are scripts for preventing serious speech by scrambling it. To prevent the scrambling, we need to expose the rhetorical devices in the document.*[102] The secrets imposed by the church are, therefore, not revealed in the documents themselves but in how the church lives out its faith.

The second form, therefore, of speech about the church's secrets is that of bearing testimony. Jordan's example describes a gay man's decision to "come out" as a gay Christian man who belongs to a particular community of faith.[103] Giving personal testimony involves the awareness that the speaker inevitably edits his witness though a complex pattern of individual and cultural motives. He notes, therefore, that the way to understanding the church's secrets and silence about its embedded homoeroticism is not though an examination of formal documents but by means of biographical witness – the lives of those men who are closest to the institutional church's center of power.[104]

An examination of *institutional arrangements* includes the genre of fragmentary history in which the archives of memory are entered. Archival memory will call up the stories of history. When one enters into discussion with these archival memories, what is cloudy but visible emerges into sight. The Christian church has a long history of experimentation with homoeroticism inside its clerical and monastic cultures. The culture of ostensibly celibate clergy inside the Roman Catholic tradition is securely rooted inside these earlier social forms or patterns of experimentation over many centuries.[105]

A final form is to draw provocative analogies between explicitly gay subcultures in the secular world and the Roman Catholic gay clergy subculture. Once one can identify the ways in which gay men create neighborhoods for themselves in secular culture, one can begin to recognize ways in which gay clergy men create such subcultures inside the priesthood.[106]

It is at this point that Jordan links these two issues for his readers – these issues of sexual violation and these issues of homoeroticism inside the Roman Catholic priesthood's clerical culture. He writes: *denied desire in seminary formation...encourages sexual abuse.* Comments about liturgies conducted by men in drag as "liturgy queens" may appear as satire but Jordan asserts that *the homoeroticism of official Catholic life is sometimes so blatant that only powerful devices keep us from laughing out loud at its solemn denials.*[107] Such laughter, once released, allows individuals and the community to release the image of every priest as heterosexual for a more factually correct one: some priests have a same gender sexual orientation while other priests have an opposite gender sexual orientation.

In looking, therefore, at the scandal of child sexual abuse inside the Roman Catholic priesthood, Jordan describes and discusses three rhetorical responses to efforts at truth-telling. These three rhetorical responses are designed to squelch truth-telling. They are not designed to facilitate it.

- Claims that making an effort at truth-telling in the religious commons is angry speech. This reaction by the official and institutional church presupposes a rule that individuals cannot be angry at the Christian Church qua institution. Jordan notes, however, that Christian scriptures teach *we can be angry – that we must be angry – when trying to tell some truth about violence, about oppression of the powerless, about cruelty or greed.*[108] The implicit institutional rule about angry speech appears to be this: trying to tell the truth about the institutional church, one must never do so in anger. Jordan properly notes that such an informal or formally expressed rule is a part of institutional strategy. Asking then what is the power of anger as a work of love,[109] as differentiated from the power of anger as a work of hatred, we can begin to separate out the passion to destroy from the passion to reform or to rebuild.[110]
- Charges of anti-Catholic bias or prejudice or hatred or bigotry. This form of response to efforts to speak truth or to search for truth-speech implies that these efforts are made by hostile outsiders or insider traitors. There is, in these charges, the implicit message that one should neither listen to nor hear the efforts at truth-speech because they represent mere prejudice writ large.[111] Issues of tribal identity come into play. *The boundary around Catholicism is a set of memories in which family life, school, and parish cult are intertwined...To speak against it in dissent is to violate family and heritage, the identifying past.*[112]
- The third general reaction is demanding proof. To Jordan, this is an interruption to truth-speech because the demand itself never specifies what counts as acceptable proofs.[113]

These three forms of official speech in response to intra-community efforts at truth-speaking mean that truth-speaking or truth-searching individuals are automatically ruled out of order by the hierarchy (and their lay cheerleaders) who seeks to protect the embedded and deeply hidden secrets of the community. The leaders in such a religious community can, therefore, deny a listening ear. Jordan comments, *in the cases around us, we are not dealing just with personal sin. We are dealing with the sin of a system for keeping secrets – about which we can no longer plausibly claim to be shocked. In that system, every sin of sexual power is multiplied by the sin of silence needed to conceal it. These sins include repeated demands for evidence that will never be acknowledged or examined.*[114] He continues by noting that keeping some kinds of secrets is a profound denial of the Christian gospel in that not only are facts denied but there is a consistent and persistent denial of our Christian responsibility for the institutional church's actions, reactions, and social arrangements. In our collective institutional silence, we deny the biblical teaching about preaching and witnessing to truth.[115] He notes, then, that national policies for dealing with pedophilia crimes which do not address these crimes' causes in institutional silence is an evasion of responsibility to tell, i.e., confess, the truth. As such these polices are complicitous actions and it is obscene to call them loyalty to the institution.[116]

What does it mean, therefore, to speak truthfully? Authentic speech begins with the cry of the afflicted.[117] The cry of the afflicted is incoherent speech. It is a cry that beseeches itself and us for words. The cries of the afflicted originate in the affliction that is experienced and has no words. These cries, I believe, also originate in the afflicted one's protest against the official voice that seeks to silence the truth and in so doing reveals its own implicit violence against the victim's and their experienced truth.

In these two chapters Jordan sets forth some of the awareness we can derive as we look at the rhetorical forms of discussion – whether this rhetoric is about same gender sexual desire, religious, spiritual and/or theological homoeroticism as a foundation for clergy formation, or same gender sexual violations done by members of the clergy. The official church's desire to keep silence about its homoerotic secrets and its abuse of lay individuals by sexually abusive clergy has provided Jordan with the opportunity to examine its institutional resistances to truth-telling even though it is clear that he believes that the Christian gospel's mandate is truth rather than complicity and silence.

Personal Reflections

As I think about Jordan's work in these two chapters, some reflections fall into place for me. One of the places we can begin to uncover some of the secrets or hidden truths of the Christian tradition is in the tradition's codified laws and teachings about sexuality. For example, the church does not need to make a law about adult males having sexual relationships with giraffes if no adult males are engaging in sexual relationships with giraffes. There is simply no reason for a civil or canonical law if there is no culturally-offending behavior which calls forth such a law. Noting the presence of a law or a code, we can, therefore, search for the historical reasons for such a code. When we do this, Jordan teaches us, it is likely we will encounter institutionalized barriers to truth telling.

In that awareness, therefore, it becomes clear that sexual violation of young adolescent boys by adult males concerned the early church just as it does today's church. The first known recorded prohibition of adult males having sexual relations with young boys occurs in the *Didache: the Teaching of the Twelve Apostles* from the late first century or the early second century Christian community.[118] The *Didache* is divided into three sections, the first of which deals with Christian ethics in the emerging Christian consciousness and Christian community. If there had been no occasion or problem with adult males engaging in sexual relationships with young boys, this ancient early catechism would not have concerned itself with this topic.

The first known prohibition against clergy and monastic sexual abuse of young boys dates from 309 CE.[119] The same principle is true. Problematic behavior yielded the turn to codified law. Codified law does not, in and of itself, yield problematic behavior. When we glimpse back over our shoulders at the centuries of Christian community, we find the presence of theological homoeroticism and we find the presence of sexual violation. In these two chapters Jordan does not discuss how we can begin to uncouple the Christian yokes that have bound these two realities together in silence and in secrecy.

For me, therefore, Jordan's discussion of the historical homoeroticism of Christian faith through the centuries needs much more work by theologians and church historians. William Lindsey writes, *there's certainly a **twisting** (emphasis his) in how the Catholic clerical elite handles all these issues , and that twisting is rooted in the simultaneous concealment of gay desire within that elite and its hostility to openly gay men. This twisting makes the approach to the abuse crisis notably toxic in the Catholic Church.*[120] Inasmuch as Lindsey – as do I – recognizes that churches with a married heterosexual clergy are as apt to abuse children, adolescents, and vulnerable men and women as is the Roman Catholic Church with its ostensibly celibate male clergy, it is essential to *do* theological and ethical dissection of the clergy abuse issue from as wide a perspective as possible.

What we know is that memes or cultural forms act similarly to a virus. To propagate themselves, they need human hosts. Usually, in my opinion at least, cultural forms are transmitted and assimilated unselfconsciously. Illusory thinking or magical thinking may play a role as well. For example, talking about the Christian Church as Christ's bride and talking about priests and minister as either an alter Christus or the voice of God may well set up the sexual tension inside the church's theology. Such a systemic theology subsequently enables priests and ministers to act out and to justify their behavior from a perverted theological sense of entitled male sexuality.

Ruth E. Krall

Yet, as a woman I am suspicious of some of these theoretical approaches. My personal sense of the matter – an intuitive sense – is that issues of male dominance and male authoritarianism are more determinative of clergy abuse than issues of gender or issues of homoeroticism. Issues of power, in my opinion, are much more prevalent than current discussions give credence. In part, I suppose, this is because so many of the voices in the debate about clergy sexual abuse and institutional clericalism are male voices. I am, it turns out, not the only skeptic.

In electronic correspondence with Roman Catholic theologian William (Bill) Lindsey, he comments on this issue of homoeroticism as an aspect of the Christian Church's abuse of same gender couples or individuals. He writes:

> *I grow impatient with folks who say that the abuse crisis is all about concealed homoeroticism in the clerical structures of the Catholic Church. This seems wrong-headed to me because (1) religious communities with no such history and with a strong antipathy to homosexuality also demonstrate potential for clergy abuse of minors and of hiding that abuse; (2) abuse of children is pedophilia and has nothing to do with issues of sexual orientation; and (3) girls are abused as well as boys including in the Catholic tradition.*[121]

In their recent book, Doyle, Sipe and Wall trace their denominational church's concern with this topic of the sexual violation of young adolescent boys by clergy through the Christian centuries.[122] By means of the paper trail of its canonical rulings about clerical sexuality, it is possible to gain a glimpse of the clergy's secret inner culture vis-à-vis a long history of clergy sexual abuse of young boys and adult women.

Today, a similar phenomenon is taking place as victims of clergy sexual abuse take their complaints into the secular courts. In settlement after settlement, the institutional Christian Church is being forced to reveal long-held secrets regarding its institutional protection of sexual violence perpetrators among ordained clergy, members of religious orders, and its religious hierarchy.

Today's American Roman Catholic Church is approaching, perhaps has already exceeded, the 4 billion dollar mark in clergy sexual abuse victim settlement agreements. This money does not include diocesan lawyers' fees nor does it include the public relations firm fees which the institutional church has paid to spin its inability to properly manage clerical sexual misconduct and acts of sexual violence done by clergy.[123] I know of no similar resources of information about other Christian denominations. I know regional conferences of the Mennonite Church have made confidential monetary settlements to victims of clergy sexual abuse. How many of these kinds of settlements have been made between church agencies and the church's victims remains hidden from view. How much money has been spent hiding and covering for perpetrators also remains hidden.

In secular political life, a common aphorism about political corruption is to *follow the money.* I conclude, therefore, that religious institution corruption and institutional secrets may also be traced *by following the money.* In these deep denominational silences around clergy sexual abuse, money also speaks a certain kind of truth – albeit not in words. The trail of money speaks to us of power, of control, of authority, of dominance, and of hidden secrets that desperately need words so that we can understand the corrupted use of power and institutional authority that the money trail reveals. Perhaps our institutionalized use of money as an analogy for corrupted power allows us to understand the true values of corrupted organized religious life.

In Jordan's third chapter he turns to questions of scandal. In his opening words he comments that scandal *managed by scandal* must be resisted. But he adds the cautionary words that it cannot be *easily overcome* (p. 34). In thinking about the church blessing same gender sexual relationships, he invokes scholastic processes regarding disputed matters. *The voices in this dispute are hardly uniform. They are articulate and stammering, established and outcast, aggressively present and almost forgotten. Our obligation for truth telling in a dispute is to hear all of the pertinent voices before speaking any determination*[124].

Utilizing the image or metaphor of a church door, he comments upon the voices inside the door and compares them to the voices on the outside of the door. Inside the church there will be doctrinal talk and, perhaps, a history of disciplinary actions. There will be the speech of its resident minister(s). There are, as well, the voices of the church's academic theologians. What is very interesting to me is his comment that private speech inside the church's doors is often very different from the speech that these same voices will admit in public. Thus, inside the church there is a public voice but there is also a private voice. And frequently - although not always - these two voices are contradictory. In the background are the layers of historical speech and these layers include written documents. Jordan writes: *The historical layers are supposed to inform or support present speeches. Often they are ignored, edited, falsified, not the least by the device of managed scandal.*[125]

Outside the church's door, a same gender couple waits – asking the church for a blessing. Their presence invokes the presence of very ancient quarrels inside the Christian Church about what constitutes marriage. Voluminous purity laws exist to guide the church in agreeing to consent to or to refuse to consent to same gender marriages.

By utilizing Jordan's imagery, it is possible to say that in many Christian churches today, the victims of clergy and religious leader violence (boys and girls, men and women) also wait outside the churches' doors – waiting for accountability, transparency, and healing. They wait for truth-telling. What is true for many victims is also true for many victim advocates – the women and men who have shared the victim's traumatizing experience of institutional disdain and active hostility.[126]

As denominational churches and institutions seek to manage the scandal of religious leader sexual abuse, too often they refuse to acknowledge the legitimate concerns of those victimized by violence. Father Thomas Doyle, in speaking and writing about the Roman Catholic denomination, frequently reminds his audiences that too often when a church institution receives information about sexual abuse done by one of its clergy persons or religious leaders or administrators, the first response is to deny that there is any truth in the accusations; the second is to consult the institution's legal counselors. He reminds his listeners that the first religious and spiritual obligation of Christian leaders and the Christian community at large in these situations is to tend to the needs of the abused victims for emotional, psychological, physical, *and* spiritual healing.[127]

Conclusions

As mentioned in the first letter, the more voices which break the silences around sexual abuse, the more likely it will be that we can cut a path out of the enchanted forest. In your reading of this chapter's first draft, you replied to me with your own *Sexual Integrity* article about these matters. Your article is more closely reasoned than this letter and I assume that is, in part, because you are living inside an ethnic Mennonite community while I live outside of any such community. You look at these Mennonite issues, as it were, through a contemporary electronic microscope while I look through an ancient Galileo-era telescope.

I have sought here, however, to begin to untangle the root systems of these two, now individuated, toxic trees in the enchanted forest of toxic theology. The goal in this short letter has been to encourage Christian churches to become self-aware.

Let me state my thinking today as a clear hypothesis: the poisonous tree of xenophobic responses to homosexuality is a completely separate tree from the poisonous tree of clergy sexual abuse. Phenomenologically, therefore, these are two separate problems for institutional Christian churches and individual Christians to address.

If we remember that authentic theological speech begins by paying attention to the cries of the afflicted – as Jordan has suggested – then we need to seek out and pay attention to those individuals which the church has marginalized because (1) they live within a same-gender sexual orientation or (2) they live inside the chains of sexual victimization. These are two separate and distinct groups of disaffiliated Christian Mennonites who need the church's attention. We must make clear in urging such compassionate, loving, and generous attention that we do not conflate both groups into one. But, we must also avoid the trap of avoiding conversations about one group as we attempt to solve the issues related to the second. Since the Christian Church over the centuries has conflated these two issues, both must be simultaneously addressed – undressed as it were.

These complex issues of hypocritical, secretive speech, and dishonest silence cuts across both populations of people who stand outside the churches' doors waiting for authentic, truthful, and spiritually faithful speech vis-à-vis their complaints and their continuing struggles to be seen and heard inside the religious community.

Following Jordan's intuitions, it is past time to open transparent, accountable truth-speaking conversations about both trees.

My understanding of these two issues now calls me to ask the churches to do several things:

- Open all conversations about the full inclusion of same-gendered sexual desire couples to individuals representing these life positions. Stop playing power and money politics long enough to recognize that there are real same-gendered Christian people with real life Christian and personal commitments. Stop holding secret conversations about them behind closed doors. Instead speak with them. Allow them to speak with you. Stop politicizing the life of gay couples and lesbian couples. Listen and pay attention. Become fully inclusive in deed as well as in word. Recognize that the Jesus path is not about sexual and liturgical purity inevitably seen through the eyes of our surrounding dominant culture but about faithfulness to the Great Commandment to live out our love for God, our love for the neighbor, and our love for the self in concrete, demonstrable ways. While Jordan does not address the truthfulness of the lived-life, we Mennonites have an ancient theology of word and deed in which deed takes precedence over word in faithfulness to the Christ path. The path of love, in my life experience, is never about abandonment, shunning, exclusion, or the creation of a pariah status for the other. Rather, the inclusion of love simply accepts what is as what it is and, on a shared foundation of truth-telling and mutual respect, builds human relationships. This kind of love is not sentimentality writ large. Rather, it is the spirit of genuine, inclusive, welcoming hospitality writ large in our hearts and in our institutions.

- Open all institutional management practices vis-à-vis sexual abuse complaints to the fresh air of truth and full institutional accountability. Where the church has made historical misjudgments about how to manage sexual perpetrators, it should acknowledge its failures and apologize, in public, for its own sins of mismanagement. Stop protecting powerful perpetrators and seek out the victims of violation to see what they need.

- For once and for all, separate these two issues (the issue of same gender sexual attraction and the issue of religious leader sexual abuse) from each other and learn how to manage each with competency, compassion, and love for everyone involved. Become intellectually competent by reading and study

Ruth E. Krall

and conversations about each issue. Know what the theologically toxic forest looks like; know what each poisonous tree in this polluted forest looks like.

- Make a commitment to truth-telling – especially in the issues which surround human sexuality. End the centuries-long theologically and behaviorally-enforced hypocrisy and dogmatically-coerced Christian silences around sexuality. We can benefit from the scientific study of sexuality as well as from the theological and ethical study of human relationships in light of the God-human one. One place to begin would be to examine the metaphorical eroticization of Christian theology in its language about the church. Jordan is correct, I think, in his analysis of the church's enduring silence and its active lying about sexuality and the need now for truth-speech that breaks that silence.

Were denominational churches to follow the principles of truth-telling in both of these matters concerning sexuality, we might find a spiritual renaissance inside of our churches. If we manage to separate these two issues, we might be able to resolve both with love, with compassion, and above all with mature adult competency.

Fourth Letter

Living inside the Hurricane's Eye, Part One

The Stories We Tell About Good and Evil

To make peace we cannot ignore war, racism, violence, greed, the injustice and suffering of the world. They must be confronted with courage and compassion. Unless we seek justice, peace will fail. Yet in whatever we do we must not let war, violence, and fear take over our own heart.

Jack Kornfield[128]

Introductory Comments

In 1988 Journalist Bill Moyers attended and filmed the proceedings of a national conference about the troubling issue of human evil. In his documentary film about this conference he covered a wide variety of the speakers and their presentations as well as the opinions and commentary of people in attendance.[129]

Maya Angelou's Warning

There in those pleated faces
I see the auction block
The chains and slavery's coffles
The whip and lash and stock....

Maya Angelou[130]

As part of her keynote address, Maya Angelou recited her poem *The Mask*. This poem is her elaboration on an earlier poem, *We Wear the Mask* (1896), written by Paul Lawrence Dunbar. In her presentation Angelou talked with the audience about the messy dangers in speaking about evil – wondering aloud what we unleash when we begin to talk about evil – wondering what misbegotten genie we un-bottle.

As I watched the documentary, it seemed to me her warning was an essential one. We should never casually enter into conversations about the generic, omnipresent nature or even the many and specific manifestations of human evil and cruelty without being certain that we and others are spiritually and psychologically protected at deep inner levels. As Anabaptist-Mennonite pacifists, when we set out to do our peace-building work in the world, we want to confront and contain the virus of evil, not spread it. We do not want, therefore, to become the inadvertent, unaware, and unwitting carriers of its virulence.

In the background of Angelou's poem are the historical realties of black slavery and the current realties of racial oppression in twentieth-first century America. The backlash against truth-bearing, in decades past, in the American eras of slavery and post-emancipation Jim Crow laws included imprisonment, sale away from families, back-scarring beatings, lynch mobs, rape of black women and other forms of murderous, controlling cruelty and rage unleashed against American blacks – especially those who were seen to be disobedient and non-subservient to whites living inside culturally insulated situations of white entitlement and privilege.[131]

Today's racial oppressiveness may seem less virulent to individuals in the dominant cultural castes, but to those who are daily surrounded by and victimized by a nation's racist consciousness, their contemporary encounters with multiple forms of deliberate cruelty and violence remain omnipresent and ever-threatening.[132] There are many ways for privileged people to enslave others and racist cultures do not apologize for their cultural and economic attitudes of entitlement and privilege. Left unattended and uncriticized these attitudes breed oppression and oppression breeds violence. Nor do the human carriers of racist beliefs apologize for the violent human consequences and often tragic outcomes of their attitudes. In far too many situations, the victims of cultural elites' ignorance or active disdain are blamed and punished for their suffering. It is rapidly becoming ordinary in the United States for attitudes of racist entitlement and racist hatred to breed acts of killing violence in the commons.[133]

Morgan Freeman perhaps reflected a similar sentiment to Angelou's when he discussed his personal decision not to watch the 2013 film *Twelve Years a Slave*.[134] Re-enactments of any kind, including the written word, do not necessarily lead to more freedom and more equality for persons in an oppressed caste. Cultural reviews and re-enactments can also serve as teachers and reinforcers of dominating and unremitting oppression. They can reinforce the violence of racist oppression rather than challenge and contain it. Re-enactments can, therefore, be manipulated inside entitlement and unearned privilege to become part of the cultural ideology which fuels new backlash movements against unpowdered truth, full inclusion, social accountability, and honorable justice. Rather than yanking the taproots of racially-motivated violence out of their cultural soil, some narrative re-enactments nourish these roots and provide them sustenance.

Phillip Halle's Warning

In my generation of Mennonites, the American Jewish ethicist-philosopher Phillip Hallie was known and praised for his studies of the Protestant Huguenot village of Le Chambon – a small village in Nazi-occupied France which rescued more than 5000 Jewish individuals, many of them children, from the Third Reich's attempt to exterminate the Jewish race in its frenzy of genocidal anti-Semitic hatred. Mid-century Mennonites celebrated his praise of the villagers of Le Chambon for their non-violent hospitality and love.

We Mennonites didn't, however, follow and praise his subsequent books. In this Texas conference Hallie, in his address and in a personal interview, revealed that he was continuing to re-work his impressions of the tiny village of Le Chambon. He talked about his childhood in the projects of Chicago where he had to learn street fighting in order to survive the attacks of bigger Christian bullies who slammed his head into the cement as they shouted, *You killed Jesus! You killed Jesus!* In this documentary Hallie talked about his participation in the liberation of Germany as a member of the artillery forces of the United States army. In the documentary it was clear he was re-thinking his earlier work on pacifism of the tiny village of Le Chambon.

One of the things I have most admired Haillie for is his refusal to move into abstractions before he considers the impact of his life on his thinking. In the documentary he discussed his inner awareness that he not only admired the villagers of Le Chambon for their rescue of Jewish individuals, but he also resented them for not stopping or attempting to stop the Nazi killing machines. His conclusion was that it took decent murderers like him to stop Hitler and the genocidal atrocities his ideology had spawned.

As we began these conversations, I went looking to see if I could find Moyers' documentary online. Initially I could not. But after Angelou's recent death (May 28, 2014), Moyers re-released some footage from that documentary and it is now available for purchase at the PBS online store. In searching for the documentary, I did, however, find treasure. I found the last book Hallie was working on before his death. The first 101 pages are a reprise of the work covered in much less depth on Moyers' documentary. In these written chapters, Haillie conducts an interrogation of his life and the lived experiences which shaped his classroom discussions and his publications.

In the book's introduction he returns to Jewish scriptures:

> *After Cain killed Abel, Cain asked God, with some asperity, "Am I my brother's keeper?" And much of the rest of the Bible is an answer to this question. The prophet Isaiah reflected his answer in these words, "Correct oppression, defend the fatherless, plead for the widow," and many pages before and after the Book of Isaiah reflect the same reply.*[135]

At times as I read, I am in tears. Here is a well-respected academic figure who chose in the last days of his life to let us look into his spiritual, emotional, psychological, and intellectual turmoil. We see his anguish. We see his dark, sometimes almost lethal, depressions. We intuit his PTSD. We hear his questions for us. We witness his preoccupation with the active pursuit of joy. We see his celebration of helpfulness when it occurs without the binding ties of incapacitating enablement. We learn about his personal commitments to helping others. Because he is so transparent about his chaotic inner life and his personal questions, we can listen more closely to his conclusions. We may not agree with these conclusions, but we must take them seriously. He will not let us look romantically at the altruistic aspects of human life without also looking closely at the immense acts of human cruelty and evil which individual and collective members of our species carry out daily. He will not allow us to wear clean white gloves without examining the filthy fingernails they conceal. He will not seek refuge in philosophical abstractions but insists that it is in the particularities of human experience where we find the issues with which we must each wrestle. Good and evil; harm and help; cruelty and rescues from cruelty are, therefore, not philosophical abstractions to Hallie. They are questions, rooted in human stories, which we must seek to understand. They are human experiences which we must encounter in all of their human rawness.

It is clear: Hallie has no respect for the pacifists of 1930's Europe – whose romantic pacifying visions of world peace did nothing to stop Hitler's march to power. It is clear: he has deeply ambivalent feelings about the spiritual teachings of nonviolence and proactive love preached by Andre Trocme – the spiritual teacher of the village of Le Chambon.

As 21st-century pacifists we should study his objections to Christian pacifism carefully. He sees those 1930's pacifists and promoters of non-violent activism as colluders with corrupt national power – those who might have stopped Hitler's genocidal destruction early on did nothing. In Hallie's words, it was decent murderers like himself who eventually stopped Hitler by their use of powerful weaponry that destroyed entire villages and their inhabitants.

I want to return to Haillie in several of these conversations. But for now I will move on to other writers – who were not represented in Moyers' documentary.

Ruth E. Krall

Elie Wiesel's Warning

> *I swore never to be silent whenever and wherever human beings endure suffering and humiliation. We must always take sides. Neutrality helps the oppressor, never the victim. Silence encourages the tormentor, never the tormented.*

Elie Wiesel[136]

Here I am informed somewhat by Elie Wiesel's novel *The Oath* in which the protagonist has taken an oath of silence about the pogrom events in his small Hungarian village. He is the remaining survivor of that event. After fifty years of silence, he meets a young man on the verge of suicide and must re-confront his earlier oath because to tell the young man what he knows may save the young man's life.

Before *The Oath's* fictional village was destroyed, Moshe – its resident madman – asks whether bearing witness and giving testimony is not death's ally. Is not, he seems to ask, the articulation of human atrocities inextricably and forever linked to the actions themselves? Moshe concluded that it was, and I paraphrase his conclusion: *therefore we will testify no more to these atrocities of our human existence.*

After the village's Jewish population has been destroyed, its lone survivor sets out to live his life – surrounded by memories of the dead. For fifty years he chooses to keep silence about his now-destroyed village and its non-existent Jewish population before breaking his oath to save a young man's life.

Yet, as we see in the Wiesel quotation above, silence about injustice and violation benefits the perpetrator of the violence, not the individual upon whom the oppressive act of violence has been perpetrated.

I am not a Wiesel literary genre specialist. I have not followed his personal career as a Nobel Prize laureate nor have I read all of his books, but when I first read this particular book during my mid-forties, the cautionary message to me was that some stories have a particular quality – they spread the virus of oppression, hatred, and irrational violence rather than curtail it. They do this by breeding hatred and urges for revenge in those previously oppressed and victimized by violence. Rather than functioning as precautionary tales, they become educational pedagogies.

One scholar-critic comments that Wiesel, a Holocaust survivor himself, is a witness, *a messenger of the dead among the living.*[137] Rather than the oath of silence, Wiesel has taken an oath to speak and to bear witness.

In a 1967 address, later published in the periodical *Conservative Judaism*, Wiesel addresses the issue of speaking in a slightly different way.

> *One day a Tzadik came to Sodom; he knew what Sodom was so he came to save it from sin, from destruction. He preached to the people. "Please do not*

murder, please do not be thieves. Do not be silent and do not be indifferent." He
went on preaching day after day, maybe even picketing. But no one listened. He
was not discouraged. He went on preaching for years. Finally, someone asked
him, "Rabbi why do you do that? Don't you see it is no use?" He said, "I know it
is no use. But I must. And I will tell you why: in the beginning I thought I had
to protest and to shout to change them. I have given up this hope. Now I know
I must picket, and scream and shout so that they should not change me." [138]

In light of Wiesel's words, it seems to me that we need to think about the stories
we tell – asking ourselves what and whose purposes these stories serve. Do our
stories foment violence by spreading their embedded ideologies like a virus, or
do they serve as precautionary tales that can help us prevent further episodes of
violence? Do the stories carry the medicine of healing, or do they carry the emotional viruses of resentment, rage, and revenge? Most importantly, in the stories
we ourselves choose to tell, do we preach to change others, or do we preach to
save ourselves?

Mary Gail Frawley-O'Dea's Warning

> *The failure to mourn impedes psychological, relational, social, political* **and**
> (hers) *spiritual growth.*

> Mary Gail Frawley-O'Dea[139]

In the winter of 2012, while the American news media regularly carried reports
of clergy sexual abuse,[140] Frawley-O'Dea, a clinical psychologist and expert trial
witness, spoke to the American Catholic reform group, Voice of the Faithful, in
its annual meeting. In that address she spoke of the need for mourning as a pre-
requisite for healing.

Not only victimized individuals need to mourn the consequences to their lives
as a result of their violation, entire communities need to do so as well. Her critique
about her church's failure to mourn its ongoing sexual abuse crisis is penetrating:

> *The failure to mourn has influenced corrupt power plays among the hierarchy;*
> *manic attempts to restore the forever gone among some victims; denial, silence*
> *and empty platitudes among many priests; and studied naïveté among a large*
> *portion of the laity.*[141]

In the following enumeration, I abstract, paraphrase, and summarize Frawley-
O'Dea's work. In successful mourning we see the following:

Ruth E. Krall

- Becoming aware that something or someone of importance has been lost or taken from our lives
- Dealing with the mixture of anger and grief which accompany meaningful losses
- Learning to manage the dance of denial (this could not have happened to me) and acknowledgment of that which has been lost (this actually did happen to me)
- Reminiscing and nostalgia for what once was but is no longer; here the individual's relationship with the dead one or even the betrayer may be idealized; the other remembered as being without fault
- Over time, however, the idealization shifts; the nostalgia changes: a more realistic and historically truthful image emerges[142]
- I would add, from my perspective on these issues, that over time, our emotional cathexis to that which we have mourned well is lessened – albeit our intense grief is probably never totally resolved.[143] Our experience of intense grief can, therefore, surface and resurface throughout our lifetimes. In each developmental phase of our life, we may need to work with our grief to manage its ongoing presence in our lives. It is quite likely, I think, that un-noticed, un-mourned, and un-managed, our inner cathexis remains untouched and continues at deeply unconscious levels of our personality to shape our behavior.
- When members of large groups, such as a denominational church, experience collective betrayal, members of the group often find themselves desensitized even as their previous sense of reality is threatened. Unable or unwilling to mourn, the inner trauma cathexis remains untouched, and individuals and entire communities can pass on incidents of historical trauma and the concomitant pathologies caused by this trauma, unnoticed and uncriticized, into the future of unborn generations.

Quoting psychoanalytic psychiatrist, Varnik Volkan, Frawley-O'Dea notes his commentary that large identify groups *are saturated with tribal, ethnic, religious, nationalistic, and/or political ideology.*[144] These identities, forged in childhood, are rarely shed in adolescence when other inherited identities are questioned, refined, or abandoned altogether. About these complex identities, she continues: *Customs, rituals, dances, folk songs, and even clothing amplify identification of the large group as "us" and not "them." When the large group identity is threatened, "we" become more tenaciously identified while "others" are equally devalued and even demonized.*[145]

In her discussion of betrayal trauma[146] Frawley-O'Dea states that the more profound the betrayal, the more likely it is that *the trauma will be denied, dissociated, or dismissed by both the victim and the bystander who consciously or unconsciously insist on maintaining attachment to the victimizer on whom they depend for some aspect of survival, including at times spiritual survival.*[147]

Reflecting on this process of idealization and denial, Frawley-O'Dea concludes that where we are *greatly dependent for psychic, physical or spiritual survival, we may maintain idealization of them and take on the blame for loss ourselves.* "*If he betrayed me, I must have deserved it. Well, it was bad but they did their best. They didn't mean for it to hurt so much*".[148] She quotes psychoanalyst Richard Fairbairn that for the abused child, *it is better to be a sinner in the world of God than to live in a world ruled by the devil.* She unpacks this in a tight exegesis of Fairburn's words: in the world ruled by God, a sinner can hope for salvation; in the world ruled by a devil, *there is NO* (emphasis hers) *hope.*[149] When there is no hope, individuals dissociate, deny, and attempt to minimize the damages done. She concludes, *Once again, mourning grinds to a halt and distortion of self, other, the world, and the Divine dominates.*[150]

Inadequate mourning is accompanied by a nostalgia that blinds the individual to reality. In light of the clergy sexual abuse issue and the Catholic bishops' inept management of sexually abusive priests inside the Roman Catholic faith heritage, she comments: *too many Catholics for too long have been enshrouded in a nostalgic haze of incense and candlelight within which longstanding perversions of power are dreamily denied.*[151]

From her position as a clinician who works with adult individuals who had been sexually abused in childhood and adolescence, she reminds us repeatedly in this important speech that mourning our losses is a complex and perhaps life-long process. Without thorough and on-going mourning, there can be no healing. This kind of mourning is a soul-rendering, gut-wrenching, lonely process that we each have to undergo alone – although we may be, and I personally believe we need to be, accompanied by others who support us in our unique journeys through our personal experiences of deep grief at what victimization has cost us: the betrayals that destroyed our abilities to trust others; the self that we will never be; the potentials we will never realize; the unremediated harm that has been done to us.

In light of Frawley-O'Dea's work, it is clear to me that in clergy and religious leader sexual abuse situations, not only victimized individuals need to mourn their losses. Members of their family, friends, extended external community, congregation, or the denomination must also mourn.

In these complex, ongoing situations of religious leader abuse, members of the complicit religious hierarchy must be coerced to be accountable. Victims of violation need to have their stories authenticated by their overlapping communities of family and faith. One aspect of institutional accountability is that religious leaders need to join the victims in mourning as they acknowledge the damages they have done to the church's institutional victims *and* to the community of faith as a whole.

Ruth E. Krall

If the religious community is to heal and prevent ongoing victimizations by other religious leader offenders, it must come to a position where denial, victim-blaming, harm-minimization, and nostalgia for a reality that never was, are replaced by a keening grief that such abuse happened, that it happened in our midst, and that we individually and collectively did nothing to stop it.

Until we are confessionally honest and truthful about our individual and collective abuse stories, I do not believe complete healing can happen – for individuals and for communities. That said, we must be careful about how we tell these stories of abuse in the commons in order to avoid spreading the abuse virus to new generations of religious leaders and laity in the pews.

The Power of Stories

We Americans have, I sometimes think, a naïve position about the power of stories to heal. Stories of violence and violation contain the potentiality for re-opening great wounds. Mary Gail Frawley-O'Dea has commented on the number of suicides among survivors related to the timing of their lawsuits against the church for its corrupt management of priest-abusers. As we think about those who have killed themselves in the aftermaths of abuse and violation, it is clear that not everyone who tells the story of their abuse survives the telling. Not everyone who hears the story of another's encounters with violence can manage the aftermath of knowing.[152] I know this to be true. While I can count the number of suicides in the network of people I know or know about on the fingers of both hands, I know there are many more symptoms of personal woundedness than outright suicide. Not every truthful story spoken out loud inside the religious commons brings automatic relief and authentic healing.

The Healer's Dilemma

Judith Herman, a Harvard-based psychiatrist who works with victims of many different forms of betrayal and trauma, has often commented upon the reality that in doing work with trauma survivors, each clinician must have a support group so that the work does not invade the clinician's mind and psychic structures; that the client's story does not become the introjected story of the therapist.[153] In her work, she talks about the invisible third party who is always present in our clinical offices whenever we work with trauma recovery processes – and that third party is the violent perpetrator who desired to intimidate and control his direct victim. The rage which the perpetrator of violence brought to his acts of intimidation and violence; the rationales for his violence; and the acts of violence: these can cross the psychic barriers between human beings and re-create themselves inside the victim's life experience. Subsequently, these can cross the psychic and emotional barriers and enter the lived experience of the helper. This is at least one of the sources of secondary, counter-transference trauma in the lives of clinicians.

The predator's rage, implanted in the psyche and terror of the victim by his or her acts of victimization, must be exorcised carefully. Care is essential that this implanted rage and fear does not cross the boundaries between client and care-giver and subsequently also invade the psyche and internal life of the healer – creating a hologram of the trauma inside the life of the clinical listener.

I personally feel this double-edge nature of sexual violence stories is true whenever we talk about specific instances of physical and sexual violation of women and their children. I suspect my caution is somewhat similar to Angelou's when she talks about the slavery and rape of her people in the Americas. Those who choose to dominate and rape and exploit others do not want to hear a critique of their behavior. Those who most demonstrate the perversions of power do not believe they need to change. We do not, therefore, know what genie of future violation and violence we unleash with our stories. We must learn, therefore, to pay attention. We should not speak casually in moments of deep frustration and anger. We should proceed, not with the arrogance of being right, but with compassionate humility, as we face our own complicity in maintaining the cultural (or ideological) soil in which such forms of violence take root.

Fifth Letter

Living inside the Hurricane's Eye, Part Two

A Conversation with Phillip Hallie

Introductory Comments

In a recent letter you wrote:

> *I know and like Judith Herman's work on Trauma.*[154] *When I teach the non-violence class at Eastern Mennonite University,*[155] *I used to talk about these "communities of resistance." But honestly, I wrestle with the word "resistance." At first I thought I was unsettled because Mennonites talk so much about "non-resistance." But then I realized that it was that the word made me feel less powerful. It feels to me like I must "resist" and "respond" to them....the patriarchy, the corporations, the violence perpetrators. I see an image of me pushing against a wall coming down on me, resisting this huge power. That word just doesn't work for me.*

> *So, I started teaching about "communities of transformation" that saw themselves as empowered, as the planners, as the creators, as the gardeners. Our job is not to resist but to transform. There is evil out there and, yes, we absorb its paradigms every day. But we have to see ourselves as powerful witches who can heal wounds and transform structures like the Pentagon into planners for something else. With an image of transformation, I am not pushing against a wall. I instead try aikido moves that redirect the oppression and turn it against itself. I help those in the system who want to do something different to find the strength and the words to join in the work to end oppression. It's just a different*

image and it has been helpful for working within the Mennonite patriarchy and the military. I wouldn't do either if I thought of it as "resisting."

But I agree with Herman that we need "communities" of people who support our work.[156]

This is an example, I think, of the ways in which our personalities, our various life experiences, and perhaps even our academic disciplines and classroom teachers have shaped the languages we find useful in our conceptual work. Since I am comfortable with Herman's language regarding the need for *communities of resistance* which struggle to find alternatives to violence and systemic corruption, I am going to use that language in my exploration below. This is in no way to be construed as a criticism of your choice to use the language of transformation as in *communities of transformation*. It is simply the way I have learned to think about these "communities of resistance" on location in Nicaragua and Guatemala during their years of war in the 1980's and the 1990's.

It is how, as a young feminist woman, I learned to manage my anger at workplace discriminatory processes that affected me and other women. In my head, I coined several variations of the following: *I do not now and I never will accept these multiple forms of sexism and cultural violence against women. Wherever I can I will push back. Whenever I can intervene I will make efforts to be helpful to other women who are being abused or unfairly treated because of their gender or their sexual orientation. I may be abused by my culture and by individuals from that culture, but I will never consent to being abused. I will push back in non-violent* [similar to what you call non-lethal] *ways in my own defense. Therefore, I refuse to define myself by the standards of abusive others. I can't control what other people do, but I do have some control over my own responses to what they do. Inside my mind and inside my body, I will never yield on this principle of active resistance. To the best of my ability, I will protect myself from accepting others' abusiveness towards me and towards others. As part of this commitment to myself, I also frequently commit and re-commit myself to work for others' safety from abuse and violence wherever I can do so.*

In my personal experiences with life to date, these commitments mean I need active and supportive individuals in my life – individuals who also understand and practice proactive resistance to abusive and violent behaviors.

Pushing Back the Hurricane's Walls

The men and women I most admire, therefore, are men and women who actively seek to protect others and who refuse to collude with violations of the basic human rights of women and their children to be safe. Whether this is the villagers of Le Chambon in France rescuing Jewish children during World War Two;[157]

Thich Nhat Hanh's activism on behalf of peace during the Vietnamese War;[158] the mothers and grandmothers in black in Argentina during years of political repression protesting the disappearances of their children and grandchildren;[159] French Cistercian monks living our their faith in Tiburine, Algeria;[160] Bishop Tutu in South Africa asking for economic sanctions during the last years of Apartheid;[161] Barbara Deming, as a lesbian woman, questioning the need for war's violence;[162] Julia Esquivel in Guatemala documenting the stories of indigenous people during that nation's long repressive internal war in Guatemala's highlands;[163] American Trappist Monk Thomas Merton writing against America's war in Vietnam;[164] Fanny Lou Hamer leading black activists in song inside southern jails;[165] American Archbishop Raymond Hunthaussen[166] and American Bishop Gumbleton[167] bearing witness against nuclear weapons. Martin Luther King preaching against the evils of multiple forms of American violence at home and abroad;[168] Claude Anshin Thomas, as a mendicant Buddhist monk, walking and working for active peace;[169] Barbara Blaine forming and guiding the Survivors Network of Those Abused by Priests;[170] or Dominican priest Father Thomas Doyle bearing witness against the sexual violation of children by the priests of his denominational church – an institution which has repeatedly provided cover for and given sanctuary to pedophiles, abusive priests, and corrupt bishops.[171]

I am aware that a basic personal stance of standing against and actively resisting injustice as one simultaneously stands for basic human rights is a costly prophetic decision. It is very unlikely that unjust social systems will yield without attacking those who work for transparency and justice. This insistence upon not accepting injustice wherever we witness it does not contain a de facto masochistic desire to be a martyr or one more victimized individual. It is a matter of seeing what needs to be done to bring about positive change (fairness, justice, proactive peace) and tirelessly working towards that objective.

At its most basic level I think these choices to resist colluding with injustice, violence, and oppressive governance structures have their roots in human compassion. Individuals who risk their own lives and their own careers in order to help others usually intuit that there will be some institutional push-back against them. Yet, because of their integrity and their compassion, they continue to do what is needed to create change. As I think about each of these named individuals, for each there was a community of friends or a community of resistance that has helped them to stand firm in their resolve at critical periods of danger and self-doubt.[172]

I strongly intuit, but do not know for certain, that there was a moment – very early in their lives of activism – where protesting individuals took stock of the situation, weighed costs, and decided to pursue that which they perceived to be essential, right, moral, necessary, or proper. It is hard to believe, for example, that they did not know, or at least anticipate, the social consequences of disobedience to the social expectations of loyalty and conformity. It is unlikely that they did not anticipate the likelihood of ostracism and social punishment for refusing to accept and go along with the status quo. They most likely did not know the precise costs and consequences of their decision to work for justice, but they knew there would be costs and consequences. They most likely wrestled with the decision – knowing what was easy and knowing what was right – and putting their potential futures in the balance while they wrestled and struggled.[173]

If we Christians could re-define the Eucharistic meal as a meal of full inclusion rather than as a meal of exclusion and church discipline; as a pragmatic ethic and action of orthopraxis rather than an abstract ethic and theology of doctrinal purity and orthodoxy, I think we might well find ourselves in a time of theological renewal and Christian hope for those whose lives seem most hopeless.

Psychiatrist Judith Herman has been a very influential trauma theorist in sexual violence and trauma issues for me. I have tended to borrow and use her language. Even more influential are the various theologies of liberation that have emerged in the twentieth-century in Africa, Asia, South America, and North America (Mexico, Canada and the United States): feminist, womanist, Mujerista, Latino, Black, post-colonial, etc.

Latin American processes of conscienticization are essentially a process of learning to resist the deep-seated cultural contamination of one's own consciousness by the dominating worldview of patriarchy. The same thing is true of feminist consciousness-raising.

Learning from Latin American Women

As I talked with women in one of the squatter's communities in Guatemala City – a village that was filled with indigenous people who had run from the killing fields of the high lands in search of the relative safety and anonymity of Guatemala City, I learned that in their tiny barrio, resistance and solidarity on behalf of impoverished women and their families had begun quite simply and quite directly. When the city refused to connect clean water and sewage systems, the women decided one morning to walk with a newly deceased baby in their collective arms. As one woman's arms tired, another woman took the baby's dead body. As they walked, they educated the bystanders who wondered aloud about what was happening in this macabre, spontaneous, all-female parade. Arriving at the city's central plaza, the women took a collective stance that the government was responsible for this baby's death. This was a very dangerous time in Guatemala. There was no guarantee that any of these women would be allowed to return safely to their homes. But the collective moral force of these impoverished peasant women pushing against their government's reluctance to help them by providing safe water was actually effective. Before another twelve months had passed, this impoverished barrio had a running water pipe which could be used for drinking water, for doing laundry, and for basic sanitation.

When I talk about communities of resistance, this community comes to mind. These women were pushing back against oppression; they were resisting the powers of death; they were stating forcefully to the powers that *we too are human beings with basic rights – the rights to live and to raise our children in safety.*[174]

By the time I first visited this community, there were latrines that worked; there was ongoing literacy work; and there was a work room with sewing machines where women could make things to sell – thus minimizing their dependency on the fates or men to protect them and their children. On my first visit, some of their homes were still constructed of junk lumber, scrap corrugated tin, and large sheets of plastic. But as the community became more stable, homes were built from more substantial and safe building materials. Some homes were even waterproof from the torrential tropical rain storms that occurred regularly. In the course of the ten years I repeatedly visited this community with students, the standard of living kept improving for most of the families who lived there. On one of our last visits, we discovered that the community, with some European financial help, had built a community center complete with a mother and baby health clinic. In the center's tiny kitchen the women proudly prepared lunch for us before they shared what was happening in their tiny barrio.

Their only outside helpers were a missionary couple who were not there to convert them but to help them move from poverty into a livable life. The woman was an able grant writer and provided them with international financial help they could not have accessed on their own. I often wondered if this couple's quite visible presence in the community saved its indigenous inhabitants the disappearances that so often happened in the wake of informed political activism. She was a daily witness to their pain and to the social oppression that surrounded them. She lent her international stature to them and their cause – a safe habitat in which to live and raise their children. To me, this is an example of communities of resistance in action.

Consciousness-raising

For almost fifty years, women whose consciousness has been liberated by the worldwide women's movement have been questioning and resisting the dominant theology of the white man's Christian patriarchy. A patriarchal worldview privileges the powerful, the male, the elite, and the economically entitled. The Christian patriarchy maintains that women's inferior status is God-ordained and cannot be changed without offending God. Women and also some men from many different denominations continue to challenge this offensive, *gender-demeaning* form of Christian ideology.

To me, as an Anabaptist-Mennonite feminist woman, such a belief system reeks of idolatry. In this case it is the idolatry of maleness. It denies that the male and the female were both co-made in the image of God. Thinking that only the male was/is made in God's image, such a theology sets up the ground cover for the enchanted toxic forest of male domination and opens the way for male violence against women and their children.

It very well may be that as we, together, explore the nuances of our multiple vocabularies (for example, personal and professional vocabularies), we may uncover insights which can assist other on-location peace advocates in their daily encounters with that which is un-peaceful and violent in their churches, their communities, and their homes.

The Languages of Personal and Social Empowerment

I do agree with you that the language we use to diagnose the problems we see is important. I also agree with you that the language we choose to use should empower us and it should help us to empower others.

It well may be that my personality is simply more naturally resistive than yours. It was during the American Civil Rights era and the American Vietnam War era that I abandoned the American Mennonite construct of non-resistance as a viable model for my own understanding of a Christian's calling and task in the face of my nation's war, my nation's proclivity to use violence to solve pervasive issues of racism, and my nation's participation in the social oppression of various minority groups.

As I have mentioned before in some of my writings, the black comedian Dick Gregory played a very influential role in teaching me about white racism.[175] His incisive and never reverent humor was a very potent form of social resistance – teaching other black people to stop being complicit with social and governmental systems that continued to violate the basic human rights of every black person in America. That some of these inner city black communities allowed me to listen in without insisting that I didn't belong and should, therefore, leave Gregory's performances was one of the greatest blessings of my two years of graduate study in Cincinnati. In modeling resistance, he taught me about how to resist with grace, biting humor, and persistence.

Philip Hallie's Metaphor of Living inside the Hurricane's Eye

In addition, I have been deeply influenced by Philip Haillie's metaphor of the hurricane for situations of human cruelty and structural oppression.

In the eye of a hurricane, the sky is blue and birds can fly there without suffering harm. The eye of the hurricane is in the very middle of destructive power and that power is always near, surrounding that blue beauty and threatening to invade it....

In a world of moral hurricanes some people can and do carve out rather large ethical spaces. In a natural world and social world swirling in cruelty and love we can make room. We who are not pure ethical beings can push away the choking circle of brutal force that is around us and within us. We may not be able to push it far...but when we have made as much room as we can, we may know a blue peace that the storm does not know.

Philip Hallie[176]

As I mentioned in my earlier letter to you, I first encountered Hallie's work in his book, *Lest Innocent Blood Be Shed: The story of the village of Le Chambon and how goodness happened there.*[177]

Sometime after this book was published, I watched a Bill Moyers' PBS documentary on the topic of evil. In this documentary Hallie talked openly about his reservations and hesitations regarding the Christian pacifism of the village of Le Chambon – asserting that it was decent killers like him who stopped Hitler. It was not Europe's Christian pacifists. It was men like himself (not the villagers of Le Chambon) who had put an end to the genocidal violence of the Holocaust done by the Third Reich against Europe's Jewish populations.

I ended up purchasing this documentary and showed it to successive generations of peace studies students because I felt it raised important questions about the nature of violence, evil, and peace-advocacy work. Thus, in this manner, I became Hallie's student. Each year I listened to Hallie talk about his personal life history. Each year I listened to him as he discussed his ideas about pushing back the wall of the hurricane of human evil and human cruelty; resisting the swirling forces of evil even as we all need to recognize and know that the capacity to do cruel acts of harm to others is a reality which lives inside of each one us as well as in others outside of us.

Each year the students and I wrestled with these complex issues of resistance – pacifist resistance in the face of violence as contrasted with our culture's ideas about the redemptive or restorative need for active violence as a form of necessary resistance against others' violence and the communal presence of collective evil.

Cultural Lessons in Hate

You've got to be taught to hate and fear; You've got to be taught from year to year; It's got to be drummed in your dear little ear; You've got to be carefully taught.

Oscar Hammerstein, II [178]

Thirteen years after the ending of World War Two and during the cold war (1945-1991) Richard Rodgers and Oscar Hammerstein wrote the musical *South Pacific*. They wrote it after the end of World War Two and the Korean War and during the opening moments of a prolonged Civil Rights struggle (1954-1968) led by African-American religious and civic leaders. It was not too hard during those years (1945-1968) to find people who were the "good" objects for white middle-class Americans *to hate and fear*. A very strong sub-theme of this musical, therefore, was the issue of fearing and hating people who are different in some way or another (cultural and individual xenophobia).

For many years I have held that violence is never the permanent solution to violence; that enacted violence simply spreads the complex virus of human hate. Violence, inevitably blended with human cruelty, builds internalized individual and communal wishes or fantasies about revenge and creates individual and communal desires to retaliate. Each new generation in its turn absorbs the collective narrative of hate from their ancestors as the motivating rationale for their own actions of violence in history vis-à-vis *the enemy*.[179] As they encounter the historical realities and narratives of victimizing violence in their cultural and familial history, new generations absorb prejudices and cultural hatreds as easily as their bodies absorb the water they drink.

For many years, I have believed that hating and fearing others due to inherited prejudices is a form of individual *and* social pathology. While those who are hated and feared bear the brunt of their victimization, it is also clear to me that those who do the hating and fearing create an inner world of dissonance, anxiety, and pain as well as an external world of fear and paranoia. In this very human game of hating and fearing there are absolutely no winners anywhere.

As an old woman, I still hold to these opinions. However, I revisit these opinions each time that violence erupts in very ambiguous situations. This is especially true in situations where competing religious fundamentalisms seem to motivate the acts of violence, for example, the current civil war in Syria; the rise of ISIS; the recent kidnappings of school girls in parts of Nigeria; or the repetitive eruption of armed political resistance and counter-resistant violence in Israel/Palestine. Each time I ask myself if this is perhaps the situation where restorative acts of redemptive violence can successfully resolve these complex cultural issues of embodied

Ruth E. Krall

social oppression and violation. Each time I ask myself this: for Christian pacifists is this situation the exception to the rule? Is this the needed time for hatred to rule the human heart and the human actors?

By watching Hallie year after year, I came to recognize that the Christian pacifism of the 1930's did nothing to counteract the growing menace of Hitler's politicization of Europe vis-à-vis the Jews. I have understood for many years that Christian history, tradition, and theology are deeply complicit in what happened between 1930 and 1945. I have understood that Christian ecclesiology is deeply complicit because of the Christian Church's folk customs and worship patterns regarding the crucifixion narratives of the Gospels. Centuries of blaming the Jewish people for Christ's crucifixion set the stage for many pogroms over many centuries.[180]

This wild harvest of separatism and prejudice sown in previous centuries was reaped in Adolf Hitler's Third Reich. In my opinion, it continues to re-seed itself.

For example, in a 1985 series of videotaped interviews about the European Holocaust interviewers went into the countries where the Hitler's Third Reich death camps had flourished. Here they interviewed Christians who lived then and continued to live now in close proximity to the camps.[181] I repeatedly watched one of these documentary investigations about Christian beliefs and the events of the Shoah with multiple generations of students. We then talked about religious bigotry, another form of cultural idolatry, as one cause of the world's violence.

In one of the tapes, peasants discussed the camp's presence with stunning simplicity. They continued to blame the Jews for Christ's death and, implicitly therefore, blamed the Jews for the mid-century holocaust which had consumed living Jewish bodies in fire. As I watched these practicing Christian men and women vigorously defend a Christianity based on hatred of the Jewish people as Christ-killers, I worried about future pogroms in that geographical area of Christianity's ideological power.[182]

Some years later the former Paulist priest and Catholic journalist James Carroll traveled to Poland to document the crosses placed outside Auschwitz at the time of Pope John Paul the Second's 1975 visit there. Carroll's work in re-theologizing the cross as Christianity's dominant symbol is, in my opinion, one of the most significant books about the cross as icon and as a violence-fomenting ideology during centuries of Christian violence against Jewish communities.[183]

A more recent book by Protestant thealogians Rebecca Parker and Rita Nakashima Brock explored the imagery of the cross as it emerged in the iconic representations of early Eastern and Western Christianity and came to similar conclusions as those made by Carroll.[184] See also Stanley Cohen's discussion of the Nazi era.[185]

All of this is to say that Hallie's concept of resistance to evil now informs my understandings of the work Christian peacemakers need to do in the world. That understanding is pervaded by his insistence that there is no human purity when it comes to violence and cruelty. We are all implicated. Hallie's work, in many ways, prepared me to understand Carroll's work. Hallie's work, in other ways, prepared me to repeatedly question my Mennonite understandings of war and violence.

> *The village of Le Chambon did nothing to shorten the war. Some of my early criticisms against pacifism kept surfacing. Pacifists can be patient as far as ending a war is concerned. They can even contribute to the defeat of the side they are influencing. While they are patiently refusing to kill, the mass murder of war can go on and on and – in the case of World War Two, so can the concentration camps that are killing thousands and thousands of human beings ever day.*[186]

Until active pacifists understand this external critique of collusion with violence, we risk becoming colluders. Our resistance to the violence we are called to witness by our location in the social history of our times needs to be immediate, vigorous, and principled. It needs to take risks. And, in my opinion, it needs to be guided by compassionate, hard-minded love.

We need to enter the struggle, guided by Jack Kornfield's admonition that to have peace, we must compassionately work for justice. To do this successfully, I believe we must do our work in the outer world guided by inner spiritual work: creating an inner world that does not need hate or fear or rage as our motivating energy or fuel. We need to do our work motivated by love for all participants in the spiral of violence rather than from a spirit of judgmental rage or debilitating anger at the injustice we see and experience.[187]

Ruth E. Krall

Sixth Letter

Living inside the Eye of the Hurricane, Part Three

A Conversation with Mark Nepo

Introduction

In 2000 the United States poet and new age spiritual teacher Mark Nepo wrote about hurricanes as metaphors for the spiritual journey. In his use of this metaphor he invited his readers to consider deliberate removal of the ego away from the turbulence of strong negative emotions such as anger or rage.

> *A deeper paradox is carried here. For the gull flies through the peaceful center; it does not live there. The work, it seems for us is to draw sustenance from that central eternal space without denying the experience of the storm.*
>
> *Repeatedly we are thrown into the storm and into the center. When in the storm we are exacerbated by our humanness. When in the center, we are relieved by our spiritual place in the Oneness of all things. So to find the center and spread our battered wings is to feel the God within.* [188]

Nepo reminds his reader of the reality that the gull does not live in the center but must fly into and through the whirling storm in order to get to the center. In addition, the gull knows, when caught in the hurricane's wind, that flying inside the violent storm, it can only survive the fierce winds by getting to the center – the hurricane's eye.

In the background of my reading of Nepo are my internal conversations with Philip Hallie about the nature of evil and good; about human cruelty and helpfulness. In the background is my life-history as a clinician who knows that unresolved human stress caused by the intense emotions of anxiety, anger and rage are life-body-spirit killers.

By the time I first read Nepo, I was already accustomed to thinking about peace and justice work as work which existed inside the moral hurricane, inside structures of injustice and oppression and violence. I could feel, therefore, the urgency of pushing back against the inner walls of the hurricane to create as much blue space as was possible. This was Hallie's contribution to my understanding of this metaphor of living inside the hurricane's eye.

Nepo's work took my awareness to another plane – to the realm of personal spirituality. His spiritual lesson for us in light of Hallie's work is threefold: first, we must learn how to navigate our way, repeatedly, into and then free of the violent storms that surround the work we do in the world; secondly, we must work together to push back the eye of the storm to make more space in our individual and collective work for the blue and sunny center. Third, we must cultivate an inner spirituality that is as calm as the storm is violent. It is in this focused spiritual center of our lives where we develop the moral courage *and* the emotional stamina to do the work of sexual violence advocacy. When we work from this calm, focused center, we no longer need the emergency fuels of anger and rage to sustain our work. We no longer need to run from the terrors of the work we do. We can simply embrace the work which needs to be done. Finally, we can then begin to do this work. Inside the blue space of the center, we can work from an informed sense of compassion and an urgent sense of justice combined with mercy.

We need other people in our lives to support our work. But, perhaps most importantly, we need this internal space of calm where our inner spirit (and our body too) is nourished and refreshed; where we live in the eternal quiet of the present moment. It is from this space of inner calm (right in the center of the swirling hurricane) that we do the best and most needed work.

When I choose to work from the peaceful center in the middle of violent moral and spiritual hurricanes, I am much less likely to make tactical mistakes in the outer world. As I free up the center from the clutter of internalized negativity, I am more able to listen to that still inner voice of guidance and wisdom – the voice that seeks to inform me about what, in this particular situation, is necessary and right to do. Christians in many eras have called this inner voice of stillness the voice of the Holy Spirit.

Seventh Letter

Living in the Hurricane's Eye, Part Four

Encounters with Prophets, Priests, Mystics and Peacemakers

*What I am hoping to communicate, however, is the need for resistance more broadly defined than civil disobedience. Perhaps a better word would be **rebellion**, or...that following Jesus ought to be **subversive** again for the cause of love.*

Robin Meyers[189]

Introductory Comments

For many months now, I have been pondering your embodied wisdom about the word *resistance*[190] as an enervating force in your body-psyche-spirit and your strong academic preference for the word *transformation*. In this letter, written many months later than our initial correspondence about resistance and transformation and months after the other hurricane letters were written, I want to return to this question and look at it slant – this time through my eyes as a feminist thealogian.

Once again, please understand, I am not attacking your personal and professional languages. I am supportive of your deep personal intuitions that the language of resistance is damaging to your body, your spirit and your will to persist in doing peace advocacy work. You may very well be correct: unthinking use of such language damages the cause of peace because it damages our own bodies, minds, and spirits. My return, to this topic of resistance, is not, therefore, a conversational wrestling match in which one of us wins and one of us loses.

I personally believe we need as many languages and as many allies as we can find and muster because the more circumscribed and cliché-like the personal and professional languages we use to clarify cultural nuances in situations of violence and violation, the less damage we do to the patriarchy; the less able we are in carrying out our Christian feminist task of dismantling the patriarchy and its oppressive orthodoxies for our sons' and daughters' futures.

I am seeking, therefore, to understand your world and work from inside my world and work. Also believing in the need for cultural and personal communities of subversive resistance *and* transformation, I am perhaps seeking, in some sense, to understand my own preference for the language and praxis of cultural disobedience and spiritually-infused defiant resistance. Believing I am called, as a Jesus path follower and as a healer to resist injustice, gives me courage when I am most afraid of the principalities and powers.[191] It comforts me when I am most anxious and overcome with doubts about how to proceed. Saying, *I do not agree with the multiple forms of violence in this situation and I will not be complicit with any of them:* these seem to me to be words and acts of subversive resistance. Saying, *I will work to overcome unjust systems that harm individuals and entire communities*: perhaps that is the work of transformation. But quite truthfully, in my daily life I don't really see a line dividing morally-principled works of disobedient subversion or resistance to injustice and morally-principled acts of transformation inside violent and repressive social institutions and systems.

Scripture's Prophetic Trajectory

> *Do justice and righteousness; deliver from the hand of the oppressor him who has been robbed; do no wrong or violence to the resident alien, the fatherless, the widow; do not shed innocent blood in this place.*

> Jeremiah 22:3 (ESV)

For many years Jewish scriptures and their prophetic trajectory have supported my thealogical and clinical spine. When I most desire the comfortable and passive silence of cultural obedience and conflict avoidance, I turn to these ancient prophets. When I most long for deep anonymity in the face of injustice and violence, I remember their outspoken heroism and courage in the commons. When I most want to run away from the world's killing and raping fields, I remember their dogged persistence in what appears to us to be their failures. When most in doubt about how to proceed, I borrow their wisdom and their words, The urgency of their messages about the need for compassion, mercy, justice, love of the unlovely, economic and friendship support for the unwanted stranger or alien in their land, assistance to the impoverished widow, and many other verses about justice, mercy, hospitality, healing, and generosity as markers of God's presence in their midst – these messages have sustained me in rainy seasons and in times of drought. They sustain me when I feel most desperately alienated from my people. Using the guiding metaphor of this short series of hurricane letters, they help me to find the calm center of the violence storm. They help me to push back (i.e., resist) against its claustrophobic and catastrophic walls as I seek to make more blue space in which I and others can live and work.

Most of these ancient Jewish prophets, just like me, would have preferred to relax with an icy cold drink as they propped their feet up under the palm trees in the oasis where their camels drank. Most of them, just like me, would have preferred God's calling voice, the incessant inner voice of Spirit demanding accountability, justice and a cessation of idolatry as the foundation for peace, to be silent. I don't see these ancient prophets as overjoyed at the notion that they, as individuals, are continuously and internally called upon to confront the cozy and familiar idolatries of corrupted institutional power and religiously-inspired orthodoxies of un-love. I fantasize that sometimes they complained to God (or to God's human informant at their back door) saying: *Can't you see I am busy right now? Give me a break! Get somebody else to speak up. Besides, I desperately need a nap.*

The clarion message of the prophets confronts me in the many moments of my complicity with injustice, in the moments when I rely on inherited skin and class privilege rather than compassion to get by. These prophets were not ecstatically burbling to the world about the gorgeous prayers, sermons, liturgies, and aesthetically correct vestments of the priestly and ruling castes. They did not hire expensive public relations firms to make their message more palatable. They did not create fancy advertising slogans, unforgettable jingles, and billboard campaigns to build an ideologically correct and ruler-supported membership in the temple. They did not create study committees or accountability review boards and panels. They were not sycophants. They did not seek followers. They did not pander to their corrupt rulers' wealth and institutionalized power.

They were, to the ruling elites and cultural insiders of their society, obnoxious folk. They were seen as trouble-makers. As whistle-blowers they were often seen by the ruling elites as treasonous. To put it bluntly: they were hated. Most of us, I suspect, would never have invited any of them to dinner. Most of us would have crossed the street to avoid being seen talking with them. We would not have befriended them on Facebook. Friends, extended kin networks, and foes alike turned against them. Things in their neighborhoods often turned nasty when they appeared. They were outcastes and exiles living inside their communities of origin.

These were not ignorant or naïve individuals. They were quite clear about the reasons they were so disdained by others. They knew precisely what they needed to do to be acceptable. Understanding the true social costs of their work, they could not keep silent.

For example, Jeremiah names his dilemma:

But if I say, *I will not mention his word or speak anymore in his name; his word is in my heart like a fire, a fire shut up in my bones. I am weary of holding it in. Indeed, I cannot.*[192]

These prophets repeatedly complain to God, *Why me?* When they think God is not looking, they head to the caves and hide. They cover their ears with pillows and their eyes with blankets. They curl up in a fetal position and beg to die. But even in the deepest and darkest of caves, the dangers of their time in history *to their beloved people* are everywhere evident to them. They see the imminent disaster on the future's horizon and insist on shouting the warning cry. The need for human justice and human accountability as the foundation for a sustainable and livable society burns within them.

Being a Hebrew prophet, I suspect, was like living every night with un-medicated restless leg syndrome. There is no relief to be found. Eventually one just gets up and starts walking.

I understand these prophets. They feel like kin to me. Not one volunteers ahead of time for coerced exile and doing jail time. No one volunteers for hate stares, hate phone calls and hostile email messages. No one volunteers to have the evening news reporters outside one's front door. No one volunteers to be hounded by the paparazzi. No one volunteers to be named as public enemy number one for religious treason. No one volunteers for communal shunning. No one volunteers to be betrayed by one's professional colleagues, family, and friends. No one volunteers for stoning, assassination, or crucifixion. No one volunteers for the dark night of the soul.

Yet, in haunting ways, it seems to me, these ancient prophets all knew ahead of time the likelihood of living in social and personal exile from their people. They most likely knew in our language today that they would soon be out of a paying job with good benefits. They likely knew they would no longer be welcome at family birthday parties. They all probably intuited that personal suffering and exclusion from their society's halls of power and prestige was a predictable and likely outcome of saying truthful things out loud and in public about oppressive national idolatry and religious-political-cultural corruptness. None were naïve enough to expect grand gestures of gratitude for their public service from the king and his court or honorary titles from the temple leaders and their followers. None, I am quite certain, hoped for their nation-state's Medal of Freedom. None hoped for their temple's annual Man of the Year designation.

Witnessing the systemic or structural evils of their time in history and making an educated guess about their long term outcomes, they resisted these evils with ferocity, liturgical genius, and integrity. Seeing the inevitable outcome of corrupt nations and corrupt centers of worship as death and desolation, they pronounced the inevitable and the uncomfortable. They spoke the inexorable word of God's judgment on their king's many economic idolatries and the words of warning about institutionalized and idolatrous forms of unfaithfulness among the leaders of the temple and its worship cult.

No wonder these biblical prophets were hated. No wonder they were locked into stocks in their town's center square where all so-inclined citizens could spit on them. No wonder they were tossed into dungeons and deep wells and left to die.

Distrusting that Which Is and Longing for that Which Is Not

> This is what the sovereign Lord says: *Woe to you Shepherds...who only take care of yourselves. Should not shepherds take care of the flock? You eat the curds; clothe yourself with the wool; slaughter the choice animals. You have not strengthened the weak or healed the sick or bound up the injured. You have not brought back the strays or searched for the lost. You have ruled them harshly and brutally...*This is what the Lord says: *I am against the shepherds and will hold them accountable for my flock. I will remove them from tending my flock so that they can no longer feed themselves. I will rescue my flock from their mouths, and it will no longer be food for them.*[193]

My personal distrust of religious institutions qua institutions as bearers of spiritual idolatry and corruption began quite naively. It began when I first heard stories of sexualized violence and domestic violence done by Mennonite evangelists preaching the one and only true way to salvation; violence done by the denomination's Biblical scholars; violence done by Mennonite missionaries, preachers, and teachers of peace orthodoxies; violence done by Mennonite administrators of social welfare agencies and mission agencies; violence done by Mennonite therapists inside Mennonite hospitals and outpatient clinics; violence done by Mennonite teachers and administrators in academic settings.

As a woman, it seemed quite reasonable to me that the gospel of peace and the gospel of service to others proclaimed by sexual abusers, sexual harassers, and by domestic violence abusers was not a Jesus-based gospel of peace and compassionate service at all – no matter how orthodox it was; no matter how others viewed the message as essential gospel; no matter how powerful, well-connected, compelling, and exalted the message bearer.

Whenever I needed to teach peace-work in a Mennonite context I was cautious because I didn't want to be a female carrier of the religious patriarchy's orthodoxy loaded violence against women and their children. Most especially, I didn't want to be a female acolyte by hiding and complicitly covering up real-time incidents of sexual and physical abuse of women and their children by religious leaders and by their Mennonite spouses, parents, and siblings. Most especially, I didn't want to lie to my students about the real world they were inheriting from their elders.

As a clinician and as a teacher of the young, witnessing our proclivity as Mennonites to solve interpersonal conflicts and issues of authority and dominance with intra-community and interpersonal forms of social or relational violence, I have frequently needed to re-think my own pacifism. I have both witnessed and been targeted by active hate stares, back-stabbing character assassination, and passive shunning. That my pacifism has survived is quite remarkable. In doing the work of the church that the church itself asked me to do, other church employees subsequent to my actual doing of that work have said nasty things about me, my character, my motivations, and my work. Thus, that I still claim a Mennonite identity is even more remarkable. There have been far too many days when I have actively wished for an eternal destination in hell for this abusive individual or that abusive individual. There have been many more days of doubt than certainty in my lifetime about the spiritual and political wisdom of being a Mennonite pacifist.

On Being a Plain Child

I often wonder whether I learned socio-cultural resistance as a plain child listening to Mennonite sermons against war in my childhood congregation.[194] But, by early adolescence some of the things I heard in sincerely-preached sermons by honorable and kind men made no sense to me. In the conflict of science and its factual truth with gospel and its miraculous teachings, science won hands down. My late adolescent and young adult mantra became *Galileo was right!* Sometimes, therefore, I think that maybe what my braids and plain dress taught me in the long-run was how to disobediently resist a church which saw more sin in lipstick, dancing, and wedding bands than it did in the socially-accepted denial of civil rights to black citizens of its nation-state; a church which refused to acknowledge sexual violence inside its communal boundaries as equivalent to warfare's violence external to them; a church which hid the presence of a wide variety of sexual and gender abuse perpetrators under the pious talk of redemptive suffering and community demands for victims to forgive on demand.

However, as an old woman now, I think another reality than my Mennonite childhood, is perhaps a more important one. This reality continues to be present in my personal search for a gospel of peace inside the Jesus path. I have not only heard Mennonite voices in my lifetime. I have heard the voices of socially-informed spiritual seekers and teachers in a wide variety of religious and social settings. I have also both read and heard the voices of morally-principled agnostics and atheists.

I have been a polyglot reader all of my life – and through much of my adolescence and early adult life I sought to understand conflicting ideas inside Christianity about theology, lifestyle, spirituality and peace-making. In essence, these conflicting messages were about inclusion and exclusion. Who belonged inside the circle of faith? Who didn't belong? What were the social reasons for belonging or not-belonging? Most of all I tried to understand why I was a plain child with braids I hated in an extended family where my great aunts, aunts and female cousins had short hair and wore lipstick. Why did the Mennonite God care if my Mennonite hair was plaited into pigtails rather than allowed to feel the wind? Why did it bother Him enough to threaten me with eternal damnation because I wanted to look pretty? Was wearing nail polish really a sure sign of my social location outside of God's love? What about starched crinolines? What about sheer seamless taupe nylons instead of seamed black cotton hose? What and whose were these arbitrary salvation markers anyway?

I personally never believed God cared about these matters of women's dress and female appearance. If "He" did, heaven was going to be sparsely populated and hell was going to need a massive influx of capital just to house and feed all of its female inmates. I was probably abetted in my doubts by my Lutheran father who often joked inside our family that Mennonites thought they would be the only ones in heaven.

My paternal grandparents, my father, his siblings, their spouses and my first cousins were neither Mennonites nor pacifists. Some were not Christian by their own self-definitions. Most of them, even the marginally Christian ones, were not practicing Christians. They were, as other denominations call them, Christmas Eve and Easter Morning Christians. Taken together, all of my grandparents, aunts, uncles and cousins represented a religious smorgasbord of Christian denominations from high church Anglican and Roman Catholic to low church groups such as, for example, nondenominational evangelical groups. Whatever their religious take on the world, I experienced my relations to be kind and loving individuals. They lived honorable lives in the commons and they cared for people who were not privileged in material goods or in health. They had a strong internal sense of personal integrity. Most important, perhaps, was the fact that they were seen as honorable and trustworthy individuals in the commons. They did not lie to themselves or others about who they were and what they thought. In short, they were not hypocrites.

In the process of becoming an adult, I needed, therefore, to resolve this conundrum of loving people who were so very different than I was in terms of religious identities, religious beliefs, religious practices, and personal values. My warrior uncles and cousins loved me and, in return, I loved and trusted them. They were my family. Yet, somehow or other, I was also absorbing a Mennonite-inspired sense of justice without violence and violation. My baptism into the Mennonite Church was not a revolutionary act of conversion in my psyche. It was a predictable rite of passage into my Mennonite adolescence. I said all of the right words but with metaphorically-crossed fingers behind my back. I kept my doubts to myself.

My decision to stay Mennonite-affiliated after I graduated from college was, therefore, a much more revolutionary and thought-through act. The reason was quite simple: in four years of undergraduate study and polyglot reading, I had become a Mennonite pacifist.

Living in a television-free home, I read. Attending a television-free undergraduate college, I read. Forbidden to go to Saturday matinees with my friends, I read.

Encountering the Mystics

By the time I left college I had met the mystics. I wrote a senior paper on the Jewish mystic and philosopher Martin Buber and he made sense to me. I had an inchoate understanding, therefore, that a maturing personal spirituality and pious communal religiosity were not exactly the same things. I was helped in this by a senior elective course about the sociology of religion. In that course, I began to understand that the human church was not primarily a God-inspired spiritual entity; it was a human-created sociological one. Thus, I had a nascent intuition that the institutional church was as full of the social ills of its time as other cultural institutions.

When I read, sometime in the early sixties, Dr. Martin Luther King's *Letter from a Birmingham Jail,* I began to collect social justice case material in my mind. Subscribing to the Methodist Church's *Motive Magazine for Young Adults,* I became aware of the connection of the visual arts to social justice movements. Somewhat later becoming aware of Dr. Vincent Harding's growing alienation from the Mennonite Church because of its structural racism, I began to know that a peace-proclaiming church was not necessarily a peace-living church. I did not personally know Dr. King or the editors of *Motive Magazine* but I did know Vince and Rosemarie Harding. My personal sympathies lay with them rather than with the institutional church in this matter. In my late twenties and early thirties I was deeply offended by the manner in which my denomination refused to respond to their urgent calls for help in combating societal and denominational racism. The Christian-Mennonite-racism paradigm weakened my personal commitment to a practicing denominational membership. When I first met Jewish individuals in large numbers in the secular academy, I heard the concept of non-practicing Jews. By my early thirties, I had concluded that I was a non-practicing Mennonite. My sense of a Mennonite pacifist identity was intact. I simply didn't practice religious institution membership.

In addition, as I left my college years behind me to begin my professional career as a psychiatric nurse, I had deeper intuitions about and urgent longings for a justice-based worldwide peace than I had words for. In books and midnight chats with friends, I sought answers for myself to unanswerable questions. What I wondered, would a just inter-racial peace look like. What, I wondered, would a world without war, ethnic hatred and economically excluded others look like? What would a world without economic slavery look like? What, I often wondered, would authentic freedom for everyone look like? What would a genuinely inclusive church look like? How, I worried, did I manage my white skin and middle class background inside a racist culture? Was I a racist? I didn't want to be but I finally concluded that white skin privileged me in too many ways to avoid culturally-embedded racism in my body-Self. Seeking to live a more open and inclusive life, I slowly began to make friends across color, language, sexual orientation, and religious boundaries.

My membership in the anti-Vietnam generation – *hell, no, we won't go* – further alienated me from my denominational church. Its passivity in claiming its privilege of conscientious objection as a pacifist church for its own young men - while simultaneously refusing to actively preach/protest against this war was offensive to me. As a nurse administrator in a large university hospital I hired several Roman Catholic young men and trained them as mental health technicians so that they might successfully claim to be conscientious objectors and thus escape the draft and jail. Needless to say in a state-funded institution located in a military town, this was a controversial decision and some of my staff protested these young men's presence in our workplace community. In addition, I provided character references to their draft boards when asked to do so. Not living inside the Mennonite commons, nevertheless, I sought to live out my Mennonite-inculcated values vis-à-vis war – most particularly, the American-Vietnamese war.

As a fully participating member of the generation which decided the American War with Vietnam was unjust, I read widely – educating myself. As I read, marched and sang in demonstrations for the ending of that unjust war: I witnessed the institutional church's mistrust of its mystics *and* of its anti-war street activists. I found I had more in common with violence-protesting marchers in the streets than I did with all of the silent and war-complicit Christians in the pews. Along the way, I learned to distrust piety and religious rhetoric dressed as required orthodoxy. I learned to actively distrust congregations which side-stepped a radical peace witness for a safer practice of offering pious and harmless words about God's peace. I learned to distrust religious teachings co-opted by the powers and principalities in the service of injustice.

As part of the generation of Mennonite girls and women that discarded plain clothing, I also discarded much more. I discarded the notion that Mennonites were God's only children. I figured in a world of racism, war and sexual violence, God had more important things to worry over than whether I wore skirts or slacks to work. It took me many more years to realize He wasn't, in fact, a He at all.

In most social situations, I stayed silent about my spiritual-religious questions and my intrapersonal experiences of awe *and* doubt until, by chance, I met Notre Dame faculty member Morton Kelsey at a conference. Since that chance conversation – in which he sent me to more books to read – it has taken me a lifetime of reading and conversations with a wide variety of spiritual seekers and teachers to understand institutional religion's refusal to listen to the spiritual wisdom of its mystics. It has taken me a lifetime to understand the institutional church's refusal to listen to its sexual violence victims and their advocates. In truth, I am not sure I understand either one yet.

I remain puzzled and troubled by the institutional church's all-too-easy rejection of its contemporary prophets. I am puzzled by the church's insistence on clinging to its troubled past and outgrown orthodoxies when the openness of the present moment in which to do justice and to seek healing for wounds of the past has already announced itself. So, I keep reading. I keep talking with lifetime friends, professional colleagues, and former students such as you. I am really not certain anymore that I will ever find satisfying answers to my questions. Thus, I continue to live my personal spiritual life inside ambiguity: inside my doubts and inside my questions. Inside these ambiguities, doubts and questions, I cling to the mystical vision of a peaceable world in much the same way that a shipwreck survivor clings to a plank of wood on very choppy waters.

These Little Ones of Any Age

For example: in reading about and studying the phenomenon of Roman Catholic *clericalism,*[195] I discovered Dominican Friar Father Thomas Doyle's exegesis of Matthew 18:6 in which he added a theological gloss to the text: *If anyone causes these little ones, **these little ones of any age**, to stumble, it would be better for them to have a millstone hung around their neck and be drowned in the depths of the sea.* Some newer translations interpret the word stumble as *to lose faith.* I found myself in tears at the gloss – for I too was one of the wounded little ones who had lost faith. I too had stumbled. For the first time in many years, I felt compassionately understood and, by implication at least, included in the theological and spiritual conversation. His textual gloss made space for me, my experiences of spiritual exile, and my questions about justice and accountability inside a Christian conversation about sexualized violence and violation. It made space for my unfaith regarding religious institutions.

Reflecting on my tears and my deep sense of identification with his gloss, I began to understand that I needed, once again, very late in my life, to rethink my personal spirituality and my religious identity. I needed, once again, to re-think my pacifism. In bearing witness against a sexual violence perpetrator inside my denominational home and against all forms of sexualized and genderized abuse and violence inside my cradle faith community of belief and praxis, I had lost my spiritual moorings *and* my spiritual community. I had lost trust in the good will and faithful spirituality of Mennonite leaders and their silent or silenced people. Moving away from the spatial geography of my religious community, my homeland, I discarded my cradle faith and Mennonite identity as complicit with the sexualized and genderized violence of that community. By my own choice, I was living in theological and sociological exile. Most of what I had once believed about the people of God living in peace together inside a beloved community now made no sense to me whatsoever.

In more than thirty years of working for Mennonite institutions I had witnessed much more overt hostility and had experienced much more covert passive-aggressive hypocrisy than I knew what to do with. Now, living outside the Mennonite community, I needed to re-think what being the people of God, the living church, and the body of Jesus really meant to me. Who were my people? Who was my family? What two or three *gathered together* sustained me, for example, in doing my anti-rape, anti-violence activism work?[196]

Sexual abuse cover-up issues[197] inside the boundaries of my cradle faith denomination led me to doubt my religious heritage and its long legacy of pacifist resistance to militarism and other forms of socio-cultural violence such as the death penalty. The cover-ups of sexual abuse by Mennonite institutional leaders led me to question the integrity of Mennonite communal life and praxis. If the male Mennonite God and His – usually – male representatives did not protest the sexual violation of women and their children as evil, for example, then this patriarchal and parochial God and his *teachings* were not now and never could be good news for Mennonite women, for their Mennonite children.

My intellectual dilemma was quite simple: if our major Mennonite theologians, biblical scholars, seminary officials, institutional board members, and members of its teaching faculties hid sexual violence perpetrators from sight and refused to hold them fully and publicly accountable for their actions, then their teachings about Christian pacifism were a form of complicity with evil. If our major theologians and church administrators were, themselves, sexual violence perpetrators, then their teachings about Christian or even Mennonite pacifism were not worth even a penny.

Instead, their many words were merely self-justification for their actions of hostility towards and dominance over women. If the church refused to reach out with compassion and healing to the victims of violation – *these little ones of any age* – there was no place I could sit inside the denomination's boundary walls and not be complicit with its structural and covered-up acts of physical violence. As a healer, being complicit was more than I could bear. For the second time in my adult life, I shuffled my Mennonite identity, my Mennonite pacifism and my

Mennonite spirituality of community to the bottom of the deck and put the deck on the shelf. Once again I became a non-practicing Mennonite in exile.

Re-thinking Anabaptist History

In very recent conversations with a sympathetic friend, he told me about Hans Denk (1495-1527),[198] a sixteenth-century Anabaptist reformer I knew nothing about. For the first time I encountered the theology and mysticism of Hans Denk – one of the earliest Anabaptist reformers and a humanist. I still don't know much about him but his presence, as an Anabaptist, as a mystic and as an academically-educated humanist, in my cradle faith lineage is important to me. He does not appear to have been a rabid ideologue. He does not appear preoccupied with excluding others because of different ideas about faithfulness or social boundary markers such as race and class. Perhaps, more importantly, in an ethnic church which has too often intellectually sanctified the suffering of its martyrs as redemptive, he was not a martyr.

He was, from what I can read about him, an eloquent orator and teacher. That he dropped off the radar of Anabaptist theologians, philosophers and humanists is not an accident. The Anabaptist-Mennonite church, as it moved to the Americas in the eighteenth century and made a home for itself by the nineteenth century, preferred orthodox beliefs and regulated communal worship practices over mystical experiences of God's living and luring presence in the world. Distrust of the secular world, particularly its educated humanists, pervaded daily life in many American Old Mennonite communities. Avoiding conformity with the world – took precedence over embodying compassion for the world. What one looked like and how one dressed became more important than one's inner life; indeed, more important than one's character. What one professed in the religious commons was more important than how one treated one's next door neighbor or the homeless hobo who showed up asking for a meal. Thus, all-too-frequently, a communally-learned hypocrisy about right-appearances became a way of life for individuals and entire congregations.

The mystical presence of God was, as I look back, notably absent. In its place were human-created orthodoxies passing themselves off as God's.

Denk's presence teaches me and others like me that we are not forever trapped in some toxic ecclesial swamp of hypocrisy, dogma, orthodoxy, clericalism, and denominationally organized purity code rules about belonging or not-belonging. We as mystics, prophets, true priests, and healers, have faith ancestors who both knew and taught others about the presence and intuitive guidance of the divine presence or holy wisdom within.[199]

Twentieth-century Mystics and Peace Activists

In terms of twentieth-century mystics, I kept stumbling over them in books, at conferences, and in person. In my mid-life career years, I learned that all of the world's great religions and wisdom traditions have mystics for whom a direct encounter with the divine is more important than theological abstractions in a theology book or creed. Meeting the life and work of world religion scholar Huston Smith[200] on an academic sabbatical in my mid-fifties finally gave me the interior freedom to openly follow the spiritual path I had followed privately for many, many years.[201] I acknowledged to myself that I had many more doubts about institutionally-organized religious life than I had certainties. I had much more distrust for institutionally credentialed religious leaders and preachers than trust. I acknowledged that there were creeds I could no longer honestly recite and hymns I could no longer sing if I wished to be honest in my interior faith.

Simultaneously, I acknowledged my deep interest in the interior spiritual life which sustains public activism in the outer world. It was not that I was an atheist, for I wasn't. But my inner experience of the silent void and quiet intuition meant I lived a spiritual life of ambiguity and doubt. It wasn't even that God was absent. It was that whatever I intuited about the divine presence in the world was more mystery than anything else. The only certainty I could find – as a tiny toehold in communal spirituality – was the intuitive sense that love, compassion, tenderness, beauty, friendship, joy and awe were not commodities to be dispensed by morally corrupt institutions. Whatever salvation was, it had to be here in the present moment rather than hoped for pie in the sky by and by. Whatever healing was, it too existed in the present moment. Its potentiality was always with us. Whatever peace was, its gossamer fragility only appeared in the present moment.

For many years, I had held on to my pacifism as the badge *and* rationale of my Mennonite identity. In this mid-career academic sabbatical year (seriously wounded in body, psyche, and soul) I began more actively and openly to nurture the spirituality of healing. I began to search for spiritual elders and wise teachers whose words *and* life made sense to me. I personally didn't care what their religious affiliations were as long as they touched to my inner neediness for something more than hastily mumbled rote prayers, communal conformity, tolerance of violence against women and their children, and long, predictable, boring sermons.

Both, spirituality and activism, I slowly came to understand were essential to my life: a deep, inner spirituality and a deep commitment to the disempowered and culturally dis-privileged as an essential act of faith in the divine Spirit. However I knew this, I knew I had been called early in my life to the work of healing. From early mid-life on, I had never doubted this calling. Social and religious contexts for my work would change at times but the inner calling to be a healer did not.

I have felt no similar deep awareness of my calling to be Mennonite in my institutional arrangements. Once I decided to live in a Mennonite community, what I did feel called to do was simple to name but complex to do. I felt called to assist Mennonite women find healing for the wounds created by the secular and religious patriarchy, in particular, the wounds of sexualized and genderized violence. I felt called to help young Mennonites consolidate their personal identities as young adults by assisting them to find their own unique pathways into adult life; pathways into spiritual freedom and maturity that had integrity for them.

Unlike the deep inner need for a rich spirituality, being a Mennonite college professor was a pragmatic decision. There was, and still is, therefore, an ethnic aspect to my personal faith and its institutional arrangements that I have never denied. Had I been born into a Roman Catholic family, I would most likely be a Roman Catholic. Had I been born into a Buddhist family, I would most likely be a practicing Buddhist. Had I been born into a family with two practicing Mennonite parents, I probably would have lived my entire life without questioning my religious and spiritual identity. In any of these hypothetical life situations, I may never have needed or encountered the Jewish prophets and the Christian and other-than-Christian mystics.

Mystics as Peace Activists: Peace Activists as Mystics

Inside the writings of Thomas Merton and the Berrigan brothers, I learned, for example, about the mysticism and peace witness of Vietnamese Buddhist Thich Nhat Hanh. Inside the American civil rights movement, I learned about Gandhi's influence on Martin Luther King, Jr. In the course of my professional life, I met Roman Catholic and Protestant peace activists at conferences. In graduate school, I met some young and idealistic Catholic Worker House staff members. In the secular academy, I met socially-informed Jewish activists.

At Claremont during my graduate school years, I had a North American Buddhist friend. We played pick-up volleyball together every week in a motley group of graduate and undergraduate students. Many evenings, long after the net had been taken down and the ball stored away, he and I sat on the curb outside his dorm room talking about his Buddhist studies, my Christian studies, the inner silence, God and mysticism. These conversations were my first introduction to the idea of Buddhist meditation as a mystical spiritual practice – as a way to approach living non-violently in the world.[202]

At a conference, in my late sixties or early seventies, I heard Rabbi Rami Shapiro speak and began to read as many of his books and articles as I could find. I found Mathew Fox's body of work on creation spirituality, the *via positiva*, and his personal activism on behalf of creation itself to speak to my inner thirst. Through Fox's work, I encountered the medieval mystics and these voices included women's testimonies to female spiritual experience.

Slowly, in the past two years, I have begun to rebuild my Jesus path spirituality and my Mennonite-inspired pacifism. But it is no longer institutional. It is no longer inherited. It is no longer singularly dependent upon Mennonite theologians and ethicists. It is no longer solely dependent upon a Mennonite exegesis of the biblical narratives. Quite frankly, it is no longer denominational. I have quietly slipped outside the back door of my cradle faith community. It is my impression that my absence has not been noted nor have I been missed.

These days I have almost no interest in a denominational praxis of control, orthodoxy and the religiously-motivated impulse to exclude others from belonging. Indeed, I am deeply disturbed by the Mennonite Church and its denominational politicized insistence upon excluding its own children from full fellowship simply because they do not fit a white, male, dominant, middle-class, heterosexual mold.

Understanding Peace through the Cultural Narrative of Sexualized Violence

Childhood's denominational lessons about the Jesus peace and my ideas about how to be a peace-maker have been scrutinized by and continuously re-evaluated by a professional lifetime of listening to the victims and survivors of violence in its militarized forms, its domestic forms, its genderized forms, and in its sexualized forms. Only late in life, in my fifties, sixties and seventies, have I frontally faced and confronted out-loud and in public various denominational forms of religious hypocrisy and associated manifestations of social and structural violence. My thealogy of peace-work, therefore, has been deeply shaped by listening to, observing and experiencing the often-hidden and culturally embedded violence and violation narratives of my culture inside and outside of my childhood's denominational home.

Demonization and Dehumanization Re-visited

We don't just live in the empire. The empire lives in us.

Robin Meyers[203]

In my clinical work, I gradually learned that demonization and its concomitant dehumanization of any human being – no matter how violent he or she was/is – was counter-productive to the healing work I felt called to do. I gradually came to realize that the wounds of violence were present in every participant and in every witness to the story of violence and violation. As a clinical witness to multiple violence narratives of cultural and structural violence, I began to realize how wounded *I* was by the patriarchal story of sexualized, genderized, and economic violence against women. Seeking to find some way I could be helpful to others when I most wanted to run away to some distant land where I didn't understand or speak the local language and to put my feet up under the palms at the camel oasis, I began the spiritual practices of meditation and gratitude. These began, quite simply, as ways of healing my own embodied physical, spiritual and emotional wounds. But, they soon began to shape my professional understandings about how peace and justice are murdered *and* how an active, vibrant work of activism on behalf of peace and justice in the commons is both born and sustained.

Perhaps most importantly, my thealogy of active peace-making and active justice-making has been shaped by reading and encountering in person some of the world's spiritual mystics and activists. I am intrigued by the combination of a deep well of inner spirituality that expresses itself in efforts to heal the self, others, and the cosmos by a spirit-infused activism. I have come to believe that both aspects of this narrative are essential: (1) the individual's direct encounters with Spirit in moments of awe and silence *and* (2) the deep healing these moments bring to the individual and her or his decisions to work for the healing of the world.

Now, as a practitioner of meditation and gratitude, I deliberately work at no longer sending people to hell in my irritated and enraged imagination. But, this has been a journey of deliberately working to hear the monkey mind, its mischief-creating anger and its interminable and contentious desires for spite and for revenge. It has been a continuous journey since I began to meditate in 1996 – a journey of learning to recognize, acknowledge and to resist negative, spiteful, hostile imagery as damaging to my personal spirituality, damaging to others, and damaging to the cosmos.

The principle is now quite clear to me: who we are today internally is what we will become or demonstrate tomorrow in the external world. It is impossible for us to manifest something in the outer world that we are not already manifesting in the inner world. Thus, it is our behavior with others – not our words - which announces most presciently who we are. It is not our words but our actions that declare our deepest faiths. It is, therefore, not our beliefs but our behaviors that define our spirituality and our character.

Ancient scriptures have taught us this; it is not some New Age heresy. *As a human being thinks in his or her heart, s/he is that.*[204] This is the wisdom of the ages. A healthy, vibrant, and living spirituality does not manifest itself in prejudiced, malicious, hostile, enraged, violent and abusive actions towards others. Rather, a healthy and maturing inner spirituality moves us away from illusion. It moves us away from selfishness. It moves us away from living in the need to make disdainful judgments about other's lives. It moves us always in the direction of compassion and helpfulness to others. It moves us towards inclusion. It moves us towards caring for the troubled and wounded *little ones of any age.*

Jesus' parable of the Good Samaritan[205] has become the expanding center of my spirituality. Its embedded mantra about the Jesus path provides a beacon for finding a life's direction: *when seeing someone who is obviously suffering, stop the inner noise, pause, and, whenever possible, provide concrete, compassionate and knowledgeable help.*[206]

Genuine, transformative peace-work or healing work, of any kind, therefore is a combined work of the Great Spirit and our inner human spirit. That said: I think we probably need to feel called to do this work of confronting evil and attempting to shape shift and neutralize its ongoing damaging presence in the world of human lives.

At the very least, it is not readily apparent to me that normal and ordinary people want to be contaminated with knowing about and preoccupied with frontally confronting evil. Nevertheless, we peace workers, prophets, true priests, and healers will inevitably encounter evil. To avoid confronting the evil we witness is to become complicit, inept and inconsequential. But, facing it, there are dangers to our bodies, our spirits, and our souls. We must, in my opinion, take care of our bodies, spirits, and psyches if we are to avoid being overtaken by an inner spirit of rage and of violence; to avoid becoming carriers of evil's intolerant presence in our society and in our religious institutions.

Our task, as I see it, therefore, is to become, with God, co-creators of the world's peace; co-healers of the inner life and compassionate, informed co-guardians of the outer cosmos. In this manner we become co-participants in the divine folly of redemption, restoration, reconciliation, and healing. Our central calling as peace-workers, true priests, prophets, and healers is mysticism writ large – now on the world stage rather than in our inner life.

As we have talked about this elsewhere, my own personal mantra tells the story of my personal journey toward understanding the prophetic call in an abbreviated form.

- God does not call healers to places of health; instead, they are called to live and work in places of serious illness;
- God does not call conflict mediators to places of no conflict; instead, they are called to live and work in places of great conflict;
- God does not call peace-workers to places of peace; instead, they are called to live and work in places of unthinkable and unspeakable violence;
- God does not call prophets to witness to healthy institutions; instead the true and authentic prophets are called to places of moral corruption and spiritual idolatry;
- God does not call true priests and faithful ministers to places where the people already know and walk the path to spiritual maturity; instead they

are called to places of abysmal spiritual ignorance and endemic, religiously-inspired prejudice, hatred, and violence.

- In addition, God does not call any of us to do work where we have no natural aptitude for the work, no identification with the work, and where we find no satisfaction in the doing of the work. A resentful attitude does not foster hospitality (making room for the needy, wounded and usually victimized other to enter) nor does it foster personal acts of compassionate mercy, generosity of spirit and resources, healing, forgiveness, reconciliation, and transformation of the cosmos. Eventually personal and communal resentment, writ large, at doing work one hates with un-nameable rages and hatreds, will damage our physical body, out inner spirit, our relationships with others, and our outer work in the commons.

In summary

> Since there will never cease to be some need on earth, I therefore command you, *open your hand to the poor and needy neighbor in your land.*
>
> Deuteronomy 15:11 (NSRV)

When I think about the spirituality of the mystics, the spirituality of the prophets, the spirituality of true priests/authentic ministers, the spirituality of those who seek to transform conflict, and the spirituality of the peace-makers, they often merge in my mind. In part, I think this is because individuals in each of these groups are gripped by an image writ large of the divine in a compassionate relationship with collective humanity as well as with individuals. Once captured by the Jesus promise of a beloved and loving community caring for each other as neighbors, we change the direction of our lives in the social commons forever. Individuals in each of these groups (the mystics in search of the divine, the whistle-blowing prophets in search of truth, the priests guiding the people, the conflict negotiators in their search for reconciliation; and the justice-minded peace-makers in search of an accountable restoration of humanity with all of God's creation) seek to remove human blinders about the divine call to unity. Each urges us to form direct and personal connections with the divine as the way to understanding our personal lives in the context of the world's need. Each causes us to embrace each other as sharing in the imago dei. Each is highly suspicious of all rigid pieties and orthodoxies that exclude others from the commons. Each distrusts following and promulgating human ideologies that promote greed, selfishness, violence of any kind, and self-other-hatred. In short, the genuine mystics, priests, prophets, conflict mediators, and peace-makers resist human teachings and a community praxis that excludes anyone from their full and equal humanity. They resist exclusion of anyone from equal and full participation inside the beloved human community.

Thus, to me at least, each (prophet, true priest, conflict mediator, authentic minister, healer and peace-maker) resists the patriarchal temptations of power, authority, money, success, self-importance, sexual domination, greed and other forms of narcissistic excess. Each resists the cruelties of idolatrous lusts for power, authoritarian control of others, and domination of the cosmos itself. Each refuses to exclude anyone from God's enduring love for all of God's creation. Each engages in active hospitality as defined in Henri Nouwen's beautiful phrase, *making space for the other to enter.*

Our culture's need to produce winners and to exclude losers is an idolatrous lust because the thirst to be number one means that many, many others are trampled upon and discarded as non-essential and non-valuable participants in the human commons. The temptations of the powers to use, manipulate, and finally exclude others as they lust for success and its trappings must be resisted in the name of the full humanity of everyone – even those most despised, maligned, and hated by winners.

Seeking to be number one, we do not trust the mystical spiritual teaching that *those who seek to be first will be last and that those who are last will be first.*[207] This is foreign to our culture's way of life. Insisting upon *my way or the highway* is not a mark of spiritual maturity.

What is very interesting about the Jeremiah stories in Jewish scriptures is that many of today's biblical commentators believe that Jeremiah and his warning messages – almost singlehandedly rescued his people from cultural extinction and oblivion during their exile years in Babylon. Inside the moral and ethical corruption of today's religious and denominational institutions, it seems to me that resistance to false ideology and false praxis as witnessed to by its mystics, prophets, honorable priests, authentic ministers, and compassionate peace-workers may rescue today's Christian churches from irrelevance and oblivion. It may be in the divine patience that today's whistleblowers on sexual abuse inside the religious commons, for example, may be seen by historians as rescuing their contemporary church from moral and spiritual corruption, cultural extinction, oblivion, and total non-relevance.

Where we most see various forms of healing and prophetic resistance today, therefore, is in the various sexual victim advocacy movements such as SNAP[208] or Road to Recovery.[209] We see it in the work of institutional whistleblowers and in the lives of those who work alongside victims of violence and corporate evil in compassionate ministries of healing and justice.[210] We see it in the activist work of contemporary mystics such as Bishop Desmond Tutu of South Africa[211] and we see it in the mystical poetry of Julia Esquivel of Guatemala.[212] We see it in the sexual victim advocacy and education work done by Dominican Friar Thomas Doyle.[213]

We see it in the ongoing work of Thich Nhat Hanh and the inhabitants of Plum Village to assist North American Veterans with severe war-related PTSD by means of Buddhist spiritual practices and meditation.[214] We see ii in the work of Christian Peacemaker Teams on location in war zones.[215] We see it in the efforts of Pink Menno to reclaim a Mennonite spirituality of hospitality and a genuinely welcoming spirituality of inclusion.[216] We see it in the annual gatherings of Jews and Muslims in Tucson – seeking to befriend each other.[217] We see it in blogs such as Bilgrimage which gather Christians together from around the Christian world in a new form of church: cyber-church.[218] We see it in Rae Halder's decision to begin blogging about rape and sexual abuse.[219] We even occasionally see it in the work of Christian preachers, teachers and academics.[220]

Everywhere we look, if we look carefully, we can see that the Great Sower of seeds is still planting tiny mustard seeds of faithfulness. None of us feeling called to the works of healing, preaching, conflict transformation, prophecy or peacemaking is, therefore, totally alone in the cosmos. The divine Spirit not only lures us but her guiding Wisdom is present with us in the work we are called to do.

Our human task, as simple and as complex as any task, is to form the beloved community on earth. In my words, this is a community of resistance. In your words, this is a community of transformation. In Robin Meyer's words, it is a community of rebellion, subversion and defiance. In Tom Doyle's words, this is the people of God, the re-configured and non-abusive church.[221]

In biblical words, this beloved community of resistance is the people of God, the Way, the Jesus people, and the living mystical presence of the divine Spirit in our midst.

Eighth Letter

Living inside the Hurricane's Eye, Part Five

Encountering and Surviving Academic Idolatry

To let go means to give up coercing, resisting, struggling, in exchange for something more powerful and wholesome which comes out of allowing things to be as they are without getting caught up in your attraction to or rejection of them, in the intrinsic sickness of liking and disliking.

Jon Kabat-Zinn[222]

Introductory Comments

In several of our recent letters we have been talking about the physical and spiritual exhaustion that occurs in the lives of peace and justice advocates. In various seasons of my life, I felt I could not go on doing the work I was committed to doing because of the emotional, physical, and spiritual toll it was taking on my embodied self and its inner spirit.

I firmly believe that as we pursue the wholeness of the world, we need to simultaneously pursue the wholeness of our physical body and its inner world of spirit. Without deliberate self-care, we are inadequate workers in the world of other-care. If we do not seek to understand our particular selves, our own body's needs for rest and respite, our psyche's need for play, our spirit's need for friends, our soul's need for silence, and our continuous needs to monitor and manage our deep anxieties and our unique personal fault lines, we are less astute in our assessments of the external world and its needs.

When we are overwhelmed by our own emotional, spiritual, or physical wounds and neediness, we often lose sight of the way(s) we might be harmful to others. We stop tracking the inner hurricanes of rage, anger, despair, hopelessness, anxiety, fear, terror, etc. We become a part, therefore, of the social hurricanes' damaging winds.

This is particularly true for those of us who do anti-violence work in any of its many forms. We too carry the enculturated seeds of violence deep within our personal and social selves. The internal hologram of our culture's deeply rooted need or desire to control others as the solution to world violence is a temptation to let go. The internalized hologram of the violence we witness every day in our work is always present.

Unless it has been deliberately eradicated or encapsulated, we human beings have a strong emotional response to human suffering. Prolonged contact with suffering can, therefore, desensitize us to its presence.[223] When this happens, we become callous to the needs of other people. When this internal callousness occurs, we become part of the problem rather than one component of the solution.

The strong internal impetus to use our anger and rage at systemic corruption and injustice as the fuel of choice for our activism is, I am personally convinced, a dead end. When we internally respond to others we perceive to be the cause of human suffering (whether out of rage or the well-meaning desire to change them) we can damage the fragile emotional and spiritual balance inside us. When we sit in positions of harsh judgment over against other people, we lose sight of their personal struggles and the temptation is to demonize them for their behaviors or even for disagreeing with us.

The Difference between Blaming and Holding Accountable

Holding people accountable and being a blamer of others are two separate behavioral phenomenons.[224] Perpetrators of violence need to be held accountable for their actions for their own healing as well as for the healing of their victims. In contrast, blaming actions by those who are the blamers – these behaviors often fail to hold perpetrators, in person, as accountable for their own behaviors. Becoming a chronic blamer, therefore, is counter-productive to peace work. Learning how to hold people and institutions accountable for their wrong-doing, on the other hand, is an essential skill for those who wish to work for long-term peace and reconciliation in the commons.

Pushing back against the hurricane force gales of injustice and systemic violence by holding perpetrators accountable is, therefore, a dangerous work. Kabat-Zinn's warning above tells us that while we seek to be change agents in the service of justice, peace, compassion, etc, we must be wary of believing that we are in charge of changing other people. This is particularly so if they are resistant to our ideas of change. Judging and blaming others in our rush to do good deeds is a real snare for those of us who seek to shape-shift violence in the commons. We can so easily trample others and harm them in pursuing our ideologies about the good.

Too often, I think, we get stuck in defending certain methods and theories of social change. Defending our work begins at times to be more important than the work itself. Buddhists warn us about this in their discussions of attachment, illusion, and suffering. It is so clear to me. Ideologies about healing do not heal wounds.

As hard as this is to believe, what is important in these situations of complex violence is the need to recognize that we share a common humanity with all parties to the violence. None can be excluded from holding a share of the divine imago dei. This awareness is the calm center of the violence storm.

In the memorable words of clinical psychologist Albert Ellis, *everyone is both fallible and mortal.* Beginning with that awareness, peace-makers can resist the dual anxiety-producing temptations of catastrophizing and blaming. What is needed, I think, to look evil in the face is the need to know ourselves and our own fault lines and then to develop compassion for our self, our mortality and our personal fallibility. When we do this, our heart chakra opens to the suffering of others and we can work compassionately with perpetrators and victims of perpetration. Inside the open heart chakra of compassion we can hold perpetrators of violence accountable for their violent actions without blaming and demonizing them. In addition, we will protect our own inner being from being overwhelmed and destroyed by the evil they have perpetrated on others.

Mindfulness, paying attention, observing dispassionately our likes and dislikes (and their intensity) is a very useful corrective to our enraged, impassioned yet often insensitive, ill-informed, and un-self-aware activism in the commons. Resisting violence and transforming injustice, therefore, is not about resisting and transforming others – particularly against their will. The resistance I am talking about is the resistance of taking a principled, moral stand and working to put an end to violence and violation in the commons. It is the resistance of speaking out on behalf of those who are most wounded. It is the resistance of doing the needed inner spiritual work of paying attention. It is the hard work of holding perpetrators fully accountable for their own decisions without simultaneously excluding them from their share of full humanity. Indeed, to successfully hold each other fully accountable without shunning each other as something other than fully human is probably the marker of a mature individual spirituality and a spiritually mature community.

Sometimes I think about muscle-training as a metaphor. When I used to work out in the weight room at Goshen College, I utilized weights to build muscle strength. That is a form of resistance. In a like manner, when I first hesitantly speak out against a specific form of injustice, I am building my character incrementally much as I built leg and arm strength. When I swim with weights, I am building all kinds of strength: heart and lung capacity, muscle strength, and deep capacities for body flexibility, endurance, etc. In a similar manner, when I speak out, I grow stronger. In essence, with each lecture or conversation, I learn about future possibilities for speaking out. I correct faulty skills as I become aware of them. As I continue to speak out, I grow even more skills in speaking out. More importantly, my courage strengthens. Slowly, almost imperceptibly, I begin to build the skills of effective confrontation. As the inevitable feedback loop plays, I keep learning about how to support victims and about how to confront victimizers in ways which do not damage my body and my soul....*or theirs.*

Bearing witness to injustice and protesting the presence of violence, therefore, is a very complex skill. Pausing in our own lives to help others who have been wounded by their personal encounters with injustice and violence is an equally complex skill. Both call for, I believe, a disciplined inner spirit – not disciplined in the sense of self-punishment or self-judgment – but, rather, disciplined in the sense of self-awareness and self-management.

This concern for avoiding the trap of demonizing the other is, by the way, not an argument against discernment. We cannot do proactive work on behalf of social tranquility and a just peace or honorable institutions if we do not comprehend the roots and manifestations of violence. We cannot intervene effectively against injustice if we do not discern the essential nature of its many manifestations in the social world.

Suffering and Compassion

I think the Buddhist teaching on suffering and compassion is one way forward here. There may be others. But if we never lose sight of the essential humanity of those who perpetrate great violence and great injustice, we may be able to reach out to them in redemptive and compassionate ways that urge them to reclaim and, in Bishop Tutu's inimitable words, assist them to re-humanize their essential humanity. For example, when we understand that everyone captured in the interpersonal narrative of human affinity violence suffers, then we do not need to demonize any participant.

This means, however, that we must be able to discern who the perpetrator is and who the victims are. We must learn how to hold perpetrators accountable for their actions as one aspect of our compassion for their suffering. It is only by the painful and self-incriminating route of full accountability *and* by grief-stricken repentance that affinity violence perpetrators can be released from their addictions to violence and from the basic inhumanity of their actions.

As you well know, there are no clinical guarantees of healing for perpetrators here. Recidivism is writ large in the narratives of human violence. Nevertheless, I

Ruth E. Krall

remain convinced that demonization and blaming of violence perpetrators is not the path for peacemakers and healers to walk. Everyone in every story of human violation and violence is fully and uniquely human. Each in his or her humanity suffers. Each, irrespective of behavior, personal or clan identities, or other social markers, carries the divine image within. Each individual, therefore, no matter how remote this possibility seems to us, carries the human potential for re-humanization, healing, reclamation and transformation.

Physician-therapist Emmett Miller speaks at times about the multi-generation effects of human pathology.[225] Everyone in the violence narrative has a history. Everyone in the many varied systems of violence is affected. No one escapes. There is, in many situations of great injustice, a generational effect. This awareness does not excuse today's perpetrators from being held accountable in the commons as the necessary consequences of their violent actions. But this awareness of the generational lineage of violence allows healers and peace-makers to work with the perpetrators of great violence in a compassionate manner. In thinking about this concept in light of Bishop Tutu's work with the South African re-humanization project with Apartheid's abusers and perpetrators, it takes a human being to help another human being in acts of re-humanization; it takes other human beings to help perpetrators and victims move towards restoration to the community and, just maybe, an honorable reconciliation of victim and victimizer.

I know, however, that we must be realistic. In many situations there can be no restoration and no reconciliation because perpetrators cling to their identities and behaviors as perpetrators. They refuse to acknowledge wrong-doing. In many situations it is simply unsafe for the victims of violence to be in close physical, emotional, or spiritual proximity to the individuals who did or who continue to do violence to them.

All of us are, I think, deeply and sometimes imperceptibly shaped by the patriarchal culture of violation and violence which surrounds us. We are embedded inside the pre-existing violence of our culture (and its language system) from the moment we are born. Our common language and our common experiences shape us. We introject our culture's sustaining values about violence as essential along with the air we breathe and the water we drink. As we mature, we can learn to critique this cultural influence and we can shape both our experiences and expressions of it, but its formative template is one that we carry until we die. We can learn to both name and resist this culture and, at times, we can begin to shape-shift it away from its encompassing ideology, prejudice and violence so that future generations are spared its noxious influences.

For example, I can live in a second culture and dress and act in ways which are congruent with that culture, but my own cultural template always identifies me as an outsider and as a North American. The way I walk; the amount of interpersonal distance I need to feel comfortable in conversations with strangers or even with close friends; the way I make or refuse to make eye contact; the way I listen to others: all of these and more carry a strong first culture shaping of my personal style and identify. Even the things I embrace (as well as the things I reject) as I go through the culture shock of learning to live in a second language culture, are shaped by this culturally bred template I carry with me everywhere.

I talk about this because, as a citizen of the world's most powerful militarized nation and one of the world's wealthiest nations, I live every day in a cultural milieu that celebrates this nation's firepower superiority. Daily this culture provides me with instructional pedagogies to reinforce the use of political, social, militarized and economic violence as part of my identity. My way of life, I am frequently told, depends on my nation's military defensive and offensive actions somewhere in the world to protect it.

There is no doubt that as an American woman I benefit from my citizenship. My passport identifies me as someone who has known a certain kind of personal freedom and privilege. If need be, in a foreign country, I can visit my country's embassy and get help in solving a problem. Showing my passport and stating my problem, it is very likely that I will be treated courteously and helpfully.

There have been many times when re-entering United States customs' lines that I have been welcomed home. I often tear up with this greeting because I am indeed home. I know that I now know the rules for social conduct and I can stop paying such continuously focused and extremely tiring attention to my own behaviors as essential to not offending people who have a different national or ethnic heritage. There is something to be said for feeling utterly at home in my skin because I am at home in the social world that surrounds me.

Coming home, however, does not alter the reality that I have learned some very damaging information about the harmful actions of my government and wealthy elite countrymen while living abroad. Coming home, therefore, I have an obligation to talk about what I have learned as a form of socially correcting my own people's way of life – a way of life that is harmful to the peace of the world.

The Witnesses' Dilemma

As we travel in the world and as we pay attention, we will see suffering and injustice. When we waver and vacillate between helpless pities on the one hand and helpless rages on the other, we often encounter the deep-seated need to remove ourselves from the situation. The temptation is to look away and to deny the importance of what we are seeing and experiencing. There is a strong temptation to move away.[226] We want, as much as possible, to normalize the situation by refusing to interrogate and integrate its systemic narrative of injustice and suffering into our own personal life narrative.

Ruth E. Krall

Witnessing a woman begging on the streets of an impoverished nation, with a physically handicapped baby on a dirty blanket in front of her, we may quickly deposit our peso, colon, euro, quetzal, or quarter in the woman's outstretched hand and move on before she can ask more of us. We do not want to make eye contact with her suffering or her baby's suffering. We do not want to stop and ask, *what in your life has brought you and your baby to such a desperate life position?* As someone who has personally experienced this reality over and over, I am haunted by my willingness to remain aloof from her suffering and her baby's suffering. In short, I am haunted by my own share of insensitive and non-responsive cruelty.

Learning how to be an effective witness to another's suffering is a skill I think that may take a lifetime. In all of my professional travels in the world, I have met only one man whom I saw and still see as a world citizen. His home nation was a small island in the Atlantic Ocean. He was bilingual from childhood. His ancestors had once upon a time been slaves. When I met him, he was his nation's minister of health. His open-hearted graciousness embraced everyone he met, and he was deeply intuitive about others' social uneasiness in the face of human tragedy. He had the innate ability to put people at ease in his presence – no matter what their social circumstances were. He was personally committed to making positive changes in the life circumstances of some of the world's most impoverished people. In addition, he was never naïve about the immensity of the challenges he faced in his daily work on their behalf.

He has been a role model for my life since I met him in my early thirties. I wanted to know how he did what he did and I wanted to be able to do it. I have not met this goal in my life. I am still socially awkward at times. I often choose to look the other way. I am more like the two men in the Good Samaritan story who walked by on the opposite side of the road than I am like the obvious hero in Jesus' parable. There are still too many times in my life when I don't want to know the details of another's suffering; too many times when I can't be bothered to stop and see if I can help.

For example, recently an inner dialogue or conversation just before going to sleep has been telling me that I carry too many sexual violence stories for too many people. I know too much. When I stop to pay attention and to interrogate that nagging inner voice, it is the voice of my sadness, my exhaustion, my absolute resistance to learning yet another story about sexual violence in the religious context of denominations or spiritual teaching centers. Sexual violence activism work, in my impatient exhaustion just before sleep, is a carousel I want to exit. There is no golden ring to capture that brings relief from my sadness and my rage.

After a good night's sleep, I wake renewed and I pick up the work I feel called to do. I am no longer overwhelmed by what I know.

The lesson here, for me, is that none of us can do the work of violence healing and violence prevention 365/24/. We must have times of rest, play, companionship with safe and loving others, time-out spaces so that we are not personally overwhelmed by the violence we bear witness to in our work. In fact, we need extended times away from our work so we can consolidate what we know. We need extended times away – the principle of the academic sabbatical – to refuel our inner reserves. If we are entrusted with the care of others – and who, in real life, is not so entrusted, we need times away from our anti-violence work to tend to the needs of our social and familial relationships. We need to spend time with those we love. We need to nourish the relationships that sustain us.

Taking the kids to Disneyland can restore our own inner child if we do this in a spirit of love and play. Sitting on a bench in our garden and watching humming-birds feed at bottlebrush bushes can restore our sense of the goodness of creation. Walking the labyrinth or meditating on the teachings of the Amerindian medicine wheel can renew our sense of unity with the divine. Deliberately maintaining the safety of our inner world is essential work and cannot be overlooked if we do not want to burn out or become physically ill.

During my working years, one of my favorite short-term anger releases was to go into the parking lot behind my office building and blow soap bubbles with my wand. Watching the bubbles form and then float free of their wand was to let my angers, rages, tensions, and fears evaporate. Even two or three minutes were all I needed to become my inner child and let adult worries vanish. What is nice about this paragraph is that, having no bubble solution, I can still visit the memory of soft breezes and bubbles floating into the bright sunshine. By imagery alone, I can release the inner tension. When I supplement this imagery with deliberate breath work, in two or three minutes my body has returned to emotional and physiological homeostasis. I am refreshed and ready to go back to work.

These days when I walk in the nearby saguaro cactus forest National Park, these ancient and young giants of the Sonoran Desert nurture me in indescribable ways. There is something eternal in them and in their seasons of blooming, setting fruit and soaking up rain water for the dry seasons. Having rested in their long shadows, and pondered their nature, I can then return to my work renewed.

Social service administrators are well aware that overloaded caseloads tend to create care-providers who are emotionally cold or even hostile to the desperate needs of others for their help.[227] It is hard to be caring and compassionate to 100 or to 1000 deeply troubled individuals each day without any respite from what becomes a human services treadmill. Social science researchers are equally aware, for example, that human service workers inside impossibly overcrowded refugee camps are very prone to issues of desensitization. It is not uncommon for them to become uncaring and abusive towards the very people they have been hired to serve and help. It is not uncommon for them to display social or personal pathologies.

The Shadow

When I read Phillip Hallie's stories about the village of Le Chambon, I ask myself: *What would I have done in the situations that he writes about? Who would I have been?* To date, my answers are not easy and comfortable ones. In hindsight we know what the villagers did not know. Each day they lived inside the questions: *Is this the day that the Nazi army takes down our village? Is this the day the Gestapo takes me away to prison?* Yet, inside that village, Hallie tells us, the people lived in a spirit of joy, love, community, and service to the Jewish children of the holocaust.

My hypothesis about these matters is a simple one. If we do not do our external work in the world as self-aware embodied spiritual beings, then that work is often diminished or distorted by that which the Jungians call the archetypal shadow.

In Jungian thought the archetypal shadow is always constellating in our lives and in our relationships. Whether or not we are self-aware of its presence, it affects our work and it affects our personal well-being. If we think about the healer, for example, in light of the needs of the one who seeks healing, then we see that the healer's archetypal shadow interacts continuously with the archetypal shadow of the one who needs and seeks healing. The good that we seek to do always, in this worldview, interacts with the shadow. We can never eliminate the archetypal shadow's presence in ourselves (or others) but we can become aware of its influence and we can learn to manage it so we do the least amount of harm possible.[228]

Detoxifying the Commons

In reading your comments about being exhausted by the needs to defend your peace-work inside the Anabaptist-Mennonite commons, I conclude that one of the ways we Anabaptist-Mennonite women survive the toxicity of knowing we live inside the religious patriarchy, but unwillingly and in protest, is to find and cultivate knowledgeable and supportive colleagues. Another essential is to have supportive, compassionate friends. Both of these groups of people provide us with a sense of personal safety and self-trust. These kinds of friends and colleagues who know us and who love us can hold us to a high standard of integrity and compassion as we seek to do our work in the world. They can do this because they have taken our measure and have decided to hang out with us for a lengthy period of time – getting to know us and coming to understand our personal stash of strengths and fault lines. By their friendship with us, they help us to buffer our distress and to survive times of personal anguish; when they can do so, they resource us in a wide variety of ways.

What I have found is that these two groups over time tend to blend. While some individuals will always remain outside the margins of the central grouping of people who are both colleagues and friends, this inner or center group becomes for us that group of people who (1) know who we are; (2) know our work in the world; (3) facilitate our work in the world; and (4) learn the quirky narratives of our personal and professional lives.

In addition, as we work together, we introduce people inside our social and professional networks to other people. In turn, our friends and colleagues introduce us to individuals in their social and professional networks. Over time, a social culture of overlapping, supportive networks is born. In this manner, our work in the world develops both a rudder and an anchor. In this way, we begin to build the beloved community that academic-preacher Robin Meyers describes in his work.[229]

Of personal importance to me is that my closest friends all know how to trigger my snorts of sudden laughter and sessions of giggling. They know that my sense of the utter ridiculousness of much of life is essential to my personal sense of well-being. If I don't take myself too seriously and if I don't take life too seriously, I am healthier. This, by the way, does not mean that I do not take very seriously that which deserves to be taken seriously. I have always, therefore, taken my work and my vocation seriously. I do not laugh at other people's suffering and their anguish. I have nurtured compassion in my life and I have sought excellence as the standard for my work. But my basic irreverence about much of life helps oil the inner machinery of my personality and my friendships. Thus, my closest friends tolerate my sense of humor and noisy, outrageous laughter, or, even more importantly, encourage it. I try to spare them my biting sarcasm but I am aware that it can be a tool for social change if applied with due thought and care not to damage others in attacking them even as one attacks a social issue.

I think even in childhood, I was learning valuable lessons about the healing powers of laughter. My family told stories about itself at the dinner table. Laughter was always one aspect of our family life together. For example, my mother's younger brother was injured in adolescence and was severely handicapped for the rest of his life. One of the funniest stories I have ever heard at the family dining table was his story of needing to choose between dropping his crutches to rescue his falling pants or to rescue his falling pants and drop his crutches. He knew and we knew he could not drop his crutches and remain standing. His choice was preordained by his life circumstances. All that remained to learn from his hilarious narrative was the question: who witnessed his embarrassment and how did they respond? As a family we were not laughing at him but we were laughing with him. I often think his bravery in making fun of something primal in his life helped all of us to learn some important lessons in bravery and in not taking ourselves too seriously. This very conservative, pious, and modest middle-aged Mennonite man wearing a plain coat could literally lose his trousers in a public manner and not be destroyed by shame. At our Sunday dinner table, he transformed this event of utter helplessness and public shame into a very funny story that could be shared. As our laughter joined his, his experience was transformed from helpless shame into a story where we all recognized its inherent strength of not taking one's self too seriously. It was a positive story too. A man passing by saw his dilemma/distress and stopped without comment or judgment to help him by pulling up his pants and tightening his belt.

Friends, Family and Colleagues as Healing Resources

In terms of my closest and long-term personal friendships, it is important to me that my friends and I understand each other's ongoing life histories so that in all of our joking around we don't inadvertently tromp on each other's wounds. The family in my uncle's story above could have chosen to blame him, scold him, and thereby enlarge his shame. But we didn't. He was, instead, a beloved insider. Collectively we took the narrative story of his shame and embarrassment and transformed it into love.

All along the way this means a certain kind of vulnerability – a trust in each other that there is love between us – a love that sustains friendships over great physical, and at times, social distances. Such friendships need tending much like a garden needs tending. Weeds need to be pulled and new seeds planted. Since not all of my friends have pursued advanced degrees, this means not being obnoxious about this obvious difference. I know life teaches all of us important lessons and I am less convinced every day that Ph.D. degrees do. So, my closest friends continue to teach me about life and about the ways in which they are willing to see and encounter me; the ways they are willing to be seen and encountered. As they share their lives with me, my life is made richer and deeper. As I care deeply about them and their welfare, so too, do they care about me.

It is important, as well, that my professional colleague-friends have integrity and that they are competent in the work that they do in the world. Over the years I have learned that personal commitments to professional competency usually are accompanied by a flexible ability to be resilient and to do the work that needs doing in a timely and reasonable manner. None of us is perfect in the work we do so we all make mistakes and we all misread situations. But competent people who strive for excellence in their work are people who know how to ride the storm winds of the hurricane and survive. In my experience of these people, when they make promises to do something, to the best of their abilities they carry through on these promises.

Genuinely competent and compassionate people are an awesome, albeit somewhat rare, treasure in the world. When we encounter them, we are wise if we cultivate their friendships. When we are young, they mentor us. As we professionally mature, we mentor others. Along the way, some of these professional colleagues migrate into the zone of becoming close personal friends. Others do not. Yet each of these professional colleagues adds so much to our lives – enriching our competencies with theirs; covering our weaknesses with their strengths; enlivening conversations with their insights; generously lending their wisdom and help to us when most needed.

I have not chosen to marry or to live with children. These are perhaps the most challenging relationships peace activists can have. In the immediacy of the home, our best and worst instincts about life co-exist. The most intimate of our human relationships are the seedbeds of the future. Unlike other friendships which can sustain themselves over long periods of time with little conflict and tensions, family relationships need daily attention. These gardens of family life are the places where we renew ourselves and where we struggle most with questions of healthy intimacy with each other.

The Healing of the Healer

As a clinical healer, I have always believed that there is a time when I must seek help. Consequently, there have been various times in my life when I became the client. In times of absolute personal brokenness I have often encountered a self I did not know I was. While never pleasant to live through, these times in my life have taught me so much about others' wounds and brokenness.

In her book *Trauma and Recovery*[230] Harvard faculty member and psychiatrist Judith Lewis Herman writes eloquently about the need for therapists and other professional workers who do trauma healing work to have their own support group of skilled colleagues to help them detoxify their horror at what they are called to witness in the course of their work. She calls this aspect of her work as a psychiatrist *building communities of resistance.*[231] I agree with her. No one – except in the most abject emergency – should do interpersonal and intra-community sexual violence confrontation work while unsupported and alone. The type of work is too destructive to the human psyche and spirit. As we commit ourselves to face into and confront individual violence perpetrators and their complicit social accomplices and apologists inside religious and secular institutions, we need others who understand us. We need compassionate others to help us stay emotionally balanced and spiritually alive.

We all need time-outs from stress. We need minutes, hours, and days away from our work to rebalance the inner life. These are times, I have come to believe, when we forge the trails to our quiet and focused center. My own experience with meditation has taught me that I most readily learn the skills of meditation when I am not stressed. Having learned the skills, or the route to the calm center of this present moment, when I am stressed, I can call upon this learned skill. I do not need hours of meditation to immediately re-enter this present moment and recognize the inner calm center where I spiritually belong.

This whole notion that I was taught regarding the faithful disciple's willingness to *burn out for Christ* is a dangerous fallacy. In fact, I believe it is a dangerous lunacy. When I am most stressed by life (most burned out) is the time I often do the most damage to others in the commons near me.

In terms of Christian scriptures, we learn that Jesus sometimes sought refuge from the growing crowds that surrounded him: escaping in a boat or heading alone into the isolation of the desert. He enjoyed a glass of wine at parties, danced at weddings, and hosted intimate dinner parties for small groups of his closest friends. His last recorded time of prayer was in an isolated garden where one assumes he was surrounded by the comfort of trees, birds, small animals, insects, flowers, and soft breezes. Even, I suspect, in this hour of anguish, he was not totally cut off from the life force that flowed in his veins.

I have, therefore, also concluded that we need a deliberate, daily, and robust spiritual practice. In addition, we need times of rest. We need times of laughter. We need time with our closest friends. In short, we need to love and to be loved and we need to laugh and play. And we need to learn how to be alone with ourselves in times of quiet introspection and, dare I say it, prayer.

The Spiritual Practice of Gratitude

For me, I have adopted the spiritual practice of gratitude – trying to see in each circumstance of my life something which yields an ability to be grateful. I know other advocates for human justice who meditate every morning. I know others who read a passage of scripture and who pray as part of their preparation for the day.

As I mentioned to you, a prayer of gratitude begins my mornings. I am somewhat informed by Native American spiritual leaders who get up before dawn to greet the arrival of the sun with prayers to the Great Spirit. While our theologies about God are likely very different ones, the Amerindian notion of a disciplined daily prayer of gratitude as the way to begin the day has become very important to me.

Good morning, world, earth, life, God
Thank you for my life
I am so grateful to be alive on this day.
In this day may I do nothing to harm others
May no one do harm to me
May I live this day so that by nightfall I am not ashamed

In this desert climate where I live, there is always a longing for rain and when it occurs, there is deep gratitude for its sounds and its wetness. In a desert, that which is wet brings gratitude home to me. If I am alone when I swim and interesting critters chatter on the outside of the pool, I may thank them out loud for sharing my swim time and making it more interesting. I seek to be pleasant and express my gratitude to the mentally handicapped and somewhat slow young man who bags my weekly groceries. I seek, therefore, throughout the day for reasons to be grateful and to express my gratitude to others for their presence in my world.

Since I am not by nature a patient person, this spiritual practice helps me to curb my impatient tendency towards social rudeness when people do not move out of my way fast enough. I remind myself by this practice that *I am mortal and fallible and so is everyone else I meet.* I can, therefore, cut them slack. I can choose to acknowledge my rudeness, then, when I catch myself in the middle of behavior that I will by day's end be ashamed of doing.

Allow me to talk very personally here. It is not always easy to be grateful. We get overwhelmed by life's twists and turns. We get annoyed at others for their stupidities even as we overlook our own. We become physically exhausted and ill. But deliberately practicing gratitude as a spiritual discipline began after my endometrial cancer surgeries. I was not only physically wounded. I was emotionally and spiritually wounded as well. It seemed to me that I was fraying around every edge of my life. But I *was* grateful to be alive. For me, personally, therefore receiving a cancer diagnosis was a turning point in my life. I deliberately stopped whatever I was doing and in that year-long pause sought help at multiple levels: medical/physical, therapy/emotional, body work, social, spiritual/religious, and cognitive/professional. In addition, I engaged in voice lessons with a skilled Bay area professional. I regularly attended church services where inclusion, not exclusion, was practiced. Severely introverted and unwell, I made a point of staying for the social hour. On several occasions I even preached.[232] In this year I decided to join the Methodist Church and I also decided not to return to a Mennonite congregation when I returned home to a Mennonite ethnic community at the end of my sabbatical. I did not remove my Mennonite membership as I returned to a non-practicing life inside the Mennonite commons. It took my congregation five or six years before officially noticing my absence and inquiring about it.

In this Berkeley sabbatical, in this sabbatical year after a very botched surgery, I worked with physician Emmett Miller, a therapist who taught me beginning meditation skills. He also talked with me about joy – and asked me if I knew joy and where I found joy. This was a needed reminder, and sometime during that year I learned about Brother Steindl-Rast and his work of teaching the spiritual practice of gratitude. I began to experiment and to practice. There are still days when I am quarrelsome with the universe, but what I have found is that when I stop, pause, and ask, *where is joy and gratitude to be found,* my day brightens and I am able to tolerate the impossible in a more sure-footed way.

Ruth E. Krall

This is the origin of my morning prayer which I shared with you above. I can face the rising sun in the East and remember that I am alive and that while this day unpredictable, with an internal spiritual practice I can meet its challenges head on. With this prayer, I remember that the Great Spirit guides me with gentle wisdom and helps me to develop a generous spirit as I move through my day. To stay calm during the day's "whatevers", I have to be willing to stay in the present moment and I have to be willing to pay attention.

My Life's Journey to Today

For me personally, then, it has not been the evil which abusive clergy have done which has been most challenging to confront. My clinical training has given me many tools to understand and to manage the deeply embedded pathologies of individuals. It has been, rather, the evil which *my church* did by the actions (well, in reality, the non-actions) of its administrators and personnel managers that wounded my spirit and forever altered my inner compass of family and church-instilled beliefs. It has been the sustained – and to me – totally irrational hostility of some church leaders and some church academics to my very existence as an Anabaptist-Mennonite anti-violence scholar and peace studies activist which has so devastated my own inner spirit.

Thinking that I belonged to this community of faith because of its values about active peace work in the world, over the years I slowly realized I was first de-valued and then eventually discounted and excluded because of my concerns for women's lives and women's healing; for children's lives and for their domestic safety. Over the course of many years, I first needed to realize and then secondly to acknowledge to myself that my voice and my work in sexual violence activism were not welcomed in the contemporary Anabaptist-Mennonite denominational commons. The reason seemed simple to me: rather than studying, at a distance, other people's addiction to violence, I was studying and critiquing affinity violence *inside* the community. In addition, in a religious denomination which, in the 20th century, oriented most of its peace witness theology to an ideology of redemptive suffering and non-resistance to evil, I was suggesting that there was no such thing as redemptive suffering in the lives of sexual violence survivors and that nonresistance was a blind alley when women and small children confronted abusive individuals – usually but not always male – in their lives. Active resistance, non-lethal resistance, public protests, and utilization of police protection seemed to me to be a better way for victimized individuals to proceed.

Once, in my Anabaptist-Mennonite childhood, a loved and included insider, in my professional maturity I have become a disliked, distrusted, often ignored, and frequently shunned outsider. Needing some external source of validation that my work had value, I utilized my professional connections and collegial friendships outside the denomination for critique and conversation. Thus, I deliberately developed a dual professional track – one inside the Mennonite community of faith and one outside it. Experiencing the reality that my professional and academic work was usually valued more outside the Mennonite Church than inside its borders made it possible for me to continue to work inside it where my work was often devalued and ignored. Since I knew that not everyone inside the extended boundaries of Christian faith considered me a hopeless heretic or a clueless ignoramus, I pursued a vigorous life of academic scholarship in the greater external academy and was thus content to pursue a more humble and socially-isolated teaching career inside the smaller boundaries of the Mennonite cultural world.

Some Mennonite male academics in the fields of religion, theology, and peace studies, therefore, do not see me as a scholar. As you have so forcefully noted in your correspondence with Mennonite men about me, my academic work is ignored and I am not included in the conversations where I probably do have something to offer to the greater community. I am seen, instead, as someone who has personal agendas or personal vendettas against the church and its leaders.

In the last two decades of my career, I often thought to myself that my students understood me better than my academic colleagues. I worked very hard at never lying to students and tried to share honestly and humbly with them what I thought and what I was learning in the external world. I tried to bring the scholarship of my outer world to their campus world.

As you noted from your correspondence with others about me, I asked students in my classrooms to read books and articles from a wide variety of perspectives on peace and non-violent conflict resolution. Some students despised (or perhaps a better choice of words might be *despaired over*) my assigned reading lists, but perhaps more former students than I might have expected have talked with me in the years since they left college about how those reading lists shaped the first ten years of their post-college work. There are some fifty-year-old Goshen College graduates who tell me they continue to keep and access those by now outdated reading lists – almost as a talisman of hope or courage. I often get teased by some former students when we correspond about this issue or that issue in their professional or personal lives that I am still requiring them to read and to think for themselves. I love this form of teasing because it means these former students are comfortable enough with themselves to know that I, like everyone else, do not walk on water. Nor, for that matter, were any of my classroom ideas written in stone. They each and all deserved to be tested in the commons where real life takes precedence over academic abstractions.

Ruth E. Krall

Academic Idolatry

I distrust academic idolatry almost more than any other academic sin. The reason for this distrust is very elemental. No idea is perfect – no matter how brilliant its author. Every theological idea, for example, must be tested in the academic commons to see if it supports the patriarchy or if it supports the critique of the patriarchy. These ideas must also be tested to see if they express a preferential option for that which oppresses other human beings or if they express a preferential option for vulnerable, abused, and often discarded human beings. I distrust all forms of theological orthodoxy which are not grounded in an awakened, compassionate self-and-world orthopraxis. If an idea or theological construct does not help folks in the pews live more compassionate daily lives, then the idea must be seen as suspect. If it does not help individuals live through their individual dark nights of the soul with a semblance of serenity and perhaps even gratitude to life for life, then the idea or theology probably should be abandoned.

We are living in a time of great paradigm shifts and the worldviews we are so comfortable with are being challenged by the emerging science and technologies of our era in history. This is especially true about the science of the human body; about our understandings regarding the complexities of sexual identity and diversity; and it is true about the science of outer space and the expanding cosmos. Our contemporary technologies and research methodologies are leading us to new understandings and to new hypotheses to be explored.

For the church to dogmatically refuse to participate in these experimental conversations is futile. For the institutional church to deny the imminent arrival of the future is dangerous and disingenuous. The future will arrive – with or without the church's full and engaged participation.

When you were my student, I was much less concerned, therefore, about indoctrinating you to a particular worldview than I was about exposing you to an adequate critique of patriarchal violence and violation in its many forms. I wanted you to be able to assess the world, think on your feet for yourself, and then act responsibly. In addition, as the peace, justice and conflict studies curriculum manager, I sought to hire part-time faculty whose expertise in the real world outside the religious academy could supplement mine. Again, I was looking for a plurality of voices. Some of these guest lecturers were Anabaptist-Mennonites. Other guest faculty and scholars-in-residence represented other faith traditions. But each person was doing valuable work for peace, for social accountability, and for justice in the world. Each, I felt, enriched students' understandings of the complexity of peace and justice advocacy.

I am convinced, now ten years after my retirement from classroom teaching, that this was a good model. I was not interested in cloning myself or my opinions. I was not interested in recruiting disciples and clones. I was interested in opening the world to students so they could find their own unique way in the world as they sought to become peace advocates in many different violent locations in the world. I was interested in helping students open their minds to the many possibilities the world would present to them during their lifetimes.

Whenever I heard, therefore, that it was impossible to inculcate an Anabaptist-Mennonite peace studies curriculum inside the Mennonite Academy without teaching John Howard Yoder, I simply disagreed. I learned Mennonite beliefs in nonviolence and nonresistance at home. I learned Mennonite history at Eastern Mennonite College from a wonderful professor named I. B. Horst. At Goshen College I met, but had no classes with, Guy F. Hershberger. Instead my theology and ethics professor was the young J. Lawrence Burkholder. Horst, Hershberger, and Burkholder anchored, therefore, my growing awareness of justice and accountability issues inside my own culture – the growing civil rights movement in the American South; the injustice done to aboriginal peoples during the time of the Western European (and in Alaska, the Russian) conquest of America; and, in my professional life, the profound injustices of the nation's state mental hospital systems. Because of Burkholder's presence in my college years and the presence of a young professor of religious sociology named Cal Redekop, I have sought to understand theological and sociological aspects of many different social issues; religiosity, war, poverty, civil war in Latin America, homelessness, the Shoah, and most importantly sexual and domestic violence in women's and children's lives. My college professors simply forced me to think about these Anabaptist-Mennonite values and beliefs at ever deepening levels of my own consciousness. They provided the foundation upon which my life of work has been built.

My Mennonite mother's insistence that her children would not own toy guns and that they would not play with toy guns morphed into my adult awareness that aggression, dominance, and violence were not the pathway for Christians to solve interpersonal conflicts. It is interesting to note, however, that my mother did allow my middle brother during his adolescence to own and use fire power (guns). In late adolescence he owned a rifle which he used to shoot rats and other varmints on the farm where he worked. I only discovered the presence of this weapon after he went to college and it was shoved among other family relics in the attic. In retrospect, I assume her lesson to each of us was that human life should not be tampered with and ended by our hands even as we cleaned out disease-bearing and crop-destroying nests of rodents and woodchucks.

By the time I was teaching students about Mennonite beliefs and values regarding active peace-making in the world, I had bridged the worlds between Mennonite, Protestant, and Roman Catholic forms of Christian thought on these matters. I looked inside these traditions to find and then re-create a way of examining violence that also included feminist principles. In the last ten years of my teaching career, I also looked east to find teachers of non-violent wisdom there – Gandhi, the Dalai Lama, Ram Das, Pema Chodron, Jack Kornfield, Jon Kabat-Zinn,

Jean Shinoda Bolen, Bernie Glassman, Huston Smith, and Thich Nhat Hanh come to mind.

Yet, despite sensing that I was not valued for my work and that, in the opinion of many of my Anabaptist-Mennonite academic colleagues I no longer belonged, I still held to the core values of adult confessions of Christian faith; to biblical teachings about God's prophetic preferential option for the weak; the vulnerable, the widow, the orphan, and the stranger in our midst. I clung to the need for the followers of the Jesus path to make informed protests and create acts of non-violent (what you call non-lethal) activism in the face of human evil. In short, I understood the Christian mission in the world as that of serving the world as a healing presence – imitating Jesus' compassion for the weakest and the most vulnerable among us.

Believing, as I do, that all activists need a community, I needed to mourn the loss of my cradle faith community as a vital and viable resource for sustaining my personal spirituality. In addition, I needed to rebuild the inner spiritual rudder which was nearly destroyed when I realized I was no longer a valued or welcome member of the Mennonite academic community.

Speaking openly about sexual violence inside my particular community of faith made me a pariah for many Mennonite academics, church institution administrators, some colleagues, and many members of the clergy. Consequently, I needed to learn how to tolerate and manage being excluded in a manner that did not destroy me or cancel my voice nor violate my Mennonite-instilled-values of non-violence and non-hatred in the face of formidable enemies.

The Damages of Shunning and Exclusion

I have come, therefore, to hold the opinion that intra-Mennonite shunning (either of an informal and individual nature or of a formalized communal one) is one of the most violent actions we Anabaptist-Mennonite academics do to each other when we disagree. This form of passive-aggressive behavior denies each other any recognition of our shared humanity. When we shun another, we actively seek to invalidate his or her contributions to the commons and we simultaneously disavow his or her creation in God's image.

I knew I was not, during the last ten years of living inside the Mennonite academic commons, being shunned by my academic peers and church administrators for overt or covert acts of personal misbehavior. By subtle forms of institutional shunning, I was being punished for my persistent witness about the active presence of affinity violence inside the community. I was being non-verbally informed that my ideas about peace-building work in these areas of sexual and domestic violence were unacceptable inside the academic and religious institution commons. I was, it seems to me now, being shunned for the unique person I was becoming in light of my ideas and my work. It was not what I did or did not do in my personal life that was being judged. It was the very person that I was becoming. That person was not accepted as worthy of full inclusion at the table. That person was relegated to the outside edges of the community. That person's gifts and contributions were ignored or actively judged as unworthy.

The irony, Lisa (and we have talked a bit about this in our correspondence), is that as my academic peers devalued me and actively hazed my work, students in my classrooms blossomed as junior scholars and beginning activists and that reality protected me. They hunkered down, did their assignments, and then wrote strong and positive classroom evaluations of their learning inside the PJCS[233] curriculum. I became aware of the presence of this student protectiveness towards me somewhat inadvertently during one commencement program when a male colleague (not generally a friend) pointed at the names of all of the PJCS graduates and commented on their intellectual abilities and their academic achievements. When we talked briefly about this previously, you reflected on your own classroom experiences and said, *I think we students were aware that you were endangered and we were very protective of your presence as our teacher.*

This little whispered commentary as diplomas were being handed over to seniors in their ritual handshakes with the academic dean and college president was not necessarily a friendly chat although it seemed that way on the surface. It served to alert me that some rather unfriendly men of the faculty were paying close attention to my work, and that the growing strength of the PJCS program and the intellectual abilities of its graduating seniors were providing me with an academic buffer zone in which I was safer than I knew.

Paying Attention to the Inner Spirit

When I realized that my denominational church and my local congregation had absolutely no concern for my personal well-being or for my inner spiritual life, when I became aware that I was unacceptable just because of who I was, I became a seeker of spiritual truth where it could be found. When I became aware that my absence and silence were valued far more than my presence and my speaking or writing, I began to distance myself from the gathered community. I joined the contemporary Christian Diaspora.

One consequence of my search for a more authentic spirituality is that I became convinced that every peace worker and every justice advocate needed to address her or his own inner life as well as the outer deeds of others. The necessary spiritual task was to confront the violence within as well as the violence without.[234] The task, as I came to understand it, was not to absorb the violence – as a blotter absorbed excess ink. Rather, the task was to find a place of inner quiet so that one could confront injustice from within a spiritual position of equanimity, fairness,

Ruth E. Krall

compassion, and integrity. Hallie talks about pushing back the walls of the hurricane. I like that imagery. It implies that, as witnesses to violence and violation, we do not open our spiritual pores to absorb the violence and violations of others, but that we actively protect ourselves in the presence of evil. We need, to speak metaphorically, to install protective hurricane-resistant windows and doors. Some authors talk about deliberately choosing when and how to open and close the empathic barriers between and among humans. These are, they teach us, empathic self-management processes that each human being potentially possesses.

In terms of Philip Hallie's metaphor, I needed to teach myself how to push back the swirling currents of hostility and cruelty and violence to yield more blue space. In terms of Mark Nepo's metaphor, I needed to fly through the storm, repeatedly, to get into the calm center. In terms of contemplative spirituality, I needed to learn the pathway into silence and inner peacefulness.

In Erik Erikson's biography of the Hindu spiritual leader Gandhi, he writes a personal letter to the now-dead teacher of non-violence. In that letter he notes that the future of Satygraha must include peace and peace-making within the family and within the domestic sphere as well as in the national and international spheres.[235] If we think of Anabaptist-Mennonite communities as constituting a certain family of faith, then in light of Erikson's commentary, it grows clear to me that the future of an Anabaptist-Mennonite witness against violence must include informed protests against the violence that lives, unchallenged, inside the community of faith.

There must be a difference in how we live our private lives as Anabaptist-Mennonite pacifists if our witness against the state's violence is to have integrity. If we continue to do violence against each other in the name of some obscure, now obsolete, sixteenth-century orthodoxy, then we have no moral or ethical high ground from which to critique our nation's violence in its orthodoxy of national security as the guiding spiritual value for the twenty-first century.

Shunning those who speak out against such interpersonal forms of Mennonite abuse as clergy and religious leader sexual violation, affinity rape, sexual harassment, incest, molestation of children and adolescents, and domestic violence is counterproductive to the future wholeness of the Anabaptist-Mennonite vision of the world. It is counterproductive to the spiritual health and well-being of the future church. When we Anabaptist-Mennonites critique the nation-state's proclivity to use violence and coercive force while we simultaneously tolerate or even promulgate issues of interpersonal authoritarianism and domination in God's name, the faith community is in great danger of losing its unique witness to the violent world in which the church is located.

Rejecting and isolating the prophets among us (those individuals who see hypocrisy and idolatry inside the community of faith) can, perhaps, silence their message. But the underlying moral rot (that moral rot which Jesus identified in his historical era as the uncleanness of the white-washed tombs of the dead filled only with decaying bones) will continue to stifle and smother the good news Jesus proclaimed as essential for the faithful religious community of his time.[236]

In his delivery of the Lyman-Beecher Lectures at Yale University, United Church of Christ minister and college professor Robin Meyers addresses the decline of Christianity inside mainline Protestant denominations. In the course of his lecture he stated, *the church many of us grew up inside is dying right before our eyes.* The Roman Catholic experience in America reveals similar declines with perhaps the second biggest denomination in America – were it a denomination – the group of individuals who identify themselves in national polls as former Catholics or as non-practicing Catholics. Myers, in his claim that there is still potential life inside the Christian community concludes:

> *The Beloved Community was born in resistance to the established order of death and indignity. It was concealed like the leaven in the imperial loaf, germinating as a secret and subversive "colony of heaven," a body of noncompliance with the principalities and powers. Now we are as complicit as the subjects of any empire, embracing what we are taught to value, and resisting nothing that threatens our comfort, our success, our reputation, or our safety...There will be no recovery of the Beloved Community until we resist taking the purity of "right beliefs" and "right worship" too seriously (orthodoxy): and until we resist taking our marching orders from the powers that be (empire) too seriously. Instead, we can renew the church but one way – taking the "narrow way" much more seriously.[237]*

It is not enough to challenge the state on its corrupt use of power and violence in the service of security and world dominance. If we wish to see the Anabaptist-Mennonite theology of active peace survive in the twenty-first century world, we must do a better job of addressing interpersonal forms of violence which thrive inside our congregations, our faith communities.[238] To accept this as one aspect of our vocational call to work for peace in the world means we must come to terms with being on the margins of institutional power. We must learn how to tolerate being a shunned outsider, a silenced voice, and an unwelcome pariah. We must learn, in Jack Kornfield's vision of wholeness, how to avoid the spirits of hate and revenge as our motivation for doing our work in the world. And, as difficult as this is, we must learn how to refuse hate and anger as the driving motivations for our responses to those who hate and despise us. Seeking to become peace-bearers in the world, we must first learn how to become peace.

Clinical therapy adds another variable to this wisdom. Our job as clinicians is not to change the other. Our job is to make the relationship safe enough so that the other person, on his or her own initiative, begins to make the changes he or she needs to make. Obviously there is a caveat here. If the client is an active danger to others, to the therapist, or to him or herself, then the therapist is obligated to directly, efficiently and effectively intervene. In short, the therapist must assume control of the other's lethality towards the self or others. But this control is, and must necessarily be, short-term and directed at the individual re-gaining self-control.

But, in general, the principle holds. I am not responsible to change and manage you. I am not responsible to manage and change the church, my church, any church. I am not responsible to change and manage my culture. But I do have a voice and I am responsible to use that voice in a violent-culture-challenging manner. I am responsible to manage my own person in the world and to com-municate as effectively as I can that violence is never acceptable in the commons – whether this is affinity violence, structural economic violence, the violence of sexual orientation xenophobia, the violence of weaponry, or the structural vio-lence of corrupted institutions.

Our job as peace makers, true priests, prophets, and healers is to persuade others not to coerce them. To do this we need intellectual clarity and spiritual wisdom. Our job is not to resist others or to demonize them and exclude them. Our job, rather, is to see them as fully human and engage them in meaningful conversations. Our job is to resist evil, not the evil doer.

Ninth Letter

Uncovering the Roots of Sexual Violence

Introduction

In one of your letters to me you commented something to the effect that at this moment in your life, working with sexual abuse survivors or with situations of institutional clericalism in the aftermath of clergy sexual abuse seems outside your reach. Yet, when I look at some of your online work I see that you are teaching conflict-transformation principles and doing international anti-violence and peace-building work with members of the United States military establishment.[239] Your work has included advocacy for women who have been sexually abused in that context.

The reason I mention this is that I do not think, as Anabaptist-Mennonite professional women, that we are all called to do the same work. In other words, we are not obliged by some arcane feminist principle to be clones. Our individual work, rather than detracting from each other's work, in my opinion at least, usually supplements or complements the work of other women. We can affirm each other's gifts and each other's work in the world by not demanding that every other woman in the world has the same concerns and does the same work that we, ourselves, do. When we are able, we can then lend each other our emotional, spiritual, and practical support without demanding perfect reciprocity of values and work. We are not clones of each other; we are not holograms of each other; we are not even mirror images of each other. We each have a unique package of skills and gifts and perhaps even a unique spiritual calling.

We are each called by our individual experience of faith and our personal commitments to the work of non-violent peace advocacy to use our unique gifts in the service of others. Awareness of our deep intuitions and differing abilities and interests can inform each of us about our personal identities and our personal vocation in the world. This awareness can inform us of the complexity of anti-violence work. No one woman can possibly do all the work that needs to be done. We need to make allies wherever and whenever we can. I think we need to be prepared for surprise when we see who shows up in our lives. I am enough of a mystic to believe in serendipity and synchronicity. Our presence in each other's lives at this moment in our denomination's history and in our personal lives as peace and justice scholar-advocates is, therefore, likely no accident. We have work to do together and we can support each other in the work we, as individuals, are already doing.

There is so much male-promulgated violence in our world that none of us women who wish to foster justice-based peace in the world will see our work finished in our individual lifetimes. I think this is why first-century Christians so longed for the end of the world and why their hope for Christ's eschatological imminent return to them was so alive in their imaginations. Living as captives inside a captive nation during Rome's choking grasp on their community and witnessing the destruction of their city and temple firsthand, the apocalypse they so desired and concomitantly so feared was already present.

Today it is my nation's military power that dominates the world. It is our minority voices as Anabaptist-Mennonite pacifist women that are culturally disdained and frequently disabled by the powerful. As women we are a minority voice inside a small religious minority. The iron glove of American military dominance is perhaps more disguised than the violently brutal rule of Rome's corrupt emperors and puppet governors in first century Jerusalem but it still represents the iron glove of patriarchal domination. It furthers the interests of the ruling class of the nation state at the cost of the needs of the weak and the vulnerable. In my experience the presence of a dominating military force always carries the inherent possibility of corrupt totalitarianism and physical brutality.

You recently commented that the individual with a government-authorized weapon can function as a peace-keeper or as a peace-enforcer or s/he can be a predator. I agree. In a democracy or a republic, this brutality of government-authorized weaponry can be constrained only by the vigilance of an informed citizenry towards its elected rulers.

As you do, I find it amazing that so many of our Anabaptist-Mennonite brothers disdain their Anabaptist-Mennonite female colleagues with the same kinds of disdain, invisibility, or silencing that the external world heaps upon them as pacifist males. Rather than supporting our Anabaptist-feminist-inspired work to end male violence inside of the community, we feminist and womanist Mennonites have apparently become, inside their male experience, the dreaded voice of a theologically useless or even detracting presence from the real work of pacifism: men's work.

As your letters have noted, we are excluded from these denominational religious and academic conversations about non-violence inside the community of faith simply because of our gender or, perhaps more likely, because of the work we do. Because of this widespread exclusion of feminist and pacifist women, it seems to me that our much-needed perspective on these issues of militarism and sexual violence is actively resisted, disdained, and denied.[240] Rather than solidarity, there is hostility and covert passive-aggressive resistance to our presence in the Mennonite commons. There is resentment regarding our voices and our perspectives about the nature of patriarchal domination as the taproot of male violence against women and their children. My understanding of this phenomenon is incomplete. But my beginning analysis includes the awareness that our Anabaptist brothers share in and benefit from male entitlements within the patriarchy and they don't intend any day soon to become aware of the potential damages this entitlement carries for genuine, long-lasting peace in the world. Protected by male privilege, power, and entitlement *and* seduced by the enjoyable perquisites of privilege and power, they don't see the dangers and damages of patriarchal thinking and living. They do not see the spiritual dangers of the patriarchy to their own inner soft self and soul.

In recent months Roman Catholic theologian William "Bill" Lindsey's blog *Bilgrimage* has been fostering a discussion of the connections between masculine identity formation, testosterone, heterosexism, misogyny, racism and America's preoccupation with guns.[241] All of these function as part of the root system of patriarchal cultures. But I don't think they are the taproot for Christendom.

Rape and the Culture of Militarism

Other authors, much more able than I, have addressed the intersection of feminist thought regarding the patriarchal connection of rape and militarism.[242] But it is an incontrovertible fact that war and rape grow together like cloned trees that have over the years become one tree. Each probably has a separate cultural root system. But like the giant sequoia trees, their roots interpenetrate every other root system in close proximity. In such a manner, the invisible roots (which lie just below the forest floor) support the visible forest above. These interpenetrated cultural roots or ideologies of male dominance and female subordination; of male superiority and female inferiority; of male authority and female obedience; and of the patriarchal and angry male god and his placating subjects: these ideologies support militarism *and* the rape and battering of women *and* the physical, sexual, emotional, or spiritual abuse of small children.

The Many Perversions of Power

In her important paper, *The Perversion of Power: When Mourning Never Comes*, psychotherapist Mary Gail Frawley-O'Dea notes that one way to derail the needed mourning in communities is to mis-name or mis-categorize. I agree. I will extensively quote her below because I think her insight is vital to this question you raised about the root systems of sexual abuse and violence done by religious leaders.

As do many other authors, including Tom Doyle, Richard Sipe, and Patrick Wall,[243] Frawley-O'Dea notes that talking about the clergy sexual abuse crisis in the Roman Catholic Church as if it began in 2000 or in 1984 is a mislabeling. She writes:

> *Similarly, the Catholic "sexual abuse crisis" which ostensibly began or at least was noticed by many within and without the Church in 2002, neither began in 2002 nor primarily is about sexual abuse. Rather, the crisis of Catholicism began on the shores of Galilee shortly after Jesus' death and has always been about power – Who wields it? Over whom? How do they keep it for themselves? What do they do when somebody tries to get power over them?*[244]

Several paragraphs later, she continues:

> *When we name a sexual abuse crisis as the essential problem, we imply that if we stop sexual abuse, if we make some kind of recompense to the victims, the crisis is over. There is a size and a shape to the problem and we just have to figure out how to solve it. And many people, Catholic and otherwise, have spent the last decade trying to do just that. ...It is all hogwash of course..... And it all comes tumbling down when we rename the crisis as a centuries long attack on the teachings of Jesus perpetrated by an all-male kyriarchy whose primary consistency has been to maintain their own power no matter the cost to anyone.*[245]

Several paragraphs later, she concludes:

> *These imperial bouncers, however, from Constantine to Benedict have had no clothes on. Or rather, their ermines, silks, and jewels always have been cloaks elegantly draped to obscure naked power.*

> *We, former and current Catholic laypeople, have to mourn what this has cost us to live into the myth that the Catholic Church was the only Jesus-approved path to the Divine and to spiritual authenticity and fullness. The sexual and spiritual ravaging of our young is only part of the price we paid.*[246]

Abandoning Jesus for Institutional Power

It well may be that the taproot of clergy leader sexual violence is, therefore, a theological and sociological one – a taproot of the Christian Church's very early abandonment of the radicality of the human Jesus and his message of full inclusion for everyone: the wandering baptizer John, the tax-collector, the prostitute, the leper, the rich young ruler, the thief Dismas, the crippled man by the pool of still water, Mary who studied, Magdalene who healed, Mary and Martha who squabbled over household chores, the Samaritan woman, the possessed man living in caves, the Roman centurion, the woman with a menstrual disorder, the small and helpless child, etc. As the early church changed from a persecuted minority to a persecuting majority, its theology shifted from a preferential option for the weak, the vulnerable, and the alien in the land to a preferential option for the powerful, the wealthy, and the culturally elite.[247]

While I personally dislike Pope Francis' metaphor of the need for priests to smell like sheep, his intentionality is clear. Members of the laity are to be served rather than to be servants of the church's elites – its popes, its cardinals, its bishops, its religious monastics, and its priests.[248] As a girl who in childhood and adolescence witnessed sheep on a regular basis, they do not seem like highly intelligent animals with a mind of their own. I would prefer not being seen by my ministers as a member of the sheep clan. Here in Arizona my rancher friends talk about rogue cattle – those cattle which have learned how to escape the branding iron, the round up, and how to survive on their own away from the ranch, often breeding and creating their own mini-herds in the wild. My rancher friends do not talk about rogue sheep. I identify much more, therefore, with the rancher's rogue cattle than with the pope's smelly sheep.

The pope and the Roman Catholic Church's kyriarchy[249] need to first realize and then accept that members of the laity (especially female members) are, indeed, not smelly, mindless sheep but human beings who have much to offer him and his church...and that many of these lay citizens of the church have been sexually plundered and viciously wounded by their so-called priest (and bishop) shepherds.[250]

As I prepare this manuscript for publication, I am re-thinking these words. Perhaps the model offered by the Jesus' path is more complex. Perhaps clergy and laity are meant serve each other as co-seekers of *The Way*. Maybe there is some form of reciprocity in our desire to mutually be fully present to each other and to the work of the world. Maybe *Shepherd and Sheep* or *Leader and Follower* or *Pastor and the People* models need to change. Maybe we need, as contemporary followers of The Way, to begin to develop new models for our faith communities – models based on a deepening awareness: by our confessing faith in the Jesus call to community we are called to be a people of constantly maturing co-seekers on a spiritual path, co-healers of the world's wounds.

The Victims' Voices Emerge

A clinical aphorism states that *one person holding onto and proclaiming new and strange or unwelcome ideas may be a lunatic. Two or three individuals of a like mind, however, form a community of peers. As part of a community of like-minded peers, no matter how small, individuals are less likely to be socially judged as lunatics.*

Until the middle of the twentieth century, there was very little public advocacy for raped and sexually assaulted individuals. Indeed, victim-blaming was extremely common as victimized people were usually seen as the precipitators of their victimization.[251] Their behavior, their physical appearance, or their personal character was seen as the direct and immediate cause of their victimization. According to the United States' Federal Bureau of Investigation's annual *Uniform Crime Index,* these crimes of affinity sexual violation were known by law enforcement officers to be under-reported by victims. In addition, however, many local police jurisdictions unfounded the complaints which they did receive and thus the crimes went uninvestigated and uncounted in local, regional, and national crime tallies. Consequently, the incidence data available was known by 1970's era criminologists to be under-representative of the actual demography of sexual violence in the United States.

The dual realities of under-reporting and criminal justice system unfounding slowly began to change in the last third of the twentieth century when radical feminist women began to speak out about rape, about domestic violence, and about other forms of individual and collective violence against women and their children.[252] The seeds of social change were small: a speak-out against rape in New York City; a domestic violence shelter opened in San Francisco; a rape crisis line in Washington, D.C. followed in very short order by one in Los Angeles County. As feminist activists held sexual and domestic violence consciousness-raising events across the nation, feminist clinicians and academic scholars began to collect and analyze factual data. Research protocols were designed to gather more accurate data. The magnitude of the sexual violence reality in women's and children's lives slowly over the last decades of the twentieth century began to come into a more focused view.[253] What we all know today about the incidence of sexual and physical violence in women's and children's lives, we know in part because of these early radical feminist women in urban and academic locations. Radical feminist women did the research that was needed to address the absence of reliable demographic data.

In response to this more accurate and more readily available demographic data, the nation's and various states' legal codes about sexual violence and about domestic violence began to change. Definitions of sexual crimes became clearer. Penalties became more uniform. Social institutions such as hospitals and police departments created new victim-sensitive protocols for managing sexual violence and sexual harassment complaints.

Ruth E. Krall

The emergence in the 1970's and 1980's of American feminist activism regarding male violence is correlated with the 1980's and 1990's clergy sexual abuse victim-advocacy movements inside the Roman Catholic Church.[254] Both movements drew awareness to the presence of sexually violent clergy as one aspect of the larger whole of male violence against women. Affinity sexual violence done by members of the clergy became acknowledged as a possibility rather than a denied one. It became possible for victims and their advocates to refute the Church's claim that their victimization was self-precipitated and constituted, therefore, a mutually consensual relationship.[255] Within the past thirty years awareness of clergy and religious leader violations of the laity or of the church's female and male employees has now spread to many different Christian and Jewish denominations.

As victimized Roman Catholic laity and reform-minded clergy and religious led the way by forming self-help movements such as SNAP,[256] Road to Recovery,[257] and Catholic Whistleblowers[258] victims in other denominations also began to address issues of their abuse by religious leaders.[259]

In a similar fashion, Mennonites have also begun to address the need for reform. Blogs such as *Our Stories Untold* provide women and men with a place to safely tell their stories of abuse and victimization.[260] The new Anabaptist-Mennonite Chapter of SNAP was formed in August, 2015 to be a peer support resource for Anabaptist and Mennonite survivors of sexual and physical abuse.[261] In the summer of 2015, the Mennonite Central Committee announced that it was joining with other groups in *We Will Speak Out* "*to break the silence about sexualized abuse in our communities.*"[262]

With increased advocacy, public awareness of the severity of these issues has begun to happen. Juries began to convict clergy child sexual abusers. In addition, over time, awareness grew about the systemic issues of structural violence which supported and covered up individual acts of violation in efforts to maintain and protect the church's projected image of religious leader holiness and sexual purity. Eventually, two separate states convicted Roman Catholic clerical bureaucrats of enabling and covering-up sexual abuse by the clergy they supervised.[263]

In 2017, this discussion in the United States about clergy sexual abuse of the laity includes theologically liberal denominations as well as theologically conservative or fundamentalist ones.[264] It includes Christian churches as well as other-than-Christian groups. Many denominations, therefore, are experiencing an internal ideological split between members who seek leader transparency, accountability, a more equitable system of governance, and those members who continue to support authoritarian control by a few male leaders whom they believe to hold autocratic power and spiritual authority given to them by God at their ordination.[265]

Mennonite Women Unite

As we Anabaptist-Mennonite women join together across generational divides to protest intra-denomination male-gendered sexual violence against women and their children, we can be reassured that it is truth about male dominance and male violence that we persist in seeking (and speaking) not lunacy. We are not alone. Women, and a few enlightened men, across this nation are speaking up about the endemic violence of rape and child abuse.[266] We may still be perceived by the male and female Greek chorus of the Christian patriarchy/kyriarchy as lunatics, but we know, by our solidarity with each other, as well as by the work we do with victimized others, that we are not lunatics.

Your letter, this week, therefore tells me you have become a member of a growing group of Anabaptist-Mennonite women – a few of whom have kept insisting for more than thirty-five years that the John Howard Yoder-Mennonite Church story[267] must be truthfully and factually addressed by the church *for the church to heal its own woundedness.* Our concern for Yoder's victims' healing and for the church's victims' healing has not been a vendetta against the church or against Yoder. It has never been an act of lunacy. Our ongoing concern about this historical narrative and its ongoing socio-theological trajectory in the heart of the Anabaptist-Mennonite community of faith has been rooted in our clinical and socio-psychological-spiritual concerns for the healing of victimized women *and* for the socio-religious-theological wholeness of the institutional church. Our concern is now (as it has been for more than thirty-five years) to prevent future similar violations and victimizations inside the socio-cultural and theo-religious borders of Anabaptist-Mennonite communities.

In her discussion of the Roman Catholic Church's childhood victims who are now speaking up as adults, Frawley-O'Dea notes:

> *The survivor victims crying out in the public square are who they are AND* (emphasis hers) *they are the symbolic heralds of realities, of crimes, of truths that many Catholics still refuse to hear or see or feel within their hearts. The victims are, in one of their incarnations, modern day prophets warning the hierarchy, "But woe you Pharisees! For you pay the tithe of mint and rue and every kind of garden herb, and you disregard justice and the love of God: but those are the things you should have done without neglecting the others. Woe to you Pharisees! For you love the chief seats in the synagogues and the respectful greeting in the market place. Woe to You! For you are like unmarked graves, and people walk over them without knowing it."*[268]

We Anabaptist-Mennonite women are neither lunatics nor are we anti-church propagandists. We do not have a personal vendetta against the historical memory of Yoder's life and his work. While some among us have been treated as pariahs by the male-led denominational church because of our advocacy for institutional integrity and transparency in this matter, we have, nonetheless, banded together as Anabaptist-Mennonite women in search of healing and truth. We have supported each other when the patriarchal church and its administrators attacked our economic security and our financial well-being. We have provided counsel to each other when some members of our faith community claimed we were vindictive and no longer should be called Christian. We continue to support each other when our various forms of scholarship are ignored as irrelevant or attacked as spurious by well-entrenched male members of the Anabaptist-Mennonite academic establishment. Most importantly, we have believed and we have supported the victims of the church's sexual and systemic violations as they have sought healing for their wounds.

We are Anabaptist-Mennonite women. We are concerned about justice and peace-making *inside* the church's own boundaries as well as inside the state's boundaries. My own perspective on this is very clear. Today the Mennonite Church's historical anti-war stance is compromised by every insider act of unchallenged sexual abuse *and* every ignored incident of insider domestic violence against women and their children. Each one of these violent episodes in women's and children's lives that the church ignores, tolerates, or excuses as unimportant to the church's peace theology, undercuts that very theology – making it increasingly irrelevant in the world.

Since some women physically, sexually, emotionally, verbally, and spiritually abuse children, they too must be held accountable. Women, as well as men, perceive that they benefit from supporting the patriarchy and its rewards for unthinking obedience and uncritical silence about violence inside the commons. Nothing could be further from the truth.

Every voice that denies this principle of factual truth-telling or that excuses male *or* female enactors of interpersonal violence for any reason participates in patriarchal reasoning. Every spoken or written voice that exempts powerful male or female religious leaders from accountability for their acts of interpersonal violence or for the acts of structural violence they ignore (and thus implicitly condone) promotes the patriarchy. Every voice that actively or tacitly condones such violence as God's will for human relationships is a violence-complicit voice that supports the patriarchal values of power-over, domination, corrupted authority, and control. Each of these many voices both speaks for and prolongs the patriarchy.[269]

This kind of double-think reasoning declares that what the nation state does in war-making against enemies or in using the death penalty as punishment for crimes done in the commons is violence, but the harmful actions that members of the church do to each other inside their interpersonal intimate relationships is not violence. This kind of double standard makes absolutely no sense to me. I neither agree with it nor do I consent to the institutional behavior that it enables.

The presence of PTSD as a form of war trauma in veterans and PTSD as a form of sexual trauma in rape and domestic battering survivors both testify to the historical presence of lived encounters with violence as an active wound in survivors' lives. These kinds of violence and their subsequent wounds call for a more adequate and proactive Anabaptist-Mennonite theology of peace-making in the midst of these kinds of violation.

Thus I believe that the work which you do in the world and the work which I do in the world complement each other. Our individual actions on behalf of individuals victimized by many different forms of violence do not, therefore, cancel out each other's acts of compassion and solidarity with the violated. Our respective tasks in the world do not detract from our potential abilities to support each other and to discover the interconnected roots of violence – those roots which support the toxic and enchanted forest of endemic violence.

Tenth Letter

Encountering Social Nastiness Inside Church Doors

Introductory Comments

I woke up this morning thinking about these letters and how they shouldn't be too pious – because I distrust orthodox, sentimental, and rigid piety inside religious institutions and theological conversations in the same way I distrust the presence of MRSA (methicillin-resistant staphylococcus aureus) inside health care facilities. If one can avoid contact with those infected by these institutional viruses and bacteria, it is better to do so. If one can't avoid contact, then one should have a good supply of sterile gloves, sanitizing deodorants, and disinfectants on hand.

In that light I got to thinking about the venerable older Mennonite statesman I knew in my young adult years. He would talk about the nastiness of church politics and then warn his all-male audience of admirers and hangers-on about the dangers of pissing with skunks. While, as a much younger female colleague, I never personally heard him speak these words, my male academic contemporaries did.

In the years since then, I have often resorted to his folk wisdom as a personal guide. There are some interactions which are futile to begin because their conclusion is foreknown. There are some relationships which are so toxic that we would do well to avoid them if at all possible. There are some conflicts which are best avoided because more heat than light will result. There are some fights which will only yield bruised egos and infected spirits. There are some adversaries whose only goal is to harm or to destroy us. Jesus taught his disciples, be *as shrewd as serpents and harmless as doves,* before he sent them out *among wolves.*[270]

The Wisdom to Discern

The wisdom to discern the essential work we must do in our own backyards from these totally useless and insanity-making destructive encounters comes, I am positive, only with age. Or, maybe I was just a very naïve and slow learner. It has taken me a lifetime to learn how to tolerate hostility-embedded conflict enough to manage it. When I was very young in my professional life, I ran from hostile professional conflicts over power. As I matured inside the life-container of the work I did, I learned to use my clinical skills as an asset. I learned to assess and diagnose my adversaries' motivations as well as their behaviors. Determined not to be an unguarded prey animal, I kept trying "not to be where the predator was" at any given moment.[271] This determination to protect myself and my work included assessing the situations in which battles for power and control erupted. Gradually, I learned how to navigate these difficult situations in ways which did not damage my inner self and which did not destroy my personal integrity by compromising it. In short, I learned to pick my fights very carefully. When they picked me, I paid close attention and decided whether or not I would enter the conflict as a combatant.

Eventually, I learned that my sense of humor – inherited and nurtured inside my family of origin – was a powerful tool for retaining (or regaining) my equanimity. If I could see the ridiculous side of some of the inane power struggles and conflicts in academic settings, then my sense of idealism was not destroyed and my commitment to making a personal difference in oppressive situations was not derailed. Over time I learned that I could stop engaging in futile efforts to change others who clearly did not want to change. I could focus my energies on building alliances and doing the work of healing, building peace, and education which could actually be done. I could seek for common ground wherever it might be found.

In some sense, I learned to flow with the river in which I found myself. Facing strong negative currents, I refused to waste my fragile share of life's energy in futile efforts trying to change that patriarchal negativity and its concomitant lust for arbitrary and controlling power – a deep-seated malicious lust for power and control when it so clearly declared its presence. Since swimming upstream seemed so futile, I learned to look for safe harbors in which I could ride out the storms. I also learned to look for sturdier boats.

Here Buddhism (and therapy) has helped me with its emphasis on staying in the present moment and doing the work of the present moment. If I stop catastrophizing long enough to pay attention, I can usually figure out how to walk through the needle's eye and continue on my journey. This, of necessity, means paying attention to places and relationships where positive change can occur. It usually means seeking to facilitate positive change rather than attacking negative resistances to change. I am a firm believer in systems analysis. A small positive change in the desired direction (for example, fewer on-campus rapes this year than last) can begin to alter the supporting environments for violence.

Civil Rights Activism: Heterosexism

We are seeing this at work right now in the Mennonite Church's negative and controlling debates about what full inclusion for individuals inside the Mennonite LBTGQ community means.[272] With each new welcoming congregation, for example, the movement for a positive decision takes on possibilities for continuing change in these directions that affirm the present moment. It seems to me that the reasonable goal here is to continue to recruit inclusive congregations rather than attacking non-inclusive ones. But it also means protecting inclusive congregations from the attacks of those who would destroy them in the name of an ideology of exclusion.

This means we must develop the courage to withstand negative verbal assaults on our persons, our characters, and our careers because those who resist this kind of positive change are locked in self-deluding illusions. Deflecting the overt and covert hostility and the raw hatred of their attacks is probably more useful than engaging them frontally.[273] Pink Menno, therefore, engages in activism by singing hymns, "street theater", speaking as delegates, worshipping together, and by running educational symposia.[274]

Civil Rights Activism: Racism

Civil rights movements always seem to elicit these kinds of mean-spirited efforts to exclude others. Eventually as courageous leaders and prophets continue their witness inside *and* outside a particular faith tradition, positive change slowly but surely begins to happen. It generally begins to happen among the young who are not willing to live within the blinders of their elders. I doubt that Martin Luther King, Jr. ever thought in the first decade of a new millennium a gifted black man would occupy the White House. It is difficult when you are claiming equal rights to use a public toilet, a public drinking fountain, or a vinyl-covered seat at a dime store lunch counter, to see the future imminently arriving in which the racist fight is about this question: *Can a black man or a woman be an elected president of the United States?* I know Martin talked about the mountaintop and I know he hoped his children would know a life without racism. But he was so realistic in his work it is hard to believe that he thought permanent cultural change would occur in less than forty years after his death. As testimony to the unbelievable happening, witness Jessie Jackson's tears on the night in 2008 when it became clear that President Barack Obama was headed for the White House. That which had been unimaginable in 1968 had, in fact, happened. Part of the African-American dream for equality and full inclusion had happened more rapidly than any of us could have hoped for in the 1950's. This is not to say, Lisa, that anti-racism work in the United States is finished and that racial justice has been accomplished.[275] That kind of thinking is a dangerous illusion.

But the first two term black presidency of the United States has happened. This is, I think, akin to the first black baseball players in integrated baseball. The racist mantra *a black person should never, therefore, can never be elected president* has been conclusively disproved – twice.

Civil Rights Activism: Sexism

We United States women are less than 100 years away from universal suffrage. It took the suffragettes about 60 to 70 years of activism to bring this about. And, yet, we women in the United States in 2016 have seen a historical moment in Hilary Clinton's serious candidacy for the presidency.[276] I remain uncertain that I will see a woman president in my lifetime – but I am certain that you will in yours. The second wave of the American feminist movement is more or less 50 years old. The American anti-rape movement is slightly more than 40 years old. Both movements have changed women's and children's lives in the United States. Both movements have also impacted world-wide women and children.

Authors such as Jungian analyst Jean Shinoda Bolen note that when a cultural worldview tipping point is reached, all of a sudden change locks into place and a new world is born.[277] Our task as peace advocates therefore is to use our time and energy wisely – working for positive change rather than helplessly flailing in the face of resistance to our work. We may not live to see the results of our collective work and activism – but as we work and build alliances, we are creating the milieu for that tipping point to happen.

Refusal to Engage in Mean-spirited Discourse

One place I refuse to fight is in religious environments where the judgment is made about me that I am not pious enough, Christian enough, Mennonite enough, politically correct enough, or whatever. Whether this is because I refuse to speak the clichés that, in my opinion, destroy genuine faith rather than reflect it or this is because of some other perceived defect in my personality, I am never quite certain. I have a strong suspicion that one value taught to me in childhood is not a shared value with the overtly, authoritatively, and restrictively pious. I was taught to question and to seek reasonable information when I was confused about how to proceed in life.

When pious and overly scrupulous individuals begin to speak prejudice of any kind as God's truth, or when they speak in rigid and unchanging theological cliches and only honor the traditional ways of understanding truth, I tend to cut out. When they judge the victims of violence to be the cause of their own victimization, I know we are not on the same page.

The value of questioning and doubting for one's own self as a way of determining the guiding principles and values of one's own life is one of the core values of my life. It is linked with a pantheon of heroes – men and women who have done or are still doing critical peace and justice work without resorting to obnoxious controlling piety or male hormone bullying to defend themselves. Unthinking and uncaring belief in the hairy verities and patriarchal entitlements of a religious culture is simply not acceptable to me as a way to live my life.

We have to live in our own era of history and we have to understand that we are culturally shaped by that era's environment. As the world around us shifts and changes, we need to keep adapting. For example, contemporary astrophysics is changing our world's scientific understanding of the cosmos and the beginnings of human life and consciousness. We now know we live in an expanding universe of multiple galaxies. There appears to be no outer edge to the space in which these galaxies hang. This emerging scientific frame has already challenged Western theologies of the cosmos and its creation.

In a similar way, modern technologies are changing our understanding of the human brain. Of necessity, this is changing our understanding of human selves and the neuroplasticity of the brain in continuously shaping our personalities, our behaviors, and consciousness itself.

As people on the Jesus path, we do not need, therefore, to accept our cultural heritage, faith environment, and inherited exegetical understandings unquestioned. Where we can, we need to look for human works of compassion and justice. But not every dumb conversation or inane academic debate is profitable in unearthing truth or in creating justice.

It is one thing to speak truth to power. It is another to helplessly and hopelessly argue and flail against unthinking, unseeing, and unrelentingly hostile fundamentalist, orthodox pieties – especially when these are ideological academic pieties or fundamentalist denominational ones.

When, therefore, someone speaks meanness or speaks exclusion or speaks addictive and obsessive-compulsive religious scrupulosity, or creates unnecessary restrictions on living life fully and happily and then simultaneously links the meanness, the obsessions, the scrupulosity, or even their own obsessive-compulsive sense of entitled exclusivity to Holy Scriptures – in any religious tradition – the fur rises on my back and I am warned that any in-depth encounter may leave me smelling for days.[278]

Civil Rights Activism: Clergy Sexual Abuse of the Laity

The estimates range from minuscule to something like ten percent of all clergy and religious leaders are abusive – and we know a certain percentage of those abusive leaders are sociopaths. One of the unsolved enigmas of the Roman Catholic clergy sexual abuse crisis is the question of whether abusers seek out the priesthood for the access to victims and for the safety it offers abusers, or whether seminarians are kept infantile in their socio-emotional-spiritual development and journey to maturity and are, therefore, inevitably shaped, formed, and educated by the church's seminary system to become abusers.

We Anabaptist-Mennonites would do well to ponder this question. Are abusive and power-hungry authoritarian people drawn to ministry? Indeed, we can refine the question further. Are individuals with character disorders drawn to ministry as a profession? If so, how do we identify these individuals and refuse to certify them by ordination? Theo-ethical debates with sociopaths are, in my opinion, useless because they are not arguing from a search for truth. They are shaping their arguments in a continuous search for domination, control, and power. Rather than seeking to heal the wounds of the people and community they serve, they seek to inflict new wounds – often under the guise and overtly pious language of spirituality and religiosity. The symptoms to watch out for are authoritarianism, strong control needs, charismatic manipulativeness, a willingness to lie, and an inability to listen to or learn from others.

I am not speaking out against placing one's opinion in the open marketplace of ideas. But in my old age, I have a better picture in my mind of what a rabid skunk looks like and where one might be found inside the enchanted cultural forests we all live inside. I seek to avoid its natural habitats and breeding grounds whenever possible. Like the now-deceased elder statesman mentioned above, I too refuse to piss with skunks.

Ruth E. Krall

Eleventh Letter

The Mennonite Phallacy

Do not copy the patterns and customs of this world but let God transform you into a new person by changing the way you think.

Romans 12: 2 (NLT)

For just as we have many members in one body and all the members do not have the same function, so we who are many, are one body in Christ and individuals members one of another. Since we have gifts that differ according to the grace given to us, each of us is to exercise them accordingly, if prophecy, according to the proportion of his faith; if service, in his serving; or he who teaches, , in his teaching; or he who exhorts, in his exhortation; he who gives, with liberality; he who leads with diligence. if it is giving, then give generously; if it is to lead, do it diligently; he who shows mercy with cheerfulness. Let love be without hypocrisy. Abhor what is evil. Cling to what is good.

Romans 12: 4-9 (NASB)

Introductory Comments

This morning your short note about your encounters with Mennonite men (and their difficulties in accepting your particular peace-making work in the world) distressed me immensely because it again reveals that many Mennonites in positions of denominational agency leadership would rather fight and gossip than try to understand another's divergent point of view. Even progressive Mennonites seem to be encapsulated in ancient multi-generational patterns of relating to each other as if it was desirable for every Mennonite to be a clone of every other Mennonite.

Socialization Plays its Part

As Mennonite women we are taught from little on up to value the community and to de-value the individual. We are both implicitly and explicitly taught that mature individuation of the female self is the same as secular individualism (a most dreaded set of words among many Mennonite academics).

What I think this Mennonite charge against feminine individualism usually means under the cover of innocent-sounding words is something like this: *you, a mere woman, do not see the same world I, God's chosen and therefore favored one, sees; you do not think the same grand thoughts that I think: therefore, since I alone, as a male, am made in God's image and since I, therefore, see the world as God sees the world, you are wrong. Since you are wrong-minded in your vision of your personal share of the peace-building work needing to be done in the world, it is quite necessary for me as I do God's work in the world to oppose your work and, if you do not yield your will to mine, to shun you. Part of my share of God's work in the world, therefore, is to self-righteously oppose you and your work. When I have made your world of work miserable for you, I know I have done God's work in the world. When I have made you doubt yourself as worthy and faithful, then I see God's hand at work in my words. When you stop working, then I know I have won.*

In addition, as part of our socialization processes as Mennonite women, we are taught explicitly and implicitly that women are expected to be subordinate to men who are in positions of power: fathers, husbands, preachers, teachers, even our adult sons, etc. Women's role inside the community is rather narrowly defined – we are to serve men and we are to obey them.

I call this model of female nature the pineapple and carrot model. We are to make this ubiquitous Mennonite salad and we are to bring it to the potlucks that celebrate the success of our male superiors. But we are to be humble about our offering. We are expected to believingly protest that every other woman's pineapple and carrot salad is much better than our own – although we have worked for twenty-four hours to make certain ours is the best.

No wonder so many Mennonite women are depressed. Their unique gifts to the world have been denied expression for so long. In addition, far too many Mennonite women and children live inside abusive relationships with the dominant men in their lives: grandfathers, fathers, husbands, uncles, sons, preachers, church leaders, etc.

Anabaptist-Mennonite women who question these deeply en-cultured assumptions about male entitlement, male privilege, male authority, and male power as God-ordained realities are, in common language, dissed by the men (and their female acolytes) whose voices determine orthodoxy, establish the rules for spiritual faithfulness, and enforce denominational purity codes for proper female behavior.

Not living in a female body, these dominant alpha males of the Mennonite Church have no clue about the dangers of female life, nor do they, in their demands for women to see the world their way, understand women's unique sensitivity to their surrounding environments and their ability to read when their work is welcome and when their work is unwelcome. They do not, therefore, honor women's unique gifts as birth-givers, peacemakers, and healers of the communal wound.

For far too long, we Mennonites have focused our attention on the way that we appear in the world: the way we dress, the way we move, the way we avoid the prohibited acts of the world, the way we act. Even our most profound artistic liturgy (the four-part hymn unaccompanied by instruments) is communal. There has been way too little attention focused on identifying individual gifts, honoring those gifts, and celebrating the work each individual is called to do by virtue of her or his individuation and vocation.

As I got breakfast this morning; I started ranting to myself about this behavior which is seen in both Mennonite men and women. It is as if we must be the Bobbsey twins in our experiences of faith and in our witness to our faith. Failure to be conformed as women to the faith community into which we were born is our current faith anathema. This is most surely one major rootlet in the Mennonite Church's response to complex and deeply theological, therefore ideological, issues such as abortion, war, the death penalty, other-than-marital sexual activity, or civil unions for sexual minorities.

It is either this patriarch's vision of peace work in the Arab and Jewish worlds or none. It is either this patriarch's theology of peacemaking in the inner city or none. It is either this patriarch's beliefs about sexual minorities or none. Once accepted as the bearer of communal orthodoxy, the Mennonite academic community rallies round these carriers of orthodoxy as if they knew and, thus, pronounced, absolute truth. Challenging voices and alternative visions of peace work are not welcomed. To keep the internal peace, passive-aggressive solutions such as malicious gossip or overt shunning are preferred.

To stretch the Christian scriptures' metaphor of the Christian Church or even the Mennonite church as Christ's body, it is as if we all need to be livers and lungs. No kidneys and hearts are needed. For sure the eyes are reserved for those who are orthodox. The same is true of the ears. Visionaries in the pews are undesirable, perhaps even detestable, aliens.

The Mennonite Militia

As you noted, dominant voices in the Mennonite community tend to avoid direct contact and conflict about issues of theological orthodoxy. You and I have been joking about the presence of a Mennonite militia – academic men and denominational religious leaders whose weaponry includes excommunication, employment termination, shunning, excluding, isolating, outright lying, money manipulation, character assassination, and demeaning back-stabbing gossip.

But in the moment when an Anabaptist-Mennonite academic woman is targeted by the Mennonite militia for denominational annihilation, it is no joke to her at all. Her wounds, though nursed alone and in isolated silence, are nevertheless life-and-spirit-endangering wounds. After such attacks, the woman usually finds her inner life forever changed. Eventually, over time, these inner life changes will transform her outer life as well.

In many situations, such as those involving the doing of peace work in the world, such controlling and passive-aggressive exclusionary views not only attempt to silence women from the dominant caste, but they also directly or indirectly silence the voice and wisdom of many women from specific minority groups inside the community: women of color, physically unattractive women, aging women, women academics, women from different nationalities, lesbian and queer women, physically or emotionally handicapped women, impoverished women, raped and abused women, etc.

Each Mennonite woman, who has been sensitized to this issue inside her particular Mennonite community, can supply the names of male academics or the names of male religious leaders who have sought to block her way and to undercut her work on behalf of the world's peace. Many Mennonite women who have sought to serve their church can, therefore, name the men (and their female acolytes) who engage in secretive back-stabbing and in character defamation activities just outside their victims' awareness zones.

Resistance and Confrontation: Staying or Leaving

When feminist and womanist women face this issue inside the Mennonite academy, they need to make decisions about resistance and confrontation. They need to make decisions about staying inside or leaving the community. If they decide to stay inside the margins of the community they need to develop strategies for professional development and survival that do not involve the men who seek to control them or even to exclude them altogether. To survive, they need to move as rapidly as they can towards career excellence and survival – which usually means pursuing a double career: one inside the Mennonite community of faith and one outside it.

Mennonite men (and to be truthful, some Mennonite women too) in the Mennonite academy seem unable to find beauty in an unpredictable diversity of opinions and they fail to find hope for the future in the multiple paths to truthtelling or in the collective wisdom of theological diversity.

This is also true in our branches of mission work and in our service organizations. There is, for example, a certain personality style and a certain take on the world which is required to work for these Mennonite organizations. I have known for years that I would be unacceptable to Mennonite mission organizations and to Mennonite service organizations abroad – despite, as a college faculty member, having lived very successfully in a second-language nation, making close friends in that nation, and working there with mission and service workers in a variety of denominational locations. I don't have the proper physical appearance and I don't speak the proper languages of piety and orthodoxy. The very aspects of my personality which helped me to succeed in daily life and build meaningful relationships inside a second culture are, therefore, liabilities inside my faith community.

My personality is more comfortable with questions than with answers; I am not much interested in orthodoxy. I want to know how people live their lives. I want to know the actual stories of their lives – rather than the doctored stories they have created to survive in the patriarchy. Are they kind? Do they demonstrate compassion for others' suffering? Do they live with integrity? Are they tolerant of diversity or even celebratory in its midst? Is their spirit welcoming or rejecting? Are they competent in the work they do? Can they accept human diversity as the way life is? Are they curious about why people do what they do, or are they immediately judgmental and harshly critical? Can they live within conflict and not need to settle it immediately – but rather allow the conflict of ideas and opinions to ripen so that it can teach them flexibility, resiliency, and curiosity? Do they express curiosity about life, or do they already know everything there is to be known? Are they interested in truth or just ideology?

My own diagnosis of the Mennonite phallacy, therefore, is rooted in this deep embedded belief that there is only one narrow way to be a proper Mennonite woman. As a Mennonite woman there is only one narrow way to work for peace in human encounters with each other. All other ways are suspect. This kind of cultural notion is truly absurd in its demand for spiritual, intellectual and cultural conformity.

If there is anything the divine source of all life celebrates, it is diversity. Look at the Gila monster, the sea turtle, the brown recluse spider, the Harris Hawk, the toucan, the silver-back gorilla, or even the lowly pack burro. Each is beautiful in its own way. Each has a role to play in the ecosystem where it lives. And then look deeply into each species and see great intra-species diversity. Why, then do we Mennonites insist that to be faithful to the Creator of all this human diversity must fit into narrow boxes of appropriate and inappropriate; faithful or unfaithful; prophetic or wrong-minded?

I am not arguing this morning that we abandon critical thinking. Quite the contrary: I am arguing that we begin to think with our minds – not with our inherited prejudices and not with our childhood's indoctrination to uniformity.

Your critics who don't believe you should work with the military or who believe that you should work inside the Islamic world rather than in your own world

– have lost sight of your unique gifts in the body of Christ. If you are a leg, they are asking you to be a gallbladder. They do not trust your individuated sense of call. They do not listen. They judge you by their own sense of their own call or even more absurdly by what they think your call should be.

These critics have no sense of the deep weariness in your spirit-body and world right now. They do not, in Henri Nouwen's words, understand that the healer must unbind her or his own wounds and rebind them one at a time so that she or he can touch others' wounds with love and compassion; so that they can see others' gifts in the world and celebrate them. They want you to clone yourself to their patriarchal vision of the world.[279] They don't care if you burn out if, at the same time, you can demonstrate to them that you accept their particular version of burning out for the kingdom. This is truly absurd. It is lunacy writ large.

This kind of not paying attention and then judging what is misunderstood is exacerbated in male-privileged and male-entitled cultures. Men get to judge women and to call us by their own names for us. Because they think God put them in charge of the universe, they get to do the defining and the naming. This is equally absurd and, in addition, it is heretical.

I personally refuse to play this game. I will name myself. I will listen to your naming of yourself. I will seek to pay attention to the gifts given to me by my human creation at my birth. I will seek to pay attention to the gifts given to you at your birth. I refuse to insist that you clone yourself to my vision of the world and the work of peacemaking in this world. Certainly there is more than enough work to go around for both of us. We cannot and, therefore, we should not seek to clone ourselves to others' vision of who we are and what we *should be doing that we are not doing.*

The Mennonite Phallacy

So, what is this contemporary Mennonite phallacy?

- Individuation is evil; one must avoid individuation at all costs; we should all be ears or gallbladders or livers. There is no need at all for eyes, hearts, and hands
- Individuation equals individualism and individualism is the greatest sin
- Yielding to the community's sense of truth takes precedence over listening to one's own inner intuitive, perhaps Holy Spirit- led, sense of our own personal skills and interests and calling or vocation
- The male voice is entitled to judge the female voice and should never be called to account for the inappropriate harshness of its judgment; people may report to you the gossip they hear about you but I want to know if they have, on your behalf, ever confronted the gossiper about the inappropriate nature of his behind-your-back-and, therefore, hidden-criticism of you

- Gossip about others' failures and wrong-mindedness is to be preferred to direct conversations about divergences of opinion and behavior
- Individuals prefer the sureness of knowledge to the insecurity of the question – even though it is in the question that the future lies
- There is a strong preference for conformity in outward matters such as personal appearance and a stunning resistance to the unique and individuated spirituality of the inner life
- In many ways the popular phrase *my way or the highway* dominates our social relationships with others inside the community of faith. This is particularly true of those of us who are socially entitled to speak for the community by virtue of position, family and clan connectedness, or personal charisma

In Conclusion

In conclusion, I think there is a central principle which we can follow. Each of us is unique – there is no one like us in the entire world. There never has been and there never again will be. Therefore, we have an individual calling inside of the social worlds into which we were born. If we use a metaphor from the natural world, maybe we can see this. We live inside a social and human termites' nest. To some alien from outer space, we would appear as if we were clones of some master designer. But, were the alien able to enter the nest undetected, he would see individual termites at work – each doing the task they do best – thus creating the mounded universe in which they live.

We are social beings as humans. There is no way to deny this. None of us would survive to adult life if other human beings did not care for us along the way. But we have individual gifts and these gifts in the form of personal abilities form the basis of our adult work in the world. We are not clones; we are individuals. It is as individuals that we carry our gifts and our talents out into the world. It is as individuals that we encounter the needs of the world for our work and for our help.

The existentialists who write about our essential aloneness in the world speak to me because the reality of our embodiment is that we are created with a deep and permanent sense of our own individuality in the context of a social world that swirls around us. Some of us are more comfortable in this social skin than are others. This is part of the nature of the human community. We are not clones. We are not holograms. We are not mechanical robots.

We are physical and energetic beings. We are physical bodies deeply shaped by human consciousness. We are spirits embodied in human flesh. We are thinking, feeling and intuiting beings. In our essential nature we are ensouled beings yet we live in a physical body and a physical universe. We all live inside inherited and shared cultures. These multiple, yet discrete, shared cultures first of all shape us – especially in infancy by nonverbal languages of care. Then, as we mature, especially after we gain and can use language, we begin in our turn to shape this once-inherited culture for future generations. This is the pervasive and lasting enigma of our lives – how can we live in community and not be submerged or drowned by its social pressures and the comforts of conformity? How can we function as individuals living inside our own skin, our own share of human consciousness, *and* simultaneously be full participating members of our particular communities?

For modern individuals and for post-modern ones as well, these questions are complex: we moderns and post-moderns live in overlapping communities and these communities elicit, as it were, different selves. American psychological theorist Kenneth Gergen hypothesizes that we live as saturated selves – impacted from within and without by multiple identities that are shaped by the multiple communities in which we live.[280] As we increasingly live inside the global village, the termite mound in which we live makes more and more demands on our always personal stash of human consciousness. No longer, in my opinion, do we live with a simple question of conformity and nonconformity to the world (church versus state, for example). We live with the growingly complex question of personal identities and communal identities inside overlapping yet discrete communities. Perhaps, just perhaps, we have more in common with the man in the story from Luke 8: 29-31 than we know. No longer believing in demons and supernatural possession, yet we live in a time when our personal identities are increasingly fragmented by the multiple cultures in which we live.

The temptation in such a time is to cling to outmoded and outworn personal and communal identities in a very small termite mound. This is a temptation to be resisted.

Ruth E. Krall

Twelfth Letter

Tales from the Reptile House

If your theology does not affect the way you use your body and how you treat other people's bodies, then it isn't theology. Perhaps it is a philosophy but don't fool yourself by calling it theology.

Adrian Jacobs[281]

Introductory Comments

This is a late addition to these letters. But I've been pondering its originating document and that document's proximity and relevance to the Mennonite Church-John Howard Yoder narrative for many years. This particular document, *Tales from the Reptile House* (1994), was created by an anonymous author who was clearly annoyed.[282] His annoyance (what you and I might in the common vernacular call *venting one's spleen*) was written in the context of the Mennonite Church's institutional need to make sense of the emerging Mennonite Church-John Howard Yoder narrative. This particular document floated in the Mennonite underground. I don't know where or when I first saw it but I had a personal copy in my sexual abuse files. I have been told by people I believe to be credibly informed that the document originated in Scottdale, PA and was written by an employee of the Mennonite Publishing House. However, as it floated free of its author's name, it did so anonymously.

1991 to 1992

The history surrounding the document is quite simple. In the 1990's when the Mennonite Church, and, in particular, Indiana-Michigan Conference and Prairie Street Mennonite Church in Elkhart, IN were attempting to deal with John Howard Yoder as a multiply-accused sexual harasser and abuser, people who supported Yoder worked in silence behind the scenes. In a sense – to the public church – they were anonymous, submerged, invisible figures at the time. Behind the scenes they lobbied the church's denominational officers for a quick resolution to their work with Yoder.[283] What seemed uppermost in these behind-the-scenes lobbying efforts was the institutional return of Yoder to theological respectability in order that his corpus of intellectual work should not be questioned or abandoned. At the time almost none of this lobbying was evident on the surface of the denomination's public face. These backdoor lobbyists for Yoder's quick restitution included Mennonites in positions of academic or institutional power as well as powerful evangelical apologists for Yoder's work – men from other denominational backgrounds as diverse as Southern Baptist (Glenn Stassen), Methodist/Episcopal (Stanley Hauerwas) and baptist with a small-case letter self-identification (James William McClendon).

As details about Yoder's sexual activities slowly emerged into a public view (particularly after the 1992 Bethel (KS) College decision to disinvite Yoder as a speaker on its campus[284]), the evangelical establishment immediately recognized the threat that this publicity about Yoder's private life posed to the permanency and definitive theo-ethical impact of Yoder's work on the religious academy and its sponsoring denominational churches. Learning, for example, that Yoder might choose not to cooperate with Mennonite Church disciplinary processes inasmuch as he was no longer employed at the Associated Mennonite Biblical Seminaries in Elkhart, Indiana, Hauerwas, McClendon, and Stassen staged an emergency conference phone call intervention with Yoder urging him to cooperate with Mennonite Church disciplinary processes.[285] Part of their argument focused on damages to his theological legacy if he decided to be uncooperative.

Many years later it seems to me that they knew – or at least strongly intuited – that appealing to common-sense morality or to a sense of compassion for his victims would be futile tactics in persuading Yoder to cooperate. What mattered, according to their own words and, in their assessment of Yoder, himself, was his theo-ethical-ecclesial legacy of written words.

As evidence, for example, of their concerns that the future Christian Church was likely to judge Yoder's life in ways which damaged his intellectual legacy, in 1992 James McClendon was quoted as saying:

> *There's an enormous burden of the church to protect the heritage he is part of,* said James William McClendon, distinguished scholar-in-residence at the evangelical Fuller Theological Seminary in Pasadena, Calif. *If he is slandered, and defamed, and abused, that is going to hurt all of us who are grateful for the enormously important work he's done for half a century.*[286]

I don't think it is too paranoid to read McClendon's words as a pejorative and reactive push-back against the Mennonite women who had brought their personal charges against Yoder's lifestyle to his denominational church. *Slandered, defamed, and abused* are very strong words for conveying a warning to the Mennonite Church about its need to protect Yoder's theo-ethical and ecclesial legacy. In McClendon's public statement, as quoted, there is absolutely no awareness or recognition of the presence of victimized women other than as individuals who can *slander, defame and abuse* McClendon's theological, ethical, and ecclesial hero.

Yoder's chief apologist Stanley Hauerwas led the evangelical infantry charge in an effort to restore Yoder as soon as possible. He preached a forgiveness sermon at Goshen College's April, 1992 commencement – in advance of the Church's formal announcements of its actions with Yoder – later revealed in the *Elkhart Truth's* June and July, 1992 series of articles about Yoder's sexual behaviors.[287] In this sermon, there was little evidenced concern for the experiences of victims of violence and violation or, so it seemed to me when I re-listened to this sermon several years ago. There was little evidence of a theological or psychological awareness for a religious leader victimizer's need, in all reconciliation processes, to be accountable to his victims, as well as to his church.[288] I heard no awareness that a Roman Catholic form of institutional absolution is totally inappropriate in an Anabaptist-Mennonite confession of faith and communally-embodied-polity. I no longer remember who first said to me that the Mennonite process with Yoder was essentially one of absolution rather than repentance and reconciliation. Whoever this individual was, I continue to hold the opinion that s/he was correct in this penetrating analysis of what went wrong in the Yoder discipline process.

Parenthetically, I think of this commencement address[289] as the single worst and most inappropriate commencement address I witnessed in my long academic career. Hauerwas interminably harangued graduates and their families about forgiveness – knowing full well, I believe, that the Yoder issue was not big on the graduates' collective mind on this celebratory day in their individual lives. So much for (1) *members of the class of 1992, you have done well*; (2) *congratulations on your academic success and personal achievements*; (3) your *families, friends, and faculty are proud of you*; (4) *your faculty and I wish you much success and happiness in your future life*; and (5) *now go and serve God and your fellow human beings with joy and compassion*.

Instead Hauerwas used his commencement bully pulpit to address Mennonite Church administrators who were present, members from Goshen's board of overseers, its teaching faculty and the college's top administrators – admonishing all of us in not-very nuanced or even well-thought-through words that the unilateral Christian obligation in situations of great injustice was to forgive and then forgive again those who transgress. Forgive and forget: this is the message he gave. We might have understood the sermon better had he named its context.[290]

It is more likely that John Howard Yoder's need for denominational respectability and institutional absolution, and not each graduate's academic milestone, was uppermost on Hauerwas' mind as he prepared this most inappropriate and ill-thought-through sermon. For, on this weekend, he was, most also assuredly, also thinking of Mennonite Church politics in light of Yoder's transgressions. During this 1992 Goshen College commencement weekend, his 2010 autobiography reveals, he also met with Indiana-Michigan Conference officials regarding their plans and time-schedule for the denomination's disciplinary work with Yoder. His 1992 opinion about forgiveness was summarized by the Tom Price-authored July 16th *Elkhart Truth* article.[291]

> Hauerwas stressed those themes in an April 18 commencement address at Goshen College. *Forgiveness is (not) simply a matter of being told God has forgiven us*, he said. *Unless we are able to tell one another the truth through the practice of forgiveness and reconciliation, we are condemned to live in a world of violence and destruction.*[292]

At the same time as the evangelical Yoderian apologists were creating glowing personal testimonies to Yoder's writings about church discipline,[293] the Indiana-Michigan Accountability and Support committee encountered Yoder's elaborate theological rationalizations for his private sexual behaviors – behaviors which were, at best, adulterous and, at worst, sexually abusive.[294] Whatever repentance means when dealing with recidivist sexual offenders, it must surely mean (1) shame and grief over one's personal failings and addictions; (2) acknowledging the truth of what actually happened and making sincere and unthreatening apologies to every individual one has harmed in the course of one's personal abusiveness; (3) acknowledgment of and respect for the validity of one's victims' fears and ongoing concerns about the sexual abuser's safety; and (4) offering to make meaningful and public amends; and (5) a deliberate and choiceful turning one's life's ongoing trajectory away from all future acts of abuse and towards different behaviors and different thoughts about one's behaviors.[295]

The Wisdom of Twelve Step Programs

Twelve step recovery programs state that it is essential to admit to God, to one's own self, and then to another human being the exact nature of the wrongs we have done.[296] This is often explained as the first step in an ongoing process of developing personal integrity and subsequently regaining sobriety in one's personal life. In following and working the twelve steps, individuals identify all those they have harmed and seek to make amends for this harm. These now well-worn steps of addiction recovery programs teach all of us that to move forward in the spiritual life, we must first honestly acknowledge to ourselves and to others who we are and what we have done. For the healing of the self and for the healing of our relationships with others, therefore, radical and transformational honesty is called for.

In context: where Yoder's Messianic rationalizations for his personal behaviors and his non-scientific, idiosyncratic ideas about female sexuality were challenged by the factual reality of many women's complaints, Indiana-Michigan Conference's Accountability and Support Group rapidly discovered Yoder was highly resistive to the idea of personal change. He was, to put it quite simply, deeply committed to his intellectual rationalizations vis-à-vis his theology or philosophy of sexual behavior. From mid-1992 until December, 1995, the committee met with Yoder thirty-one times and they also insisted on a psychological evaluation and a course of therapy.[297]

During those years (1992-1996) mean-spirited conversations and gossip floated – unfettered - in the greater church community vis-à-vis a variety of women's accusatory charges.

In addition, the Yoder revelations spawned a decade of Mennonite women's activism on behalf of victimized women and children (1992-2002) that had previously been abused by other-than-Yoder abusive individuals. During this decade other abusive denominational religious leaders were identified and disciplined by their congregations and conferences.[298]

It was, for example, during this decade, that the Women's Concerns Desk at the Mennonite Central Committee in Akron, PA sponsored a series of church-wide awareness-raising conferences on the topics of domestic abuse *and* sexual abuse inside Mennonite communities. Many of the denomination's individual conference structures also sponsored regional conferences. There were also instances of individual congregations sponsoring informational and awareness-raising events. The denomination's church press reported on these conferences as well as denominational disciplinary procedures. In all of these venues, speakers and consultants heard formerly unspoken stories of physical, emotional, spiritual, and/or sexual abuse in the lives of Mennonite individuals.

Thus, two contradictory processes were at work in Mennonite communities. In the first process, consciousness-raising about violence inside Mennonite families and churches was encouraging truth-telling and providing support for victimized individuals. In the second, negative criticism of these awareness-raising activities surfaced and free-floating hostility towards victims and their advocates was freed. Attempts were made to suppress information. Speakers and consultants in these events were attacked as rabble-rousing, vendetta-wielding, and rabid anti-church misanthropes. Victims were blamed for being victims. Victims were blamed for not forgiving. The church press was blamed for truthfully seeking to tell the stories of the church's various disciplinary actions. Victim advocates (and their character) were verbally attacked in private and economically attacked behind their backs.

Institutionalized Patterns of Response

In several on-line presentations and published speeches, Dominican priest Father Thomas Doyle describes a pathological pattern of religious community response which he has observed during more than thirty years of victim advocacy work.

- Institutional silence and consultation with lawyers about institutional self-protection
- Denial that the abuse happened
- Cover-up activities which hide inept or criminal institutional responses from view
- Protection of the abuser
- Protection of the institution and its financial resources
- Minimization of the amount of abuse
- Minimization of the damage that resulted from the abuse – this can include under-reporting of the financial costs to a denomination
- Outright lying
- Deflection to other issues (in my opinion, in his church, priestly celibacy and homosexuality; in my church, homosexuality)
- Re-victimization of the original victims by casting doubt on their characters or their motives for reporting abuse; refusal to seek to heal victims' wounds by recognition of the severity of the damage done to the psychological, emotional, interpersonal, and spiritual aspects of their lives
- Vilification of victims' advocates as anti-church
- Shifting blame to external factors such as the media or a sexually permissive culture
- Overt and outright attacks on those individuals who support victims in the processes of speaking out about their event (s) of victimization.[299]

Congregational Responses

In 2007 the Rev. Laurie J. Ferguson, a Presbyterian minister, published her reflections on the topic of the laity and their reactions to the accusations of clergy sexual abuse by their congregation's minister.[300] She writes:

> When lay church leaders heard there was an allegation of sexual misconduct against their minister, the most typical collective responses were a refusal to listen, hostility, dismissal of evidence, and then, if the identity of the victim became known, ostracizing the victim, the victim's family, and at times anyone who stood with them...The response of the laity was total – complete – denial.
>
> This primary defense was rigidly overused, not just by individuals, but also by congregational collectives. The defensiveness led to splitting, scapegoating,

selective amnesia, and repetitive retraumatization. Congregations "refused to know" and in this sense often functioned much as the Roman Catholic hierarchy when confronted with sexually abusive priests.[301]

In her continued discussion of laity and congregational leaders, Ferguson notes the *profound power of denial* as it moves and shifts within congregations. In her analysis, she makes a clinical interpretation. *Denial is always in the service of something.*

I personally believe there is no way to overstate Ferguson's awareness. Once we realize this, then the presence of outrageous denial becomes revelatory of deeper problems than we first thought. Pervasive denial provides us with diagnostic questions. Recognition and understanding the presence of collective denial is central to our abilities to intervene successfully in our efforts to protect those who have been victimized by religious leaders; in our efforts to heal the wounds of individuals and the entire community. Ferguson unpacks denial in this way and I both paraphrase and comment on her important work in beginning to diagnose pathological communal responses:

- Pastors and other religious leaders are seen by the laity as speaking for and on behalf of God
- Therefore, these religious leaders represent grace and forgiveness, knowledge and power in their essential being as pastors. Thus, they are often seen as being an essential conduit for lay salvation
- Congregations, therefore, often view their pastor as perfect and their congregation as a mirror image of that perfection; by identification, they therefore see themselves as living in a reflected state of salvific perfection
- Congregations, falling into this pattern of perfectionistic thinking, are filled with individuals who give up personal or individual responsibility for their own spiritual growth. They do this by forming a dependency relationship with the minister – in which they piggy-back their salvation to his spiritual charisma
- Living on borrowed godliness and goodness, the laity live, therefore, in a state of spiritual immaturity
- The minister is idealized. After accusations of sexual abuse are credibly lodged, members of the laity simply refuse to recognize any wrong-doing including the recognition of sin and the presence of betrayal in the minister's conduct. In my language, there is a cognitive disconnect between what they believe the minister to be and what the minister's accusers reveal him or her to be. This cognitive disconnect is managed by refusing to believe the minister could do wrong deeds – such as the sexual abuse of children, adolescents, or vulnerable adults. This is essentially the same process that Father Doyle calls minimization

- The laity, in their reliance upon their minister's perfection, thus feel compelled to defend the minister. As they do this they may refuse to believe and, therefore, chose to ignore the suffering of the victimized individual(s) who brings charges against the minister. They may berate the victim(s) of abuse as liars. They may choose to cast doubt on the integrity of the victims and the credibility of their accusations. This refusal to recognize the suffering of the victimized accuser is exacerbated by the community's perception of power (the minister's) and their perception of the relative powerlessness of victims (such as a child or a woman). In essence, the community that lives in denial casts its spiritual or theological preferential option for the powerful victimizer and against the victimized powerless ones[302]

I would add that in my personal experience, the presence of vigorous and hostile denial often signals the presence of additional hidden abusers in the religious commons – abusers who use congregational and church institution denial to further manipulate and abuse members of the community. They deny and verbally abuse whistleblowers in order to protect themselves, additional abusers and entire institutions. As they protest the persecution of a fellow perpetrator and protect his legacy of abuse from full investigation, they inadvertently reveal the possibility of additional abusers hidden in clear sight in the commons. It is as if they dare ordinary lay individuals to play the children's game *Where's Waldo?* At the very least, they raise questions about their personal reasons for their vigorous protection and defense of a known perpetrator.

It is clear: in Roman Catholic, Protestant, Evangelical, and Anabaptist-Mennonite communities, the response of the institutional church and the response of the laity to internal complaints about religious leader sexual abuse represent a threat to the solidarity of the religious community. In addition, they represent a threat to the personal spiritual security of each individual inside this community. They represent a threat to the very message of Jesus which I will summarize this way: *take care of the weak, the wounded and the vulnerable little ones in your midst for of such individuals is the kingdom of heaven created.*[303]

We have not talked much about this in these letters, but when an immature or even perverted spirituality overtakes the religious community, it automatically and inevitably replaces the spirit of compassionate care and genuine hospitality with a spirit of harshness and judgment. After members of the laity turn (like rabid dogs) against other members of the laity, then these congregations (or entire denominations) become unsafe spiritual homes for individuals and families. It is not uncommon for such church communities to implode and self-destruct.

I think the institutional church's protection of abusive priests, religious, and corrupt institutions is the reason so many disillusioned Roman Catholics have left their denominational church.[304] Some sources say that the second biggest denomination in the United States – were it a denomination – would be the denomination of thirty million former Roman Catholics.[305] We Mennonites have not kept track of the folks who have walked away in disgust and despair and we are too small a denomination for national polling organizations to watch. But all of us who have worked on sexual violence issues inside the Mennonite Church know men and women who have walked away from their community of faith in disgust and despair.[306] We know, in addition, formerly abused individuals for whom the church is so unsafe they can never again enter religious buildings or participate in communal worship services.

In multiple articles and in numerous public speeches, Father Thomas Doyle comments that the spiritual damages of religious leader sexual abuse and institutional clericalism may be harder to treat than the psychological, physical, and emotional sequellae to abuse.[307] I agree with him.

SNAP, The Survivors Network of those Abused by Priests, on its home webpage offers concrete and specific advice to congregations and religious communities when their priests and ministers and other religious leaders are accused of sexual abuse.[308] This is a resource for individuals to print out and for entire congregations to consult. As I read and re-read this list, this central theme emerges. Everyone needs to educate themselves about the possibilities of sexual abuse in their personal religious community. They need to recognize the symptoms of abuse and they need to act. Denial serves no one. In my professional understanding of these kinds of issues, prevention beats quarantine and treatment in both time and money effectiveness. Below I abstract and paraphrase SNAP's thirteen points.

- Instead of immediately assuming that allegations about clergy abuse are false, keep an open mind. Be enquiring rather than immediately judgmental towards these accusations
- Pray for all parties involved
- Be present to and aware of your own emotions as they arise in response to revelations of religious leader abuse
- Remember that religious leader abuse is actually quite common – across denominations
- Don't try to guess who the accuser is: don't gossip about victims: Victims of clergy rape and other forms of abuse need privacy so they can begin to heal their wounds. In addition, gossip can prevent other abused individuals from coming forward with their own stories of abuse. This is particularly true of malicious or mean-spirited gossip. I [Ruth] personally learned in years of managing psychiatric in-patient communities that one never controls or even knows who overhears gossip. In this situation of clergy sexual abuse inside religious communities, it may be one of your own family members who has been abused and who, hearing you gossip, decides on the spot that

it is never safe to talk with you or others about what happened in his or her on life

- If you know the victim, protect his or her right to confidentiality – the right to tell his or her own story in her or his own timing
- Understand that victims of clergy sexual abuse often have troubling behavioral symptoms such as alcohol or drug abuse or even sexual promiscuity. Attempts to self-medicate one's internal pain and anguish take many different forms
- Don't allow the passage of time to discredit those who choose to disclose their life history of being abused. This is true, for example, of adults who were abused as teenagers or as children. But it is also true of adults. One individual's bravery in coming forward often enables other individuals to do so as well
- Inquire of personal family members and friends if they were victimized. If they answer yes, provide them with support and assistance to get help.
- Mention victimizations to others who might have been affected – make a window for openness and truth-telling to emerge
- Where appropriate, contact police or child protective service agencies
- Confront other church members who make disparaging remarks about victims or the need for the church to investigate claims and deal appropriately with these claims
- Perhaps most importantly in terms of prevention, educate yourself, your family members, and friends about sexual abuse. If you are a minister, educate your congregation. If you are a teacher or a professor, educate your students. If you are a parent, educate your children. If you are the administrator of a church institution, educate the people you supervise

I would like to add my own impressions here for our continuing discussion about these matters.

One event or, more likely, multiple events of clergy sexual abuse in a congregation, a church institution, or an entire denomination creates an unsafe community for everyone – no matter where they are located in this particular narrative: perpetrator, victim, witness to the violation, adjudicators, family members, and previously uninvolved members of the laity at large. Everyone's religious faith is going to be tested. Everyone's sense of trust is going to be bruised – if not entirely destroyed. Everyone's sense of the spirituality of the faith community is going to be tested. Everyone's personal sense of connectedness to the divine source is going to be tested. There are no exceptions to this rule except babies in diapers who are too young to understand the currents and undercurrents which swirl around these difficult issues.

If congregations, high school and college campuses, and denominational supervisors do not recognize this very simple reality (rape and other forms of sexual abuse are emotionally, spiritually, and communally destructive), then their interventions will be ill-planned and poorly implemented. It is inevitable that there will be spiritual and religious casualties. It is likely that victimized individuals will be re-victimized by these ill-conceived efforts to intervene.

Denominational or congregational leaders need, therefore, to understand the theological or Biblical concept of a preferential option for people of faith. Whose needs do they prioritize in their efforts to contain the toxic wildfire of denial? Do they choose to believe and, therefore, to protect the victims of clerical violation? Or do they choose to believe and protect the perpetrator?

What happens when an allegation of abuse surfaces? Will they tolerate, unconfronted, the hostility of lay member to lay member? Will they challenge or refuse to challenge nasty gossip? Religious or lay leaders who seek to be healers must ask themselves: *How, in the middle of such a toxic forest, can we adjudicate fairly? How can we search out the truth of what happened? How can we avoid demonizing any of the participants inside this particular abuse narrative? How can we assist everyone to avoid the denial that defends the perpetrator and his, or her, implicit rights to abuse others in God's name?*

Here it seems to me, as I write, that the skills of your profession enter this arena, for most surely these forms of congregational and denominational confrontations need the skills you and your colleagues have developed in conflict transformation inside other kinds of intransigent conflicts and intractable arenas of human discord. I don't think biblical theology is enough to manage clergy sexual abuse accusations. I think we need to develop entire cadres of people who have skills and can move into angry and denying communities on demand. In a sense my model for this originates in my awareness of the teams of clinicians who move into schools where children have killed other children. The healing worker(s) need to be trained in skilled crisis intervention and their help needs to be immediate. Otherwise, I believe (because I have witnessed this first hand) religious communities and congregations will begin to self-destruct and permanent hostilities will develop – responses which are much harder to diagnose, treat, and resolve.

Community mental health models teach me that the more immediate and effective the crisis intervention response to experienced trauma, the more likely it is that individuals can heal with support; the more likely it is that entire communities can mature. The longer traumatic stress syndromes go unaddressed, the more secondary supports there are for the trauma to go underground. Then, for example, in work with individuals, clinicians are not only treating trauma, they are treating alcoholism or sexual addictions or sexual performance problems, or marital problems, or child abuse problems. These dual and triple diagnosis disorders are much harder to manage and to treat, and positive clinical outcomes are less certain.

In addition, inside the healing community, we have learned that for victims to heal, they need to be able to tell their story in a narrative form and that their story needs to be believed *and* acknowledged.[309] There are some indications that if the first person to hear a victim's story is compassionate and believes that story then victims heal more rapidly than if they are disbelieved, judged, and scolded.

I personally believe the same kinds of issues are present in communities which refuse to deal appropriately with religious leader abuses. Communities tend to adapt to the abuse and then they integrate the narratives of abuse into the ongoing life of the community. Interventions then must be, of necessity, more complex.

We are seeing this right now in the international Mennonite Church. Institutional and academic resistance to dealing with the factual truth of the John Howard Yoder and Mennonite Church legacies of abuse of power is now well-anchored in place. Faculty members, for example, in the church's seminaries have historically accommodated to the history and they have built elaborate intellectual defenses and rationalizations which make any attempt to heal this narrative much more difficult.[310] Academics, in their spirited defense of Yoder and the church's historical mis-management of his behavior, cannot, therefore, see the ongoing dangers of denial and minimization to the spiritual life of the Mennonite community. Given this until very recently largely unexamined history of sexual abuse in the life of the denomination's major 20th century theologian-ethicist-ecclesiologist, very little has been learned about diagnosis and prevention of future situations of religious leader abuse. You and I both know and have read our academic colleagues' institutional and personal blogs which blame victims and, consequently, put Yoder's work on an idolatrous pedestal. They ignore the already-harmful consequences to the denomination of their denial and their minimization of the consequences of that denial that have already happened.[311]

Parenthetically, in my opinion, more heat on this topic is just going to build more resistance. What we need are carefully constructed models and analyses of this case study – as a case study – so we can learn from it. We need to bring to this study as many intellectual perspectives as are relevant. Deliberately excluding, for example, clinical wisdom from these discussions means that these case study protocols will be inadequate. The same is true for the social sciences and their analysis of power and authoritarianism. Unless these case study protocols are rooted and grounded in a study of institutional issues, we will fail to comprehend the depth and width of the problems unleashed by the Mennonite Church's inept management of John Howard Yoder's abusiveness.

The warnings to God's people about the prevalence of religious leader abuse are now in the secular newspapers. The warnings are in American court rooms and court procedures.[312] They are, as of 2015, in the cutting rooms of American entertainment media.[313] It is not only the Roman Catholic Church which struggles with denial and faulty bureaucratic procedures. The headlines tell us about Jewish study-centers for the young, Mormon communities, Baptist churches, mainline Protestant denominations, Jehovah's Witnesses, Eastern meditation centers, small independent sectarian evangelical congregations, and even Mennonite communities.[314]

The problem of clergy and religious leader sexual abuse is pervasive inside the Christian commons.[315] To date the questions remain unanswered. What will we do – collectively and individually – about this problem? How can we address it in ways which honor the public health model: prevent, contain, and treat? How will we honor the Jesus path with its mandate to heal human disorders as part of Christ's body's mission on earth?

Father Doyle suggests that we must forthrightly recognize and theologically address the spiritual pathology of the community; Ferguson's article suggests that we must make our way through the miasmic swamp of collective denial; SNAP suggests we must make our way through the overflowing landfill of victim-blaming. I suggest victim advocates and healers must create a more secure pathway into and out of the enchanted forest by educating ourselves, in advance, about these issues so that when they occur in proximity to us, we can support everyone in this abuse narrative.

I personally believe everyone needs, indeed deserves, emotional and spiritual support in this story. Victims need to be believed; perpetrators need to be confronted and held accountable for their behavior; these stories' witnesses, for example, members of the laity, need to be guided to understand the structural meaning of the story as they encounter it so that they can behave appropriately. Most important, in light of our conversations about healing, victim advocates need a community of resistance in which they, themselves, find support for their work.

Compassion and discernment, not hostility and judgment, must reclaim the landscape, fertilizing it with our sincere desires for genuine reconciliation. This means we must recognize the true costs of reconciliation to everyone – including the perpetrator. To do this work well, we must, therefore, deal with problems of power as well as with problems in our understandings of human sexuality.

The Body of Christ

If we believe that as one metaphorical body of Christ we are the embodiment of God's work on earth, then each of us has to grow up spiritually and each of us needs to take responsibility to heal that which we can heal. Hostility, denial, victim-blaming, rage, ridicule of victims, attacks on the character of victim advocates, unacknowledged grief, and scapegoating are not the paths to healing. They are not the paths to genuine reconciliation. They are not even the paths to personal integrity. Most of all, these are detours on the path to spiritual maturity for individuals and communities.

I am personally convinced that spiritual maturity is a developmental process in our lives. What is spiritually mature at 18 is probably not spiritually mature at 75. What is true of psychological or emotional maturity is likely true of spiritual maturity. We become mature by encountering life, by recognizing factual truth, by giving up illusions, and by making personal commitments to love, justice, compassion, helpfulness, and a commitment to personal integrity in the face of adversity. In general, when we falter and when we make big mistakes in our lives, we need other people to give us a helping hand or speak a confronting word. Operation bootstrap creates inevitable failure opportunities for each one of us.

We need each other. It is as simple as that and as complex as that. This is the essential wisdom, I think, of twelve step programs. People, who themselves struggle to maintain sobriety, hear each other out, without judgment, and then someone reaches out with a nonjudgmental helping hand to someone else who is struggling. Radical honesty and nonjudgmental support: these are perhaps the keystones to healing and transformation. They most certainly are the building blocks to spiritual maturity.

No one individual will ever hold complete truthfulness in her grasp. The search for truth will be life-long. But we can avoid the pitfalls of vengefulness, rage, hatefulness, and judgmental approaches as the driving forces in our search for truth. We can become aware of our own shadow, and we can become aware of our community's collective shadow. We can give up superficial idealism for practical realism. We can, and should, cease to live in states of individual and collective illusion, denial, and delusion. We can, and should, know that radical discernment is one aspect of personal maturity in all of its forms: emotional, psychological, cognitive, and spiritual.

Our Vocabularies of Discourse Shape Our Cultural Realities

The words *alleged* and *allegations* emerged as the church's written words of choice in describing victims' accusations and complaints vis-à-vis Yoder's (or other perpetrator's) behavior. Even after Indiana-Michigan Conference and Prairie St. Mennonite Church adjudicated women's complaints and deemed them valid and accurate, the words *alleged* and *allegations* continued to define the Yoder-victim situation.[316] Even after the Tom Price article in which Yoder acknowledged in a public manner that the women's complaint were basically, if not perfectly, accurate, this practice continued.

> Yoder had told the two panels that the alleged misconduct is not taking place currently, sources said.

"They speak for me – not with perfect accuracy – but accurately enough that I don't want to debate what they say," Yoder said this morning, terming the task force's statement as "less accurate" than that of the commission. "Both of them have the right to attribute things to me that they have attributed."

Yoder declined further comment. "It's in the hands of two church agencies, one in the district level and one in the congregation," he said. "My acceptance of that structure makes it very hard to see on what grounds I should be going to the public."[317]

Use of the words *alleged* and *allegations* continued after Yoder's adjudication processes were completed in 1996 *and* after Yoder's death in 1997. Indeed, even in 2014 various authors, writing about this era in the church's life, continue to use these precise words to describe Yoder's behavior vis-à-vis the women he harassed.[318] I mention these few historical details in introducing this part of this letter because they reflect the denominational milieu and institutional bias in which women's accusations about Yoder's behavior became known to the world church. Inside some parts of the denomination, victimized women and their advocates became informally known in some male circles as *alligators*.

In 2012 I wrote the following paragraphs about the continued use of the words *allege* and *allegations* vis-à-vis known and formally adjudicated situations of sexual abuse.[319]

Another linguistic clarification which needs to be made is about the words allege *and* allegation. *To* allege *something means to make an unsupported or unproved claim. An* allegation, *therefore, according to several dictionaries is an assertion without proof. It is only a claim that must be proved. In our current culture, it is a statement asserting something without proof.*

This bit of word-sleuthing about the word allegation *is essential because one continues to hear and to read about women's and children's allegations regarding sexual abuse long after the reality of abusive behavior has been confirmed by an adjudication or legal process. As an example here, I refer to Anabaptist-Mennonite scholars and their continued use of the word* alleged *in their published and unpublished comments about John Howard Yoder's sexual abuse behavior.*

Yoder's sexualized violent behavior towards students, student wives, colleagues, and wives of colleagues and friends was alleged in rumors before the summer of 1992. According to the 1992 Prairie Street Mennonite Church Yoder Task Force, John has acknowledged the truth of the charges (T. Price, June 29, 1992, B 1-2).

After Yoder's public acknowledgement of the nature of his abusive behavior, the language needed to change. In relationship to Yoder's lived-life, continued use of allege *and* allegation *in articles or books written about his life and work after this date is no longer appropriate.*

Specific information about the exact nature of many of Yoder's offenses has been withheld. I assume this is because of legal agreements between Yoder and his various work environments and between Yoder and Indiana-Michigan Conference of the Mennonite Church. In the summer of 1992 an Indiana-Michigan Conference press release contained, however, information that Yoder had acknowledged the accusations made against him by a group of Mennonite women. Since some of the women's allegations were published in the summer of 1992 by investigative reporter Tom Price of the Elkhart Truth,[320] *the general nature of Yoder's abusive behavior is known.*[321]

Inasmuch as Yoder's acknowledgment was reported in some detail to the secular and religious press, women's accusations or complaints about Yoder's specific behaviors are no longer allegations. They have been acknowledged by Yoder and confirmed by Mennonite Church officials to be factual truth. The continued linguistic use of the words alleged and allegations casts unwarranted doubts about the victims' truthfulness. It keeps the question of Yoder's culpability for his sexual harassment open. It helps to create a church-wide public climate of disbelief and denial regarding Yoder's actual behavior. This is not helpful at all. It is a very, very subtle form of continuing to judge, blame, and intimidate victims for speaking up and breaking open the silence of Yoder's abusive behaviors towards themselves and others.[322]

Since the women's complaints as published in the Elkhart Truth *(1992) were explicitly about contact forms of sexual violence and non-contact forms of sexual harassment, the continuing use of the word* allegation *functions as a code word to deny Yoder's behaviors and their negative impact and influence on the lives of many women. It is past time for religious writers and scholars to stop their linguistic minimizing maneuver and to acknowledge that they do know, at least in part, the specifics of Yoder's actions because he, himself, acknowledged that he himself was guilty of the behaviors of which he had been accused. Secular and religious press articles both published this information. It is no secret.*[323]

In 2014 and in 2015, the Mennonite Church USA, as a denomination, re-entered its earlier examination and action processes because of various calls for the church to account *for itself* in its historical treatment of women's complaints against

Yoder. Once again the issue of proper terminology has emerged. In particular, continued use of the words *alleges* and *allegations* by church academics and the church press has surfaced as a point of contention between women victimized by Yoder, their advocates, and the church's public face as represented by its institutional announcements, the church press, and articles written by the church's academic faculty members.[324]

In light of the Mennonite Church's Discernment Group public media releases to date, it is now clear that certain Mennonite officials from 1976 and forward knew both the social contexts of Yoder's sexual misbehavior and its specific actions. The word *alleged* ceased to be appropriate in the early 1980's when Yoder admitted to Marlin Miller that he had engaged in the very behaviors about which women's accusations were already in place.[325]

Early in the summer of 2014, Dr. Carolyn Holderread Heggen, the Mennonite Church's most recognized voice on clergy sexual abuse in Mennonite communities, addressed the issue that church publications and academic scholars are using to discuss John Howard Yoder's legacy of sexual harassment and sexual abuse of adult women. She comments:

> In common usage "allegations" implies charges that are unsubstantiated and unproven. It is not appropriate to continue to use the term "allegations" in reference to Yoder's sexual abuse and immoral relations with women.[326]

She then reviews personal history for her readers and describes a meeting of eight Yoder-victimized women with representatives of the John Howard Yoder Task Force at Prairie St. Mennonite Church (Yoder's home congregation) as well as representatives of Indiana-Michigan Conference of the Mennonite Church (the holder of Yoder's ordination credentials). Subsequent to this meeting, Indiana-Michigan Mennonite conference released a statement that said, *from this work the task force concluded that the reports are true and that Yoder has violated sexual boundaries.*[327]

Heggen concludes that *since church and conference representatives had determined that the charges were true, it is not appropriate to continue describing them as allegations.*[328]

In addition to clarifying the linguistic issues surrounding the use of the words *allege* and *allegations,* Heggen clarifies two more items of common misunderstanding: (1) women did confront Yoder and his supervisors directly and in person and (2) women did confront the Mennonite Church and its agencies directly and in person. These abused women, therefore, were known to the Mennonite Church and its agencies. They were not, therefore, throwing uninformed and anonymous darts into the religious air. In the formal 1992 complaints that the 8 women made to Prairie St. Mennonite Church and to Indiana-Michigan Conference, each woman signed her name to the statement of complaints. Once again, these women were not anonymous. They were known to the adjudicatory committees responsible for processing the complaints the church received about sexual misconduct of any form.

Heggen notes the presence of many abused women in historical situations similar to the eight women, and comments that many never had the courage, a sense of guaranteed personal safety, their community's support, or even the opportunity to complain in person to church adjudicatory committees. This lack of opportunity was perhaps especially true for international women Yoder abused during church-sponsored trips abroad.

Alligator-Infested Swamps: Truth or Fiction

I am interested in comparing my 2012 commentary and Heggen's 2014 commentary in light of the 1994 short essay by N.W. Ann Onymous [name withheld anonymous] in *Tales from the Reptile House*.[329] Stating that those who have alleged abuse inside the Mennonite Church of 1994 are alligators, the author of this anonymous (and scurrilous) piece of writing asks:

> *With new allegations popping up all over, there obviously must be a myriad of alligators out there. The question is; who are these alligators? What do they look like? In what part of the Great North American Swamp do the alligators live? What do alligators feed on? DO they really savor white, male church leaders who are already on the endangered species list?*

The elitist, sexist, and racist components to this paragraph need no additional commentary. What is striking to me, however, is that individuals, in this case Mennonite women, who were victimized and subsequently complained about clergy and religious sexual violence (the prey) and their advocates are transformed by this writer into vicious predators that dine on and thus devour white and male church leaders. Suddenly, church-authenticated preyed upon victims have been ideologically transformed into abusive and dangerous predators.

The anonymous author continues:

> *Do alligators float alone, or do they travel in packs, posing a far greater threat than we have heretofore realized. We need to know. Is it true they lurk in the shade, avoiding the light of day as much as possible. Do they really stay submerged, ready to take a bite out of the next unsuspecting passerby?*

Here, too, we have the imagery of the violent predatory alligator lurking and hiding in order to bite an innocent and unsuspecting bystander or pedestrian out for a stroll. This is most certainly victim blaming in anonymous disguise. In addition this essay casts the known sexual predator into the social role of unsuspecting victim.

In a final set of paragraphs, the writer, who is himself anonymously hidden from accountability, labels by name and geographic location known abuse victims and known victims' advocates. These are the alligators against whom he rails. He ridicules these people's work for truth-telling, justice, safety, and healing by claiming that they are in vigorous competition for the Mennonite Church's *alligator of the year* award.

This mythical award, *the Lorney,* is named for J. Loren Peachey, then editor of the Mennonite Church's official publication, the *Gospel Herald,* who (with other Mennonite editorial board members) made the 1992 editorial decision to publish stories and letters to the editor about sexual abuse and domestic violence inside Mennonite communities.

This entire essay is, therefore, a very venomous – albeit very anonymous – assault on the characters and the truthful witness of abuse victims and abuse victim advocates. It is, therefore, also an assault on truth-telling. It is an assault on bearing faithful and truthful witness.

In my opinion, this kind of hostile, mean-spirited, scurrilous, and anonymous writing makes the religious commons more unsafe for everyone – victims, victims' friends and family members, victim's' advocates, victim's therapists, and every individual called to bear witness to these kinds of events. It deters individuals from coming forth and telling the very stories they need to tell in order to find safety once again in the religious commons.

Whether by intention or not, this essay, therefore, lessened the likelihood that wounded and insecure victims would ever feel safe enough to venture forth in the commons to seek justice and healing. It is, therefore, a narrative of denial, minimization, blame-shifting, victim-vilification, victim-advocate bashing, demonization of victims, and deflection of the compassionate moral impulse. Such an anonymous essay participates in the re-victimization of individuals and entire communities. It, in essence, destroys the very community it *allegedly* seeks to protect.

Thirteenth Letter

Crumbling Temples

We were not seeing the revelation of a shameful aberration but the uncovering of a dimension of the clerical subculture, a complex pattern of thought and behavior that was a deeply embedded aspect of the "institutional church." In other words, this was not some disgusting parasite that had come from the outside and attached itself to the church. This was a dark and destructive force that had its roots deep in the institution itself. What was becoming clear was that the clergy abuse phenomenon consisted of one entity, one problem so to speak with two sides: the aberrant and destructive sexual behavior which targeted children, adolescents and adults and the integration of this behavior in the institutional church.

Thomas P. Doyle[330]

Introductory Comments

There are few sadder phenomena (in business) than a company that thinks its failed product would surely have been successful if only customers could have had its greatness fully explained to them.

Thomas Baker[331]

You and I have had several electronic conversations over the past year about religious institutions and the way some religious leaders or denominational church employees verbally manipulate others as a way of gaining and keeping control or remaining in power. Another possibility is that they do this manipulation to strip another person of the rightful share of human empowerment which is theirs. We both know that the verbal maneuver of character assassination as one way of excluding others from the religious commons is present in Mennonite communities. An additional pattern or cultural form of verbal manipulation as one road to power and institutional control includes saying one relatively positive (not to mention hypocritical) thing to a person's face and a second much more negative and critical thing in the religious commons behind that same person's back. Praising one's body of work to one's face and then denouncing it as flawed to others behind one's back is another form of this. [332] Still another form is seen in the current Roman Catholic hierarchy's management of its abusive priests. In this form, vague and generalized apologies are publicly made in the third person (*Mistakes were made; we are so sorry for the harm Father has done*) while church-employed lawyers clobber and seek to destroy victims and their advocates in hostile courtroom procedures. A fourth form is to isolate victims and their advocates by denial, shunning, and direct attacks.[333] A fifth form is outright blaming of abuse victims for their abuser's behavior or for the church's mismanagement of the abuser. A sixth form is secrecy, outright denial, and lying about matters of factual truth – usually justified internally for the *good of the church.*

In many of his on-line speeches Dominican priest Father Thomas Doyle identifies that his church's hierarchs (and I would add religious academics to his list) who seek to control others *for the good of the church* or *for the good of the institution* are really seeking to protect their own personal stash of status, control, power, and authority. It is his (as well as my own) viewpoint here that these leaders have conflated their personal identities with those of the institution. Protecting the conflated self is justified as protecting the institution. Thus, as Doyle notes, the use of the phrase *for the good of the church* is really a self-protective defensive maneuver that represents the self-serving desire to protect the good (i.e., status, power, authority, and control) of the bishops and other religious elites.[334] One consequence of this form of self-serving manipulation of language is that ultimately it directly protects the perpetrator of malicious speech or malicious action from being held accountable for his or her interpersonally predatory and socially violent behavior.

We might consider these kinds of verbal maneuvers to be equivalent to a sorcerer's sleight-of-hand movements to deceive the eyes of the watchers. What is said about motivation (*for the good of the church* or *for the good of the religious academy*) does not reflect inner and social truths about the real motivation (*for my good*) for behavior. It is, therefore, a lie.

In the Roman Catholic tradition in the United States, the sorcerer has been undressed by American courts and the stacked and marked cards inside his sleeves discovered because of the work of the church's victims and their advocates.[335] While there are likely many reasons for baptized Roman Catholic individuals to leave their faith tradition, it is clear that disgust with the church's hierarchy regarding the active presence and protection of sexual pedophiles and other sexual predators in the priesthood is a statistical factor in a Catholic faithful Exodus movement or in the formation of a Catholic Diaspora.[336]

Most other Christian denominations – including Mennonites – are only now reluctantly beginning to address their own elite community of spiritual sorcerers (those in leadership positions who have abused their followers in the pews in a wide variety of ways) and so many of the marked and stacked cards inside their sleeves, shirt pockets, and cargo pants remain unrevealed.[337] Perpetrator blaming and victim blaming take precedence over full institutional accountability. Very few denominational institutions have willingly chosen to expose and then exorcise their own culpability for hiding perpetrators behind walls of institutional silence, secrecy, and closeted conversations. Few appear capable of full transparency and accountability to the people in the pews – the people who have funded these same institutions for years. I know of no Mennonite congregation, for example, which has invited victims to come forth in a public forum – come forth out of the silence in which they've hidden themselves for self-protection. I know of no external truth and accountability commission that can and will hold denominational church institutions accountable for their complicity with clergy abuse of the laity. I do know, however, of hidden financial settlements designed to protect the church from further publicity and liability in situations where ministers have been recidivist perpetrators.

Former Dominican priest Matthew Fox notes his opinion that the Roman Catholic Church as a denomination is crumbling from the inside out because of its internal moral rot.[338] One factor in his estimation is its mismanagement of the clergy sexual abuse phenomenon. But a second, perhaps more noticeable, aspect of its inner rot, in his opinion, is the authoritarian need of the bishops, cardinals, and popes to maintain control over the people of God who sit in the pews by the use of rigid and out-dated medieval theologies and by the behavioral enactment of authoritarian discipline over ordained and non-ordained individuals who hold divergent opinions about what the Roman Catholic Church is now in a post-modern age and what it should be in the rapidly arriving and unpredictable future. The denunciations and silencing of highly-qualified reformist voices (such as Leonardo Boff of Brazil, Hans Kung of Germany, or Charles Curran and Margaret Farley of the United States) trouble Fox just as they do many other Roman Catholic intellectuals and people in the pews.

I have seen variations of these kinds of behavior vis-à-vis the denominational church's management of a wide variety of sexual abuse issues inside Mennonite religious institutions. You have seen it inside the militarism-peace building work which you do in the context of your Mennonite heritage and pacifism beliefs. Because the Mennonite Church is such a small denomination and many of its institutions are small, these kinds of hypocritical and overtly deceitful behaviors occur in the face-to-face interfaces of colleagues and people we have seen as friends. Thus the betrayal factor is huge. Our Mennonite cultural ways of silencing reformist or non-majority voices have included (1) hypocritical back-stabbing behavior, (2) discouraging, preventing, and terminating employment, (3) silencing and shunning, (4) character assassination and (5) professional or personal disparagement. In my opinion, as a denomination, we are guided more by our needs for comfort in a uniform community than by our needs for robust and open discussion of complex issues (such as sexual violence or the denominational status of sexual minorities or the interface of our pacifism with American capitalism and militarism) which need such discussion.

One of the things I would note, in general, about this kind of duplicitous and two-faced institutional behavior is that it either vitiates (or prohibits entirely) vital and often needed conversations in which diverse opinions are actively sought out and valued. When I learn, for example, that I can't trust what a powerful academic colleague says to me to my face because of what others tell me he is saying about me behind my back, my overall style is to grow more cautious in what I say inside our inevitable or necessary encounters. Once it grows clear to me that I can't trust someone's words and behavior, then I begin to protect my own inner soft-self in every encounter with that person. Over time my self-protective persona shapes all encounters with the person I no longer trust. Our conversations grow increasingly superficial and are, therefore, no longer capable of productive change or collaborative intellectual intimacy. They are no longer capable of producing synergy and shared creativity. This is, I believe a huge factor in what White above calls institutional implosion.

A lively search for truth or for a better way of approaching peace building activities together is, in this manner, tamed, imprisoned inside mistrust and, consequently, strange mutations of behavior occur. The spiritual damages as well as the emotional damages are huge. Most of us, for example, do not want to spend time working with individuals we have learned are not trustworthy or who lack integrity. We do not want to spend time with people who say nasty things about us and our work to others. We learn to shield our inner soft-self within a façade of collegiality and the language of religious "brotherhood" where, in reality, there is no intellectual intimacy, collegiality, and/or honor. This is the very ordinary birthplace of individual and institutional hypocrisy.

I know in my own situation when these kinds of betrayals occur, I retreat into formal civility. I have made a personal commitment to myself not to retaliate in kind within these situations – not because I am so pure but because vengeance-filled retaliations are so futile in accomplishing goals I may want to achieve. If I know, therefore, for certain that someone, behind my back, is trashing my character, is negatively critical of the work I do, continuously judges the quality of my life, or secretively seeks to get me fired from my position as a church employee without informing me about their critique, then I simply do one of two things: I avoid as many encounters with that individual as possible and if avoidance doesn't work, will retreat into watchful formal diplomatic civility. There will be no synergy in this relationship because there can be none.

But it is important to note that I will also engage in self-protective behaviors. Like you, I believe in non-lethal self-defense. I do not believe that institution-inflicted suffering is redemptive.

In the ninth letter I talked about my personal decisions not to piss with skunks. The greater difficulty arises when we are betrayed by friends and by colleagues we once trusted. Here, I think we must get brave and we must confront the other with what we know. We need to open a doorway to engage each other in honest conversations. Usually, at the end of such an effort, either the intimacy of the prior relationship has been restored, or we know that the relationship is irretrievably altered and cannot be repaired.

The real tricky aspects of these kinds of life betrayal experiences lie in our inner world. We need to be able to protect ourselves without betraying our own ideals about making peace in the world. In one of his books, clinical psychologist and Buddhist spiritual teacher Jack Kornfield talks about monastic living and the difficulties that arise when individuals within the same community cannot trust each other.[339] He recognizes, as do I, that we may need to quarantine ourselves from relationships with individuals which are toxic to us. But he also urges his readers to avoid hating or denigrating or revenging the self on the other. I suppose this is what Christianity declares as the spirituality of returning good behavior towards others whose untrustworthy behavior has harmed us, belittled us, or denigrated us in harmful ways.

In the years of my maturity I have come to realize that I don't control and can't control the behavior or motives of others. In fact, even if I could do this, I don't want to. I do, however, have at least a modicum of control over my own behavior. This means, therefore, that I must pay attention, simultaneously, to the outer world around me and the inner world inside me. I must be making consciously-chosen responses rather than automatic ones. Learning to live mindfully in the present moment (facing the challenges of this moment and that moment as they occur) is, I think, a life-long skill development challenge. But once we realize that the past is truly past and that the future is not yet here, then we have no realistic alternative in terms of our choices of behavior but to live mindfully in the present moment. Sometimes, at least in my experience, this is easier said than done. But it remains a working goal for me in my daily life.

One attitude that is so clearly present in my own personality is the reality that while I may be actively abused by others, I will never give my consent to their abuse. I may not be able to stop it but I can stop giving my implicit or explicit consent for the abuse to continue. I have choices. I can break off the relationship. I can confront the abuser in the hopes that we can rebuild trust. I can stay in proximity when we must work together but practice aloof civility in all encounters. Each of these choices has consequences in the emotional realm of life, in the spiritual realm of life and, I believe, in the physical and energetic body as well. Thus, these choices should never be casual ones. We need to think about these issues and be intentional in our responses to being betrayed or to being abused.

To understand these dynamics, I have, therefore, been reading and re-reading organizational management literature. For these complex issues are more than just personal issues. They affect and infect entire organizations. This reality is most visible to me in various denominational churches and their ongoing mismanagement of clergy sexual abuse situations. By maintaining institutionalized cultures of secrecy and denial and by actively engaging in cover-up behaviors, religious organizations undercut their spiritual mission in the world. This phenomenon is probably equally or even more visible to you because the work you do for peace by working directly with military institutions is both highly innovative and very unconventional in terms of Mennonite ideology and praxis regarding militarism. Thus, your work can be ideologically judged by others as inappropriate behavior for an Anabaptist-Mennonite woman.

As I write, I also think (vis-à-vis your written and consulting work) that we should not underestimate the peer jealousy factor. Some of the hostile behavior which you describe inside professional encounters in your career may have the underlying motive of personal or professional jealousy. Undercutting your work and putting you in your place behind your back function, therefore, as underhanded means of subverting your work in the service of narcissistic jealousy. Learning how to rise above these kinds of situations – refusing to play tit for tat so to speak – takes deliberate thought and conscious spiritual work. Refusing to make enemies where enemies already exist is a delicate ballet of inner and outer spiritual work in the world.

Parenthetically, we see these same kinds of dysfunctional systemic organizational behavior whenever entire denominations are confronted by sexual minorities who are asking for full inclusion in the religious life and the spiritual teachings of these denominations. The full range of people who belong at this table of conversation is simply not happening. The overt denominational statement may be that all are welcome at the Christian table and then a huge *but* (sometimes verbal and sometimes behavioral) is added. This includes the exclusion of individuals from the needed conversation about inclusion on the basis of their sexual orientation, their skin color, their gender, their economic status, their family status, or many other sociological variables we human beings use to exclude others in xenophobic reactions to human differences.

Incestuous Institutions

Ultimately the incestuous institution collapses inward upon itself and implodes.

William F. White[340]

In their concluding paragraphs about treatment processes for clergy and religious leader sexual misconduct perpetrators, Wells, Wells, and Earle[341] discuss organizational theory and management issues. Drawing on earlier published work by William F. White, they describe the way in which dysfunctional institutions or organizational systems close ranks and eventually become claustrophobic.

I want to quote several paragraphs because they can be used to illuminate denominational rank-closing when it comes to clergy and religious leader sexual misconduct – and in this paragraph I am using these two words to describe acts of consenting adultery as well as acts of sexual harassment and other forms of non-consenting sexual abuse such as rape. These words, it seems to me, can also be applied to current Mennonite Church US debates about full inclusion for sexual minorities.

There are good reasons why many organizations have rules against nepotism and social fraternizing that involves sexualized behavior. The best reason is that such behaviors are inherently disordering to the social well-being of the whole. Pillow conversations subvert the emotional neutrality of the work milieu by privileging sexually intimate conversations over the much more emotionally neutral and therefore work-productive conversations that most institutional employers expect among their employees and subordinates.

William White (1986) suggests that certain organizations predispose their employees to what he calls "organizational incest." What precedes the violation of sexual boundaries in his model is a merging process within the institution. The views and values of staff become increasingly homogeneous. Dissenters are expelled. As the staff draws yet closer together, they tend to socialize exclusively within the institution since "no one understands." The boundary between work and social life becomes less and less distinct. Staff members think about work constantly. They become their jobs.

At the same time, their jobs leave them emotionally starved. Institutions predisposed to institutional incest place intense stress upon their employees while providing little support. Generally there are strong "no-talk" rules about sexuality, although many other boundaries have been broken. The final step for the isolated, deeply depleted, rigidified players in such a system is a sexual violation of institutional boundaries. For example, the CEO sleeps with a department manager. In White's model, even if professional ethics are not involved, the dual relationship catalytically disrupts the organization by focusing and concentrating simmering feelings of resentment, alienation or deprivation among others. Ultimately, the incestuous institution collapses inward upon itself and implodes.[342]

White's assessment is very similar to the assessment of Kramer and Alstad[343] in their discussion of guru abuses inside Eastern philosophies and religions. When the guru chooses to become sexually active with his disciples or students, the learning milieu is deeply disrupted and the spiritual or metaphysical learning process is disrupted for the entire community. Not only the sexually used student has been violated, the underlying principles of learning and relating for the entire community have been violated. In a certain sense, therefore, the entire community is the recipient of the religious leader's acts of violation – knowingly or not.

This is as true for Christian churches, in my opinion, as it is for Eastern meditation centers, Zen teaching centers, and ashrams. The individual selected by a sexual misconduct perpetrator as the focus of his erotic attention or the target of his abusive behavior is directly affected. But so is everyone else who lives in proximity to these sexually exploitive events and their narrative story – even if that is a more indirect and subtle form of abuse and betrayal of the community's trust.

If we think in a systems model we find (*at a minimum*) these recipients of harm.

1. The specific individual targeted by the religious professional for acts of adultery, sexual harassment, sexual abuse, or sexual violence
2. The directly victimized individual's family and friendship network
3. The perpetrator
4. The perpetrator's family and friendship network
5. Members of adjudicatory committees and processes and their family and friendship network
6. Members of police or legal investigatory networks if there has been a criminal aspect to the misconduct
7. Advocates for transparency, truth-telling, and healing
8. Members of the congregation or extended institutional community in which the misconduct or abuse happened

What we see, therefore, is an ever expanding network or circles of institutionally noxious and incestuous influence. In situations of institutional sexual misconduct and institutional cover-up behaviors, John Donne's wisdom becomes immediately self-evident.[344] No individual who is touched in any way by his or her proximity to these narratives can become a self-sufficient island – untouched by the sordid and toxic nature of the narrative. The very presence of a sexually abusive narrative means that everyone – close in and on the margins – is going to be called to account for their knowledge and their participation in the unfolding of the narrative.

In addition what we also see are ever expanding circles of complicity and collusion. As soon as one becomes aware of these sexual misconduct narratives – whether by company gossip or by criminal justice proceedings – we are placed in the position of needing to make decisions about how we will hear and then exegete these stories. Will we believe the accusations or will we deny their validity? Whether we believe or disbelieve the accusations, our personal moral decision-making is called first to attention and secondarily into accountability.

We will either choose to act or we will choose to refuse to act. Either of these choices carries a moral weight in our own inner lives and in our interpersonal social lives. Whatever we decide to do or we refuse to do, we will carry this legacy of moral decision-making and moral choicefulness with us into our continuing life. Walking across this personal bridge into the future, we will be forever shaped by what we have chosen to do or not to do with what we know or intuit to be factual truth.

Our moral decisions, day-by-day, affect the moral and spiritual formation of our ongoing lives. They shape our personalities. How we choose to respond, situation-by-situation, to the violation and suffering of others engages us daily in a process of spiritual and moral formation. Choosing to be perpetrators of violence; choosing to support perpetrators of violence against their victims; choosing to support the victims of violation; choosing to remain unengaged: each of these choices has direct social, emotional, cognitive, and spiritual consequences in our own lives.

When I think about corrupted religious institutions, there are several components to the corruption. One factor is that of an individual or individuals who violate the community's standards for living in the commons. These individuals may violate ordinary ethical standards for conducting financial transactions. They may violate communal practices for fair, honorable, and just treatment of others. They may violate communal standards for moral and just sexual practices. In general, in my observations of these realities, abusive interpersonal and social patterns often emerge, as it were, in one breath. This is particularly true for individuals in leadership positions who engage in sexual misconduct. It is not uncommon, for example, for sexual misconduct and financial misconduct to coincide in any given episode of individual or community betrayal. It is not uncommon for institutional bullying behavior towards subordinates to accompany administrative sexual and financial misconduct.[345]

As we have corresponded, it remains my opinion that the cultural forms – what we might call roots and rootlets – support personal behaviors. In turn, personal misconduct behaviors water and nourish these pre-existing cultural roots and rootlets of misconduct.

I want to take a short detour for a moment. One example of what I am trying to describe is the cultural presence of disaffiliated and often socially ostracized American children who take guns to school and take down their fellow students and teachers – as, for example, at Columbine or Sandy Hook. The possibility of copycat killings is always an immediate to intermediate danger for children and teachers in other schools. So, we have a cultural form in the United States called school killings and we have had individual manifestations of the form in multiple schoolyards across the nation's 50 states. If there were no cultural form, I hypothesize, there would be no replications. But if there were no manifestations, there would be no cultural form.

Such a discrete and statistically rare form of violence such as schoolyard shootings more easily demonstrates the issue of form and manifestation than the ubiquitous reality of one individual's choice to betray another by hypocritical behaviors; of one group's xenophobic decisions to exclude others in the name of its god; or one groups' internally incestuous management practices regarding the protection of employees' criminally malfeasant actions.

Perpetrators and institutional structures that protect abusers of any kind by providing cover for their actions may practice covert or overt retaliations against individuals who protest such behavior. Informed knowledge that is also principled, moral, and ethical inside corrupted institutions – what White calls incestuous institutions - usually yields negative institutional behaviors that would ordinarily demand transparency and truth-telling. Unfortunately such principled and moral behavior is quite rare.[346] It is quite common in morally or religiously or spiritually corrupt institutions that principled individuals are subjected to innuendo and rumor campaigns or even to economic reprisals as abusive individuals and their protectors seek to protect their own careers and reputations by any means possible.

Institutional Hypocrisy

The more I have pondered these issues of sexual abuse and the correlated issues of abusive cover-up behaviors in institutions, the more I have pondered issues of transparency and discretion, of truth-telling and diplomacy. Not every sexual act, for example, needs to be announced in the commons. I know of no healthy adult or healthy congregation which would want a weekly announcement about the number and kinds of their pastor's sexual acts in the week between Sundays. Most healthy adult people, in my estimation, don't want to know about the specific sexual actions of other people. There is an internal cognitive or psychological or emotional boundary that says loudly and clearly, *that is none of my business.* It is my studied opinion that healthy adults actively avoid the pornographic eye. They avoid becoming voyeurs of other's sexual acts.

Recently, for example, I've become aware of my irritation with public media and its graphic descriptions of sexual crimes. Recently, I found myself talking with one of my good male friends, saying: *I resent being made into a voyeur.* I personally was fascinated by this spontaneous comment as I heard myself saying it to my friend. In my early thirties I was part of the first group of physicians, nurses, psychologists and other clinicians taught to do sexual histories with our clients. In the service of my clients' health, I never felt like a voyeur.

Yet, by their criminal actions, sexual violence perpetrators make all of us into voyeurs. To be helpful to the individuals they victimized we need to hear the stories of perverted sexual behavior. Judith Herman, in one of her lectures or published articles was correct, I think. In our work with the victims of violation, the perpetrator is the third party in our consulting rooms. S/he is always present inside the narratives of those individuals we seek to help. We must, of necessity, deal with his/her ghostly presence. We must also protect our clients and ourselves from introjecting his perverted sexuality into our own consciousness.

It is a quite common phenomenon to hear clinicians and plaintiff's lawyers say, *I felt like I needed a shower after my client left the office.* Another phrase one often hears among professionals is this: *When I listened to my client, I felt like I was wading in a cesspool. The abuse s/he suffered was so toxic.* It was not the client's experience of violation which troubled these helpers; it was the nature and the content of the act of violation by the perpetrator. Violent sexual encounters, to be quite precise, are disturbing when they are experienced. They are often equally disturbing inside their subsequent narration by someone seeking help. The issue, however, is not the client's narrative of her experiences. The issue is the content or nature of the sexual violation itself.

I have pondered this reality in my own life. It is not the client's story and the client's pain that created a sense of the need to distance myself from his or her story. It is this introjected and thus internally experienced presence of the perpetrator and his or her perverted imagination and violent behavior which makes us all into voyeurs.

A nosy intrusiveness into the marital and sexual lives of ministers and their partners or spouses would rightfully be seen as prurient and inappropriate. What is appropriate conversation between lovers and close friends is as often as not a form of inappropriate conversation between strangers. What is appropriate in private conversations and personal self-revelations with friends can be very inappropriate inside the collective commons. What conversationally can be both appropriate and necessary in a therapist's office may be highly inappropriate in a church foyer.

Yet, when a priest or minister sexually assaults a member of his or her congregation, details of that abuse will take over the emotional and spiritual space of the congregation. Every individual will be touched by this narrative and need to make decisions about how to hear its sexual content. Every individual will be called, therefore, into the circle of information that makes the abuser's actions offensive to the ear and to the healthy personalities of the whole.

Thus, when sexual misconduct or sexual abuse occurs inside the boundaries of the religious institution or work environment, every employee or every customer becomes an inadvertent witness to misbehavior. This is so because the misbehavior (if condoned by and then hidden by) the institution makes everyone complicit. It makes everyone into a voyeur. That which is culturally seen as unacceptable, prurient and private adult behavior now becomes public. My personal sense of this is that healthy and mature adults are repelled by this behavior. Thus, there is a social tendency to the bystander effect of not paying attention and not responding to another's obvious suffering.[347]

A core issue in sexual misconduct and in the cover-up activities of institutions vis-à-vis a religious professional's sexual misconduct, therefore, appears to be the issue of hypocrisy. Several different web-based dictionaries define hypocrisy in slightly different ways. Taken together, the definitions provide us with a window into the questions of truth and accountability. Hypocrisy is, therefore:

1. *A practice of professing or claiming to have moral standards or beliefs to which one's own behavior does not conform*[348]
2. *Behavior of people who do things they tell other people not to do; behavior that does not agree with what someone claims to believe and/or feel*[349]
3. *Feigning to be what one is not or to believe what one does not believe*[350]
4. *Pretending to have virtues, moral or religious beliefs, principles, etc., that he or she does not actually have*[351]

It well may be that the central organizing taproot of clericalism in the context of clergy sexual misconduct is our quite human proclivity to practice hypocrisy.

There may be a similar root when individuals who are sexually closeted in their same-gender sexual orientation lead the denominational charge to purge the denomination of individuals who are out of the closet.

Concluding Remarks

The temples of Tikal,[352] Chichen Itza,[353] Machu Picchu[354] or Teotihuacan[355] did not crumble, I am certain, in a day. The worldviews they represented lasted many centuries. It is likely that one can find remnants of that ancient worldview – now assimilated into the religious centers and temples which succeeded their spiritual and political teachings. But the reality is sobering: no one holds community worship events in these temples in 2015. It may be that shamans and sorcerers gather there – on the days of the solstices or the nights of the full moons. But in terms of shaping a collective culture and shaping an individual soul, these ancient temples and centers of sacrifices to their gods are dead. Other temples have replaced these temples. Thus these slowly disintegrating and crumbling buildings tell us only about their past – not the present or future. The buildings have become archeological ruins to be studied and interpreted rather than vital centers of living worship and community. No longer do their priests preside over the spiritual and temporal lives of the people. Other priests in other temples have replaced these ancient temple's priests. Other rulers (than the rulers who once walked here) have moved into positions of power. Other dynasties of power have replaced these ancient dynasties.

I am of the opinion that institutionalized Christianity is slowly crumbling in its denominational or institutional forms inside a post-modern and highly techno-logical society. The surveys of neutral organizations point towards this reality.[356] It is likely that remnants of denominational Christianity will linger centuries more. However, if its central moral and spiritual core is now dead, its influence on the shaping of human consciousness and human souls will continue to decline.

You and I both know many Mennonite women who have exited the denomi-national Mennonite Church because of sexual abuse. We both know members of various sexual minorities who have also walked away without looking back. We both know people who have left because they were not spiritually nurtured by exclusionary, puritanical church governance policies and theological scrupulos-ity. No one is counting how many have already left the religious commons of the Mennonite Church and no one seems to care. We know, however, that when mothers and fathers leave, they take their children with them. We know that when the young leave, they take the future with them.

If we look back to the explosive formations of our spiritual ancestors in the Anabaptist Reformation, what we see is that this spiritual movement (with its implicit democracy) spread like wildfire and became so threatening that secular princes and religious princes joined forces to push it back into obscu-rity. Our ancestors were pursued by Roman Catholic *and* Protestant authorities. Consequently, many of us do not see ourselves as Protestants – preferring to use the name Anabaptist. The number of martyrs is probably unaccounted for because of the nature of that era's torture and slaughter. It is striking to me that a wildfire of political and religious violence against our ancestors was needed to combat the wildfire of spiritual freedom. This is not unlike the original Jesus movement.

Peasants and members of the minor nobility sensed something vital and alive in this migratory history of fleeing and witnessing. They cast their votes, there-fore, for a participatory form of spirituality that defied the institutional structures around them. They were known, at least initially, for their love for each other – sharing life and the risks of faith on a daily basis. Orthopraxis and orthodoxy were held in a certain tension.

As the centuries unfolded, however, we both know that schism piled upon schism and these multiple schisms about theological words replaced embodied acts of love. Purity codes and theological orthodoxy replaced the practice of a communal democracy based on need. In a very real sense in the past two hundred years of Mennonite life in the Americas, orthodoxy has replaced orthopraxis. In short, word has replaced deed as the theological and sociological marker of belonging.

As a result of these letters between us, I have come to the conclusion that when a religious organization becomes more concerned about status, control, power, theological agreements, sociological unity, authority, behavioral purity, and orthodox words than about embodied and compassionate love of the neighbor, justice in situations of injustice, spontaneous acts of charity and helpfulness towards the vulnerable, and mutual compassion for each other's humanity in the face of great personal and social differences, it has already crumbled on the inside. What remains is the white-washed face of the tomb where dead religions now rest.

When I think about these intersecting realities, which at a cognitive level means I am looking at discrete jigsaw puzzle pieces instead of one completed large puzzle, I cannot figure out why the following realities seem to emerge like joined Siamese sextuplets out of the cultural womb which surrounds us all: (1) multiple forms of clergy and religious leader abusiveness towards each other and towards the laity, (2) issues of institutional financial corruption; 3) interior moral rot, (4) the proliferation of sexual minority xenophobia, (5) an all-too-human proclivity to betray one another in the name of the Gods/orthodoxy and (6) conservative political beliefs about the essential needs for militarism and other forms of social aggression and violence to protect our particular view of our particular national religion – expressed in pious declarations by politicians of all stripes that this nation's political polity is particularly blessed by the Gods.

I just know that in each of these, there is an underlying foundation of patriarchal authoritarianism and moral hypocrisy about what *we* do accompanied by rigorous purity codes and punctilious scrupulosity about *what other people* should do. All too often in today's denominations there is a willingness to attack, betray and exclude others in the so-called name of theological orthodoxy, doctrinal purity, and authoritarian intents to control. A demand to be served has replaced the scriptural mandate to serve. Judgmental attitudes have replaced hospitality and purity concerns have replaced compassionate love. Protection of institutions takes priority over protecting the vulnerable human beings who live inside of them.

Ruth E. Krall

Fourteenth Letter

Managing Our Wounds

They scandalized my name

Paul Robeson[357]

Introduction

In several of our back and forth electronic letters, we have talked about physical, spiritual, and emotional fatigue and about the sense that as advocates for peace and justice our human bodies carry deep and enduring stress wounds caused by the anti-violence work we have been doing. There is a phrase which I heard often in the evangelistic revival meetings of my youth. These circuit-riding Mennonite evangelists, imported into my Mennonite childhood from distant states, urged their Christian audiences to *burn out for Christ.* I was a little kid (just on the verge of adolescence) and had no idea what they meant. Perhaps I still don't.

As a clinician who worked with very sick, emotionally traumatized, and hospitalized people for the first twenty years of my professional life, I have a very different sense of the phrase, *burned out* than I think those roaming, traveling evangelists did. As I matured professionally and as I learned about the toll emotional, psychological, physical, and spiritual stress took on the human body, I came to distrust this evangelistic admonition as an accurate or even desirable descriptor of spiritual faithfulness to the Jesus path. The more I learned about human violence, trauma, and stress, the more I believed that these human realities were extraordinarily harmful to the human body, the human personality, the human spirit, *and* to the human commons.

There is a brand new book about trauma research and trauma treatment on the market as of September, 2014.[358] It is worth reading. Since he became a psychiatrist many years ago, Harvard physician, and trauma researcher Bessel van der Kolk[359] has been a student of the human body's (most particularly the brain's) response to experienced trauma. This popularly-written book makes visible and understandable the complexities of the human mind and the human body as it responds to experienced violation and traumatic events. Each chapter has an extensive bibliography of research resources so that professional clinicians can trace the research studies which he has popularized in his chapters. This book supplements an earlier edited volume which was written for psychiatrists and other mental health practitioners.[360] Individuals who work with traumatized individuals in a wide variety of settings can benefit from owning and consulting with both books.

A Bit of History: Enduring Space

> The phrase *Enduring Space represents the present moment in time as it is experienced in an individual's human consciousness. It is in this present moment when individuals and their surrounding cultures simultaneously create and walk a living bridge from the past into the future. Thus, it is only in each present moment when individual and cultural transformation can take place.*[361]

The concept of an enduring space has been in my own awareness and thinking for almost 20 years. The phrase made its appearance in my own consciousness long before President George W. Bush declared war in the name of *enduring freedom*. The potentialities of each present moment succeeding each present moment are a key element of mindfulness.[362] Paying attention to the is-ness of the now present moment frees each one of us to access and make use of the wide open potentialities for healing in each present moment.

First Vision

Circa 1995-1996 I was at the still point during a time of focused meditation when the words and an initial intuition of what the words meant made their appearance in my psyche. Early on I envisioned *enduring space* as an actual space, a feminist place devoted to healing female healers and female peace-workers – women who are often energetically and emotionally wounded by the work they do in helping severely victimized and traumatized others. In my journals and in my night dreams, I created physical spaces devoted to healing the healers – feminist retreat spaces which had simple cabins, ready access to medical care, psychotherapists and body workers, and communal rooms with deep fire pits for healing liturgical work. I envisioned trails in a forest that contained simple lean to shelters for private meditation furnished with spiritual icons from the world's religious wisdom traditions.

I envisioned still pools of healing water. I envisioned a simple non-dogmatic and multi-faith chapel with flowing stained glass windows and simple chairs and cushions which one could use in individual and collective meditation times. I dreamed about creating healing liturgies for communities of feminist women.

But, in the middle of all of this day-dreaming, I was also a realist. I had visited a similarly-motivated space in the 1970's – carved out of the Sonoran Desert. The two lesbian feminist women who owned this space shared with me their original dream for the space and they also told me that some women who utilized the space and their services as healing women were not respectful of the desert landscape and trashed it. Some of these women also disrespected the simple physical shelters which housed them by stealing things such as towels and sheets or by breaking things such as windows, lamps, and tables – abusing the courtesy of their hosts *and* the land. They told me that this was the hardest work they had ever done as women and that this reality of their clients' disrespect for their land and their work was a factor in their own burn-out as visionary, healing, feminist women. They were, they told me, considering the reality that this was much needed work, but said that they were likely to close this ranch as an open resource for women needing healing from the earth itself. I am not certain when they closed *Healing Space* but this wonderful desert ranch nestled up against the Rincon Mountains is no longer in existence as a healing retreat space for feminist women in need of a place for taking time out from their work and their activism. *Healing Space* did not, therefore, endure.

In Henri Nouwen's wonderful book, *The Wounded Healer*,[363] he retells an ancient Jewish story in which a religious seeker asks the Prophet Elijah about how he can find the Messiah. Elijah tells him that he will find the Messiah sitting at Jerusalem's main gate. The man replies, "There are so many men sitting at the gate, how will I know which is the Messiah?" Elijah replies that the Messiah is the one who constantly unbinds, treats, and re-binds his many wounds, one at a time. He does this in order that he can continue to be accessible and available to others who seek healing for their own wounds. Nouwen's retelling of this ancient Jewish story captured my attention the first time I read it and the story has guided me for many years.

The trauma of experienced or witnessed violence wounds the body, psyche, and spirit of all who are touched by it: the primary victims, the witnesses to victimization, the first responders, the crisis intervention teams, the healers, and the mop-up crews. Violence also wounds, perhaps most dangerously, those who perpetrate acts of violence. Perpetrators of violence not only de-humanize their victims: they de-humanize themselves as well. In South African Bishop Desmond Tutu's words, the reconciling and healing process after acts of personal and systemic violence and victimization must include *re-humanization* for both parties to the cultural rituals of violent victimization.

Re-humanization, in my opinion, requires the supportive presence of compassionate and knowledgeable healers and helpers – people who know how to stay present and to unbind, treat, and rebind their own wounds without asking the victims of violence to take care of their healers. Re-humanization allows victims, working gently to heal their own wounds, to rebuild their lives. Re-humanization also requires the moral and spiritual stamina of entire communities as they seek to hold people accountable for their acts of abuse and victimization.

This is, of course, the genius of the South African experiment with truth and reconciliation. There could be no political amnesty for Apartheid's victimizers without their need to provide the commons with a full and truthful accounting of what they did. Political forgiveness was not, therefore, gratuitous. The nation's offer of forgiveness and political amnesty demanded accountability. That which had been done in secret or at night was brought into daylight and the full light of truth. Truth-telling by the perpetrators of violence and violation, however incomplete and/or self-serving it may have been, was, therefore, recognized as essential for individual healing and for the nation's healing.

Compassion Fatigue

One clinical term for this state of helper-woundedness (among those who deliberately and repeatedly put themselves in proximity to violence and its after-images in the human psyche or spirit in order to bear witness to it and to help its victims) is *compassion fatigue. Other* terms include *secondary post-traumatic stress disorder* and *traumatic counter-transference.* In essence, those who choose to bear witness as victim advocates, therapists, health care workers, volunteers, refugee camp staff, priests, ministers, shamans, and members of religious orders not only need to learn how to help others care for their post-violence wounds. They must simultaneously learn to help and care for their own wounds as well. If the healers, et al., are to survive as whole and healing persons, they must first recognize that they are at high risk for being emotionally overwhelmed and psychologically and emotionally distressed. In terms of witnessing religious institution violations, they will inevitably confront internal cognitive dissonance and spiritual wounding as well. The healers and victim advocates must, therefore, learn to manage and care for their own personal wounds even as they attend to the wounds of others.

I see compassion fatigue or traumatic counter-transference as a psychological, emotional, physical, and spiritual challenge for all helpers, victim advocates, and witnesses who work with sexually abused clients in the aftermath of their violence-filled life experiences. One reason for this is the nature of these victims' violence-filled life narratives. If these victimized individuals are to survive with their own authentic self and personal integrity intact, they must learn how to manage and care for their own appalled or indignant moral stress and aroused or enraged physical distress at the suffering they witness or encounter in the lives of victimized and violated others. This inevitably means re-visiting their memories of abuse and violation. Those who seek to help them must, therefore know how to listen and to be supportive.

If the healers cannot do this very necessary work of tending to their own woundedness, they will eventually become part of the problem they initially sought to help others solve. I believe, therefore, that people doing human violence prevention work, crisis intervention work, and healing work need periodic time outs. Those *bearing witness* need a place to learn and to actively practice self-care. They need to learn how to shelter and care for their inner spirit – what we might call their soul. They need safe places of retreat – retreat which may be denied the victims they seek to help. They will likely need to resolve massive elements of cognitive dissonance on a daily basis. They too, often need a healer or another compassionate witness to be present with them in the personal *dark nights of the soul* that their violence-challenging encounters and violence-healing work create.

Self-care is essential: it is not narcissism; it is not selfishness

For most of my professional life – certainly after I began a prolonged and serious study of human encounters with traumatic life events – I have believed that anti-violence workers, healers, and peace activists must learn that they too can be, and frequently are, wounded by the stories of human trauma which they encounter in the course of their work. By being a student of their own wounds, they can, I believe, learn about the wounds of others. I think of this psychic-physical reality as a Mobius-strip.[364] In their real-life encounters with people needing help, the helpers are drawn into relationships and narratives where the potential is always present that each person inside the healing relationship will be forever changed. Thus, there is no edge between the wounds of the healers and the wounds of those whom the healers help. There is, in essence, one trauma wound with many manifestations.[365]

That said, it is, however, the healer's responsibility to manage his or her own wounds in such a way that the primary victim of trauma is freed to learn how to manage his or her own life. This is not a mutual relationship in the sense of personal friendships. The clinical helper must maintain two boundaries. First, there is the boundary between the clinician and the client. The clinician's primary role or task is to provide care and help to the other. The reverse is not true. Secondly, however, there is the equally important need for the therapist or clinician, by means of self-care, to maintain the inner and external professional boundaries which allow him or her to focus attention on the needs of the client. This involves knowing when one cannot be helpful to another individual and making appropriate referrals to other clinicians.

This latter aspect involves the whole issue of supervision. None of us should work with traumatized individuals without having a backup community of support. To stay whole and diligently cognizant of our personal stash of human woundedness, we need a community of people – a trustworthy community where we can be ourselves in all of our complexity. When we choose to work with the survivors of violence and victimization, this becomes essential. We need safe and confidential spaces for debriefing and for support. We have talked around this issue of needing to detoxify, in one way or another, the large stash of others' violation stories which we carry inside our own body-minds. In Nouwen's frame of reference, supervision and a knowledgeable and supportive community allow us to detoxify the violence hologram in our own psyches by carefully examining it and by continually moving into the present moment.

This Mobius-strip as a model reminds me that I am not separate from the people whom I seek to serve as their helper. What affects them most deeply will, in turn, in some way or another affect me. I cannot, therefore, isolate myself from their experience of post-violation trauma and be helpful to the traumatized person. In several of these letters I have commented that we must learn, over time, how to look the evil of violence and violation in the face and not be destroyed. This is particularly true as we learn, as women, how to listen to the stories of sexual violence in the lives of other women and their children.

Somewhere psychiatrist Judith Herman wrote or lectured that just when she thinks she has heard every possible variation of violent victimization, a client tells her a story which is new in its levels of violence and degradation. I have an older clinician friend, now semi-retired, who has worked with rape, incest, and war trauma victims for most of her career. She tells me that even now, there are some clients' stories which are so vicious and trauma-filled that they deeply affect her. Her years of training and work in this field do not protect her. It is then, she tells me, that she closes her office door when they leave and cries for them and for the anguish of their story. She has learned, she tells me, that she must leave more space than ten minutes between clients so that she can continue to stay present to each client as they arrive in her office. She has learned, just as I have learned, that clinical compassion must be managed so that we do not burden successive clients with the unresolved emotional or spiritual processes of righteous anger and compassionate grief which we are carrying from a preceding client's story.

In my own hours of therapy as his client, physician Emmett Miller has been very helpful to me by teaching me practical skills in the use of my imagination, my ability to draw upon the resources of my human life – in total – as a way to proceed so that I do not become ill and so that I do not become overwhelmed by the tragedies of life that are all around me. Or, perhaps even worse, so that I do not become callous in the face of others' suffering. The principle here, I have come to call resiliency. By resiliency, I mean the ability to repeatedly enter, work within, and then leave behind, if only for a few healing time-out moments, the enchanted forest of violence and trauma.[366]

We healers and peace-workers must each of us individually and all of us collectively find our own way to emotional stability, physical health, spiritual healing and joy in the middle of the work we do. I know stories of women who clog, men who do strenuous day hikes, individuals who dive into the ocean's depths, people who are fanatical about sports teams, and still others whose hobbies such as the meticulous repair of antique pens, remove them from the stress of the work they do on behalf of others. Pursuing their own avocational interests intently (even if for only short breaks of time) they actively counterbalance the work they do in a professional world filled with trauma stories.

Giving the mind-body sufficient rest breaks from its encounters with stress and trauma is essential to its internal resiliency, healing, and ability, over time, to stay emotionally, psychologically, socially, and spiritually balanced. Emmett told me the story of one man he knew who collected small shells from the ocean's beaches. He kept a small jar of these shells in his office drawer and when highly stressed, would take a shell out of the jar and spend a few moments remembering the day on the beach when he found the shell. He would then spend a few more moments visualizing the beach and sensing, in memory and imagination, his body walking along the pounding surf. Returning to the present moment, his body-mind was refreshed and ready to move on into more work.

I sometimes choose to read inspirational biographies – about lives filled with meaning and blessing, for example, those of Hank Aaron or Bishop Tutu. At other times I dip into women's poetry, for example, Adrienne Rich or Mary Oliver. I walk in a local cactus forest and note the seasonal changes of a wide variety of plant species. I play with photography. These days I am learning how to "do" and to "process" an active and growing Soul Collage ® collection. I maintain an active correspondence with several of my college classmates – women who have become part of my friend-family – where we trade jokes, recipes, gossip, and reflections on life.

As you know, I also deliberately cultivate the inner life of silence and the inner life of imagery as a route to managing my personal distress at the violence of our culture as it is experienced by women and their children. This has been Emmett Miller's greatest gift to me as *my* helper. In the fifteen years since I exited his practice as a client, I return repeatedly to the lessons learned in his office – lessons about meditation, lessons about play, lessons about joy, lessons about deliberate breath, lessons about time out and deep relaxation, and lessons about activating healing imagery.

You and I have talked, for example, about his clinical example of the white fuzz- embedded seed heads of a dandelion as a visual image. As small children it is likely we spent time blowing dandelion seeds into a stiff breeze just to watch them blow away. As adults, finding ourselves locked in a pattern of obsessive, worrying thoughts or a paralyzing set of illness-inducing and recurring traumatic images, we can, by means of visualization and imagery blow away the seed heads of these negative or worrying thoughts just as in childhood we blew dandelion fuzz and seeds into the wind. I have talked elsewhere in these letters about taking bottled soap bubbles outside and blowing them into the wind – allowing my intense emotional state to be absorbed and to blow away in the wind as the bubbles rise and glitter in the sun. There is something about the beauty of these fragile bubbles that comforts something deep inside me, that nurtures the innocence of the still-living inner child. I suppose this is a form of inner child play but it serves the adult self's needs to be free, even momentarily, of adult issues. Kite flying on California's beaches during graduate school exam periods was another form of therapeutic play for me. The wind did the work and I simply "flew" with the kite where it dodged and darted in the air. Keeping the kite aloft took my mind away from my obsessive fears about failure.

You have written about hiking barefooted in the woods near your home as a healing activity. You have written about your garden as a healing place. From your books I have learned about your interests in individual and communal liturgies of healing.

Not everyone will do this work of self-healing in the same way for we all have unique personalities. But, for all of us to stay effective helpers for others, we must, I believe, seek, find, and then deliberately nurture our own pathway into healing the psychic-emotional wounds which we collect in our work with others – especially those others who have known overwhelming violence. Those of us who work inside the religious commons of our various denominations will likely also encounter the need to build new spiritual resources for ourselves – building upon, perhaps, those instilled in us by loving parents – yet different from those of our ancestors.

There is a common misperception in the larger culture, I think, that people who really care about the sufferings of others must enter into and fully share those sufferings. I am ambivalent about this perception because there is some truth to it. If I wish to be helpful to someone who is suffering, I must learn how to be present with that individual in the middle of his or her suffering. I cannot shield myself from his or her suffering and be a healer.

At the same time, the client's share of human suffering belongs to him or her. The task of the healer is to assist the other individual to bear that which initially to her or him seems to be unbearable.[367] The task is not – because it cannot be – the removal of his suffering. A healer's work cannot facilitate healing for others if the healer breaks down and begins to act as if the suffering one's burden is now his or her own burden to carry.

Ruth E. Krall

Another one of Emmett Miller's examples has been very helpful to me as a clinician. Knowing that healing is not the work of the healer, one must then ask, what is the work of a healer? Emmett frequently talked in workshop settings about the game of curling as a model. In the game of curling, players use brooms to remove obstacles from the granite puck's path towards its goal. As the ice is cleaned and brushed, the puck moves on its own towards its destination. When we human beings remove obstacles to healing, then healing happens of its own accord. The body-mind-self has a strong impulse towards healing and towards homeostasis. We need, as much as is possible in our ordinary human lives, to remove impediments to healing in order that the body's natural birthright of healing can occur. It is when we choke and hold on to trauma – involuntarily – that we get in the way of the body-mind's ability to heal itself.

From my recent experiences of severe physical illness, I am convinced that an essential part of healing is to work with the body-mind's strong desire to heal itself. During this extended time of working with my body and my emotions, I simply tried to pay attention to simple things: when was I thirsty; when did I need a nap: when did I need to laugh with my friends; when did I cry out of pure frustration and could I ease that frustration in any way? I paid attention to my thoughts and kept moving my consciousness back into the present moment. I kept up my spiritual practice of gratitude. It is a given that one day I will die. I have not, therefore, denied the reality that I was very ill and needed the direct intervention of American medicine to avert the crises my body was experiencing. But, once in recovery, I cooperated with my healers to the best of my ability. Told to walk more, I walked more. Told to eat lots of fruit, I ate fruit at every meal and for every snack. I took my medication as ordered and never skipped a dose.

I don't see death, therefore, as an enemy. It is a part of life. But what we know of the body/self/mind is that there is a strong desire for life, healing and health, and wholeness. As anti-violence activists, therefore, we must pay attention to our bodies and to our physical, emotional, and spiritual responses to the violence we will inevitably witness as we seek to make a difference in our world.

Some clinicians report, for example, that after hearing an especially vicious and degrading story, they, as clinicians, may begin to carry the client's paranoia and traumatic memory as if it were their own story to carry and to manage. This is the essence of traumatic counter-transference. Every clinician at some time or another in his or her life will need to learn how to manage such a clinical reality. Otherwise, over time, the clinician will become more and more internally-traumatized and will likely experience professional burn-out. The essential goodness of the universe will be lost from view. The ability to help others will weaken.

I know one individual who uses a metaphor similar to one I use. After hearing a terrible, trauma-loaded story that contains moral degradation of victims by their perpetrators, he will comment, *I need a shower.*

In my own life situation when I feel as if I need to take a shower after hearing a genuinely nasty story of abuse, I will use my hands to brush away this negative energy from my body. When I can actually do so, I may take an actual shower. And as I do so, I use guided imagery to remove the negative energy of my client's story so that I can allow her or his story to be the client's story and not my story. I not only physically wash the trauma energy away from my energetic physical body. Imagistically I deliberately remove it from my psyche at the same time. I may stand in this pouring water and cry. I may swear. I may imagine revenge on my client's victimizer and then know that this is a story that is an important story in my own professional and personal development as a healer. This is a story that stretches open my compassion and, as such, can provide my inner soft large S/Self with the spiritual vitamins of new learning and new integration that it needs. I begin, as it were, to contain the story into a manageable story for my own psyche so that I can continue to hear and to help the story's narrator.

When I was actively practicing my clinical profession, I regularly participated in group supervision activities. All of this deliberate attention to my own inner reaction process was a way of detoxifying it so that I could continue to do the work of sexual violence teaching and activism – work that felt like a vocation or a calling to me.

When I lived with a dog, walking him became a time of just being fully present to his joy in being. If I could do so, I would let him off-leash and he would announce his pleasure with such gusto, I was tugged into his world. Just as I was protective of his welfare, he was protective of mine. Sometimes when I was reading, he would jump up on the sofa and stretch out next to me, clearly just content to be with me, head tucked over my leg as I paid attention to something he could likely not fathom was interesting – words in a book.

What I am trying to illustrate is that self-care takes many forms and the more ways we learn to do this, the better work we will do in the presence of people who have experienced the lived realities of victimization and trauma. Other people – indeed even the animals that share our lives – can become healing presences to us if we allow them to be this.

The Re-vision of the Earlier Vision

It is thus my unscientific and, as yet, untested opinion that identifiable and reliable set-apart times and spaces for communities of wounded healers are essential. These days I think about retreats – in other people's facilities – where sexual violence experts, victim advocates, lawyers, and other helpers sit down with each other at long tables to tell stories and to listen. I think about having the resources of a labyrinth community or a Soul Collage® process or a yoga practitioner in residence or a skilled team of body workers on hand to guide the body-Self in healing.

I think about infinity pools to swim in. I think about Tai Chi and walking, silent meditation. I think about a daily process of deliberate, planned sitting in meditative silence with each other – breathing with each other. But most of all, I think about a quiet space in a beautiful place where a variety of non-intrusive and non-dogmatic or non-doctrinal spiritual practices can speak to the spiritual and emotional healing needs of the healers and helpers for time-out, for help and healing. I think about engaging with the spiritual wisdom of a John Shelby Spong, a Gene Robinson, a Mathew Fox, a Jack Kornfield, a Herbert Benson, a Marty Rossman, a Thomas Moore, a Lauren Artress, a Bessel van der Kolk, a Brenda Proudfoot, a Thomas Gumbleton, an Emmett Miller, a Richard Rohr, a Pema Chodron, a Joan Chittister, or a Cynthia Bourgeault – simply in attendance as human spiritual resources to listen carefully and to offer non-ideological spiritual help if such help is requested. I think about a daily – totally voluntary and re-theologized sacred meal of inclusion, with non-alcoholic beverages so that recovering alcoholics are not excluded from participation. I am no longer certain about the likelihood or the specifics of non-abusive and non-ideological communal pathways to spiritual healing, but I deeply sense their absence in my own life and in the lives of other healers and victim advocates I know.

When I think about such a gathering in a retreat setting of, say, ten or twelve activist-helper-victim advocates, I think about what it would take to create a very safe space to process in trust and confidence that which has been so often held in silence in the body-Self of the helper. I think about the benefit of being able to speak in a confidential and nonjudgmental setting that which one has chosen not to speak out of deference to the needs of victims. What I think about is the question: what would it take to create a safe enough place in order for the helper's rage, cognitive dissonance, and spiritual or emotional despair to be trustingly exposed to the light of day? How can we help healers who are in the midst of their own very personal dark night of the soul because of the work they choose to do to help other people? How many boxes of Kleenex would be sufficient? Who would be the helper and who would be the helped? If these healers – shaman like – met to take care of this often unrecognized and often unfinished business inside their own spirit-psyches, what is the spiritual energy that would be released into the universe as a consequence of such deliberate attention to healing the wound of the healers? In terms of Henri Nouwen's story of the wounded healer, where can we find or create the gate to Jerusalem where we sit down together, unbind our wounds one at a time, and collectively mourn for those whom we have not been able to help?

What is the kind of speaking, for example, which spreads the virus of violation and violence? What is the kind of speaking that spreads traumatic counter-transference? What is the manner of speaking which spreads paranoia? What are the narrative forms of our speech that seek to detoxify the inner world but which, in being unthinkingly utilized, pollute the commons? How do these forms of personal or professional speaking differ from healing speech?

Another way to ask these questions is to reflect on the question: how do we individually and collectively manage the absolutely worst and most terrifying story or the most morally degraded story we have ever heard? What, for example, was it like to be the first allied soldier to walk into Dachau as the allies freed its inhabitants? How did that soldier and his colleagues learn to manage the images, the smells, and the moral horrors of entering and liberating the death camp just minutes after its keepers ran into the surrounding countryside? What night terrors did that soldier bring home with him? What might we learn from him, and his story, that would help us?

Today's clinicians and victim advocates who listen to stories of the rape of small pre-pubescent or adolescent children are in a similar situation. In their compassionate desire to help the violated individual who sits in their presence and begins to speak, they must be both willing and able to confront the smells, the images, and the moral horrors of a desecrated human body as these are present in the victim's stories. How, for example, do we, as individuals and as communities of healing learn to tolerate listening to adult clients tell us about being repeatedly raped before puberty? How do we learn to do this work and not die a little bit inside with each new story?

These days I think so often of Nelle Morton's example of listening to a woman's pain-filled narrative in a church basement. In this story no one interrupted the woman until she was finished speaking. Then, she looked around the group of women and said: *You listened. You heard me all the way down. You heard me into my own speech.*[368] Nelle's extrapolation of her own learning from this woman's experience was to see God or the divine process as that force or power which *hears each one of us into our own authentic speech.*

If Nelle was correct, and I believe she was, it is with careful listening as healers that we hear each other's painful and traumatic first-hand or second-hand narratives into speech. And, it is in this combined speaking and hearing of inner truth where healing resides for the healer.

Many of us as activists or peace workers act from within a scarcity model. We seek out healing resources for an inner drought and often find it in thimble-sized dribbles when we need it in quarts or gallons. How, I wonder, do we heal our inner large S/Self when our inner spiritual world has been so trashed by the painful narratives we know from others? In what manner do we begin to transform the spaces between us as healers and as victim advocates into places of spiritual abundance? And what might that abundance look like?

This is not a frivolous concern on my part. We work as healers or as victim advocates from inside the homeland of our inner resources. If we are too wounded or if we are too needy, it is very likely that we will inadvertently ask the violated ones we meet to take care of us instead of offering informed care to them. When our own inner spirit is too confused, too devastated, and too broken, we may ask them to take care of our needs for support and for comfort while they are in our care. In this process we may deny them the support which they need. Or, in another model, we will begin to abuse and take advantage of those people in our personal lives who love us. In these ways, however, we spread the virus of violence. We become its carrier. We may even become its perpetrator.

What would a deliberate and voluntary therapeutic community of healers meeting with other healers look like? What kinds of safety nets would need to be in place? What would the ground rules be? Who could and would call such a community into being? Who could and would choose to become part of such a community? What are the grounding spiritual and emotional principles that could support such a gathering of healers? What practical issues, such as money and time, would need to be resolved?

What kinds of speech and what kinds of narrative shape healing speech? What are the central myths and guiding stories that bring shape to our longing and desire for individual and communal wholeness? What are the individual prayers and the communal liturgies that might shape our inner resiliency? In short, what is the grounding of our very being that allows us or enables us to help others?

When Guatemalan shamans gather at Tikal, for example, they bring with them an ancient set of beliefs and practices. Meeting at the closest full moon to the solstice or the equinox, they form a professional guild. They tell stories about the political and military violence inside their nations' borders. They renew their healing skills. They mourn their dead. They review the healing needs of their communities. They offer ancient prayers and conduct even more ancient ceremonies. What, I wonder to myself, would it look like if modern healers or victim advocates agreed to regularly meet at the full moon at the quarters of the year to heal their own wounds and to be fully present to the wounds of their fellow healers? What kind of synergy might we unleash for the healing of the world?

A Third Re-vision of the Original Vision

Gradually, as I got closer to my retirement years, I came to understand *enduring space* more as a program than a beautiful space with permanent acreage, meditation trails, spiritual icons, rich supportive liturgies of healing, and safe shelters. Finally, as I approached the actual day of my retirement, with some resigned sadness, I considered the finite personal resources of time, money, and energy. As I did this I realized that in my lifetime *enduring space* will most likely never be acreage or even a formal program of healing activities for healers. Sadly and reluctantly, but realistically, I put away the dream of creating a time-out healing space and safe/predictable program for healers, peace-makers, and others who bear witness to the suffering of violence's many victims.

As I began to actively think about what I wanted to do in retirement, my dream was not to run a retreat center, do therapy on a regular basis, or even to hit the road in public speaking and consulting events. As I allowed myself to dream, it became clear that what I wanted to do in retirement was to sort through my life and figure out if I had learned anything at all of value to others. Anthropologist Mary Catherine Bateson in her books on healthy aging calls this *composing a life.*[369] In a play on her words, I began to call it *composting a life.*

Above all, I realized in 2002 on a sabbatical trip back to Guatemala during Holy Week, that what I most wanted to do was write. During my 1995-1996 academic sabbatical in Berkeley, I had struggled to become a writer. However, once I returned to ordinary academic life, I seemed unable to get the internal space to do much creative thinking – much less writing. I was teaching *and* also administering a growing curricular program in peace, justice, and conflict studies. Both were full-time jobs. I needed to manage my own stress levels – not increase them with the self-imposed demands of a third job. It is by this slow route of self-care that the concept of *enduring space* as a place of healing has become a much more fluid space on the internet – a place for the sharing of ideas.

I gathered from your very first electronic mail message to me that this electronic room, *Enduring Space,* is how you found me after all of these years since you left my undergraduate classroom. These written conversations are, then, a result of my decisions to make at least part of the *enduring space* vision-call a reality. While I remembered you as an undergraduate college student, I had no idea of what you were doing as an adult in the middle of your own career or in your own personal life.

I have now begun to remedy that. I am reading your published books and I have visited some of your electronically-recorded interviews on the World Wide Web. Only when I mentioned Mary Catherine Bateson to you, did you tell me that she guided your dissertation at George Mason. Our shared interests in anthropology and the cultural roots of human violence bring us back full circle into this current set of conversations – now not between a teacher and her student but between two fully mature feminist Anabaptist-Mennonite women who are colleagues and friends.

The Large S/Self[370]

You have no idea how blessed I feel that you have chosen to re-enter my life to hold conversations about these issues. I thought this morning as I woke that maybe it would be helpful for you – and others – to know that the journey from one dream to another dream to another dream eventually has finally manifested itself in this present moment. In these electronic conversations about healing, we are, in essence, serving as peer healers for each other. We are listening to each other's life experiences and the questions these experiences have raised for each of us. We are creating a shared space where healing can manifest itself.

The inner observant large S/*Self* pays attention and it does listen to feedback from the external world. But it never quite gives up on us even when our energies wane and we need to seek the gates of Jerusalem to find someone to teach *us* so that we can learn how to bind up our wounds. This inner large S/*Self* continues to remind us of goodness – both in the dream and in the reality of human relationships. It reminds us, on a daily basis, if we listen, that healing our own wounds and healing the wounds of the world are always living and always interpenetrated possibilities. They are, as it were, a Mobius-strip Loop. The omnipresent possibility of healing very deep wounds may demand hard work (or, sometimes no work at all), but it is always a grace that cannot be demanded. It can only be received. In addition, the always potential grace of embodied healing can never be totally destroyed or obliterated by evil.

Whatever God is or whoever God is, she does not abandon us and she does not leave us. We simply have to get quiet enough often enough to find her living presence inside us and inside the creative, restorative, loving and healing aspects of human life. When we are silent enough and the monkey mind ceases its restless chatter, we come to realize that deep inside of every one of us there is a large inner spaciousness, an inner place of *enduring space.* I have come to believe that this inner spacious "room" is the source of all healing and of all healing work. When we can do our work anchored within the deep silence of this large inner room of grace and peace, we no longer need to do our work fueled by our anger, rage, despair, hopelessness, or any other negative energy. We become, in that moment, a bodhisattva of the divine One's always present compassionate healing Spirit.

The American shaman Hank Wesselman talks about the deliberate cultivation of our inner garden – a place we enter in a quiet desire to be helpful to others as well as a space we can enter to care for our own inner wounds. He notes a phenomenon that I too have observed. The increasing awareness of personal spirituality in our particular culture *is mainly happening outside the carefully patrolled borders of our organized religions.*[371]

Nowhere is this more evident to me than in secular organizations that are mapping the spiritual aspects of collective wisdom, ancient traditions, and contemporary action – organizations and individuals whose roots are in the secular wisdom traditions of our era in history – organizations such as IONS (The Institute of Noetic Sciences) or the *Journal of Spirituality and Health.* Individuals who are working to restore the wholeness of the world by a pro-active spirituality are reaching across many of the cultural dividing lines we know, for example, Christianity and Judaism, or Catholic and Mennonite, as they seek to create a meaningful inner spirituality that supports their activism on behalf of others *and* the world's ecosystems.

There is something about a too-rigid demand for orthodoxy in abstract beliefs (words) that cuts people off from the deep inner well of spirituality that can resource them (and us) in our efforts to remain compassionate and helpful for the long distance run. Being willing to explore the margins of their own (or others' faith traditions) is clearly allowing some victim advocates and helpers to find spiritual as well as emotional healing. When this happens, we see renewed courage and determination to persevere and to expand their work in the world. The more I mature in my own spirituality, the more I am convinced that a sign of spiritual maturity is flexibility. Learning to develop spiritual maturity and flexibility means being willing to question, being willing to seek, being willing to recognize, and finally, being willing to appropriate healing resources wherever they may be found. It means being willing to live with cognitive dissonance as a needed stimulant to personal growth in all aspects of our lives.

Cafeteria-Style Spirituality

The derogatory term for this kind of ecumenical spirituality among some fundamentalist Christians is *cafeteria-style spirituality*. I am personally offended whenever I hear this term used. I read Jewish authors such as Elie Wiesel or Abraham Joshua Heschel and my Christian spirituality and sense of the complexities of justice are deepened. I read the Sufi mystic Rumi or the Hindu poet Kabir and my awareness of the mystical dimensions of my spirituality are enhanced. I study Gandhi and in his Hindu spirituality, I see new dimensions of effective nonviolent activism. I read Simon Wiesenthal and Bishop Tutu and I revisit complex questions of what forgiveness might mean in situations of genocidal violence or clergy sexual abuse scandals. I read Rabbi Rami Shapiro and I learn about the embedded spiritual meanings of the human choices we Americans are faced with each day. In particular, he teaches me about the twelve steps of Alcoholics Anonymous as a resource for non-alcoholics. Many years ago I danced with Mathew Fox and a group of strangers in a workshop setting and reconnected with joy and a lightness of spirit. I read about the teachings and healing work of Fools Crow and Rolling Thunder. I study the spiritual teachings and earth healing work of Sun Bear and insights about aboriginal healing work flood into my awareness. I think about Amerindian sand painting healing rituals and the sand mandala-creating spirituality of Tibetan Buddhism. I make Soul Collage® cards and discover things about my life journey that I'd forgotten to honor. I study Michael Harmer's, Sandra Ingerman's, and Hank Wesselman's writings and come to understand that in sexual violence work, soul retrieval work is a concept and practice we should, as victim advocates and healers, be exploring. This is particularly true since many victims report that their experiences of childhood and adolescent sexual abuse have murdered their souls. I read Bessel van der Kolk, Peter Levine, Brooke Medicine Eagle, Carol Christ, Jon Kabat-Zinn, James Hillman, Ram Dass, Stephen Levine, Mary Oliver, Mark Nepo, Adrienne Rich, Pema Chodron, and Huston Smith, and my awareness of the spiritual dimensions of my personal embodied life and my collective life in the commons are re-shaped, refreshed and renewed.

In all of this reading, I am guided by my clinical training. Physicians and nurses have a unique relationship with the human body. We see it in all of its aspects of wellness, wholeness, illness, and pathology. We are intimately in contact with each body's multiple permutations of health and well-being and with its equally multiple permutations of illness and sickness. When a patient in search of care enters our lives, we turn to the body to ask, as it were, to tell us what it knows.[372] As we grow into professional maturity, we come to recognize the sacred nature of the human body. If, or perhaps when is a better word, we are wise, we are reverent and in awe of each individual's unique embodied presence and embodied beauty in the world. No matter how distorted the image of the divine is in a human life, it is still fully present at all times in each individual's living body and simply needs to be re-discovered and re-acknowledged.

If we actively cultivate our inner spiritual garden, we then can nurture and develop our innate compassionate ability to be present with and stand by the suffering little ones of all ages. This ability is essential to those us who seek to be healers of the world by means of active peacemaking and conflict resolution or conflict transformation activities since human suffering caused by human violence is omnipresent in the world. When we cultivate and expand this inner space that endures in each present moment, we can move into and out of the world of human suffering as priests, as healers, as shape shifters, and as shamans. As we move towards the healing of our inner world, we can then honestly and with integrity proclaim the boundless possibilities for God's healing spirit to do her work in the outer world of others through us as her hands, feet, and eyes.

Fifteenth Letter

Weaving Parachutes

I have woven a parachute out of everything broken, my scars are my shield.

William Safford[373]

Introductory Comments

I want to talk more about the spirituality of healing work, activist work on behalf of justice, and victim advocacy work. As one aspect of this discussion I want to quote at length Roman Catholic Dominican friar and ordained priest Father Thomas Doyle. These words were attached to a sexual abuse and institutional clericalism bibliography which he sent to his friends and professional colleagues in 2010. These words were my first introduction to Father Doyle's life journey and work in the world as it related to the spirituality of his inner life. They were a personal reflection on his then thirty-year spiritual journey from the early 1980's (when he was in his 4th decade) as he began his work of advocacy for the victims of Catholic clergy sexual abuse and for the victims of his church hierarchy's collective crimes of obedience[374] – those criminally malfeasant[375] actions of the Catholic Church's bishops and cardinals which he and many others call, simply, institutional clericalism.[376] Many years later, he would define spirituality as the *inner life of the soul.*[377]

That the church's bureaucratic decisions (made by his church's administrative bishops, cardinals, and popes) to stonewall victims and protect abusive priests disillusioned Father Doyle in mid-life is clear. His denomination's decisions to prevent truth from emerging in order to protect the institutional church from scandal and its administrative caste from accountability undercut the moorings in Father Doyle's cognitive faith and his personal spirituality. The levels of institutionalized moral and spiritual corruption and the bishops', cardinals', and popes' theological rationalizations for criminal cover-ups dismantled a personal spirituality of trust in and a moral posture of unquestioning obedience to his denominational institution supervisors.

In my personal experience with similar issues in my own life, once this dismantling of trust and faith begins, questions about required orthodoxy and the need for unquestioning obedience emerge. Repeatedly betrayed and disillusioned, it is rare for individuals to retain unquestioning trust or belief in the truths that their cradle communal faith group has taught as essential. When a community of faith has repeatedly proven itself to be unworthy, a logical conclusion is that the truth this community has claimed is likely to be false and unworthy as well. Kramer and Alstad, in their excellent book about guru abuses in Eastern religions, instruct their readers that when a spiritual teacher makes claims about the spirituality of a specific faith tradition which his or her personal behavior does not demonstrate, these spiritual leaders are lying about the validity of their teaching and the spiritual claims which they make to their disciples are, therefore, likely to be fraudulent ones. In short, corrupt spiritual teachers do not know whether or not their religious or spiritual teaching is valid because it is untested in their own individual lives as human beings and as spiritual teachers.[378] Indeed, when these religious or spiritual authorities actively abuse their followers, they demonstrate the inherent fallacy of their spiritual or ethical teachings.

In Christian and in Anabaptist-Mennonite circles, this wisdom is known as the wisdom of *word and deed.* For spiritual teachers to be trustworthy and for their teaching to be accepted as authoritative for the community, there needs to be congruence of word – that which they teach – and deed – that behavior which they manifest in their own daily lives as individuals and as leaders inside their religious community. When word and deed are separated (or when orthodoxy and orthopraxis are no longer held in tension), then there is a strong tendency for religious leaders to abuse the trust of their religious community and their spiritual followers or disciples. There is an equally strong tendency for their teachings to be corrupted as well.

The corrupted spirituality of abusive communities has a corrosive and toxic effect on human consciences and on compassionate spirits. In the words which follow, Father Doyle reflects on this perhaps initially inchoate and always difficult-to-express spiritual awareness in his own life.

The Art of Parachute-Making

Over the course of my years of involvement with the clergy sexual abuse "happening" I have learned that the damage done to the spirituality of victims has been considerable and in many ways, more difficult to deal with than either the emotional or psychological damage. The victims are not alone in suffering grave spiritual damage. Many of those directly or even indirectly involved with this whole complex phenomenon have found themselves in a growing quandary with their belief systems. I am one of them. For years my belief system and the object of my faith were gradually shifting, often in ways I did not even notice. Most of what I had been taught about Faith, about Beliefs, about trust in the human or earthly dimensions of the community of believers, the institutional Church, came under assault. I had believed what the official church had told me without much questioning. I accepted that the Church was what it was and I bought into all of the standard explanations for the historical departures of the institutional church and its leaders from basic Christian decency and certainly from honesty... like the inquisition, the crusades, the approval of slavery, the colonization of the new world, and the Vatican's diplomatic ties to Hitler and Mussolini. My serious questioning started when I found myself on the inside looking out as the clergy sex abuse began to unfold back in 1984. As I saw first-hand the duplicity and the institutionalized lying of the self-proclaimed 'successors' of the apostles, I slowly began to wonder if the apostles weren't actually a cabal of anti-Christian dolts or on the other hand I wondered if the infallible connection between the popes, bishops, and church monarchy was neither infallible nor divinely willed.

It was not exactly a pleasant or secure feeling as my not-quite-paralyzed brain began to ask the inevitable question "If they can easily lie about raping innocent little children, can they just as easily lie about everything else?" The next stop on the journey was actually the first stop: taking the risk of asking myself what was true and what was not true about everything else I had been told to believe. I finally paused long enough to let soak in the reality of this deeply embedded dynamic: I (and all of us actually) had been consistently told what I must believe. I had never been...offered the option of figuring out the basics for myself. This no longer worked for me....

The next stop in the journey necessarily came very soon after the first stop. The second stop was the cognitive and emotional acceptance of my right to question...anything and everything I had been taught that was supposed to be true about the institutional church, the people running the institutional church and the entire body of dogmas that were required for membership in the institutional church. Along the way I began to understand what I had for so long taken for granted: that spirituality isn't an affect, an appearance, or attitude that some acquired (to their institutional benefit) and others never seemed to get (like me). I began to realize there was a gaping hole inside of me that had a depth I never thought possible. I tried to fill that emptiness with other things for a while but none of them worked. I finally realized that spirituality is not something acquired and it certainly cannot be accurately equated with or measured by outward piety. For me, the journey into the realization of my spirituality had to reach the point where I seriously questioned the very existence and nature of God. It was at that stage when I came to the frightening acceptance of my need to get rid of the Catholic god I had feared and find someone or something that made sense. I believe I found it early on in my upward and often steep path through the Twelve Steps. The Higher Power was significantly different from the images of the supreme being I had labored under for most of my life. If the veracity of this Higher Power was in any way demonstrated in the lives of the other people I met at Twelve Step meetings, then I had come upon the real thing.

I was and still am left with figuring out where the reality of the Church, religious life, and ultimately Jesus Christ fit into a life that has this spirituality at its core. I have tried really listening to others, meditating, and reading. All three have been much more helpful than blindly accepting various and sundry ecclesiastically based pronouncements, dogmas, etc.[379]

Personal Reflections

> *It's possible to love something even if you've spent much of your life exposing its darkest secrets, its deepest shames. It's possible to have faith. But faith doesn't just permanently arrange itself to thrive in the human heart and mind – it has to be tended.*
>
> Manuel Roig-Franzia[380]

It would be arrogant and presumptuous of me to critique Father Doyle's personal experience or, as a Mennonite woman, to abstractly theologize about it. His words need to stand exactly as written. This is because I need to confront them in all of their painful rawness. Since I first read these words, I have repeatedly returned to them in order to ponder what these words have to teach me about my personal spiritual journey as an activist woman who has worked inside several administratively-corrupted religious institutions.

What about my personal share of the world's healing work inside the enchanted forest of sexual violence advocacy work has brought me into this extended dark night of the soul where I cannot bear to sing the community's music, pray the communal prayers, or listen to the weekly sermons? Why, I repeatedly ask myself, did Father Doyle's words burrow inside my consciousness and take up permanent residency there? What is the lesson of these sobering words for all of us who seek to be compassionate companions to individuals who have been beaten and sexually abused by the people and religious institutions they trusted? What does it mean to follow the Jesus path when one cannot tolerate being with the gathered Christian community?

In short, what can I learn from these words that touches my own personal share of distrust in the institutional church of my childhood – a church I loved and trusted implicitly in childhood and adolescence because it was my spiritual home?

Adult Spiritualities

I had to cut a distance between my own idea of faith and the pronouncements of the institution. I began to define my identity as a Catholic, as one much closer to the parish, the Mass, the liturgy.

Jason Berry[381]

With mature human brains and psyches in adult life, as we confront the implicit spiritual immaturity of a coercive inherited spirituality, we begin to use a spiritual microscope to examine our own lives. When we recognize the community system of rewards for our often-coerced blind obedience to men and women in positions of religious authority and power over us and simultaneously begin to recognize and reap the punishments of our growing movement into adult thinking for ourselves, we are faced with a moral conundrum. What moral-spiritual agency do we express as adult Christians: the moral and spiritual instructions of powerful, authoritative, and controlling institutions, or the moral intuitions and spiritual agency of our personal decisions about belief and practice, about word and deed? Is our spirituality, therefore, primarily an inherited reflection under the control of the religious institutions into which we were born? Or is our innate spirituality something which we slowly come to understand as we mature through the continuous process of making and learning from our life's decisions? How does our spirituality both reflect and help construct our large S/Self – that inner reality and identity which came with us at our human birth?

If, as Father Doyle so cogently argues, our spirituality is not something we acquire[382] but is innate to each person, then what does it mean for us to be spiritual beings in a physical body? What does it mean to be embodied spiritual beings in community? Do we spiritually mature inside situations of enforced obedience, or do we spiritually mature inside situations of confronting our doubts and utilizing our inner resources in the face of external challenges? What does it mean to be a spiritually mature person: obedient and subservient to external religious authorities, or questioning and discerning what is needed in each troubled and troubling confrontation with the ordinary and daily realities of life? What does it mean to tend the inner garden of our personal spirituality? What does it mean to have the spirituality of helpfulness to others – a spirituality of care and compassion? What does it mean when we begin to allow our own spirits to be deeply troubled by the troubles of others whom we encounter in our daily personal and professional lives?

If my spirituality is neither an acquired habit nor a process of magical thinking, then what is it? If my spirituality is not expressed in repeated and semi-automatic acts of religious duty or in obsessive-compulsive, self-flagellating moral scrupulosity, then what is it? If my spirituality is not narcissistic self-preoccupation, then what is it? If my spirituality is not a dramatic, pious performance on the outer stages of my professional life inside religious institutions, then what is it?

How do we discern the presence of authentic spirituality – in our own lives and in the lives of others? In many ways, I am convinced that the stories we tell each other about our lives are much more revelatory about our spirituality than the theological abstractions and orthodox dogmas we cling to in the desire for a buffering safety zone from life's encounters with outrageous suffering.[383] It is in the lived stories of our lives that we encounter our deepest values and our most fragile hopes. It is in these narratives we recite to ourselves just before going to sleep at night where we record the traumatic suffering we have endured and where we recount, if only to ourselves, the moments in which we chose to become survivors and endurers. As we reflect on the many narratives in a lived life, we can find our most private and most painful obsessions, but we can also find our most enduring loves and joys.

These real-life-narratives are, I believe, the raw material out of which a mature adult spirituality emerges. As we compassionately seek to understand ourselves and, in similar ways, as we seek to understand others, the universal nature of human suffering eventually comes into view. As we seek to become messengers of hope and healing, the inner spirituality of our being begins to send us telegrams about how we need to live our lives.

Our questions about the meaning of our lives perhaps do not begin in the ordinary and usual developmental moments of childhood, adolescence, and early adult life – eras of our lives when we tend to accept the theological and spiritual answers of our ancestors and their faith communities. These kinds of questions do not generally arise in the smooth and easy times of our lives.

My personal hypothesis – based on my life journey to date – is that we begin to question our childhood's religious indoctrination when we experience deep moments of cognitive dissonance. We become disillusioned about our religious heritage when we encounter the reality that what we have been taught by our well-meaning elders and by our community are lies. The beginnings of our descent into the dark night of the soul are often complex and multi-faceted. We can encounter dogma and doctrines about the nature of truth that are clearly not about truth; we can have doubts about orthodoxies and customary pieties that have no reasonable response or answers for our doubts and life questions; we can find no meaning-ful reassurance and guidance for our lives when we directly encounter the issues of hypocrisy, dishonesty and untrustworthiness in the religious commons; we can encounter teachings about principled morality that religious leaders do not model; we can witness cruelty wearing the mask of helpfulness; we can observe hate being described as love; we can be disastrously betrayed by physically, sexu-ally, or religiously abusive spiritual authorities and abruptly enter the enchanted forests of religious betrayal.

Ruth E. Krall

There are many reasons for the birth of agnosticism and atheism. But for individuals who reasonably and with sincere belief trusted the religious institutions of their childhood and adolescence as the carriers of God's truth, I am convinced that adolescent and adult encounters with corrupted and hypocritical religious leaders and these leaders' complicit followers are the main cause. Evil deeds and corrupted belief systems promulgated as good always bear rotten fruit.

Our growing sense of disbelief arises in the middle of our doubts, our questions, our fears, our experiences, and our sense of having lost (or even having a sense of its deliberate destruction by others) a reliable inner rudder to guide our daily decisions. Our most despairing questions of the gods and life most often arise within a deep sense of personal betrayal.

Perhaps our bodies have betrayed us and we face an early death. Perhaps a mean-spirited friend has betrayed us and we face the abrupt end of a meaningful (even essential) friendship. Perhaps a colleague or co-worker tells lies about us to other people. Perhaps someone in our family has abused us and caused us to lose a sense of personal safety in the world. Perhaps our church or religious institution has enacted its spiritual calling to lead the people of God in ignoble, callous, deceitful, cruel, narcissistic, and hateful ways. Perhaps our religious leaders have betrayed us and all routes to salvation that we previously believed in are now closed to further travel: previously posted and spiritually secure road signs regarding salvation and safety are now missing from our lives. Perhaps the visible suffering of the world is just too overwhelming to absorb and our ethical or moral sensibilities are either offended or destroyed. Perhaps our doubts about abstract and unpalatable hypotheses overtake us.

For first responders, healers, helpers, witnesses, and victim advocates a certain route to spiritual despair occurs regularly in the absence of adequate personal self-protection. Our inability to successfully buffer ourselves in the presence of others' overwhelming trauma and suffering can be devastating. This is particularly true when that suffering appears to have its roots in deliberate and planned individual, collective, and/or institutional evil-doing.

However it is that we enter the dark night of the soul, our encounters with ourselves inside its dense parameters will forever change us. It does not matter if we are priest or physician, therapist or shaman, conflict-manager or body-healer, community organizer or spiritual guru: when we enter this time of deep, dense, and even perhaps revolting despair, our inner spiritual world will inevitably change. Once trapped inside this dark night, we cannot escape our doubts and these doubts, whether denied and repressed or faced head on, will permanently mark and change us. As we seek to make sense of the "new" world we now live in, we will need to resolve intense experiences of cognitive and spiritual dissonance.

The manner in which we do the work of cognitive and spiritual resolution will shape our belief system, our characters, and our interpersonal relationships with others in the outer world. Our resolution of this intensely personal internal struggle will deeply affect our ongoing responses to others in the socio-religious world of human relationships and human need.

We have choices in the middle of our despair. We can retreat into unthinking denial, nostalgic piety, or routinized dogmatic orthodoxy. These will often, but not always, make us complicit with both the causes and manifestations of religious abuse and human suffering. Conversely, we can just keep doing what we have always been doing – even when we no longer believe the communal reasons for our doing. To me, this seems like defecting in place. We no longer believe but we act as if we believe. Finally, we can commit ourselves to self-scrutiny and the pursuit of a belief system that has integrity for us even if no one else can understand or share our precise journey back to spiritual wholeness – working to determine the belief structures that must now replace childhood's outgrown faith in order to guide us in our inner and outer decisions and ongoing lives.

Over the adult years of my life, my repeated encounters with cognitive dissonance about unreliable religious teachings and corrupt spiritual teachers have taught me that I must pay attention and I must know (or at least seek to uncover) the spiritual values that guide my life's decisions. I have found Huston Smith's[384] insistence upon the principle that all of the world's religious traditions contain repositories of human wisdom about the spiritual life to be helpful. I am not limited, therefore, to just one fountain of deep spirituality. I can drink from many wells.[385] My own spirituality, therefore, is deeply influenced by the great contemplative spiritual traditions of the world.

For me, in light of Safford's poem above, parachute construction includes (1) reading authors who reflect a justice-based spirituality of compassionate helpfulness, (2) reading spiritual teachers who guide me into practices of deep silent contemplation and pervasive gratitude; (3) doing meaningful work in the world, (4) recognizing a profound sense that there is so much I do not know about the spiritual life which is often immediately accompanied by others' insistent and usually dogmatic institutional assertions about what I must cognitively believe and do to find salvation – fervent assertions that often make no damned sense to me at all. Thus, as I discovered so long ago in my twenties, my spiritual path is a path with ambiguities, doubts, insecurities, hesitations, and outright disbelief.

My copy of Will Oursler's book, *The Road to Faith* (which was written shortly after his father Fulton Oursler's death), is now tattered and underlined in many different colors of ink.[386] Its explicit permission to doubt as part of the faith journey of an individual's personal spirituality has comforted me for many years. I do not need to have all of the answers to my questions. I just need to trust that the doubter's road to faith and an intact spirituality is well marked by the footsteps of spiritual travelers who have preceded me in walking its path.

In the past month, thanks to an internet news item, I have discovered several books written by Robin Meyers.[387] Meyers, like Oursler, acknowledges doubts as the source of faithfulness. In addition, he takes us back beyond centuries of Christian history and its creeping infallible orthodoxies and helps us to see the human Jesus and the very human people who were the friends and family of the human Jesus and, therefore, the first followers of *The Way.* In this serendipitous way, Meyer's work has infiltrated several of these letters since you saw them many months ago in their rough draft form.

This is most definitely an example of two things I have noticed in my life. The first is exemplified by the aphorism that *when a student is ready to learn, a teacher appears.* When, or more likely if, I can get my questions formulated into language, then a pathway opens to find answers for myself.

The second is the issue of synchronicity – when we pay attention that which we need to make progress in our inner life appears. I have always called this *mystical reading.* I walk into my public library and on the new book table is a book that will help me answer some current doubt or hunger to know. I open the internet to read an article and up pops a book review by a credible source.

Struggling to Understand Transcendence

Like the Jewish-American ethicist and author Philip Hallie, I struggle to understand the nature of evil and cruelty and the nature of genuine helpfulness as they are embedded in my own life and in the surrounding local and world communities in which my personal life is embedded. Like many women, I struggle to understand the ways in which my life – and the lives of many women – has been damaged by patriarchal understandings of the Source of all life and consciousness. Like the Protestant-American preacher and anti-nuclear activist William Sloane Coffin, faced with the violent evils of my church and nation, often done in my name, I simply beg for courage and for wisdom to know how to live my life. No longer believing in prayer, I still pray. No longer believing in salvation and resurrection and the power of redemptive suffering, I long for newness, wholeness, and well-being to emerge out of that which is dead and decaying in my internal life and in my culture. No longer believing in a hell at the core of earth's fire or in a physical heaven somewhere beyond the celestial clouds, still I seek for a path to the redemption of the cosmos. Despite my deep despair and many doubts about specific beliefs, I still cling to an abiding belief in the transcendent – there is something in the universe that is continuing to create newness and to create our internal and urgent senses of the need for wholeness. This transcendent something is simultaneously external *and* intrinsic to human doing and human knowing.

In his life, and now in his spiritual teachings, Father Doyle has embraced and adapted the language of Alcoholics Anonymous as a guide to his spiritual intuitions. Institutionally-disillusioned as a Roman Catholic priest, an internal sense or awareness of a *Higher Power* guides his personal experiences and understanding of the transcendent at work in his life. His particular parachute carries, therefore, the trademark of the spirituality expressed inside the meetings and principles of Alcoholics Anonymous. Father Doyle's parachute, therefore, reflects his on-going utilization of the twelve steps – a social-spiritual resource which has carried, and continues to carry, him through his own dark nights of the soul.

For a variety of reasons a *higher power* is not an intellectual construct for God-naming or God-understanding that I can adapt as a woman thealogian in my own naming of the divine Source or the divine Presence. I am, therefore, more comfortable these days with the sense that whatever we human beings can know of God, we know as the source of human consciousness, as the source of all consciousness in the universe – from the tiniest frog to the most gigantic blue whale... and of course to us as human beings as well. This transcendent consciousness of the universe, therefore, must encompass cruelty as well as helpfulness, evil as well as good. It must encompass presence as well as absence.

Rescuing One Life as an Act of Salvation

> *There may be times when we are powerless to prevent injustice, but there must never be a time when we fail to protest. The Talmud tells us that by saving a single human being, a man (sic) can save the world.*

Elie Wiesel[388]

Such a concept, therefore, places the question of doing evil and being cruel back in the lap of each human person who exists. We are the moral agents of the universe and it is our human actions which birth unthinkable and unimaginable acts of cruelty and evil just as it is our human actions which birth unimaginable acts of goodness and compassionate helpfulness. In our daily human choices we give birth to the social and physical universe which surrounds us. If we wish to live in a loving, healing, whole, and trustworthy universe, then we must strive to be loving and trustworthy. It is as simple as that and it is as overwhelmingly complex as that. It is our human choicefulness – individually and collectively – in each human present moment which determines our personal future and the future for our descendants. There is no magical grandfather (or grandmother) in the sky to rescue us from ourselves and the consequences of our human choices and actions.

But, that said, I still continue to believe that there is a great, compassionate, and loving Spirit who responds to human acts that manifest human consciousness. As we align ourselves with this Spirit in each present moment of our awareness,

Ruth E. Krall

we move slowly but inexorably towards a quiet inner center. In that inner center, we are empowered to know who we truly are as embodied spiritual beings on a spiritual path.

How this Great Spirit chooses to embody itself in human flesh remains a mystery. But the evidence is all around us. Every human being, no matter how cruel and how callous towards the needs of others, is a spiritual being. This is our common human flesh and this is our common human spirit. Therefore, no one lies outside the potential of wholeness and completeness. Every human being, no matter how derelict or how corrupt, is a bearer of this common human spirit.

It is, therefore, unwise to demonize each other as being something other than physical beings who each share in the divine spirit in some way – a way which we do not understand. In terms of the work I do in the world, this means that the sexual predator whose behaviors are most heinous shares in the same consciousness as does the most sainted individual who seeks to heal the wounds of the world by loving and generous advocacy. I must believe, therefore, in the potential for real healing and wholeness. But I know the journey will be very difficult. In order to heal one's own self and one's own relationships with those we have harmed, we must be willing to recognize our own cruelty and acknowledge the harm we have done. In addition, we must repent of it with deep and lasting grief. Knowing our imperfections and our deep inner conflicts about who we are, we must seek transformation.

At some mystical level I do not understand, predation is one shadow component of the human archetype – the antithesis of compassion, love, altruism, healing work, and sheltering care for each other. Trust kept and trust betrayed form enduring aspects of human consciousness which belong to each one of us. We do not understand human life – most particularly our own individuated life – if we distance ourselves from facing this fundamental reality – we can and do harm others; we can and do help others. We suffer because of our own actions and others suffer from these actions as well. We misunderstand others and, in turn, we are misunderstood.

My own experience of these deeply knotted spiritual questions of belief and meaning is that they arise in life moments when the traditional answers of my inherited culture no longer make sense, when the shared orthodoxies of my cradle faith community no longer serve me as reliable and faithful guides for the life I lead and the work I do. Repeated experiences of being thrust into one or more of life's relational, moral, spiritual, emotional, or cognitive hurricanes repeatedly force me, if I am paying attention, into doubt and questions and perhaps even night terrors.

Human betrayal is a major source of our very human need to re-think who we are and to re-think the communities in which we live. It is a truism that our known enemies do not betray us. This is so because they have no emotional power over us. Knowing their enmity in advance of their actions against us, they have no social currency to use in order to betray us. We do not, in the first place, trust them enough for them to have any emotional traction in our lives except the buffering traction of self-protection. Wearing the armor of mistrust and defensive self-protection, our enemies can harm us but they cannot betray us. Knowing that we have enemies is important because it helps us to make decisions about voluntary vulnerability – that vulnerability of the soft inner large S/Self that allows us to mature and to grow emotionally and spiritually.

It is, however, a well-recognized clinical truism that a too-defended spirit, psyche, or small s/self simply cannot move free of itself into that vulnerability which allows the individual to seek, to doubt, and to move into the free zone of personal change and growth – or individuation. There are times in life when something has to break us wide open in order for us to grow.

To make a new friend or to fall in love – these kinds of important relationships call for trust. Trust between human beings is, therefore, I believe the glue of our loving and caring attachments with others. When trust is betrayed, therefore, we enter a time of loss, of anger, of grief, and a sense that the world and perhaps even the gods are untrustworthy and, therefore, undeserving of our belief and trust.

Holding On and Letting Go

> We don't give up on democracy because of Watergate and I won't give up on the church because of corrupt bishops.

Jason Berry[389]

I found this quotation on American journalist Jason Berry's home page. As one of the Roman Catholic investigative reporters who have covered the sexual abuse crisis in the Roman Catholic Church from the 1980's until today, his web page reports that he experienced such deep rage about what he was uncovering that he needed to seek therapy in order to help him move back into a more nuanced and balanced life. In addition, the web page reports that he continues to worship and to pray in a Roman Catholic congregation in the parish where he lives. He has clearly found a path to his personal salvation in the parish, the liturgy, and in his participation in the Mass.

As I read this brief account of his spiritual journey inside the boundaries of his church, I am reminded of all of those for whom a similar journey is simply impossible. He gives credit to faithful priests and nuns who walked along side of him and provided meaningful spiritual guidance as he made his way out of his personal dark night of the soul.

Ruth E. Krall

Having an absence of mature spiritual leaders or compassionate spiritual friends to walk with us as we live inside the enchanted forest where the dark night of the soul pervades our lives, we must make our own way slowly and deliberately – allowing our doubts and fears to guide us.

If and when we exit our dark nights of alienation and despair safely, it seems to me we can become spiritual helpers or mentors for others like us – those others who have needed, because of the force of their life narratives, to abandon the traditional routes to salvation for the difficult mountainous paths of missteps and doubt. As we knowingly distrust the answers provided by corrupted institutions intent on preserving their own powers in the world rather than giving up those powers to serve the powerless and the wounded and the vulnerable; as we seek to assist the wounded little ones of any age who search for healing, shelter and wholeness in the midst of their brokenness, we ourselves become broken and recovering healers. It is after all not the secure who need reassurance; it is not those who are well who seek healing; it is not those needing no help from others who seek refuge; it is not those who live inside zones of peace and well-being who need to be rescued.

When we acknowledge our own brokenness and our own mortal fallibility, then and only then can we push back the internal hurricane walls of our own cruelty in order to allow our innate goodness to emerge. Only when we recognize our human solidarity with the broken little ones of all ages do we begin to repair our own souls.[390]

Sixteenth Letter

Markers of Christian Patriarchy

The oppressions are interlinked, so homophobia is buttressed by, and in turn props up sexism, racism, ablebodyism, etc. You can't end any one oppression without addressing the other inequalities.

Chris Morley[391]

Introductory Comments

In your electronic letter on July 3, 2014 you issued the following challenge.

What are the 10 things about patriarchy that people in the church need to understand? [Make it] just a page or two long. Is that something you have interest in writing?

[This would be] sort of a Dummies Guide to Patriarchy.

I am not sure I know how to respond to such a challenge. But I will give it a try. Keep in mind that there are many authors who have written entire volumes about the construction and maintenance of the patriarchy.[392] Keep in mind, also, that I distrust short-hand information sources on subjects when their topic is bone-deep in complexity. I don't think I can do what you ask in 2 pages.

In her book, *All about Love,* American social commentator bell hooks writes that the worship of death is a central component of patriarchal thinking, whether expressed by women or men. She notes that the failure of religion is one reason our world patriarchal cultures remain death-centered.[393] She notes the work of Mathew Fox in drawing our attention to Creation-centered spirituality as expressed in the *via positiva* rather than in the *via negativa*. She concludes, we move away from this worship of death by challenging patriarchy, creating peace, working for justice, and embracing a love ethic.[394]

While I seek to answer your question above with my own thinking about these matters, I am deeply moved by hooks' and her awareness that the patriarchy, in addition to being about power, authority and control is at its roots about loving death rather than loving life.

I. *Theological Roots*

There is a very strong preference for the second creation account in Genesis in which woman is created second and named by man.[395] Man in this mytho-theological narrative is made in God's image while the woman is made in the man's image. Therefore, she is, by virtue of the order of her creation, a subordinate to the man who was made first.[396] As many feminist authors have pointed out, this ancient narrative negates or seeks to counter the human reality in which it is woman who gives birth to all members of the species – male and female. This creation account, therefore, most likely contains an ancient polemic against Mesopotamian goddess worship – such as ancient Sumer's *Inanna*, the Babylon's *Ishtar*, and their descendant and corresponding female deities in the land mass surrounding the city of Jerusalem such as Ashtoreth (Astarte) or in Egypt such as Isis. As a seminarian I was told there are hints in these ancient Hebrew texts that the multiple creation narratives of Jewish scriptures contain a religious-political invective against earlier Mesopotamian and Near Eastern creation stories. [397]

In addition, there is a very strong Christian tradition that claims Eve brought evil into the world. In Genesis 3:6 we read that Eve ate the forbidden fruit first and then encouraged Adam to eat it as well. Many Christian theologians through the centuries have speculated that Eve's sin, treated metaphorically as fruit eating, was a sexual sin – tempting Adam to sexual intercourse.

What is interesting to me now as a much more informed reader of ancient scriptures is that according to the narrative's structure, Eve never heard the prohibition firsthand. It was Adam who was taught by God not to eat fruit from the forbidden tree of knowledge of good and evil.[398] Knowing what we know in this current century about men's inclination to guard esoteric knowledge in secrecy as a way to maintain systems of their power over others, one can only wonder what Adam actually told Eve. Nevertheless, the historical narrative of their shared life in Eden assures today's readers that Eve knew about the prohibition – whoever taught it to her.[399]

I have always enjoyed, indeed, laughed in glee at, the story of Lilith in Jewish extra-canonical mythology. According to some narratives of the story, when Lilith, Adam's first wife, was commanded by God and Adam to assume the subordinate and subservient position in their pair relationship, she refused and flew away to lodge outside the Garden of Eden. Some contemporary feminist authors speculate

Ruth E. Krall

about what might have happened inside the garden had Eve known about Lilith's rebellious presence outside the boundaries of Eden.[400] Would she have joined her predecessor in refusing a life of subordinated service? Would Adam and God both have trembled?[401]

There is a very strong tradition in conservative Christianity that woman is ontologically intended to be subservient to and subordinated to men. In First Corinthians 11:10 we read that *the head of every man is Christ and the head of every woman is the man.* This is also reflected in Ephesians 5:22-23 where the author writes that wives are to submit themselves to their husband as it is fit in the Lord... *for the husband is the head of his wife as Christ is the head of the church, his body, of which he is the savior.* In First Peter 3: 1, 5-6 we are instructed that the woman is to be in subjection to her husband.

Theological fundamentalists and Biblical literalists can claim, therefore, a solid scriptural foundation for male dominance and female subordination. There is much in the traditional conservative hermeneutic of scriptures which support a position that even in situations of marital violence a woman is to live in total subjection to whatever man has God's intended control over her – whether this is her father, her spouse, or her son. These kinds of discussions are forms of binary gender essentialism.[402] In the online lesbian, bisexual, gay, transgendered and queer culture encyclopedia, patriarchal society is described as *male-dominant, male-centered, and male-identified. Besides variables such as race, age and social class, the control model also hierarchically organizes gender and sexuality.*[403]

Another theological root is that God is a Trinitarian being who sits on top of a heavenly pyramid. Roman Catholic nun and theologian Elizabeth Johnson, CSJ writes:

> There is a settled country from which the quest for the living God sets out in our day. Inherited from recent centuries, this view envisions God on the model of a monarch at the very peak of the pyramid of being. Without regard to Christ or the Spirit, it focuses on what trinitarian theology would call the "first person," a single powerful individual who dwells on high, ruling the cosmos and judging human conduct. Even when this Supreme Being is portrayed with a benevolent attitude, which the best of theology does, "He," for it is the ruling male who stands for this idea, is essentially remote. At times he intervenes to affect the laws of nature and work miracles, at times not. Although he loves the world, he is uncontaminated by its messiness. And always this distantly lordly lawgiver stands at the summit of hierarchal power, reinforcing structures of authority in society, church and family.[404]

United Church of Christ pastor and college professor of social justice Robin Meyers[405] reminds his readers that after Jesus' death and after the death of all of those who remembered him in his human life, the Christian movement began to have deeply divisive fights about a wide variety of *beliefs* about the nature and meaning of Jesus' life. Reading the four Gospels in the sequential order of their writing, we see the beginnings of the struggle for human control of the Jesus movement in terms of theological orthodoxy and human power.

These internecine doctrinal fights about controlling rule, orthodoxy and heresy were often intense and were sometimes bloody as Christian fought Christian for power and control of the emerging Church. In 325 CE, the Roman Emperor Constantine convened the Christian council of Nicaea, in essence establishing the foundations of an Institutional Church that we know today. Setting a governmental structure in place for the church, Constantine vested the bishops with the governance of religion inside the Roman Empire.[406] Fights continued to break out, sometimes turning very nasty as the now-official Church with its own hierarchy attempted to establish what heresy was and what orthodoxy was. Would be popes killed other would be popes.[407] Some contemporary theologians and religious history scholars contend that it was the emperor Constantine who ordained the Christian movement as a Church or institutionalized religious body and it was under his guidance that defining issues of heresy and orthodoxy began to be established.

Perhaps after Nicaea, the Council of Chalcedon in 451 CE is most influential in the Christian movement's theological doctrines of the essential natures of God and Christ and indirectly, therefore, of human beings. By the fifth century inside the Christian movement, women had been discarded as teachers, preachers, and dispensers of the Eucharist. Women were relegated to the sidelines as unimportant. Males alone debated and then established the Christian Church's theological orthodoxy and heresy. Meyers reminds us, therefore, that most of what we know as Christian orthodoxy (right belief) has, in fact, had a human origination and not a divine one. He urges his readers to discard these man-made orthodoxies as the true measure of Christian faith. To put it in another way, that which we see as orthodoxy in the twenty-first century would have been heresy to Jesus and his disciples during his lifetime.

Inside Trinitarian theology in the twenty-first century, all three aspects of the divine being tend to be seen in male imagery although the spirit is usually represented in the visual image or icon as a bird – the dove. Thus, for most Western Christians God is male and there is no feminine aspect to his maleness. While Roman Catholicism and Eastern Orthodox Christian traditions venerate the Virgin Mary in ways that may indicate, at least psychologically and spiritually - to individuals in the pews, a portion or aspect of female divinity, most Protestants (including Mennonites) do not. No major strand of Christianity and its orthodox theology sees Mary, therefore, as carrying personal divinity. She is, therefore, not a goddess to be worshipped. Instead, she is a semi-divinized human God-bearer.

Thus, inside the gates or boundaries of orthodox Christianity women tend to be seen as inferior to the male human being who shares in the male god's preference for males over females. Early theologians such as Tertullian (155-240 CE) and Augustine (352-430 CE) created elaborate theologies about women which we have inherited. Protestants in the Reformation, for example, John Knox (1514-1572 CE) and Martin Luther (1483-1546 CE) did not reform ancient prejudices against women. These influences remain in our time as prejudices against women in the Roman Catholic priesthood and in evangelical denominations and their prohibitions of women in leadership positions.

Inside Mennonite communities, Emma (Mrs. Joe) Richards (1927-2014 CE) was the first woman in the United States to be ordained to the Mennonite pastorate and she was ordained as part of a married couple's ministry. The church at the time of her ordination was explicit: her ordination was not to serve as a template for other women's ordination. Even today, some Mennonite congregations refuse to hire ordained women.

2. Exclusion or Denigration of the Female Voice

In our correspondence you have already identified one of the markers of the living patriarchy based on the West's religious mythology. This is the marker of female invisibility and exclusion from male-defined and male-protected turf. Only in 1849, for example, did Elizabeth Blackwell become the first American woman to graduate from medical school. Only in the middle of the 20th century did medical schools discontinue their rigid quota system for female medical students – thus limiting women's access to all sub-disciplines in medicine as a career.[408] The same kinds of female-denying pressures were present in American law. Harvard, for example denied Pauli Murray's entrance on the grounds of her gender.[409] Women could be mothers, nurses and elementary school teachers. They could not, by virtue of their gender, become neurosurgeons or astro-physicists. At the turn of the twentieth-century, not allowed to have suffrage, it was inconceivable that the United States Supreme Court would have three women judges at the turn of the twenty-first century. In a similar way, at the turn of the twentieth-century, it was inconceivable that women could be ordained ministers and bishops in Protestant denominations. By the beginning days of the twenty-first century, several United States denominations – such as the Methodist Church and the Anglican or Episcopal Church were administratively led by women bishops as well as female priests.

In similar ways there has been a strong preference in the religious academy for the words of men as the authoritative word. It has been within my lifetime – within the past forty years – when women began to enter the Christian academy as theologians, biblical scholars, philosophers, ethicists, divinity students, etc. Prior to that time, for example, in the lifetime of my friend Nelle Morton (1905-1987), women were only allowed in the religious academy in the field of religious education of small children. Somewhat later in time, the Roman Catholic theologian-philosopher Mary Daly needed to go to Europe to complete her degrees in Roman Catholic philosophy and theology.[410] At this moment in time, however, women's presence in theological programs of study is nearly universal.

Parenthetically, we tend to overlook the reality that women in the United States were denied suffrage until August 18, 1920.[411] This means that only 4.5 generations (counting a generation as 20 years) of American women have had the freedom to participate as equals in American constitutional law. It took nearly 70 years of women's activism before the Amendment passed to bring about universal suffrage for women in this country. Thus, the 1920 ratification represents years of activism by women who never benefitted directly from their work on behalf of women's equality under the law.

The Equal Rights Amendment written by Alice Paul was first introduced in the United States Congress in 1923. It has been introduced into every congressional session since then. It has not yet become a ratified constitutional amendment.[412]

One consequence of our rather recent arrival as women in the Christian Academy is that – even today – we tend to be ignored as peripheral to the real work of theology, men's work. Women in a wide variety of educational and occupational settings report that in important meetings, for example, they are simply excluded from participation in programmatic decision-making. If they are physically present, their contributions are likely to be ignored. One phenomenon women report over and over again is that when they speak, their ideas are ignored; sometime later when a man repeats, verbatim, what the woman has just said, then and only then does the idea get space in the discussion and subsequent decisions. The most extreme example of this I know is from a woman I met in my forties and her fifties. Her husband was a tenured and highly respected university professor. She had literally authored all of his professional publications before tenure, and she was never given any academic mention nor did he share authorship credits with her on book covers. She said to me in a counseling session: *I can't divorce him. He owns all of my work in his name. I have no professionally recognized equity in the books and articles I wrote for him. Because of my work, he is internationally known while I am relegated to the role of his spouse.* Because she was refusing to continue to do this kind of work for him, the marriage had begun to feel like a cage to her. But economically she could see no way forward for herself and her late adolescent children but to tolerate his intellectual abusiveness towards her inside the marriage as a way of reaping some financial security out of the publication-authoring work she had already done for him.

In these kinds of situations, the man is, therefore, given credit for the insight and work which a woman colleague brought to the table. Such male behavior essentially invalidates the work, the worth, and the unique contributions of women. It is also, I have come to believe, a serious form of academic plagiarism. Men take women's ideas, use them, and then claim them as their own. Men who engage in this behavior repetitively need to be called on it by everyone who notices it. Until men learn this is unacceptable behavior, it will continue. Shaming them is probably the best pedagogy that women have devised. In these kinds of situations, we need to inform our male allies that they must begin to speak up *in situ* on our behalf.

In your own work, you have noticed this phenomenon just as I have noticed it in mine.

Women must be willing to project their ideas, and themselves, with a certain kind of intellectual fierceness if they are to be noticed at all.[413] This self/work-protective behavior then leads some men in the religious academy to label academic women in pejorative ways – ways in which forceful men are not so labeled. Cultural dynamics or stereotypes of enforced femininity are thus also in play in this particular arena of male and female relationships.

In essence, I think, women are still reduced to their sexuality – even in professional collegial relationships. This may be why we see so much sexual abuse of women graduate students in doctoral programs and so much sexual and gender harassment of women students and women faculty in the religious academy. Women, therefore, are judged by their femininity (or its absence) and their sexual attractiveness (or its absence) in ways men are not judged. This pejorative view of women allows many academic men to denigrate their female colleagues' academic abilities.

In our recent conversations about the absence of a strong and forthright female voice in the John Howard Yoder – Mennonite Church/Believer's Church conferences regarding Yoder's dual legacies, we have both also noted the almost total exclusion of women's voices from publications authored by contemporary Yoderians. It is not that there are no Yoderian women – for there are.[414] It is rather that their voices are not respected as equal to men's voices and, therefore, historically have not been included proportionately to men's voices. Many of the female Yoderians are literally invisible to the men in the religious academy of the Mennonite Church and in the religious academy of the Catholic Church. In addition, where there are known women who have studied Yoder's work in a critical and self-aware fashion, these voices have been deliberately excluded.

It is possible even today, therefore, to write an edited volume of essays about Yoder's legacy and include absolutely no women's academic voices. While there have been women speaking and writing (from the church's margins) about the dual legacies of Yoder's life, their absence from denominationally-sponsored publications becomes noticeable as soon as this question of full inclusion is raised. Something is drastically amiss in the new century's religious academy when it can continue such patterns of gender repression.

In 2007 when I began to do the research for the book which eventually became *The Elephants in God's Living Room, v.3, The Mennonite Church and John Howard Yoder, Collected Essays,*[415] I became aware of the disproportionate maleness of voice in the various festschrift volumes, book chapters, and periodical articles honoring Yoder. This is but one example. The original constitution of J. Denny Weaver's most recent book – where two women's somewhat contradictory voices were added as an afterthought is another. Each woman's voice, to a certain degree, cancels out the voice of the other.[416] Pitting woman's voice against woman's voice is, therefore, another methodology of the patriarchy. It is a methodology which denigrates both women's voices in the service of the dominant male voice.

The women who work for the peace of the world are, therefore, especially ignored when their work is about men's sexual violence in the world. You and I have talked about this on multiple occasions. Those of us who have spent a professional lifetime urging for sexual violence advocacy as a part of the church's needed peace and justice work, have become the pariahs of the pariahs in the religious academy. Our insistence upon speaking up with clarity and forcefulness is seen as *holding or creating vendettas against men or against the male-led church itself.*

I always thought it helped me as a college professor that I inhabited a large body and that I had a low register voice with lots of projective power. Even in classrooms with 200 students in them, I never needed to use a microphone to project my voice. I am not much of a believer in auras but I've been told many times that in public speaking events I project a large aura. When I spoke at a cousin's ordination, for example, he told me later that a woman in the congregation asked him who I was because of the large aura I projected when speaking, in her words, *a compelling aura that filled the entire room.* Recently, at a professional clinical workshop in the Tucson foothills, after I introduced myself, the teacher said to the gathered group of students, *what a wonderful booming voice.* Later he asked me, *Are you a singer? Have you had voice lessons?*

At Goshen I used to joke with my academic colleagues and friends that I could still the whispering in the back rows during required chapel services – the whispering of students whom I privately called *the unbaptized* and *the non-washed* because of their resentments towards the college's mandatory attendance requirement that they be there. I silently stood at the podium until the chapel auditorium grew quiet. I looked directly at these back rows of recalcitrant and hostile students. Once I had their undivided attention, then, and only then, would I begin! This was particularly true when I was introducing an honored guest speaker who would not understand and, therefore, did not deserve, the students' intentional rudeness. In addition, unlike most of my colleagues, attending chapels and convocations, I always sat in the back rows where I could directly and in close proximity stare down the students who were being deliberately noisy and rude.

Ruth E. Krall

The same was true in my classroom. I simply did not have the discipline problems many women faculty report in mixed-gender classrooms. On more than one occasion I publicly invited whispering students to go to the hallway for their private and very disruptive conversations. They would glare in anger at me but they grew quiet. And in no instance I can recall did I need to make this direct intervention a second time with any particular set of inattentive whispering miscreant students.

I generally, in public, ignored overtly hostile male students who entered the class with a huge chip on their shoulders. Recognizing them as a problem, I began to set classroom buffers in place between them and the students who wanted to learn. Since I utilized small-group discussion processes in nearly all classrooms, I would assign hostile and negative male students to the same group – thus intellectually quarantining their group contamination processes. They had to deal with each other's negativity and do the assigned work if they wanted to pass the class. Or, alternatively, I would assign them one by one to groups that each included strong male academic achievers – those male students who refused to tolerate nasty and uncaring classroom behavior by a classmate when it affected their own grades. These bright, highly motivated male students helped me, therefore, to police the intellectual safety and integrity of classroom work. Thus, small-group discussion sections were never randomized in my classrooms. There was always a motive and a purpose for the group's composition as well as its task.

My sense is that the religious academy is much more conservative about integrating women as full peers than is the secular academy. During my years in the secular academy, I rarely needed to fight for conversational space or for recognition of my contributions to the life of my department. There was collegial respect that extended both ways between me and the other folks in my department. My department chair included me as a full participant in departmental decisions that involved me and the staff I supervised. He encouraged me to publish and appointed me to various boards and committees where I represented not only the department but my own thinking as well. Approximately fifteen years older than I was, he actively mentored me and promoted me. I was, therefore, as comfortable having conversations with him in his palatial office as I was in my tiny one.

In contrast, inside the religious academy, I often felt personally devalued as a scholar-teacher and I thought my work was also often devalued. I was frequently excluded from decisions that involved me or involved the department as a whole. I found some institutional administrators and colleagues were more interested in intimidating me than in supervising me or respectfully inquiring about what I thought.

As the first non-ordained woman inside the Mennonite Academy to be tenured in a particular Goshen College department, I endured hours, days, and indeed years of pre-tenure academic hazing. I used all of my clinical and diagnostic skills to understand this hazing and to circumvent it whenever possible. I was rarely, therefore, ever boxed into the corner of departmental or personal failure caused by hostile male colleagues who so clearly wanted me to fail. I think, therefore, that I may be the only tenured Goshen College faculty member in recent history whose tenure nomination originated outside of the departmental home in which tenure was eventually located. This faculty governance irregularity was tolerated – perhaps even welcomed – by the college's rank and tenure committee and by the academic dean in place at the time. Without the active support of sympathetic mid-level administrators and faculty colleagues, and good classroom evaluations, I would never have stood in front of you as your classroom teacher. I would simply have been one more female academic consigned to the academic discard pile.

There were notable exceptions to this general pattern of silencing in the Mennonite Academy, and these welcoming and including male colleagues and former supervisors remain my friends in retirement. They often inconvenienced themselves on my behalf – extending me protective cover and even emotional support when I most needed it. They recognized my academic strengths and sought to buffer me from some of the irrational male antagonism and intellectual hazing that was faced by so many of the women faculty in my age cohort. They befriended me in order that my academic strengths could be used on behalf of the students who sat in my classrooms.

Many years ago I had a conversation with a black woman academic faculty member at a prestigious woman's college. She told me that when she applied to the university as an undergraduate, she left ambiguous the questions of her gender and race. Her first name could have been male or female. Her last name was Dutch in origin and she capitalized on that. She told me that for the first year of university course work, she never spoke in class or identified herself as the African-American woman with the Dutch name. She took the computerized tests and aced them. She was convinced that this strategy had allowed her to succeed and build an academic reputation on paper that she could then later transform into a more personal relationship inside graduate schools with her major professors. I've been told more recently that very bright and highly motivated Asian-American women utilize similar strategies when applying to prestigious Ivy League colleges. They anglicize and masculinize their names if at all possible to escape the formal or informal Asian female quota system.

These kinds of discriminatory behavior and academic hazing are all markers of the patriarchy in motion.

3. Pyramidal Power Structures

Starhawk, to my way of thinking, has the best description of patriarchal world-views as hierarchical and pyramidal.[417] They are based on conceptions of power as

Ruth E. Krall

a limited human resource. They are based on the ideal of power-over rather than on notions of internal empowerment or collective empowerment.

It is likely that some of these notions of pyramidal power have, in reality, helped individuals accumulate great personal wealth and have helped societies develop elite collective communities which do the same. However, the resources of wealth and power do not necessarily filter down the pyramid. Thus, what we see when we look at societies based on the pyramid is that huge numbers of individuals are disempowered and unable to gain the necessary traction of power that is needed to succeed in hierarchical societies. It is common wisdom that most people trapped in poverty and in illiteracy do not have the needed skills and interpersonal connections to power in order to compete in highly organized societies based on literacy and a modicum of economic goods.

Studies of infant brains and the brains of children throughout childhood and adolescence are demonstrating that privileged children have bigger vocabularies by the time they enter primary education years. This advantage plays itself out in academic success. Children with fewer than 500 words by the age of four simply lose their ability to compete in their earliest primary years. This increasingly computes into academic failure. In its turn, such academic failure guarantees that an individual is likely to live into poverty throughout their own lifespan and to replicate this pattern in their own children's lives.[418] In my opinion, such research demonstrates the omnipresent hazards of the patriarchy for those who are least privileged in any society – and therefore are the most vulnerable.

Here is where we begin to see the interstitial connections of racism, sexism, heterosexism, classism, ethnocentrism, anti-Semitism, and other forms of prejudice with authoritarianism, dehumanization, depersonalization, culturally enacted crimes of obedience, and socially enacted violence based on innate human differences – in short the prejudices, cultural actions, and crimes of xenophobia. When cultural elites determine who belongs and who doesn't belong, who should survive and who is expendable, there are huge consequences in the lives of those who belong *and* in the lives of those who don't belong. Usually the gatekeepers are those who do the work delegated to them by those who are higher up in the channel of command.

One story that I often return to as my example here is about the very young and very gifted vocal musician Marian Anderson. In her biography she describes making her way to one of the premier vocal training studios in the United States in order to apply for admission. She did not get past the secretary-receptionist at the front desk who told her bluntly that *we don't admit your kind here.* Anderson had to go to Europe to receive the necessary advanced vocal training which is always essential for the classically educated voice. The irony in this story is that Anderson's voice was almost universally recognized by mid-career as one of the most exceptional voices of the twentieth-century – vocal equipment that comes along perhaps once in every several hundred years. Everyone who ever heard Anderson sing knew they were hearing a unique voice on the classical and operatic stage. Eventually, long after her prime as a singer, the Metropolitan Opera Company honored her achievements by admitting her to its ranks as its first black singer. If you have never read her biography, I recommend it highly. In her life after this admission to membership in the Met, she was a tireless friend to younger African-American operatic hopefuls who continued to honor her as a mentor and friend until the end of Anderson's life.

4. The Male Body and Self as the Prototype for the Human Body and Self

Here my example is from medical research. For years only male rats or other male research animals were used in the basic research protocols for new medications – medications that would later be used by both genders. One part of the rationale was that the male rats or other animals did not have the hormonal fluctuations that female animals did, thus one variable in research animals could be controlled. As feminist women in the medical research academy have been insisting for more than fifty years, such a scientific practice is absurd. If the medications are to be prescribed to women as well as men, then more nuanced basic and applied research is needed to determine the safety of these medications as treatment modalities.

Only recently have the nation's major research-funding institutes begun to address this very obvious discriminatory problem.[419]

5. Mankind = Humankind: He = He and She

Another example of the privileging of the male as the human prototype is the now-academically-discredited use of the word *mankind* to be the inclusive term for both men and women. Research has consistently shown that when the word *mankind* is used, the overwhelming perception is that what is being discussed is male. The same is true of the universal word *he* to stand for both he and she. I distinctly remember repeatedly arguing this issue in the educational academy of the last century. Initially, this insight was met with protesting laughter and ridicule. By now, however, publishing companies rather routinely insist upon authors using inclusive language where both genders are included in the discussion. But this is a relatively new phenomenon in American academic publishing. Many remnants of the older practice can be found in daily life.

The female voice, when subordinated by and absorbed by the male voice, cannot be heard as her own voice. It is as simple and as complex a reality as that.

Ruth E. Krall

6. Fear of the Female Menstruating Body

This absurd, albeit ancient, notion that the menstruating female body is somehow ontologically unclean and contaminates the purity of the commons means that the woman who menstruates is, as a consequence, unfit for important forms of human work and leadership. Monthly bleeds have been used to question a woman's personal and professional fitness for other human roles and activities. Would you [gasp] want a menstruating woman as a nation's president – controlling its atomic arsenal? Would you [gasp] want her to be an astronaut? Would you [gasp] want her to be a priest? Would you [gasp] even want her to be a bishop? Would you [gasp| allow her to consecrate [and, by implication, contaminate] the sacramental elements of the Eucharistic meal?

The orthodox theological answer to these questions appears to be that women were only created to help men procreate a new generation of humans. Indeed some of the earliest and most revered Christian theologians held that women were misbegotten males – in short, the womb as incubator failed in some major way and produced an inferior product.[420] These men, in all of their robust theological wisdom, simply could not find another reason for a woman's presence on planet earth than her sexuality and reproductive abilities. In this pre-scientific view of procreation, the perfect male seed [now known as the sperm] was believed to contain the entire human being and simply needed to be incubated properly inside the female body to create another male human being. There was no sense of the human zygote as a creation of two gamete cells sexually merging to form the first new cell of a human being.

Even though we now can look, with the assistance of powerful electronic microscopes, at these cells merging and then beginning to multiply, these ancient hysterical prejudices against bleeding and pregnant women still persist in the larger culture which surrounds a woman's life, in the social world of work, and the private world of family life.

7. Only Males Can Inherit the Kingdom

In addition, we have the long monarchical tradition of male primogeniture in which only a king-fathered firstborn son can, by law, assume his deceased father's throne. Only in the absence of a male heir is the now-dead king's eldest daughter allowed to assume the inherited position of rule. In the sixteenth-century, the Scottish Protestant reformer John Knox argued that female rulers and their female regents were an abomination and contrary to God's will.[421]

This prejudice remains deeply ingrained in the Roman Catholic Church where only males can be priests and only males can be popes. The subordination of Roman Catholic nuns to the all-male hierarchy comes into clear view whenever the papacy decides to crack down on this group or that group of nuns for inappropriate female behavior such as speaking up and participating in social activism on behalf of the poor.[422]

A remnant of this prejudice about the essential maleness of political rule remains. In 2017, women have yet to assume, for example, the United States presidency. In part, I think this has been due to women's historical, and now-changing, exclusion from combat roles in the American military and from participation in the nation's military academies. In part, it has been due to the relatively recent phenomenon of women governors and women congressmen and women mayors – these traditional training grounds for candidates with presidential aspirations. In part, it has been the reluctance of individuals with great wealth to underwrite the political campaigns of women. Feminist PAC organizations such as Emily's List[423] have focused on identifying electable women and have raised the funds to underwrite their campaigns. While these efforts have been hugely successful in many situations of a woman's candidacy, there is still no proportionate representation of women in these electoral positions.

In addition to the legislative and executive branches of government, the number of women judges in positions of real power is also not proportionate to their numbers in the general population. The current United States Supreme Court, for example, has only three women judges. It has no protestant judges.

8. Disproportionate Shares of Financial Capital

While some women independently control great wealth, the majority of women do not. Wealth creation and wealth maintenance are, therefore, seen as masculine activities. In particular, women who represent ethnic diversities – such as new immigrants – or women who grew up in relative poverty rarely control vast wealth empires. There are, of course, exceptions to this general rule such as Oprah Winfrey who controls a vast empire related to the public media. But, in general, middle-class and working-class women are excluded from the possibilities of wealth generation.

9. Sex Goddesses

Western culture's obsession with sexualizing the female body is definitely a clue that the patriarchy is alive, well, and busy colonizing the consciousness of men and women, boys and girls. We do not know why menarche is now occurring at younger and younger ages for girls in the West's industrialized nations. I suspect (in addition to the electric light hypothesis) that the girl child's female body is responding to the omnipresent imagery of girls and women as sex objects. If one is not "sexy" (even as a ten-year-old girl) then one has no implicit value in a sex-addicted culture.

When I open the Sunday newspaper and look through the advertising flyers, I am often appalled at the clothing advertisements for very young girls. Then I go to the grocery store, a shopping mall, or to the public library, and see these clothing items actually being worn. I simply have to look away because it is so painful to me to see children being allowed, indeed encouraged, to look whorish before they are old enough to know what the word *whorish* means.

10. Rape

Rape is, I think, the ultimate symbol and the penultimate weapon of patriarchal cultures and of deeply enculturated beliefs or patriarchal understandings of women's and children's essential nature. Rape's cultural sibling, domestic violence, is also a powerful reality and symbol. When men feel entitled to rape or to beat a woman, we know the patriarchy is alive and well. When men who rape or beat a woman face no consequences for their actions, we know the patriarchy is alive and well.[424] When the surrounding culture does not teach nor hold men responsible to live with women in pacific manners, we know the culture is rooted in patriarchal values about women's subordination and subservience.

The current discussion about rape on American college campuses is a much needed one.[425] It is essentially an extension of the feminist anti-rape movement which began in the 1970's. Women academics have known since Mary Koss's important research that rape is omnipresent on most – if not all – college campuses.[426]

As we have corresponded briefly about sexual violence accusations against Bill Cosby and John Howard Yoder, it is not only *bad* men in dangerous neighborhoods who sexually violate women. Rape and women's accusations about rape are endemic in the world and rapists are present in every layer of society and in every culture.[427]

Concluding Commentary

Perhaps my reflections here can provide you with your own personal gateway into this topic. I am certain that you have identified other markers of the patriarchy. If we surveyed fifty of our collective feminist and womanist Mennonite friends, I wonder what other markers would be identified. Most assuredly, our social location in life affects what we see. This list, therefore, reflects to some degree, my white skin, blue eyes, and large body. Indubitably, it reflects my life inside the religious academy as a sexual violence educator. It reflects my years as a clinician. It reflects my years as a student of religious mythology and culture wars. It reflects my cultural status as middle-class and heterosexual.

I tend to think in stories and in narratives so this response to you is peppered with examples. Thus, I have failed to meet your challenge of two pages.

Seventeenth Letter

Case Study
A Disciple of the Buddha does
not Misuse Sexuality[428]

The archetype is a universal and regularly occurring pattern. It exists in the heart and soul of humanity. We can see its individual expression, therefore, as an individual hologram of a universal cultural form.

Michael Conforti[429]

Introductory Comments

Some of our recent electronic correspondence has touched upon spiritual conversation matters. Many of these seem to me to have emerged as Eastern philosophies have entered mainstream awareness in Western cultures. In particular, we have been talking about physical movement, therapeutic touch, guided imagery, prayer, massage, Yoga, and meditation practices as useful aids in helping sick minds and sick bodies heal.[430] While I think that you and I are both clear about our social and religious identities as Christian and Mennonite, it seems necessary for me to state my own thinking here. I remain committed to the Jesus path, once historically known as *The Way,* as it has been understood and taught to me *in an Anabaptist voice.* That said, I do not believe that my faithfulness to that path excludes or excuses me from the necessity of thinking critically about my ethnic faith tradition. For example, I do not now and never have believed that only Mennonites represent God's people.

Reading Roman Catholic theologian Mark Jordan[431] was helpful in his elucidation of the principle that because Christianity has historically insisted that it is a confessing church, individual Christians, by their confession of faith, are obliged to bear witness against the deeply embedded lies and entrenched repressive secrets held inside their church's institutional organizations. These lies and secrets, for example, the hidden presence of sexual violations by religious leaders, are, therefore, endemic, ideologically embedded, and usually denied aspects of Christianity's institutional life and praxis. In Jungian thought, they represent the institution's shadow – that endemic reality which Father Tom Doyle calls religion's *dark side*.[432]

Throughout the institutional church's history, these denied aspects of religious communal life have historically been covered over and lodged deep inside walls of secrecy. We see, therefore, the continuing presence of ethical, moral, or spiritual corruption inside the church's power and governance structures. One clue to their presence is authoritarianism. Another is the religious institution's reluctance or total unwillingness to be transparent about moral lapses inside its leadership caste. In multiple speeches, book chapters, and articles Father Doyle notes the presence of abusive narcissism among the clerical castes.[433] The altars of power, control, authority, and money interact and intersect. Over the course of many years, a systemic and endemic moral rot is the consequence.

I take Jordan's concern here to include corrupt moral actions of individuals such as clergy sexual abuse of children, adolescents, and vulnerable adults. But it also includes corrupted and economically or scientifically suspect doctrinal teachings that privilege the powerful at the expense of the vulnerable. I also include religious doctrines and theologically repressive teachings which claim that some human beings have an intrinsically disordered sexuality because they live within a same-gender sexual orientation.[434] I also include here the practices of institutional clericalism.[435] In short, these church teachings, contrary to Jewish and Christian scriptures, claim that not all human beings are made in the divine image. Some are born, therefore, as evil. I consider this to be heresy. In addition, it is partly pornographic because it obsesses about the sexual behaviors of other adults. It is also gender orientation idolatry. *Me and mine but not you and yours: we who are culturally dominant alone belong inside God's love.*

In this series of letters, I have looked inside several denominational versions of Christianity. In particular, I have looked towards the work being done to understand clergy sexual violence and clergy practices of clericalism as these have been studied and written about inside the world-wide Roman Catholic faith tradition. This is a shared tradition with our Anabaptist-Mennonite one inasmuch as our denominational ancestors were Roman Catholic Church reformers. In the sixteenth century they, and their critique of the social and ethical corruptness of the Christian Church of their era, were rejected outright by the mother church as heretical. Consequently, our faith ancestors in the Anabaptist tradition were hunted down, persecuted, and sometimes murdered by the mother church for their efforts to form a more faithful Christian community. Bearing witness to endemic, internalized, systemic, doctrinal, or structural corruptness is, therefore, part of our spiritual heritage as Anabaptist-Mennonites.

In addition, I do not believe that my Anabaptist-Mennonite ethnic and religious identity prohibits me from learning from individuals and communities who have chosen somewhat different spiritual paths. My choice to live inside the sociological margins of the Anabaptist-Mennonite religious faith community does not isolate me from a desire to deepen my own inner spiritual formation by learning from other religious or philosophical traditions.

No one human individual or community knows truth in its fullness. In my open-ness, therefore, to learning from other spiritual traditions, I am deeply indebted to the books, articles, and lectures of Huston Smith, son of Methodist missionaries to China, a Methodist layman, and a former Professor of World Religions.[436] I am also indebted to my Lutheran father, his parents and siblings and my cousins – none of whom were - or are - Mennonite.

There are enough similarities, for example, between centering prayer and con-templative prayer in the Christian tradition and sitting meditation in the Buddhist tradition that we can explore the wisdom and methodologies of both as resources for our own inner lives. During the Vietnam War, the interfaith resources of mutual respect, dialogue and learning about spirituality (and its connections to anti-war and pro-active social justice witness movements) became visible, for example, to Barbara Deming (Quaker), Thomas Merton (Trappist monk), Martin Luther King, Jr. (Black Baptist preacher), Doug Hostetter (Mennonite peace activist), Thich Nhat Hanh (Buddhist monk), Abraham Joshua Herschel (Jewish philosopher, theologian, mystic, activist, and rabbi), Phillip Berrigan (Josephine Priest) and his older brother Daniel Berrigan (Jesuit priest).

In the United States we can see the influence of Gandhi's spiritual teachings about Satygraha (truth force)[437] on the work of mid-century Black civil rights activists such as Rosa Parks and Martin Luther King, Jr. In addition, we can also see the influence of Gandhi's life and work in the civil rights activism work of Nelson Mandela and Bishop Tutu inside South African protest movements vis-à-vis repressive state-sponsored and state-enforced Apartheid.

During the past seven years of reading and study about clergy sexual abuse and the related phenomenon of institutional clericalism, it has become clear to me that religion's shadow side, that *dark side of organized religion,* can be found wher-ever there is supposed to be light. Father Doyle states that these phenomenons of clergy sexual abuse and their concomitant structural components of cover-up abuses are not parasites or barnacles that attach themselves from the secular outside to religious structures. Rather, they are well integrated internal aspects of the church qua church as an institution.

When we look at world religions, including Eastern philosophies and guru-dis-ciple communities, what we find is that they are no freer of these disturbing and disciple dis-enablement issues of spiritual teacher abusiveness than are Western theologies and their communities. The problems of religious leader abuse of their disciples and members of the laity are, therefore, endemic spirituality-disabling problems in human religious institutional structures and in the spirituality of human psyches.

The principle I talked about in an earlier letter comes in to play. If no adult males are having abusive, illicit sexual relationships with giraffes, there is no need for a code, a law, a precept, or a spiritual teaching about the harmfulness of such behavior. Without manifested behavior, there is no need for a warning or a prohibition. Thus the same principle underlies Christian laws and Buddhist precepts. Christian teaching and Buddhist teaching, therefore, agree on some common issues of human morality and ethical behavior.

The precepts address potentially problematic areas of human relatedness in a search to guide individuals and communities to a life which is whole and well. The first precept, for example, is actually very akin to a therapeutic principle known to all Western physicians, nurses and other clinical specialists: *do no harm!*

This brief summary of my current approach to these matters is important because in the case study which follows I want to access and reflect upon a situation of spiritual teacher abuse of disciples and students inside the Soto Zen Sect of Buddhism in the United States. Such a case study must be seen in the context of my earlier work about the presence of sexual violence and institutional clericalism *inside* Christian – indeed, inside Mennonite - communities.[438] Inasmuch as I am not a practicing Buddhist, I will include some background work I did earlier about the missionary-like emergence of Soto Sect Zen's teaching centers or communities insides the United States during the twentieth century. This will help establish the sociological and religious context of the case study which follows.

My personal intuitions about the need to include case studies in my academic work are lodged inside my history as a clinician. Medical and nursing grand rounds, for example, utilize a case study methodology. Clinical training programs emphasize the case study method as one which is essential to gain an in-depth awareness of clinical complexity. Case studies, therefore, help us to locate and anchor our theorizing inside real life examples. Thus, case studies can help serve as correctives to our theoretical work even as they serve to provide us with exemplars and models.

The cultural forms (or archetypal patterns) of religious leader abuse are present in many, perhaps all, world religions. Thus, religious abuse of spiritual disciples and members of the laity by the priest, the guru, the minister, the imam, the rabbi, the shaman, or other spiritual leader is a regularly repeating pattern of organized religious life. These abusive violations represent repetitive disruptive patterns of authority initiated or enacted by an individual with systemic or structural power. They are received by an individual with less power. In religious communities this power or the human priest or minister, in most religious traditions, is spiritually tied to the non-visible power of the divine. Thus, it can be named as an archetype in terms of the individual's unconscious *and* in terms of the community's collective unconscious.

To summarize: this archetype of the abusive religious leader resides inside individual consciousness at pre-conscious or unconscious levels. In Jungian thought, it also, therefore, resides in humanity's collective unconscious.

If we look closely at Gugenbuhl-Craig's[439] discussion of the constellating archetypes in the helper relationship, we begin to get a model to examine. For example, the archetype of a healing physician needs the correlating archetype of a sick patient. In the actual world of medicine, there can be no healing relationship without both a healer and a sick person. To make matters more interesting, the healer has an inner archetypal healer but she also has an inner archetypal sick person. The patient, likewise, has an inner archetypal sick person but he also has an inner archetypal healer. The ways these archetypes repeatedly constellate inside any healer-sick person relationship will largely determine how well or how poorly that relationship works in the service of healing or in the service of anti-healing.

If we look, therefore, at these issues of a religious leader's sexual abuse of his or her disciples or followers, we can see that the guru, priest, rabbi, shaman, or imam has an activating inner archetypal spiritual leader, guru or priest and an inner archetypal disciple while the disciple has an inner archetypal disciple and an inner archetypal spiritual leader, guru or priest. When the priest or the guru chooses to become abusive by sexual involvements with a disciple or member of the laity, ancient and pre-verbal patterns of manifested behavior come into play. It is as if both parties become actors in an ancient tragedy whose roots lie in their personal identities, their personal life histories, their community's history, and in the collective unconscious. They become pre-scripted actors in the story they will create together in the present moment by their interaction with each other. I am tempted to say that if there were no archetypal cultural form of religious leader sexual abuse there would not be, indeed there could not be, any abuse. But this is too shallow and simplistic a reading of the relationship of archetypal form to individual acts of abusive behavior.

These contemporary stories of religious leader sexual abuse become, therefore, complex and tragic meta-stories of human sexuality in the service of authoritarian power, narcissism, and domination. They also function as complex and tragic meta-stories of human evil.

No matter if the enactment of the tragic story of religious or spiritual leader sexual abuse is adult to child abuse or adult to adult abuse, the story's basic structure is first of all a cultural form. In these chapters, and elsewhere,[440] I have argued that the organizing social pattern (perhaps that which Jung identifies as the complex) that activates the embodiment of these cultural forms is the patriarchy itself.

Exegesis of the Third Precept

A disciple of the Buddha does not misuse sexuality.

I found a discussion of the Third Precept on an internet web site and I will abstract that discussion in order to assist us to see how Buddhist teachings about sexual misconduct from within a Buddhist context (rather than from outside within a Christian context) intersect with historical events of sexual misconduct. I am indebted to Josho Pat Phelan who heads the Chapel Hill Zen Center in North Carolina.[441] She is in the spiritual-teaching lineage of Suzuki Roshi of the San Francisco Soto Sect Zen Center and was ordained by Richard Baker Roshi. Her interpretation of this precept regarding sexual misconduct occurs in a larger discussion of the *Ten Basic Precepts* and is, therefore, part of her on-going practice of teaching the precepts to her students and readers.

According to Thich Nhat Hanh the Sanskrit word *sila* or its English correlative *precept* indicates *an intention of mind that manifests in body and speech.*[442] A precept, therefore, is not a prohibition. Nor, is it a prescription. Rather, precepts are guidelines or reminders for practitioners to live and act mindfully. Thus, fundamentally, the precepts are disciplines for the mind – part of the pathway to the mindfulness of awakening. As Nhat Hanh so clearly writes, *our own life is the instrument through which we experiment with truth.*[443] In the embodied life of the Buddhist practitioner, precepts provide guidance about how to proceed inside the dual spiritual disciplines of individual meditation and living in community.

Phelan comments that the Third Precept originally was a prohibition against any sexual activity for all Zen monks. She remarks of this era, [f]*or monks this list (from the Brahma Chinese Net Sutra) prohibits any kind of sexual activity – with the opposite sex, with animals, with gods, goddesses, ghosts or spirits, and other forms of lustful behavior, as well as all kinds of 'perverse' (punctuation hers) sexual conduct.*[444]

Later, after lay individuals began to live by the Ten Precepts, this prohibition came to mean *no adultery*. Phelan comments that to her the precept applies to any *lustful or sticky desire* whether it is sex or some other object of the senses.[445]

Buddhist Dharma, as I understand it from the outsider's position, is not a teaching that moralizes about good or bad behavior. Rather, it is a set of mental guidelines for training the mind to live mindfully and in equanimity in each present moment. The Third Precept, therefore, attempts to guide the practitioner's insight about ways in which self-centered desire shuts individuals off from mindfulness and from one another. By means of paying attention to self-centered desire, the Buddhist practitioner can come to realize that sexual misconduct is *often facilitated by misusing speech to manipulate others, and self-centeredness leads to treating people like possessions or objects.*[446]

Yet another way, according to Phelan, to misuse sexuality is to indulge in intoxicating fantasies about sex or being carried away by euphoric feelings. Here she clarifies that she is not talking about ordinary sexual fantasies but about indulging in sexual fantasies to the extent that this mental activity replaces a larger and larger portion of the practitioner's real daily life.[447]

She concludes that the point of the Ten Precepts is to help individuals become aware of how they separate themselves from everything else, and, in regard to this specific Third Precept, *by not misusing the original intimacy of relationship between the self and other.*[448]

Soto Sect Zen Arrives in Los Angeles

According to James Ishmael Ford[449] Japanese Soto Sect Zen came to the continental United States in 1923 when Hosen Isobe established a Zen mission center in Los Angeles. Dying after four years, the Isobe-founded mission became the immediate forerunner of the Los Angeles area Zenshuji Mission.

In this manner Japanese Soto Sect Zen set down its first roots in the United States. At first serving Japanese-descent and Japanese-speaking individuals, gradually the population of spiritual seekers and disciples spread to include individuals who represent America's cultural diversity. Over time, people of European and African descent found their way to study at an expanding network of Soto Sect Zen temples or meditation centers.[450]

Today, Soto Sect Zen remains the largest Zen presence in America. Fifty Soto Sect Zen temples and centers dot the American landscape and less than 15 of these serve congregations made up primarily of Japanese-speaking individuals or people with a Japanese ancestry.

Soto Sect Zen Settles in San Francisco

The founding teacher of the San Francisco Soto Sect Zen Center was Shunryu Suzuki Roshi. He was born in 1904 to parents with long family histories of priestly Zen practice. With a (then) newly-allowed monastery policy allowing monks to marry, a married priest system developed. Suzuki's mother was among the first group of married women to live within the temple complex. Since the temple had no married quarters, the young couple and their young son lived in the large Buddha hall. Growing up inside the temple, it was here that Suzuki received his first Zen instruction.

Migrating from Japan to San Francisco in 1959, Suzuki settled in the city's Japantown where he began to build a community around sitting meditation practices. By 1962, the Zen Center of San Francisco was formally incorporated. Today the San Francisco Soto Sect Zen Center is the formative nucleus of the largest network of Buddhist centers in North America.

Sexual Scandal and the San Francisco Soto Zen Community

According to Downing[451] and Ford[452], Richard Baker Roshi was a gifted American Soto Sect Zen disciple and practitioner to whom Suzuki gave the Dharma transmission.[453] Upon Suzuki's death in 1976, Baker became Abbott at the San Francisco Soto Sect Zen Center.

In March, 1983 Baker's tenure as the resident Abbott began to unravel when allegations were first revealed and then validated that he'd been having multiple sexual relationships with the center's students. In 1984, under intense pressure from community donors and member practitioners, Baker resigned from his position as the Center's teaching Abbott. Parenthetically, Wikipedia reports that *former students have said that he was addicted to power, abusive of his position, extravagant in his personal spending, and inappropriate in his love life.*[454] Downing and Ford both note that Richard Baker, in the wake of sexual misconduct revelations in San Francisco, continues to have a world-wide Zen spiritual teaching practice.

Wikipedia also reports that Vietnamese Buddhist teacher Thich Nhat Hanh has said of Baker that *to me he embodies very much the future of Buddhism in the West with his creative intelligence and his aliveness.*[455] It is quite clear as one researches Baker's spiritual teaching career after leaving San Francisco that he remains a vital and active force in Western Soto Sect Zen Buddhism. He, in short, landed on his feet.

After Baker's resignation, Jakal Dainin Katagiri Roshi of the Minneapolis Soto Sect Zen Center became the interim Abbott (1984-1986) in San Francisco as the community sought to re-organize and re-orient itself. His task was to help the San Francisco Soto Sect Zen community heal the divisive effects of Baker's misconduct and to regroup. In part Katagiri was asked to help the San Francisco community regain its spiritual equilibrium and internal unity because he was seen in American Soto Sect Zen as one of its morally impeccable leaders.

One long-term consequence of the sexual misconduct allegations towards Baker has been the development of a code of ethics for Soto Sect Zen teachers and practitioners. The San Francisco Zen Center has led the way in the development of this ethical code. This code not only clarifies what sexual misconduct is, it establishes a set of procedural protocols for resolving the conflicts and dealing with the social and spiritual problems such misconduct inevitably causes.[456]

Thirty years after his coerced resignation, Richard Baker Roshi is reported to have said *I don't think the gossipy or the official versions of what happened are right, but I definitely feel if I were back in this situation again and the person I am now, it wouldn't have happened. Which means it's basically my fault. I had a kind of insecurity and self-importance, which I didn't see for a long time; that was a bad dynamic in the community.*[457]

Dainin Katagiri, Standing Upright Zen: A Short Biography

To not be real about our teacher is to not be real about ourselves. It is to twist the Dharma.

Natalie Goldberg[458]

For biographical details about Katagiri's life, unless otherwise noted, I rely on Ishmael Ford's 2006 book.[459] In 1928, Dainin Katagiri was born in Osaka to a Shin (Pure Land) Buddhist family. He was the youngest of nine children. According to Ford his youngest sister drowned shortly before he was born. He and his family believed that he was her reincarnation. His mother died when he was fourteen.

Natalie Goldberg, in her book about Katagiri written after his death, recalled an early conversation in which he talked about his childhood. His very busy mother, he said, barely had time for him. In his entire childhood he remembered only one occasion when she and he were alone together on a shopping trip. In this treasured memory he recalled how much he enjoyed having his mother *to* himself.

During World War Two[460] Katagiri was drafted into the Japanese air force. He knew that he didn't want to kill anyone and he later told Goldberg that he deliberately mis-fired his weaponry to avoid doing so.

In 1946, at age eighteen, he decided to become a monk. His first teacher was Roshi Daicho Hayashi. Katagiri was ordained during the years that he studied with Hayashii. After two years of concentrated practice and study, he transferred to the Eiheji Monastery – the intellectual and spiritual home for Soto Sect Zen practice in Japan. His second teacher was Roshi Eko Hashimoto. Katagiri lived in this monastery for 3 years. From Eiheji he was sent to the Soto Sect Zen affiliated Komazawa University where he completed his undergraduate and graduate degrees – earning a master's degree in Buddhist psychology.

When, at age 35, a position opened in Los Angeles in 1963, he applied and was accepted. Shortly after arrival in America, Shunryu Suzuki invited him to join the newly incorporated Zen Center of San Francisco and he accepted. Arriving in San Francisco he studied English. Goldberg's personal reminiscences supplement Ford's work. Katagiri told her, she writes, that upon his arrival in America he hated all Americans.

In 1982 (when he was 54), at a time when accusations about Baker were swirling in San Francisco's Zen Center, Katagiri decided it was time to practice and teach independently, he moved from San Francisco to Minneapolis where he became the Abbott for a small group of meditation practitioners in what would eventually become the Minneapolis Zen Meditation Center. Somewhat later, he founded Hokoyoji Zen Practice Community near the Mississippi River in southeastern Minnesota. In the course of the 1980s and 1990s he sent many of his North American students to train in Japan. Dharma heirs and practitioners from the Minnesota Zen Meditation Center would eventually establish similar centers in Kansas, Nebraska, Iowa, and Wisconsin. By the late 1980s, Katagiri was a widely-recognized and respected spiritual teacher and administrative problem-solver inside the United States Soto Sect Zen community.

In 1984, Katagiri returned to San Francisco to serve as interim Abbott of the San Francisco Zen Center as that center attempted to repair the traumatized community after the coerced departure of its former Abbott Richard Baker. After the San Francisco Zen community re-established stability, Katagiri, in 1985, returned to his own community in Minneapolis.

During the final year of Katagiri's life in residence at the Minnesota Zen Meditation Center he named twelve Dharma heirs in his spiritual lineage. In this group were both men and women – one (Rev. Karen Sunna) after his death followed him as the community's spiritual leader.

He died of cancer in March, 1990 (age 62). Katagiri had three marriages. The first ended in divorce. His second wife was murdered. His third wife (Tamoe) and his two sons (Yasuihko and Eijo) outlived him.

Sexual Scandal and the Minnesota Zen Community

It was nearly six years after Katagiri's death that information surfaced about sexual misconduct. During his years as Abbott and Zen Teacher in Minneapolis he had engaged in sexual relationships with a number of his students and spiritual disciples.

In Natalie Goldberg's book, *The Great Failure*[461] she discusses the nature of her spiritual relationship with Jakal Dainin Katagiri.[462] Goldberg, a dedicated Soto Sect Zen practitioner, was one of Katagiri's disciples. In earlier books Goldberg had written about the importance of his teaching to her inner life and spiritual practice. In *The Great Failure* she describes that time in her life, six years after his death, when she first learned about sexual misconduct accusations made against him by some of his former students and disciples. After the first of these stories surfaced, several more did as well. Rumors began to collect and circulate about still others.

As Goldberg and the guiding members of the community investigated these early stories and rumors, the Minneapolis Soto Zen community discovered that before his death Katagiri had been sexually involved with several of his Minnesota students. Inasmuch as the Abbott before his death had been seen as one of the teachers of Zen in the United States to have avoided extra-marital sexual encounters and sexual scandal, these posthumous revelations came as a shock to his Minneapolis disciples and to the American Soto Zen community at large.

In at least one situation described by Goldberg, one of the students with whom he had a sexual relationship subsequently became suicidal. As this affair threatened to become public knowledge, Katagiri concocted an elaborate cover-up scheme to prevent awareness of his actions. In addition, he isolated himself and the Zen Center from this former student's family and their phone calls.

At Issue: Abusive Sexual Activity, Hypocrisy, and Active Deception

In mid-November (2014), in the wake of new accusations of rape lodged inside America's public media against American comedian Bill Cosby, you wrote:

> ...what I was trying to say [in an earlier electronic note] was that we need a term, a special adjective for the Bill Cosby's and JHY's[463] of the world. There are many shades of patriarchy. Just like there are many types of racism. African-American authors have created a more nuanced way of understanding the pervasive forms of racism since it comes in so many forms but shares the same basic assumptions.

> It seems we need a new way of talking about sexual violence that is done by men who pretend to be some new kind of gentle man. There is a level of self-denial and hypocrisy that puts these men in a different category than the Woody Allens of the world that don't pretend to be good men.[464]

I have been pondering your question for more than a week. I am not personally certain that we need new language – although that may certainly be useful. We need, as women who live inside religious cultures with male spiritual leaders, to get clear that public religiosity, social status, educational achievements, celebrity status, or other social markers of desirable masculine identity do not create rape-free zones for women. Rape happens in every world culture. Religious leader sexual abuse of women and other vulnerable individuals occurs in most, if not all, world religions.

Marie Fortune raises the question in this manner: *The recent death of Joshu Sasaki Roshi and the publication of an extensive article on John Howard Yoder raise once again the contradiction of beneficial teaching and abusive leaders. What legacies do these prominent faith leaders leave?*[465] Fortune continues:

> I look at Yoder's body of work with great skepticism because it appears that for him, what happens to women doesn't count.... I can only conclude that women

are excluded from his theology. This means his theology, grand as it may sound on paper, is of no use to me.[466]

In my previous work, I have maintained, for example, that while John Howard Yoder had an IQ that topped the charts and while he had a prestigious academic career, he was a very ordinary sexual predator.[467] The levels and the quantity of abusive sexual violence which he carried out unmasked his inner moral character – no matter how religiously, spiritually, or ethically advanced he, or his male academic apologists, claimed he was.

Whenever a man rapes or sexually abuses women (and/or their children), he reveals his inner character. This is true no matter how wealthy, how well-dressed, how well-spoken, how culturally-accepted, or how well-educated this man might be; no matter his family connections; no matter what his career choices might be: theologian, priest, guru, comedian, physician, attorney, farmer, missionary, college professor, astronaut, hardware store owner, plumber, etc. In other words, a rapist is a rapist. He may be a Christian rapist or a Buddhist rapist. He may be an atheist rapist or an agnostic rapist. He may be a farmer rapist or he may be a theologian rapist. He may be a seminary president rapist or a seminarian rapist. His behavioral decision to rape speaks truth to us about the moral and ethical characteristics of his inner personality. In a certain sense, his decision to rape and the actual rape undress his inner spirituality – or its absence – for us. In the manifested behavior of rape, we learn a bit about the inner unconscious and its processes. We learn, therefore, what kind of man this is. We learn his true faith.

In this essay I am choosing to look towards Eastern philosophies and their "good guys." These are the spiritual teachers, the gurus, the so-called advanced spiritual beings.[468] Perhaps looking away from Christianity for a moment can help us examine your important question by turning our inquiring gaze away from our corporate, communal Mennonite navel.

A Disciple's Response to Revelations of Sexual Misconduct

Natalie Goldberg studied with Dainin Katagiri for twelve years before his death. About his death she later wrote:

> *What a shock it was for me to see my great teacher's stiff body. This was for real? The man I had studied with for twelve years was gone? Stars, moon, hope stopped. Ocean waves and ants froze. Even rocks would not grow. This truth I could not bear.* [469]

Regarding the process of Zen master-student relationships, Goldberg notes that the student projects onto the teacher his or her interior issues. In the practices of

Ruth E. Krall

sitting meditation and personal instruction given to the student by the teacher-guru, the student gradually reclaims these projected aspects of the inner life. This process allows the student to discover the *largeness of psyche* that belongs to her or him. She notes,

> As the student-teacher relationship matures, the student manifests these [admired teacher] qualities herself and learns to stand on her own two feet. The projections are reclaimed. What we saw in him is also inside us. We close the gap between who we think the teacher is and who we think we are not. We become whole. [470]

In Goldberg's life situation, the teacher died before the process was complete. She adds,

> I felt like a green fruit. I still needed the sun. The nutrients of the tree. Instead the great oak withered. I dangled for a while and then fell to the ground. Very undernourished. [471]

In a 2006 web-page interview Goldberg spoke about the reality that she loved Dainin Katagiri very much.[472] As his student she had begun to find her own voice and self-empowerment. In learning about his sexual relationships with other female students in the Zen Meditation Center she felt deeply and personally betrayed by his behavior. She correlates his betrayal with former betrayals of her sexuality by her father when she was a child and adolescent.

Regarding the time, six years after Katagiri's death, when the secret of Katagiri's sexual activity with the Zen Center's students first became public knowledge, she writes about the first moment of information. *I tried to keep my balance after the landslide of this new knowledge.... the hurricane I felt inside.*[473]

There was gratitude towards her male friend at the Zen Center who called her as soon as he knew the information.

> I felt gratitude to Peter for calling directly, before the information was covered-up or reduced to some half rumor, allowed into a secret silence, people turning their backs if someone poked around. I'd seen this happen before in other communities. I could not find an easy conclusion. I no longer had any ground below me. Every time I tried to find my feet the foothold crumbled. [474]

Revealing her inner psychological state, she wrote, *my mind began to unravel. The old world, the one I constructed for so many years with Roshi at the helm was collapsing and no logic I perfunctorily grabbed was going to stop it.*[475] In her home, she retreated into silence and tears. *I cried a lot in that rocker. The shock finally shattered any veneer I attempted to create. I didn't want to know these things. I didn't want to know how human Roshi was.*[476]

As months passed, Goldberg continued to question and to uncover internal issues regarding the Zen community's relationship with Katagiri Roshi. In so doing, she came to the following realizations. I summarize a much longer section of her book and audiotape.

- Something *had been going on*; the earlier misread signs now made sense
- His breach of trust was shocking
- He not only betrayed the women students with whom he had sexual relations, he betrayed the entire community
- Part of his own self was cut off from another part. *Roshi was sincere about his vows. But in a split, the one part does not live by the same rules as the other part. So a person could practice deeply, have a great understanding of and aspiration for compassion, and simultaneously act out in a way that blurs boundaries between teacher and student.*[477] The teacher qua teacher was radiant. *It was hard to see the darkness at his back. But unless I could see his, I was vulnerable in being shortsighted to my own*[478]

In her perception, not-knowing the factual truth created individual *and* communal misconceptions of what had factually happened. For her own integrity and for the integrity of the Zen community she decided that she needed to write about Katagiri's unacceptable sexual transgressions. As she began to research and write, she discovered that she needed to do two things: (1) confront her own inner emotional realities and (2) confront the responses and reactions of other Zen practitioners and the community where his violations had occurred.

Regarding her own interior practice, she became aware of anger and needed to distinguish between clinging rage and *the red-hot flash of energy*. There is, she writes, a pure anger that *comes through us, cleanses us, and passes through us.*[479]

In addition to this flash of anger-energy, she commented that a kind of grief-work needed to be done as she integrated the factual reality of his multiple betrayals. In a type of obsessive preoccupation, she writes that she went over and over what had happened. There was a certain shattering of her inner world. As part of her decision not to continue to react blindly and erratically, she began a search for factual truth. She began to write about this factual truth as she uncovered it. She slowly came to the realization that no one knew the full extent of Katagiri's sexual misconduct with his students and disciples.

As her work of reconstructing factual truth began to be noticed inside the American Zen community (that community which had believed Katagiri to be one of the *good* gurus who had not sexually abused his disciples), a wide variety of responses began to manifest in others' relationships with her. In her Beliefnet interview with Lisa Schneider,[480] Goldberg noted that her decision to write about

Dainin Katagiri's sexual transgressions has cost her many friends inside the Zen community. She interprets this response as happening because other Zen practitioners wish to protect their teacher's image and his reputation. Parenthetically, I found Ford's 2006 book very interesting in light of Goldberg's commentary about community denial. While he is quite forthright about Richard Baker's sexual misconduct at the San Francisco Zen Center, there is no mention of Dainin Katagiri's in Minnesota.

In *The Great Failure*, Goldberg describes a wide variety of responses to her investigatory work. Before the book was fully written and published, she began to observe her Zen community's reactions. I will summarize some of these below.

- One former student estranged from the Zen community because *she had known* (italics mine) at the time about his sexual behavior before his death and had wanted to protect him, was *relieved* to talk with Goldberg about what she personally knew
- Another said p*eople exaggerate. No one knows for sure*
- Still others asked *what about the Roshi's wife? You will hurt her*
- Goldberg reported feeling very alone and perceived that others wanted to minimize his sexual misconduct or stay unaware of it
- She reports that no one was happy with her decision to seek information. They wondered why she was making such a big deal about the story of the long-dead teacher's sexual misconduct with students
- People turned their backs on her and she lost friendships she valued
- The Zen center eventually issued such a vague statement that if she had not already known the facts, the information was totally veiled and hidden
- A Zen teacher asked her, *why write anything? It will just cause trouble*
- Five years after the revelations, one of his Dharma heirs claimed that Dainin Katagiri *had immaculate morality*. Goldberg comments that he knew this was not true

After Katagiri's death two of his Dharma heirs also crossed the teacher-student boundary and had sexual relationships with their disciples and students. One of these was a licensed clinician who, when accused by one of his students, surrendered his right to do licensed clinical therapeutic work. Goldberg eventually went to the Minnesota licensing bureau and read the details of his behavior and reviewed, for her own understanding, the decisions made by the state's professional licensure board. She notes, however, that as a Zen teacher, this individual continues to teach the Dharma.

Goldberg writes that in such situations of abuse by a Zen master of his disciples and students, *the Dharma, the teachings of Zen, cannot grow straight (emphasis mine)*. In addition, in situations of such abuse and secrecy, the suffering or trauma caused to individuals by the abuser is inevitably passed into the entire community and into the future itself. Not only is the present moment of community life con-taminated and weakened by the spiritual toxicity of guru sexual abuse, its future life is contaminated and weakened as well.

Not So Impeccable Teachers: Hierarchies of Preference and Hierarchies of Abuse

As I continue, I simply want to say that I have perhaps learned more about clergy sexual abuse in Western cultures by looking at guru abuse in Eastern ones. In par-ticular, Kramer and Alstad's important book[481] should be read by all of us for the insights which it contains about abusive spiritual leadership in any community. We should be assigning it to our students to read and discuss.

In this book Kramer and Alstad note that for a religious leader, spiritual teacher or guru to become sexually involved with some and non-involved with others is harmful because it establishes *a hierarchy of preference* inside the community. They write: *Since the guru's appeal is his offer of unconditional love to all, this [preferment] causes an undercurrent of jealousy and resentment among the followers.*[482]

In discussing the transplanting of Eastern religions in Western soils, the authors comment, *When a religion is transplanted from a conservative culture to a more experimental one, its leaders are no longer constrained by tradition.*[483] *Since the West, in general, has looser sexual mores than do many Eastern cultures, gurus face "irresistible temptation" as they encounter female disciples.*[484]

> *Without deep cultural constraints against it, sex scandals go with the occupa-tion of guru because of its emotional isolation and eventual boredom. Disciples are just there to serve and amuse the guru, who after all, has given them so much. The guru's temptation is exacerbated by the deep conditioning in some women to be attracted to men in power*[485]

Kramer and Alstad reflect on issues of betrayal in such a guru-disciple situa-tion. First, the guru puts his own needs, desires, and pleasures before the needs of the disciple. This is one form of exploitation and *unabashed dominance (emphasis mine)*. They ask how a disciple can disobey – especially one who is spiritually com-mitted and culturally conditioned to obedience as part of her devotional practice.

Second, the male guru rewards women for their sexuality by tapping into ancient cultural forms of social conditioning. In traditional female roles, women gained power by sexual involvement with powerful men. The women that gurus choose to exploit often have deep-seated issues related to their own sense of power and self-worth (or, more likely, its absence). The more the disciple needs, trusts, and depends upon the guru for her sense of self-worth and empowerment, the more power he holds over her in their relationship.

Sexual relations with a guru are, therefore, implicitly incestuous because he functions as the woman's spiritual father, one to whom she owes obedience. Having sexual encounters with a spiritual father reinforces the old and often unconscious cultural idea of women gaining power by using sex. When dropped by the guru, lasting patterns of shame, confusion, and guilt remain for the disciple to cope with and resolve for herself.

Third, whether overt and visible to the community or covert and hidden, sexual encounters between a guru and disciple set up hierarchies of preference. When overt behavior is openly present in the community, disciples become competitive – seeking more of his attention than is available to their peers. When covert behavior defines the hidden relationship(s), the reality of lies and secrecy is omnipresent. *The presence of secrecy and lying inside the community inevitably distorts the teaching* (summary statement and italics mine).

Goldberg's narrative illustrates some of Kramer's and Alstad's contentions. Keep in mind that Dainin Katagiri's sexual misconduct behavior was deeply hidden from the Minneapolis and American Zen community's awareness until six years after his death. In one place Goldberg muttered to herself: *Why did he choose her? She got more time with him. I was glad I didn't know about it when it was happening. There would have been only confusion in the Zendo.*[486]

In another place, she notes that to keep a secret for so long, meant that Katagiri was cut off and isolated, *alone with the alone.* His life's sadness and loneliness became more visible to her after his death. Behaviors that once had one interpretation in his community of disciples now were re-interpreted in light of his now-known sexual misconduct. In her book she writes that eventually she came to understand:

> *I had a glimmer then of the chasm between the Zen master and the lonely insecure man. That moment was an opportunity to hold contradictory parts of him, to understand life doesn't work in a neat package the way I wanted. I could have come closer to his humanity and mine. But I wasn't ready or willing. I had needed him to be great, to hold my projections. In freezing him on a pedestal, I had only contributed to his isolation.*[487]

In another place she notes that he was so unclear in his behavior towards the women students he had sex with and so clear in his spiritual teachings to the Zen community. This dichotomy of life and teachings became an issue which his disciples and students needed to resolve after his death.

During one of their individual teaching sessions Goldberg recalled, she had asked Katagiri a teaching question about another Zen leader in a different Zen community – a man who had just been revealed as a sexual abuser of his students. Inexplicably to her at that time, Katagiri became incensed at her question, shouting, *Buddhism is Buddhism.* Intimidated by the explosive heat of his response, she did not pursue her question any further. Only after his death and the surfacing of other women's allegations of sexual misconduct did she revisit her remembered inner confusion that day about the strength of his response to her question. Only after she knew his Zen Center sexual history could she piece together the historical data. Her question to him occurred in the middle of his intense, sexually-charged relationship with a woman student. Years after his death, Goldberg reports, the woman involved in this affair remained in love with him.

Having some awareness of how transpersonal human consciousness operates in communal settings is helpful here. Below levels of the Zen Center's students' cognitive awareness, behavioral signs and signals were being sent by the Zen master about his adulterous relationship(s) with his student disciples. These were received below the perceptual level of consciousness by individuals inside the Zen Center community. During his lifetime, Zen Center residents and disciples saw intimations and hints about sexual interactions between Katagiri and his female disciples. After his death individual members of the Zen community re-visited their memories of these behavior patterns and re-constructed a new narrative about the meaning of the behavior they had earlier observed. With new factual information, they could create a more accurate story of his life (as their spiritual teacher) during the years they knew him. His abusive behavior had been hidden in clear sight of the community's students and disciples. But during his lifetime, his visible behavior was not recognized not understood for what it was, abusive sexual misconduct by the spiritually venerated Zen master.

While Goldberg does not comment on it, it is quite likely that her question and its timing were not coincidental to his abusive behaviors. Just below the surface of the community's communal consciousness, a student's individual watching mind was processing information from the sensory observational data it was continually receiving. The non-conscious watching mind – as opposed to the conscious mind of the human ego – is rarely deceived. Goldberg relates her question about spiritual teacher sexual abuse vis-à-vis the behavior of another Zen teacher – one that the Zen disciple's conscious mind could acceptably know about. It is much safer to ask a spiritual father the question, *what about his sexual behavior* than it is to ask, *what about your sexual behavior.* It is striking, therefore, that she later pegged Katagiri's outburst to the time of his intense sexual relationship with a particular student-disciple inside the Zen Center's walls.

In a certain sense, the Zen community's shared illusion that Katagiri was one of the impeccable teachers protected him from being discovered during his lifetime. It may also be that the force of his personality prevented others from correctly perceiving and interpreting the actual behaviors they witnessed inside the Zen Center. As Kramer and Alstad note, the students' and disciples' position of spiritual dependency on the guru prevents them from being able to question his

Ruth E. Krall

teachings or to disobey him. Finally, it may have been possible that because his teaching was so powerful and so influential in their own interior lives that his disciples may have been unable to deal with the cognitive dissonance of studying with and obeying a sexually abusive master.

Human beings use denial of factual reality (that complex mental process which Buddhists identify as addiction to illusion) as a powerful psychological means to avoid dealing with something they feel unable to acknowledge and work with. The human experience of cognitive dissonance is so painful that the cognitive human mind, or the ego, constructs an alternative mental picture of reality which becomes the substitute interpretive narrative for factual truthfulness.

Luminous hugs in the laundry room, deeply intimate laughter in the corridors: these and other memories surfaced six years after Katagiri's death. One student explained to Goldberg that during Katagiri's lifetime he'd had no framework to interpret the behavior he had actually witnessed.

It is quite likely, I think, that at slightly-below-personal-and-group-consciousness levels, the Zen center's students and disciples picked up behavioral hints of the Roshi's improper relationships with others. Unable to accept the factual reality of what they were seeing and hearing, they became unable to accurately interpret it. The group's collective or transpersonal consciousness allowed for no factual knowledge or awareness to emerge. Not only did individuals deny the factual reality and meaning of what they were seeing. The entire community did so as well.

One student however had directly challenged the living spiritual master about *those noises I heard in the night*. Katagiri, utilizing the power of his position as the center's Abbott, forcefully told the young man to mind his own business. The student precipitously left the Center. Years later, in her search for factual truth, Goldberg hunted him down and reviewed what he had observed and knew during their earlier shared time as Zen Center students and disciples.

In their analysis of a guru's sexual misconduct, Kramer and Alstad note that individuals often focus upon the sexual – even to the point of being glad *that he* [the guru] *is getting some.* However, these authors note – accurately I think – that the issue of teacher and community lying is the greater of the moral complexities.

> *It's the lie – not the sex – that's the real issue. The lie indicates that the guru's entire persona is a lie, that his image as selfless and being beyond ego is a core deception. Many think that though a guru lies about his personal behavior, his message is still essentially true. Lying here as elsewhere is done to cover-up self-interest. If the guru's message is that purity without self-interest is the ultimate achievement, not only did he not achieve it, but he does not even know if it is achievable. If being self-centered is an unavoidable aspect of being human,*

then any ideology that denies this will necessarily corrupt its promoters and believers. This is why images of purity corrupt.[488]

When East and West collide in the spiritual relationship of an Eastern-born guru and a Western-born disciple, there are abundant opportunities for sexual misunderstanding and sexual misconduct. When the guru (who has primarily known same-gender monastic communities) works in the context of Western spiritual communities (where male and female disciples are more commonly present) cultural issues surface almost immediately. Some of these issues are lodged within human sexual desires. Issues of position and personal authority, position, power, and the need to control others intermingle with sexuality.

I think, however, that this is a more strictly-drawn statement of East-West cultural misunderstandings about sexuality than is perhaps warranted. In his book about living a Zen-infused year in Kyoto, *Time Magazine* essayist Pico Iyre (1992) notes in many places – but in passing – that unmarried and theoretically celibate Japanese Buddhist monks had special female friends or they had special on-going relationships with specific Geishas.[489] Clearly, restricted gender relationships, monastic celibacy, monastic purity or sexual restraint was also tested inside a more rigidly stratified Japanese culture in late twentieth-century traditional Kyoto.

Many monastic traditions in Buddhism now have married gurus, admit married disciples, and ordain women priests. Increasingly, in North America, the teachers of the Dharma have a North American cultural heritage as well as a Japanese Buddhist lineage. Some of the abusers inside Soto Sect Zen Buddhist spiritual centers are of Japanese descent. But increasingly, they are of American descent.

Concluding Comments

Looking closely at a guru's inner circle is extremely revealing. Those closest to him, his most dedicated students, display better than anyone else displays where his teaching leads after years of exposure. What is also displayed is who he prefers to have around him: Are they strong and interesting in their own right, or are they boring sycophants who continually feed his ego? Do disciples ever "graduate" and become self-defining adults, or do they remain obedient and tied to the guru?[490]

Joel Kramer and Diana Alstad

While Christianity and Soto Sect Zen Buddhism have very different world-views, the structure of community responses to religious leader abuse inside a religious or spiritual community is very similar. As Goldberg so cogently notes, damage to individuals, to the community, and to the abusive guru's spiritual teachings are inevitable. For one thing, the wounds of the victims, the wounds of the community, and the wounds to the spiritual teachings, themselves, are structurally equivalent in these two world philosophies or religions. Secondarily, by looking east, another principle comes into view. The underlying ideologies or theologies of these various religious traditions are contributing factors to the development of abusive spiritual teachers. Thus, we need to look at the role of our ideologies and theologies as the feeder roots of these deeply embedded sexual corruptness problems within the world's religious communities.

Once again: Father Thomas Doyle has reminded all of us that these sexual abuse problems are not parasites or barnacles which have attacked the church or spiritual teaching centers from the outside. Instead, they are endemic structural realities – well-rooted and actively nurtured systemic realities inside our various world religions.[491]

If, as Mary Daly has often asserted, the world's encompassing religion is patriarchy, then we must begin to seriously de-construct the presence of patriarchal thinking as one contributing factor to the sexual abuse scandal inside many world religions.

If Goldberg is correct that the teachings of Buddhism are contaminated by the presence of sexually abusive leaders, then we Mennonites need to look where our theological and ecclesiological teachings have been similarly corrupted by our own sexually abusive theologians, biblical scholars, ethicists, and ministers.

If Kramer and Alstad are correct that the issue is not the sexual abuse per se but the lie embedded within the teachings and the teachers, then we Mennonites need to look at this issue of lying and hypocrisy as it is embedded in the writings of our sexually abusive theologians, ethicists, and ecclesiologists.

If Father Doyle is correct (and I think he is) that there are two issues embedded in every act of institution-protected act of sexual abuse by religious leaders [(a) the act of sexual violence and abuse and (b) the cover-up activities done by church authorities in institution-protective actions], then we lay members of the Mennonite world-wide community of Anabaptists must assertively insist that the institutional church not only focus on disciplining and controlling individual abusers but, more importantly, it must also focus on transforming its own corrupted institutional structures and abusive management behaviors.

The institutional church must be held accountable for the members of the religious hierarchy who covered up and, implicitly therefore, lied to members of the church. For the healing of the institutional church, we must collectively grow in truthfulness about the presence of sexual abusers inside the religious elite – those Mennonite Church leaders and administrators who have been (and currently are) responsible for managing the church's personnel and financial matters.

I will close by quoting Marie Fortune:

The profound theological and existential question here is does the value of the message depend on the character of the messenger. To which I must answer "yes" and "no." Hopefully the value of the message or teaching stands on its own, sometimes in spite of the teacher. If the teaching is true, you receive it with a grateful heart and mind. But do not allow the value of the teaching message to blind you to the serious faults of the teacher or the message.[492]

Ruth E. Krall

Eighteenth Letter

Resurrection Morning

They live in an ante chamber of fear and ignorance
too timid to open the doors of their hearts, and minds and bodies...
Perhaps what gets us most is the pastoral lie,
The utter dismissal of the real needs of the people
Hungry for justice, and, at times, the failure to acknowledge
That hatred and cruelty and thievery and despicable lies are in play-
Precious lives are at stake...completely discarded.

Rachel Fitzgerald[493]

They have threatened us with resurrection,
because they do not know life (poor things)

This is the whirlwind,
which does not let us sleep,
the reason why sleeping, we keep watch,
and awake, we dream.

Julia Esquivel[494]

Introductory Comments

We can say where the church is but we cannot say where the church is not.

Bishop Kallistos Ware[495]

In this letter I want to leave some rocky cairns by the side of the road for others to think about as they get ready to exit this book of letters. Rock cairns can be utilitarian – as when they identify the correct trail to take at an obscure trail juncture or while bushwhacking and hiking toward a mountain's saddle where one might easily get lost. Rock cairns can represent places of grief – where an ancestor, beloved animal companion, or some ancient dream has been buried. In addition, cairns can indicate or mark places of spiritual centering, places of prayer. Many rock cairns, therefore, identify a spiritual pilgrimage, a spiritual path, or draw attention to a specific holy place. Others appear to have been created solely for the beauty or joy or self-expression – a signifier, if you will, of our human need to create and to play.

The Building of Cairns

Cairns are constructed of Mother Earth's bounty – her rocks, boulders and stones. Stones, say some Native American tribes, carry their own unique form of consciousness, just as humans, animals, and plants do. It is just a much slower paced form of consciousness. Stones, boulders, and rocky outcroppings, therefore, in Native American wisdom, have their own part to play in the ever-moving and always contracting or expanding transpersonal sea of consciousness that surrounds everything and is embodied within everything on planet earth.

Thus, the question: do we select the rocks from which we make cairns? Or did the rocks call to us to move them and create a cairn – a new form of collective rock consciousness? Of, even more complex to fathom, did the gods call rocks and humans together at this juncture point on this particular trail at this particular moment for a purpose only the gods know? What ancient Ley lines do these rock cairns now, in this present moment, represent to us in a culture which knows little of sacred geometry, which disbelieves that everything in the universe is connected in some mysterious way, which disavows the notion of the sacred in nature, which sees the *true gods* dressed only in anthropomorphic far-away, all-powerful and omni-potent maleness?

Cairns are placed, one balancing stone at a time, by individuals living in the present moment. Each cairn-creating person is perhaps thinking about those who will walk, perhaps years later, on the same path, following the same trail. If this is so, then these cairn creators set trail markers in their present moment as they looked forward into the future, a future they might not live to see. They set out these trail markers which we note, in our passing, that at some past moment another human being was at this very space where we now stand. We see – but hesitantly and indistinctly, perhaps, a remnant energy of his or her (or in the case of many sacred cairns, their) personal consciousness in the moment of the cairn's creation. We guess at the meaning of this particular cairn, of that particular cairn.

Ruth E. Krall

But, just perhaps, when we pause to ponder their presence, we sense the sacred nature of these balanced and balancing rocks. In this letter I want to stack rocks. I want to build a cairn for the future.

Selected at Random: First Rock

Every human life is both unique and precious. At a cellular and transpersonal level, we, collective humanity, form one living and always moving sea of human consciousness. We are each embedded within this great transpersonal sea of consciousness at the moment of our conception. Throughout our lifetimes, we will add to it and shape it for future generations. The great mystics in the world's spiritual and philosophical traditions have always known this. What affects one of us, affects all of the rest of us. The web of human consciousness, the very web of being itself, pulses with our individual thoughts, decisions, and actions. Whether or not we realize this, there is a seven generations effect carried deep within each of our motivations, thoughts, decisions and actions.

If we choose to live in prejudice and hate, what we pass on to future generations is a web of personal and transpersonal consciousness in which prejudice and hate are stronger because we, as one embodied organism in the web of being, have chosen to live inside, indeed, to become, prejudicial forms of hate. We become, inside the human sea of transpersonal consciousness, therefore, the carriers of prejudice and its accompanying dehumanizing and demonizing hatred of others.

If we are driven to live in paranoia, we create a more paranoid world around us. If, in our paranoia, we choose to perpetuate violence against others inside our most personal relationships (or even against the stranger in the village), then we pass on a culture of paranoid violence to the generations that succeed us. Our descendents inherit, sometimes unaware, the consequences of our individual and collective decisions and actions. Repetitions occur in future generations and the cultural matrix of prejudice, paranoia, hatred and violence grows stronger. Cultural permission to hate and to kill becomes more emboldened and, consequently, embodied violence becomes more the norm than the exception to the norm.

Writing about Russian Mennonite experiences of slaughter and rape in Russia during the Russian revolution, Canadian novelist Miriam Toews writes:

> *Plautdietsch was the language of shame. Mennonites had learned to remain silent, to shoulder their pain. My grandfather's parents were murdered in a field beside their barn but their son, my father's father, survived by burying himself in a pile of manure. Then a few days later he was put in a cattle car and taken with thousands of other Mennonites to Moscow. From there he was sent off to Canada....When my mother went to university to become a therapist she learned that suffering, even though it may have happened a long time ago, is*

something that passed from one generation to the next to the next, like flex-
ibility, or grace or dyslexia. My grandfather had big green eyes and dimly lit
scenes of slaughter, blood on snow, played out behind them all the time, even
when he smiled.[496]

If, on the other hand, we choose to live in a spirit of compassion towards all suffering beings – including, parenthetically, ourselves – then we move our own consciousness towards behaviors which do not cause suffering in ourselves and in others. This too has a multiple generation's effect – as a spirit of compassionate generosity tends to sprout and spread inside the human commons.

Pro-active peace work, therefore, begins inside our embodied human cells of consciousness. As Anabaptist-Mennonites, carrying the inherited memory of church and state violence against our ancestors,[497] we seek to transform this bloody history into contemporary works of non-violence and peace. As we seek individually and collectively to become transformed away from the spirit (or, metaphorically now, the virus) of violence which all too readily pervades our human cultures, we eventually engage in peace-creating actions. We not only seek to change the violent outer world: it is inevitable: seeking external peace, we must seek to calm the violent and troubled storms of our inner world. As we seek to make the external world less violent, we must also seek to become peaceable beings in our internal world. It is a truism: *we cannot stop violence by using violence as the cure for violence.* Clinical psychologist and Buddhist spiritual teacher Jack Kornfield writes:

> *For great injustice, coming to forgiveness may include a long process of grief,*
> *outrage, sadness, loss, and pain. True forgiveness does not paper over what has*
> *happened in a superficial way. It is not a misguided effort to suppress or ignore*
> *our past. It cannot be hurried. It is a deep process repeated over and over in our*
> *heart which honors the grief and betrayal and in its own time ripens into the*
> *freedom to truly forgive.* [498]

If we live in an honorable community which seeks to live in justice and in peace, we soon learn that this transformation of human consciousness away from violence is a mighty work. For, to put it quite simply, we human beings get on each other's nerves. Inadvertently *and* deliberately we betray each other. We intrude where we are not welcome and we are bothersome, at times even noxious, where we intrude. Our noisy and always restless monkey minds seek mischief as much as they seek the common good. We are always testing the boundaries of my and mine as we encounter the embodied and social boundaries of others and theirs. Each one of us, I often think, is convinced that if only everyone else would conform to his or her [i. e., *my*] way of thinking and being in the world, there would be global peace. This is, of course, utter nonsense.

The patriarchal and xenophobic ideologies of hate and human prejudice do not spring, unseeded, into life. Acts of injustice, acts of paranoia, acts of narcissistic ambition, acts of betrayal, acts of violation and acts of violence are deeply rooted in transpersonal ideologies of power-over, deeply personal needs to control others, irrational prejudices against others often manifested in phobic public behaviors towards them, clan-motivated hatred, and our contentious personal desires to revenge ordinary slights and betrayals.

Second Rock

Shunning among Mennonites has many forms – not all are as formalized as shunning among the Amish or Orthodox Jews in which total silence and total non-inclusion after excommunication is the practice. Shunning is essentially a social act of community rejection of individuals or external groups. One individual or group places another individual or group at a social distance by means of exclusion from the commons. This act of exclusion and rejection can be a formal action such as excommunication by a religious denomination. When this happens, all individuals of the community are urged to avoid association with the shunned individual. The individual is banned from communal religious participation.

In less extreme situations, it involves individuals and groups socially avoiding contact whenever possible. In undeclared shunning, the behaviors may involve refusing to acknowledge or speak with a person when the parties' collective paths cross, as for example, at church services or in post offices, stores, and banks. Targets of informal shunning can include people judged as apostates, heretics, sinners, dissidents, troublemakers, whistleblowers, or individuals that the shunning individual or group perceives as a threat to its internal security and well-being. Some shunning occurs in the context of false, baseless, frequently derogatory, and often malicious rumors. Its intention is to coerce or punish the human object of shunning for some aspect of his behavior or her personality. These authoritarian forms of social rejection can and often do cause trauma and psychological damage to their recipient.

Watching and, at times, experiencing shunning inside the Christian commons for more than a quarter of a century, I have come to the opinion that those who initiate shunning behaviors are themselves spiritually damaged and emotionally hobbled. In part, this is due to the psychological mechanism of projection. In the defense mechanism of projection, that which we most fear or disdain in others often originates within our rejection of some aspect of our own selves and is, therefore, an aspect of our own denied shadow. When we subsequently reject and expel others by blame and shunning, we damage our own spirit and our own community. By projecting our own shadow or our own self-fears onto others, we covertly deny ourselves the opportunity to spiritually and emotionally mature and we often damage, sometimes irreparably, the personality, spirit, and imago dei in the second person.

Secondarily, the harm done to initiators of shunning is, in large part, due to inner processes of casting judgment. Projection, paranoia, religious scrupulosity, and spiritual judgmentalism are all toxic personal and communal responses to an outer world or others. Perceiving others to be threatening or evil in some way or another, we demonize them, we dehumanize them, and we cast them out of the commons with little or no regard for their well-being. When, in this manner, we break off relationships with others (and we all do this at times) we harm ourselves perhaps more than we harm them.

When we live in fear and hatred of the other, we reveal our inner soul damages. But tragically, in our expression of these troublesome attitudes and motivations, we further harm our personal inner soft large S/Self because we reinforce, and thus magnify, our inner world's troubles by projecting them onto the outside world. With each repetition of hateful behavior towards others, we are shaping our inner personality into a personal identity as a person who hates.

My own sense of the matter, therefore, is that shunning is a passive-aggressive form of behaviorally expressing disdain, hatred, and an absence of love. It is a form of coercive rejection. All too often it is conducted in a spirit of dehumanizing hate or self-righteous judgment. It is form of controlling and authoritarian behavior justified by pious language and strict observances of a community's self-imposed codes of purity and holiness. It is the antithesis of the Jesus path of hospitality, inclusion, reconciliation, welcome, and communal shalom.[499] Shunning behavior refuses to acknowledge the human rights of the other for recognition, community and inclusion.

Social awareness of shunning as ridiculous religious behavior in the face of human difference is the source of the Mennonite joke, *only thee and me, Jake, are faithful and recently I've come to have my doubts about thee.* This is also the source of another Mennonite joke, *there is only one true, pure, and holy Church and only I belong to it.*

Shunning, as practiced by Mennonites, is a form of communal behavior in which an individual or an entire community chooses to deny the full humanity of another person – usually in the name of purity codes, ideology, orthodoxy, piety, and power. Shunning, therefore, is more about exclusion, punishment, ostracism and shaming the other than it is about welcoming love, forgiveness, mercy, restoration, and reconciliation. Mennonite shunning includes the refusal to speak to another; creating or spreading malicious gossip, rumor-mongering, and exclusion from ordinary communal social events because of some perceived ideological or personal fault line in the undesirable person being shunned.

Right now (2015) Mennonite Church USA institutional shunning includes denominational policies that refuse to welcome lbgtq individuals as married couples or as partnered singles into congregations and into ordinary community social events. It includes formally mandated denominational excommunications of entire congregations and conferences because of their practices of welcoming inclusion: membership, marriage, and ordination.[500] It includes social rudeness and isolation of lbgtq individuals from the commons. It includes hate stares and the derogatory words of hate speech.[501]

Shunning, as Mennonites practice it is, therefore, more about coercion than it is about restoration of right relationships between and among people. Shunning is an interpersonally violent form of social abusiveness. Those who shun others violate the full humanity of those who are shunned. In their actions of shunning; those who shun others betray and behaviorally refute their proclaimed spiritual messages of welcome, inclusion, love and peace-making. Thus, those who shun others directly contradict the message of the gospels: all who show up are welcome to follow the Jesus path; none are to be coerced. Ultimately, of course, they refute Jesus' teachings by their otherizing and isolating behaviors.

To be shunned as a pariah, as a social outcast, as a non-included other is to know that one has been disdained and discarded. It is to know that one is unacceptable for some known or unknown personal characteristic or behavior. It is to feel actively unsafe in the commons.

One response of individuals who are shunned by their peers or their culture is the experience of shame. In her discussion of shame in the context of her work on Post-traumatic Stress Disorder, Psychiatrist Judith Herman says:

> *Shame is a signal just the way fear is a signal. Only it's a signal that something has gone wrong in a social connection, something that threatens a relationship that matters.*[502]

One purpose of shaming actions is to coerce an individual – by shaming them - to yield to another individual or group. In shaming another, I actively seek to coerce him or her to yield to my opinion about social propriety, belief systems, ethics, or morality.

When I experience shame, I am aware that I have violated some internalized as well as externalized common code of *what I should be* or *should think* or *should do*. In a certain sense, shame is that internal emotional experience which places the needs and desires of the community above the needs and desires of the individual.

I have personally come to believe over many years of watching shaming and shunning behaviors inside the Mennonite world that these pressuring forms of human behavior, much like the violence of killing, deny the gospel of peace. Those who most insistently shun others for declared or undeclared faults are often the most vigorous defenders of word-encoded creeds, beliefs, purity codes and ortho-doxy. The only two outcomes of a shunning individual or a shunning community are social conformity or social ostracism. I suppose a third one is also possible: the total destruction of the life of the now-shunned person. I doubt, however, that suicide and murder are desired outcomes of Mennonite shunning and shaming behaviors.

The stated or unstated goal of shaming and shunning is to bring people to their knees in submission to the group mind. A secondary goal, when submission does not occur, is to exclude them from the commons. Since shunning may also be formally done in order to protect some usually paranoid ideology about what *ought to be* or *what ought not to be,* it represents a very low threshold for cogni-tive dissonance.

As I have both experienced and thought about these matters, another much more elusive interpersonal objective for these isolating interpersonal behaviors comes into view. Since it slips in and out of words for me, I may not be able to describe it clearly. But I will do the best I can.

Another goal of shunning and shaming is to shut down conversations about conflicted matters. When we refuse to listen to another's perspective by shaming and shunning behaviors, we essentially invalidate them as a person who is equal to us in worth and value. We also invalidate their concerns. When we, in essence, close our hearts to them, we elevate ourselves above them. In short, we establish ourselves as their judge and jury. We become the right-minded ones and they are, by virtue of their disagreements with us inside our shared commons, wrong-minded. Essentially, therefore, acts of shunning are about the demonstration of power-over. Thus, in their very essence, these acts are not about truth, truthful-ness, faithfulness, or any other high ground ethical or intellectual imperative. Rather, they represent the iron hand of power and position enclosed in the soft glove of silence.

The ability to exclude a person from their social family (be that family a bio-logical one or a religious one) represents a view of the self that goes like this: *I am morally or spiritually or socially superior to you. As my inferior, you will yield to my will or I will shove you outside of this family, community, relationship.* These messages reveal, therefore, another and yet deeper layer of abusiveness. Excommunication, shaming and shunning are, therefore, hostile acts. They are also violent acts of control and domination.

What these shunning and shaming individuals fail to see (in their acts of harsh judgment and exclusion) is actually quite evident: their embodied actions of coercive interpersonal social warfare against a fellow human being concomitantly declare an absence of welcoming love and hospitality. This embodied behavioral declaration of love's absence is a much more powerful witness to the shunning individual's daily lived faith than all of their pious words. Their now-empty words

Ruth E. Krall

about Christ's welcoming love, Christ's inclusive peace, and human salvation are revealed as false words by their contemptuous actions towards the disdained and shunned other.

Busily proclaiming Christ's redemptive peace, the scrupulosity and orthodoxy patrol spreads hate, disdain, and eventually interpersonal violence. Diligently patrolling and guarding the borders of who belongs and who doesn't belong, they create and then spread the virus of interpersonal and communal contentiousness.

I want to add a personal footnote to this particular rock. There have been four academic individuals (inside the religious academy during my professional career) who have gone out of their way to avoid acknowledging my presence and to avoid speaking with me. Initially, I was quite puzzled about why this was happening since I had previously been on a first-name basis with each of them in different settings. When I finally figured out (1) their connections with each other and (2) what behavior of mine had triggered these public events of socially rude behavior, lots of pieces fell into place and I realized that these apparently disparate acts of sunning (at a variety of academic conferences and lectures) were indeed related. They had a narrative structure that could be de-coded and understood.

A collective decision had been made by these four individuals to punish me for something I had shared in confidence with one of them – a concern I had about a specific atmosphere of incompetency and injustice inside the boundary of a particular academic community. I had been, in other words an informal whistle-blower raising a concern I thought my older professional confidante might be able to address. This man had obviously gossiped about my conversation and its concerns inside his academic-social-peer-intimate group. Once a friend-colleague to all four individuals, de facto, I was now excluded by these four individuals from any kind of social recognition. They refused to acknowledge my presence in the commons.[503] I had clearly become the unwelcome ghost in the room to be looked through.

This kind of informal professional shunning can backfire. For one thing, I would not be thinking and writing about shunning if this sequence of events had not happened in my life. Inasmuch as none of these shunning individuals could personally or professionally harm me in significant ways, I found the whole scene puzzling. Once, however, I lined up the sequence of shunning events and the four players, I understood their causality. At the moment, when all became clear, I laughed and laughed and laughed out of sheer relief. My paranoia evaporated. I both knew and understood what my social *sin* was; I had a realistic causative narrative to understand what had been a very puzzling sequence of shunning events.

In the instant of my understanding, the whole professional shunning scene became ridiculous. Never again would I trust these venerable theologians and their high-priced theological words about the Christian Church as a living and worshipping community which reflected God's love. I stopped reading their work;

I stopped teaching their work. I stopped trying to have conversations with them in public meetings. Perhaps most of all, I stopped honoring and admiring them as my elders.

Their shunning behavior which was collectively designed and implemented in order to shame and humiliate me actually reinforced my moral spine. In a certain sense, their behaviors taught me more about their spirituality, an innate hostility and an absence of professional collegiality than they understood.

As a consequence of their very public actions of shaming and shunning I have continued to reflect on the intrapersonal and interpersonal effects of these very public and therefore very complex acts. I sometimes wonder who else might be part of this obviously organized network of people who have agreed to shun me in professional settings. I wonder if some day in some future professional organization, someone else will refuse to see me, shake my hand or otherwise acknowledge my living presence.

My reflections have led me to conclude that this very petty act of male academic shunning – paying me back – said much more about the patriarchal male will to dominate (and the associated character and spirituality of those doing the shunning) than it did about my adult personal character and my professional behavior. Whatever I had learned about Christian theology, Christian faith, welcoming hospitality, and a spirituality of inclusion from these patriarchal male individuals, was now called into question. No longer could I trust them to be either objective scholars or faithful personal witnesses to Jesus' teachings.

In one situation, at a mentor-colleague's funeral, I forced one of these shunning individuals to recognize me, acknowledge me, and speak with me. With the three other individuals, I have not forced the issue of a handshake and a conversation. I have not forced the issue of eye contact. I have made no public scenes. I suppose they can interpret my willingness to be their "shunnee" as a confession of fault. If so, they are dead wrong. Could I go back in time twenty-six years, I would once more choose to be a whistle-blower. I might do it differently in order to be more effective than by having a private conversation. But I would do something to see if I could rectify an ongoing and troubling institutional injustice. And I would do it because it was the right and principled thing to do.

Initially puzzled about what I had done to deserve this rude social behavior, I tried to recall being offensive. Initially, I had no key to unlock the puzzle. When I did figure it out, I became highly amused by these individuals' sense of righteous self-importance and their shared belief that their social rejection of me would be personally chastening and devastating.

Eventually, as this game played itself out in the final years of my employed career, my sense of amazement and amusement went hand in hand with my attempts to do some theological deconstructive work on shunning inside the religious establishment. I don't think that my description and deconstruction of these colleagues' behavior would amuse or educate any of these individuals. The reason for this private assumption is simple. By deconstructing this social, yet very personal, reality in my life, I claim my personal authority. I refuse to accept their implicit – and probably explicit – judgment as having done something shameful, something deserving of their moral and social judgment.

Three of these four individuals have already crossed over and one is very, very elderly. It is doubtful that their fancy theologies of reconciliation and right relationships will affect their behavior towards me in this lifetime. The remaining one will soon die and only I will know who these individuals were, what they did to me, and why. The survivor of these negating and socially vicious interpersonal behaviors has, in essence, the last word. My personal evaluation is, therefore, that none of these four individuals, in their acts of public shunning and shaming, demonstrated a believable praxis of Christian faith. Since their behavior towards me was patronizingly unchristian, by that very reality their theologies of Christ's compassionate welcoming love can be assumed to be faulty. Their individual and collective ecclesiology of the church as a place of welcoming hospitality to all have been disproved by their actual, embodied behavior.

I have concluded, therefore, that their theologies and ethical reflections about human relationships inside the people of God are almost totally invalidated by their deliberate and collective decisions to refuse to recognize me, acknowledge me and speak to me. At some level of my personality, this whole scene is just so ridiculous as to be hilarious. At another level, it is a serious breach of these theological elders' ethical responsibility to live by the code of ethics that they taught during their long professional careers as Christian theologians and ethicists.

Being actively shunned has not caused me to regret the behavior that has triggered it. I would choose, were I forty again, to do the very thing I did then – which was to act on behalf of others whose voices were weaker, more vulnerable, and more muted than mine. I would confront the institutional lie about itself. I would choose to be a whistle-blower in a very corrupted institutional setting where institutional lies littered the landscape.

These individual's sense of self-importance, therefore, has told me more about their interior moral and spiritual characters than they can imagine. It has shown a flashlight on their professional *and* personal narcissism. Make no mistake: this particular collective act of shunning, now that I understand it, continues to amuse me. It has, therefore, not forced me into a fawning and frightened submission. I sometimes think with my clinical mind: *I know these four people at a psychological and spiritual depth they cannot imagine. In a sense, I have recognized them for what and who they are.*

Third Rock

In the same way that it takes a community to create exclusion, paranoia, prejudice, clan hatred, interpersonal contentiousness, social isolation, and violence, it takes a community to create peace, compassion, harmony and justice. It takes a committed community to heal a world broken by hate and violence. It takes many such communities to build, brick by brick, stone by stone, cell by cell, a world where justice, mercy and compassion kiss.[504]

Without a rich cultural soil for peace-work, an individual's contributions to peace remain solitary and diffuse, that is to say, unshared. This is not to say that one solitary person can make no contributions. That is absurd. World history is filled with the accounts of individuals who made a difference in tilting the world's ideological fulcrum points. It is simply to argue that an individual's actions on behalf of the peace of the commons are usually grounded in that individual's personal psyche *and* in that individual's community.

Many years ago, I met and became friends with a venerable Quaker, an elderly man connected to many global peace activist movements. One day he confessed to me that he'd become enraged at his meeting the Sunday before our conversation. A family with a mentally handicapped son sat beside him and just as he entered the quiet zone of meditation the boy would poke him in the side and say, *Andy* [not his real name], *what time is it? Andy, can I have a piece of your gum? Andy, your shoes are not on your feet, why?* He said, *I took the boy by the hand and led him outdoors so as not to further disrupt the meeting.* Disrupted, the spiritual discipline of seeking to hear God's voice in the silence, kept him from hearing God's voice in the life and voice of this young boy. He was chagrined, he told me, after the fact, at his spontaneous intense anger towards a young boy who had sought to make a connection with him inside the deep silence of a Quaker meeting. From such homely and daily narratives, we construct our spirituality of peace or our spirituality of violence.

My own personal confessional reality is that I continually must wrestle with my inner contentiousness towards others. Patience is not a natural virtue for me – so I must catch my impatience and tame it before I unleash my social and interpersonal irritation and violence into the world. I suspect I fail more than I succeed.

Fourth Rock

For more than 18 years my own personal experiences as a fully participating member of the academic peace studies guild and the religious studies guild led me to conclude that there were no other professional guilds in my life where I witnessed and experienced more interpersonal mean-spirited behavior and professional violence in terms of human conflicts about ideology. As academic colleague strove mightily against academic colleague to score some point or another, I came

Ruth E. Krall

away with headaches that lasted for hours. The deep shadow side of the peace movement is its ideologically driven forces for *doing peace advocacy work the right way,* i.e., *my way.* Authoritarian needs to control and individual needs for dominance and personal needs for national or international prestige and prominence were very evident to me. Male dominance and skin color dominance issues were evident to me. Sexual harassment and sexual boundary issues were evident to me. Over time, I found that my academic and professional engagement in organizational academic peace studies and religious studies guild work was too challenging for my own spiritual sense of the matters at hand. I was much too tempted to join these academic skirmishes. Once entering, I was as determined to win as were others in whatever academic battle was under way. When these determinations to win, no matter how we win, enter conversations between academic peers, wisdom departs by the back door. In striving for our own vision of peace advocacy – whatever that vision might be – we all too often forgot the peace needs of the human commons right in front of us. We all too often forget the living tenderness of the human spirit in our intellectual and academic adversaries.

We tend, in these contentious, and all too often contemptuous, academic and religious institution debates, to forget the full humanity of our adversaries. We make enemies where we need to make colleagues. We create the despised other where we need to search for and create allies. We create the pariah where we need to make a beloved friend. We create divisions where we need to create community.

Jungian analysts and therapists talk about the always-present archetypal shadow in any regularly recurring encounter between and among human beings. Unaware of its presence, the shadow can direct our behaviors with others as much as – or even more so – than our declared intentions. In St. Paul's language, *I do not do that which I know I ought to do and I do that which I know I ought not to do.*[505]

Fifth Rock

The archetypal shadow was present in these academic peace societies and religious studies guilds just as it is now present within our Anabaptist-Mennonite denomination as we endlessly and tirelessly debate who can belong to our family of faith and who cannot; as we interminably debate the fine points of our Anabaptist-Mennonite purity codes; as we argue endlessly about our ecclesial theologies for belonging or not belonging; as we vote for including or casting aside other Anabaptist-Mennonite individuals as undesirables because of gender and sexual orientation issues.

The Mennonite shadow is not difficult to see. We have a very useful theology from our ancestors about the need to live peaceably in a discerning community but we are immensely schismatic. We are conflict phobic or avoidant and thus we prefer conformity to disagreement. In addition, many of us are biblical literalists.

Thus, we can fight about the meaning of words at the drop of a hat. Consequently, many of us are passive aggressive in how we manage conflict in our religious lives. As noted above we prefer shunning and ostracization to conversation and compromise. If my/our viewpoint does not carry the day, I/we will take my/our ideological marbles and go home. And, as I/we walk out the door, I/we will verbally trash the work, ideas, and character of those who remain inside. In such a situation, the ideology of my/our opinion takes precedence over the need to live and work in a we-filled community for the good of all.

In these interminable debates about purity codes, about who belongs, and who doesn't, judgment takes precedence over compassion; exclusion takes precedence over a welcoming, hospitable and including spirit. A paranoid decision to avoid and exclude the hated other eventually blunts and then overtakes our awareness that all whom Christ calls belong to Christ: tax collectors, adulterous men and women, ceremonially unclean bleeding women, rich young men, studious women, impoverished fishermen, people of different skin colors, dish-washers in the kitchen, carpenters, physicians, men and women with ritually unclean sexual histories such as the castrated Ethiopian in Acts 8:26-40. Indeed, in a Gospel-based story about faith, Jesus even includes a professional Roman soldier in Matthew 8: 5-13. It is a cultural given: we Mennonites don't hear too many church-authorized sermons based on these latter texts.

Emerging as an adult from a culture which taught him to disdain and avoid all contact with Samaritans and perhaps women too, Jesus picked up a friendly conversation with a Samaritan woman and, at that conversation's conclusion, stayed two nights as her village's guest. Jesus, by his ordinary acts of eating and drinking with the despised ones, sleeping under the same roofs, and being conversationally friendly with his culture's hated other, made converts in that town. Nowhere in this Gospel conversion narrative do we see any teaching of ritual or purity laws. While we have been taught to see his conversation with the Samaritan woman as critical about her lifestyle, when we read it fresh, we see Jesus made a simple declarative observation and then offered her and her village full inclusion.[506] The conclusion of this simple narrative is that by his refusal to disdain the hated other, Jesus made friends and welcomed the theologically and culturally despised Samaritans of this village into his new family – the family of shared faith.

Sixth Rock

In addition, our contemporary religious institutional awareness is blunted about creation itself. In my theological opinion, we do not hold to a faithful theology of creation: that each and every human life is made in God's image. When this happens, the community splinters in its dissent about lesser matters. Consequently, we lose our witness to the world because we cannot live in peace with each other.

Inside the religious world of his day, Jesus addressed the religious leaders of his time: *Woe to you, scribes and Pharisees. You have neglected the more important matters of the law: justice, mercy and faithfulness.*[507]

The more we collectively gather the horses around the patriarchal tribal boundaries or around ecclesial ideologies of purity and their associated praxis of shunning and exclusion, the more likely we are to do damage to those *precious lives we so disdainfully discard as not made, **like we are**, in God's image.* The more we pursue exclusionary ideological, ecclesiastical and liturgical purity, the more we become the embodied *pastoral lie that dismisses and discards the real needs of the people.* Pure and simple: this is bad theology; this is bad science and it is essentially a form of self-idolatry.

Seventh Rock

Our collective history as Mennonites should teach us to know better than to shun and exclude others as unacceptable. But it appears to me in the twenty-first century that we have forgotten and idealized the sixteenth-century pain of being shunned, hunted and murdered for differences in thought and praxis. We have forgotten that our faith ancestors once needed to worship in caves at the end of a long stream which they forded or waded in so they could not be traced as they gathered to sing the songs of peace. Now we have become the hunters, the enforcers of the purity laws, and the shunning ones. The genetic descendants of the once hated other, now we are the ones who hate. In our individual and collective paranoia and hatred, we force others to find welcoming caves of security and peace far away from our Mennonite church institutions and our homes.

Generations and generations of Mennonites have carried the stories of violent hatred towards our faith ancestors. We carry them in our ancestral bones. But, the transformation of this narrative about our hunted and persecuted ancestors now seems to be nearing its completion. It is now, apparently, payback time. Now, in our ecclesial structures, we hunt down the so-called heretics and the so-called outsiders only to exclude and shun them from our individual and communal presence. Our hate stares reveal our true faith: *you people do not belong here.* Now, in our communal and religious professional lives, we seek to stamp out others – those others who share our ethnic genes – simply because of a biologically embedded difference – their gendered sexual orientation. Our purity codes no longer protect the community from sin. Now, they are an occasion and excuse to sin.

I am haunted by the words of Rachel Fitzgerald above as she describes her church's hierarchy in its direct assault on the humanity of LBGTQ individuals – denying that they were made, like straight people, in God's image. Her words: *perhaps what gets us most is the pastoral lie; the utter dismissal of the real needs of the people, hungry for justice, and, at times, the failure to acknowledge that hatred and cruelty and thievery and despicable lies are in play.* As my old-fashioned Quaker friend might say it, *thy testimony, Rachel, resounds within me.* In these aging moments of my life, from inside the Mennonite Diaspora, I simply refuse to collude with this exclusionary teaching that refuses to accept all of Christ's little ones as belonging to Christ's community. Like Rachel, what gets me most is the pastoral lie.

Eighth Rock

For many years I have pondered some of these difficult questions of peace in situations where peace-maker is at odds with peace-maker about the work of making peace, indeed, about the very nature of the peace which is sought. Somewhere in the very distant past, I was at a conference and one workshop leader gave me one clue or one puzzle piece to help me to understand the archetypal issues in play. He said, and this is definitely from memory: *to be really good, i.e., successful in mediating conflict, it is essential that the conflict mediator love and is energized by conflict.* In memory, then and now, I recalled a personal conversation with clinician-philosopher Rollo May about the impact of disordered childhoods on adult psychotherapy clinicians. Again I paraphrase from memory. In that long-ago conversation May talked about his often troubled childhood/adolescence and the extensive therapy and supervision processes that brought him competency as a clinician and wisdom as a clinician-philosopher. *Some of the best therapists, Ruth, have had the most difficult childhoods; some are much wounded individuals in their personal lives.*[508] More recently, ordained minister and psychotherapist Wayne Muller has reflected on this same theme.[509]

In this context, I also remembered a long-ago personal conversation with another wounded therapeutic genius, Virginia Satir, who said to me that as therapists we must always look at the pathology-inducing systems which surround clinical pathology in individuals. During my graduate studies, anthropologist Margaret Mead in her clinical supervisory conferences also emphasized the need to know every client's context as well as her or his presenting symptomatology.

As I remember and invoke these ancient messages that live in my memory, I wonder, therefore, if we need to love violence in order to do effective anti-violence work. I wonder if we need to be wounded by violence in order to counter its toxicity in our midst. To use a medical metaphor, do we need to know violence first hand in order to immunize and protect our soft inner selves so that we can work for peace in its presence and avoid being destroyed by the psychological, spiritual and physical impact of the violence to which we bear witness?

If so, this conundrum of being wounded by life, of inheriting and living inside systems of violence and violation, of caring for and managing our own woundedness, of loving conflict for its own sake, and loving violence as a tool of managing our rage becomes present to us. It demands resolution if we are not to transmit to others our culture's historical wounds and our personal wounds in a never-ending generational lineage of pain and suffering.

The keystone for holding together the complexities of this conundrum is our continuous need for spiritual and emotional metamorphosis. It seems as if a wide variety of the world's religious wisdom traditions teach us about this paradox of loving violence while seeking peace. It appears as if we must have an intimate acquaintance with conflict, wounding, and violence if we are to become effective healers, mediators, victim advocates, and peace-workers. We must know, these traditions' spiritual elders seem to be saying, wounds, violence and conflict from the inside out. We must recognize them for what they really are and, in that process of gaining self-knowledge, we will come to know and acknowledge our love/hate relationship with violence. They seem to be telling us that before we seek to address violence of any kind as a problem in the commons, we must learn to recognize it internally. Therefore, I conclude from these wisdom teachers and their precautionary advice to the young person I once was that we must learn how to recognize the subtle and not-so-subtle private manifestations of violence in our own individual spirit/soul before we seek to de-fang its dragon-like presence in the public commons.

In many cultures of antiquity, including the Hebrew people, if human beings knew the name of the God to whom the community and individuals prayed then mortals gained control over that god. Since this was an undesirable outcome in terms of the peace and security of the human community, the name of God became unsayable. This is ancient spiritual wisdom we Christians need to re-learn. All too often we fight about our anthropomorphic human name for God and our anthropomorphized human understanding of God – as if this ineffable mysterious universal consciousness is ours to name, define, defend, and thus manipulate. We act as if our prejudices and hatreds have originated with this divine higher being who lives somewhere on the other side of the sky. We defend our mean-spirited and exclusionary behaviors by claiming that God demands such behaviors. We invoke God's name as we club each other to death.

The novelist and essayist Anne Lamont reminds her readers of their need to be self-aware and self-critical in their loves and hates:

> *You can safely assume that you have created God in your own image when it turns out your God hates all the same people you do.*[510]

Jesus, as an itinerant and probably illiterate Jewish spiritual teacher, reminded his listeners and questioners of the moral and spiritual essentials: *love of God and love of the neighbor.* It is a psychological given: in the presence of love, there is no hatred of the neighbor, no irrational prejudice, and no malice. Love seeks union rather than separation. It seeks unity not divisiveness. Not only does active, well-grounded compassionate love cast out fear; it also creates an interpersonal soil where violence cannot breed and grow.

To be effective peace-makers, healers, victim advocates, and conflict mediators, therefore, we must deal not only with the dangerous fire-breathing dragons roaming free in the commons. We must deal with our internalized dragons. Perhaps the sequence matters. Perhaps we must first acknowledge and deal with our internalized dragons before we enter the commons as dragon hunters. No matter the sequence: once we become actively engaged in seeking to create peace and justice in the commons, we will need to engage simultaneously and continuously with our world's internalized *and* externalized dragons.

I presume, therefore, from these comments made by my clinical elders at various times in my life that the best dragon hunters are those rare individuals who have come to know and to love their inner dragons and to love and respect the outer dragons because to do otherwise would mean they know nothing of substance about dragons.

How do we learn to love and to respect violence enough to contain and then transform it? That is a question which must be asked but will probably not be easily answered.

Ninth Rock

Over the years I have come to believe, therefore, that the hardest work of peace-making, conflict mediating, and victim advocacy work that any of us will ever do begins inside our individual human psyches. For it is inside the human psyche that we plot acts of revenge and fantasize acts of revenge. And it is there that we must begin the life-long journey of personal transformation and metamorphosis.

It is a clinical aphorism that the only person an individual can change is that person's own unique self. None of us can coerce desired personal and social change in the commons. We can persuade but we cannot coerce unless we are willing to engage in the very acts of violence we decry in others.

It is true that murderous dictators can create a nation-state in which no one is free or safe from harm. But these states tend to be short-lived and come to violent ends. In a relatively free state, human beings cannot be coerced into personal and cultural change. We are, therefore, as peace advocates and as conflict mediators engaged in the persuasive work of bringing about social change. It is inevitable that we must, therefore, deal with the issue of change and transformation of our own individual lives as we seek the peace of the commons, as we seek to create and then mark the path to a community where truth-telling, justice, mercy and compassion meet and merge. Without this merger, there can be no lasting peace.

The decision, however we make it and whenever we make it, to work for the peace and healing of individuals and of the commons inevitably sets us on the path to conflict. When we decide to do anti-violence work in whatever venue we do it, we will inevitably encounter more conflict and violence. We enter the possibility or the realm, therefore, of spiritual transformation. If we neglect our own inner spiritual metamorphosis, we will inevitably become one more violent peacemaker; one more violent healer; one more violent victim advocate.

We can no more coerce the peace and healing of the world than we can control the wind. Yet, as we seek to become one of the world's peace workers, one of its conflict mediators, one of its victim's advocates, or one of its healers, we must also seek to find a secure path to our own peace and our own healing. We must find a way to manage our inevitable conflicts of ideology, opinion and action so that we and others are not destroyed. To become one of the world's healers, peacemakers, or one of its conflict mediators and transformers, we must, therefore, tend our inner garden so that it manifests in the outer world with beauty, integrity and compassion.[511]

Creating situations of external peace and healing our inner world are, therefore, co-terminus actions with each other: failing to heal our own inner sources of, inclinations for, and motivations to do harm, we have little more to offer the world than ideology. Failing to bind up our own wounds, we spread their purulent virus into the world. Even as we diligently seek to create a healthier external world for others, if we do not do our own spiritual work, we continue to spread – inadvertently – the spirit of violence and violation. Failing to do our own spiritual work, day by day, hour by hour, minute by minute, we become the violence virus carriers.

Tenth Rock

While we may never enact violence in the world by killing, for example, we can become the carriers of the very ideologies which support killing in its various forms. Instead of becoming part of the needed solutions to the problem of killing, we have now become part of the problem. I am personally convinced by my life-experiences to date that we all carry the culturally-embedded virus of violence inside of ourselves. When I think, *I hope that individual spends eternity in hell* or I find myself in a midnight fantasy of *revenge killing and rapacious rage or* when I want to win an argument at any cost: *doing and being any of these,* I encounter the introjected violence virus of my culture inside my own psyche.

Not only do our overt actions corrupt the sea of consciousness. So, too, do our hostile thoughts and fantasies. We must learn, therefore, how to manage this aspect of our individual consciousness inside the various commons where we live and work. That behavior or personal social conduct which we will eventually manifest in interpersonal or social realms has its motivating and invigorating origins deep within the private imagination or psyche.

In a professional conference many years ago anthropologist Angeles Arrien, taught us that when we mindfully catch the monkey mind having hostile thoughts and hostile fantasies about others, we should deliberately stop the inner narrative and self-correct it by saying to the monkey mind, *that's a narrative that does not need to happen. That's a story that does not need to manifest.* I have personally found this to be a powerful way to educate my own monkey mind away from fantasies of revenge, of violation, etc. It is metaphorically like placing a road block which causes the mind to detour away from its personal stash of stored hostility and negativity.

Encountering somewhat later in time, Brother David Steindl-Rast's spiritual teaching about living in gratitude,[512] I began deliberately to substitute images and narratives of gratitude for these spontaneously-appearing monkey mind images of anger, violation and revenge. I began to search for gratitude in very ordinary places. I sought to replace these so-called spontaneous fantasies, images and narratives of anger, revenge, hatred, and violence with images of stillness, calm, beauty and peace. This is, I have found, a constant work of the spirit in process and I am humbled by how hard this spiritual discipline of gratitude in the service of peace is for me.

Inevitably, I think, this means that when we begin to practice a form of spirituality as a buttressing support for our peace and social justice activism in the world, our own lives become the experiment in peace from which we can reach out to a world filled with violation and pain. Buddhist Monk Thich Nhat Hanh says this so well. He writes: *our own life is the instrument with which we experiment with truth.*[513] We seek to become, in these sometimes difficult and begrudging moments of our spiritual transformation, the hands or the feet of God.

Eleventh Rock

Conversion, in our culture's Christian sensibility, is often seen as a onetime *born-again* event of *right belief*. I have come to understand following the Jesus path as a continuous process of being spiritually, psychologically and emotionally converted away from my own stash of internalized motives for betrayal, revenge, violence and violation. In my personal life and in my professional life as a clinician-thealogian, I have come to understand conversion as a life-long process of behavior. In the supposed conflict of word and deed, I prioritize deed (orthopraxis) above word (orthodoxy). But I deeply hold to the premise that all of our actions are rooted in our interior consciousness. Thus, in some perhaps inexplicable ways, word/thought and deed are inseparable.

Conversion, therefore, to me, is like walking up a very steep and sometimes treacherous mountain path where there are many cairns placed by my ancestors to help me. There are many moments of decision on such a path and each can contribute to my ongoing conversion: a journey towards healing and peace-making. Or, each cairn, if ignored or misunderstood, can lead me away into subtle [or even, not-so-subtle] forms of interpersonal violation and violence. Only by paying attention – by being mindful – do I stay on my path.

Each present moment carries, therefore, the potential for doing good or for doing evil. As we are mindful, each present moment, therefore, is a potential moment of deep and lasting transformation in ourselves and in our culture. This is, I believe, the real message of the Jesus teaching that we must, to enter the reign of God, be born again.[514] This message is not, therefore, about proper beliefs or thinking right. It is, therefore, not about orthodoxy. Rather, it is about continuous metamorphosis. It is about orthopraxis. It is about right behavior and, in its specifics it is about behaving towards others in ways which do not violate their bodies, their spirits, or their full humanity.

Twelfth Rock

When we choose to diminish another's life for any reason at all, we diminish our own. In so doing, we dim the lamp inside us which searches for wholeness, for well-being, for peace.

As Mennonite men and women we have been taught that the deliberate killing of another human being is against the divine will for human life in the commons. Our denomination has been clear in its teaching that Christians do not enter the killing fields to kill – be these fields the death penalty, armed combat or racially-inspired police actions inside one of our nation's ghettos. When we do choose denominationally to enter the killing fields, we carry quilts and blankets for warmth, rice for food, potable water for drinking and bathing, medicines for healing, and canvas tents for temporary shelter.[515] We are more apt, therefore, to send carpenters and plumbers than we are to call a theological conclave about the problems at hand. We have been well-taught that the Jesus path is a path of peace. We have been well-taught that discipleship – *faithfully following after the faithful [and peaceful] Christ* – is the center of our religious faith and communal praxis.

Yet, in our homes within the Mennonite commons, children are beaten in God's name; spouses are battered and emotionally abused in God's name; and all manner of vulnerable people are sexually harassed, abused, and violated...*inside the community of faith*. Spouse abuse, elder abuse, incest and affinity rape are all more common than we might suppose. Prejudice against people of color and prejudice against people with non-dominant genderized sexual orientations are rampant in our various communities. Emotional and verbal abuse is everywhere among us. We are skilled at the arts of shunning and thus we tend to avoid and to exclude those with whom we disagree. In situations of interpersonal conflict, we become verbally and behaviorally passive aggressive.

We have had, as a Mennonite people, almost no teaching over the centuries that these forms of domestic affinity violence and violations are as costly to the human personality and human community as the violence of the state. Other than the sermons which Mennonite women have occasionally preached – and we can only speculate about how many of those sermons there have been since the ordination of women began in the Mennonite church,[516] I don't think I have ever heard domestic abuse and violence against vulnerable people inside the boundaries of the faith community spoken against by Mennonite pastors in a regular Sunday morning service until very recently. I have never heard regularly preached sermons in which the internal violence of the community has been addressed as a peace and justice issue. I do not think I have ever heard a sermon critiquing the interior spirituality of violence as it is taught to us by our religious and secular cultures.

In contrast, I have heard sermons about football on Super Bowl Sundays. I have heard sermons about the evils of homosexual life styles. I have heard sermons – many years ago – about the community's demand that its young people not participate in civil rights protest marches. I have heard lengthy sermon harangues about the evils of lipstick, dancing, short hair for women, mustaches for men, worldly clothing, and wedding bands. I have heard evangelistic rants against premarital sex and the use of tobacco and alcohol but none about sexual violence.

While I have personally witnessed the Mennonite community of faith excommunicate young men who enrolled in military service, I have never witnessed the excommunication of individuals who have perpetrated rape, battery, incest, emotional abuse, etc., inside the Mennonite commons. I have never witnessed an abusive spouse or parent publicly criticized or disciplined for the violence he or she has done inside the family. I have never witnessed excommunication of abusive and authoritarian institutional administrators. Until very recently, I have never heard sermons against abusive and corrupt church institutions.

I am not arguing for excommunication and shunning. I really don't believe in shunning or expelling people from the religious commons for any reason I can think of – including adultery, pedophilia, grand theft, rape, and murder... or the wearing of eye shadow. While I believe that criminal elements need to be restrained to protect the commons, their humanity is intact and it should be honored by humane treatment inside their restricted area of movement – whether this is a city jail or a federal prison. Efforts should be made to rehabilitate these individuals for a shared, now safe, and restored life in the commons. To put it quite simply: accused and/or convicted Mennonite criminals need knowledgeable and compassionate pastoral care inside the various jails where they reside. This too is peace work.

Punitive measures clearly don't work and often exacerbate the underlying motives for violence in the prisoner's psyche – damaging it further and making it more unlikely that these individuals can and will be able to live in the shared

Ruth E. Krall

commons as peers. If we only address the violence of behavior and we never address the violence of the inner world, the motivating forces for violence will continue to shred our human communities.

Parenthetically, Phillip Zimbardo's important work[517] demonstrates that those who guard the criminal element often become de-sensitized to the full humanity of those whom they guard. They move into devastating forms of personal and structural violence. We should, I think, teach Zimbardo's work inside the church. In the same general arena is Sam Keen's important work about enemy making.[518]

Not only are the keepers corrupted inside prison facilities. We find the same realities present in the isolated refugee camps of the world – where individuals have almost no material resources and usually face restricted access to the outside world.[519] Having nearly total control of individuals within social and religious structures is almost an invitation for their guardians and keepers to abuse those who are controlled.[520]

Instead, I am commenting that whenever we, as a particular community of faith and praxis, tolerate, indeed, sanction, perhaps even promote violence inside the Mennonite community of faith, we gut our community's pacifist witness to the world's violence outside its borders. We know, now, that the human trauma response can begin inside situations of private violence – hidden from view – as well as from situations of public violence, whether or not this public violence is sanctioned by the nation-state or results from guerilla-like motivations of anarchy to disrupt the status quo of the nation-state.[521]

Thirteenth Rock

While physical crucifixions and religiously-inspired murders are less frequent, perhaps, – but not yet non-existent in the twenty-first century, social crucifixions are quite common.

As an individual who became aware of sexual violence as a clinical issue in my thirties and as a theological issue in my forties, I am very aware that my advocacy work inside the Mennonite Church on behalf of sexually traumatized individuals has made me very few friends and many enemies. As I mentioned above, I personally know what it is like to be deliberately shunned. As you and I have talked, you have reported to me that you know that a sub-group group of the Mennonite Church's academic theologians consider me to hold personal vendettas against my church home. My own short hand form of this is to call myself a *denominational pariah*. Quite frankly, there are a lot of Mennonites – in the academic world and outside of it – who would be quite happy if I became an Episcopalian or a Buddhist. I doubt they are consigning me to hell on a regular basis. They just wish I would go away or, at the very least, shut up. They make one thing quite clear to me in their interpersonal and professional behaviors towards me: they disapprove of the work I do; they don't like me; and they don't like being in proximity to me. In consequence, I am the recipient of their discomfort with me and their disdain towards me. A very strong social signal is sent that it is some deficiency, some personal fault line, in me that causes their judgment.

My interrogators, so to speak, are, therefore, in the self-righteous position of purity and righteousness while I am clearly in a social or religious position of wrong-mindedness, perhaps even heresy. Sometimes I refer to my reputed misconduct and bad reputation among this small but outspoken percentage of my academic peers as the equivalent of *farting at the altar rail during communion*. My spiritually-and ethically-motivated behavior (the behavior of seeking to expose the truth of the Mennonite community's internal violence problems on behalf of the victims of its social and sexual violence) is to this sub-group of Mennonite academics and church leaders, clearly unacceptable. What I personally perceive to be a moral, ethical or spiritual need to bear witness, they obviously see as unprofessional, deviant and community–destructive behavior. I often wonder if I am portrayed in their fantasies and thoughts about me, therefore, as an irrational and very angry female with a Glock Safe Action pistol cleaned, loaded and ready to do battle with all who disagree with me.

My clinical and academic work on behalf of church and family-victimized individuals (incidentally work begun in 1990 at the request of the institutional church itself) is seen as more destructive to the community than these multiple acts of victimization and violation. Bearing witness to the realities of victimization inside the Mennonite commons is seen as more violent than the acts of victimization and their subsequent cover-ups by the institutional church.

I find no internal personal support for these images of me. I own no Glock. I carry no sword. I have no vendetta against my church. I hold no ill will against it.

What I do have, however, is a deeply rooted belief in personal and societal non-violent activism as the pathway to lasting peace – peace based on social justice towards the marginalized. I am deeply committed to healing as a profession and as a belief system. To me, this means I am ethically compelled to bear witness against violence in all of its irrational forms and presences within culture and community.

When I stop long enough to feel the pain of my theological colleague's labeling, I see it as instructive pain. It is a hologram of the silence and pain known by every ostracized victim and survivor of the church's many forms of internal violence. Just as the victims of sexual violence inside the church are silenced so too are their advocates, therapists, family members, friends, and other helpers. In a similar manner as the victims of the institutional church's homophobic violence are silenced and shunned so too are their advocates, friends, family members and other helpers. Shunning, hate-staring, shaming, and silencing constitute the passive-aggressive way we Mennonites solve the need, indeed, the invitation to hold these difficult conversations with each other.

Ruth E. Krall

It is my perception that my church and some of its academics in abandoning me to my harshest critics and in refusing to hear my academic voice inside the church's narrative of non-violence have betrayed me. Much more seriously, in my opinion, the church and its academics have betrayed its own theology of peace. Most seriously of all, however, they have abandoned the little ones, *the little ones of any age,* who have been victimized by the institutional church and its official ordained representatives.

Beginning in the 1990's I was repeatedly asked to preach about and lecture about sexual and family violence in the context of Mennonite communities. Choosing to serve my denominational church in this very public way, I soon realized that I'd become an ideological lightning rod for many members of the Mennonite Church. It was not long until I realized that for many Mennonites, including some Mennonite administrators, academics and pastors, it was easier to trash me behind my back than it was to engage me in a serious conversation about the presence of sexual, physical, and verbal violence inside the community. It was easier to complain to my employer than to talk with me in person.

One well known ordained Mennonite Church administrator was cordial to my face but whenever my name was suggested for a denomination-wide committee, he would sadly shake his head, roll his eyes slightly, and say, *well, I just don't know about Ruth Krall's personal faith and her theology.* My name would be immediately withdrawn from consideration as a church theologian with something to offer to the community at large.

What fascinated me about this story when I first heard it from a concerned feminist colleague was that this male church executive did not verbally lie. He was, with his words, speaking the absolute truth. He had never once talked with me about my personal faith and my personal theology. We never had a conversation about his concerns. It was only his non-verbal behavior that conveyed the message of my unacceptability. What others heard in the non-verbal nuance was that he knew I was an inappropriate, perhaps even heretical, theologian for the church. It was this behavioral and non-verbal message that persuaded others I was morally and theologically unfit as well as unsanctified. My personal and professional character was smeared, therefore, without words, by his sad shake of the head and the roll of his troubled eyes – non-verbal behaviors which implied he did know the specifics of my heresy but was just too saintly or principled to gossip about them. He was, to all appearances therefore, deeply saddened by my fall from grace, sanctification and theological acceptability. But, as his theological and pastoral duty, he needed to protect the Mennonite Church community from my noxious presence and conversation. In more than ten years of this behavior, he never once asked me about my beliefs and my spiritual praxis. This is a form of dishonest manipulation and, while it harmed me, in my opinion it profoundly harmed him much, much more. In the service of destroying my professional service to my church, his dishonesty cost him personal integrity, spiritual honesty, and compassion.

When you talk about the deep-rooted perception in today's Mennonite academic community (at least among some of its male academics) that I have a personal vendetta against my church, I wonder how much of that current belief is rooted in this administrator's stash of personal or ideological hostility towards me – hostility I never fully understood. There is no way to know. Rumors, particularly malicious rumors, spread inside the Mennonite commons like an out-of-control and non-contained forest fire. It is the rare Mennonite academic administrator or pastor who will check out a troubling or malicious rumor to see if it is true. Thus, few academic colleagues in religious studies or theology ever asked me to define my faith or engaged me in conversations about it. Over time, therefore, I slowly became known as the unfaithful one, the unacceptable one, the one with a vendetta.[522] When this perception filtered down even into the congregation where I worshipped, I knew it was time to move on out. I joined a welcoming Methodist congregation.[523]

This kind of malicious behavior is a form of intra-community, interpersonal, and structural violence in motion. All of the fancy pious words we can conjure up do not conceal the spiritual, psychological and communal damage this kind of implicit lying, character assassination and rumor-mongering creates inside the Mennonite Community of faith.

In writing about this, I do not mean to imply this was a global phenomenon inside my denominational heritage. Rather, it appeared to be a well-orchestrated action of a few very powerful and influential individuals. They seemed to me to take offense about my feminist notion that peace activism should include anti-sexual violence activism *and all-inclusive* active caring for the victimized little ones of any age who carry the wounds of their victimization.

Fourteenth Rock

Recently, in correspondence with a young Mennonite scholar I wrote that when the church of our childhood abandons us as unworthy, there is probably no greater spiritual pain and loss. That place and that people whom we once trusted with our spiritual lives and personal well-being have tossed us to the wind. We become exiles.

I've done a lot of reading about various groups and individuals who were, in one way or another, forced into exile by the dominant group of their culture – other people forced them to do what they might not have chosen to do on their own. Whether we are talking about the Babylonian exile of the Jewish people as recorded in ancient Jewish scriptures; the forced re-location of Sephardic Jewry on July 30, 1492 by Spain; the forced marches, *the* multiple *trails of tears,* of North

Ruth E. Krall

American Amerindian nations such as the Cherokee, the Ojibwa, or the Navajo; Aleksandr Solzhenitsyn's coerced exile from Russia and his solitary and isolated sojourn (1974-1994) in New England: the status of isolation from one's geographic and spiritual homeland is extraordinarily painful. It is a wound which refuses to heal. It is a wound which not only changes our external landscape. It changes and restructures our inner world.

Betrayal and its consequent exile from one's people represent, therefore, deeply divisive forms of interpersonal and social violence. When social intimates and trusted friends deliberately choose to betray another, they usually do so in the name of personal jealousy, ideology, money, or power. But sometimes they do this also in the name of God. To be denounced by one's people as unacceptable, even or especially in God's eyes, this is a form of social *and* spiritual violation. It is a form of deep betrayal.

Fifteenth Rock

Our known enemies may harm us but they do not betray us because we do not trust them to begin with. It is only those we have trusted as friends and colleagues who have the power to betray. Religious and spiritual betrayal, therefore, is an immense spiritual problem in today's churches – inasmuch as the dominant ideology is that of exclusion under the guise and language of welcoming.

My own way of dealing with this issue of my identity as a Mennonite academic and Mennonite thealogian in an ethnic church I now barely recognize as Christian is to turn to Psalm 137:4.[524] Loving the four parts a cappella music tradition of my church, I can no longer bear to sing inside the community because the implied spiritual unity of our singing together has been broken. My communal singing voice has been silenced and destroyed because my community has turned its back on others and on me. In a form of obscurantist, perhaps narcissistic projection, it is not the Mennonite Church's academic and institutional elites who have a personal vendetta against me: rather they report to the world – albeit behind my back - that it is I who have a personal vendetta against the church. In the words of the African-American spiritual, *they scandalized my name.*[525]

I consider this entire narrative of *me as a vendetta wielding layperson,* to be absurd. I have never hated my childhood; I have never hated my childhood church. I loved its people and, ah, the a cappella music – it just fed my spirit. Most of my closest life-long personal friends have Anabaptist-Mennonite origins. Even now I often wake in the morning with hymn melodies and words singing themselves in my just awake mind.

Sixteenth Rock

But the violence of my community: I am so sad when I think about how many wounded individuals there are because of the community's willingness to tolerate its own violence; because of the community's pervasive unwillingness to confront its own very dark shadow.

Not too long ago, I asked myself this: *If my community tolerates these various forms of interpersonal, sexual and physical violence as acceptable, is my community wrong about its anti-war teachings as unacceptable?* And, in that moment, I surrendered my Mennonite peace theology vis-à-vis war based on Anabaptist-Mennonite history, theology and the Bible itself.

My personal peace theology therefore is no longer Mennonite or even institutionally Christian. Having seen the damages to individuals and human communities, violence quite simply is not the path I wish to pursue. As healers, nurses and doctors are taught a quite simple maxim: *first, do no harm!* I no longer need my denominational church to teach me that physical war and economic war is wrong. These forms of war harm precious and unique people. They destroy individual lives and they destroy entire communities. In addition, they spread the virus of violence.

This is also what sexual violence does. It destroys individual lives and communities. This is what homophobia does. It destroys lives and communities. This is what racism does. It destroys lives and communities.

War's violence and the violence of sexual abuse in any of its many forms destroy precious lives. Thus, both are morally wrong. I do not need the voice of any of the world's gods to teach me this. All I need to do is to encounter lives destroyed by the worlds killing fields, by torture, by rape or by homophobia as well as by other forms of individual and systemic abuse.

Being a healer by my profession, I seek life rather than death; I seek healing rather than destruction. I seek restoration and reconciliation rather than revenge. The universal spiritual teaching in many, perhaps most of the world's major religions is to love the neighbor as one loves the self. In our love for each other, therefore, we find the love of God. This is where I now live.

Seventeenth Rock

Even in a world filled with violence, shunning, betrayals of all kinds, and many forms of character assassination, there is hope. One thing I have learned in the past twenty years. I am not alone in spiritual exile. There is a large and vibrant spiritual Diaspora of concerned Christians, Jews, Muslims, Buddhists, etc., and its growing edges are most visible in the newly emerging cyber world *and* in so-called secular peace activism projects. For example, groups of deeply committed peace-makers are increasingly grounded in ecumenism. In Tucson, AZ, for instance, members of the local Jewish community and members of the local Islamic community have an annual get acquainted festival day of solidarity, social action and a common meal. Local community members of all faiths are also invited to participate in the day's activities.[526] All who show up in a respectful attitude are welcomed and none are disdained as feared and hated outsiders. It is a day of making acquaintances. Friendships formed during this day endure and show up in other peace action situations as well.

In my experience, this newly emerging cyber-space form of Christianity and/or ecumenical Diaspora community is based on communicating in a personal *and* behavioral way that which now defines us as a spiritual people of faith, as a spiritual people of peace. Less emphasis is placed upon institutionalized doctrinal formulations of faith and more emphasis is placed on community praxis. Whoever shows up for respectful and thoughtful conversations about faith and praxis is welcome.[527] Whoever shows up to do the work of peace is welcome.

For me the very word *Christian* has, in these aging moments of my life, become contaminated because in my lifetime it has been weaponized.[528] I find it easier to talk about following the Jesus path than I do to identify myself as a militant institutional Christian in a world where Christ's name is so frequently invoked as the reason to hate the other, to exclude the maligned other, and to do interpersonal, social and physical violence to other human beings in all kinds of ways in the name of one's religious community.

If we define, as I now do, the word church as *the people of God,* then we can ask about the behavioral characteristics of the people of God. When we do this, the definition is not about buildings or institutions or hierarchies but about personal and collective commitments at work for the healing and peace of the world.

The schismatic institutional church, based on worn out ideas and theological clichés, is divisive and spiritually concerned people are simply exiting it. The purity code churches which exclude people on the basis of skin color, an absence of personal wealth, ethnicity, sexual orientation, and other ontological and sociological factors beyond their control are not attracting the young.[529] When churches fight, split, and then re-form around false ideologies of exclusion and idolatries of prejudice and hatred, fair-minded people turn away and seek a new community in which their spirituality is nurtured and their unique image of God is honored.

The churches which openly protect sexual abusers and which concomitantly suppress information about child sexual abuse and adult sexual abuse by religious leaders: these churches routinely suppress the truth. Roman Catholic theologians and priests such as Thomas Doyle, William Lindsey, Donald Cozzens, Mark Jordan, Matthew Fox and Hans King warn their denominational church that its ideological support for faulty praxis in child sexual abuse cases is causing a slow *and* perceptible shift away from Catholic social teachings, a shift which does not bode well for the long-term survival of Roman Catholic communities of faith.

They warn as well of the spiritual and communal dangers of excluding individuals simply on the grounds of their sexual orientation.

What is most fascinating to me – as we turn now to cyber churches for our sense of community and support in activism – is that people from these communities often seek ways to meet in person. Those of us who are Jesus path pacifists find allies in this ecumenical world of cyberspace that we might never have met without the intense pain of denominational exile driving our search for a new family. There are now peace-work and justice-work coalitions of Catholics and Mennonites. There are now peace-work coalitions of Christians, Jews, and Buddhists.[530] In addition many Christians seek wisdom in Amerindian traditions of care for the earth. As members of the contemporary spiritual Diaspora we search for a new community in which to anchor our personal spirituality. At the same time we also search for allies in our activism on behalf of the world's most vulnerable little ones of all ages. We are becoming co-creators with God of the world's peace as we actively seek to create peace inside our most personal lives and spiritualities.

Eighteenth Rock

I read these words recently. I do not, for certain, know they are the words of Menno Simons. They were attributed to him. They comfort me. Perhaps they will comfort you as well.

> *I know of a certainty, that a proud, haughty, avaricious, selfish, unchaste, wrangling, envious, disobedient, idolatrous, false, lying, unfaithful, thievish, defaming, backbiting, blood-thirsty, unmerciful, and revengeful man whosoever he may be is no Christian, even if he was baptized one hundred times and attended the Lord's Supper daily.*[531]

In the context of the religious wars of his own era in time, Jesus is reputed to have given instructions to his disciples as he sent them out into the world beyond the small group gathered around Jesus. Matthew's gospel records him as saying, *I send you out as sheep into the wolf pack. Be wise as serpents and harmless as doves.*[532]

When we begin to work as healers, as peace workers, as mediators of conflict, or as victim advocates we leave a safety zone in which all is familiar. When we choose not to fight back with violence but continue to do our work, we need to pay attention. In my language (now-influenced by yours), we seek to resist violence non-lethally and to push back its walls; in your language we seek to transform violence. Both sets of language help us to see ourselves living dangerously in order to help someone who is vulnerable. We choose, I think, to put our own lives on the line; to put our own personal characters on the line; to put our own integrity on the line. When we do this, we will unavoidably be changed from the inside out. This is where the Jesus teachings about wisdom and harmlessness make sense. I probably don't need to be wise and harmless if I am sleeping in my own safe North American bed. But, when I go out into the world of violence, woundedness, and unbelievable pain seeking to help its most vulnerable ones, I must pay attention. I must be mindful. I must seek to walk in peace even as I encounter the world's suffering and pain. Enraged by the damage violence does to others, I must find a way to calm and stoke these intense emotional fires so that I, as well as others, am not destroyed by my anger.

Nineteenth Rock

One night in a small Guatemala village – a village where the military junta had recently assassinated some of the village's men in the fields while they hoed their crops, I got separated from the small group of North American students I was with. I knew where our pension was and I knew one of our Guatemalan hosts was with the students so I felt they were safe. The streets were dark and the stars over head were brilliant. I began to walk toward the small guest house where we were staying. I had the inner sense that I should walk quietly and softly in the darkness – simply being present with the night. I felt that the night would protect me if I did not move in noisy and abrupt ways that called attention to my presence. In that silky moonless night, I walked past a small house and inside that house a group of Guatemalan Christians were singing a hymn of protection and safety. I recognized the tune but did not know the Spanish words. It was a mystical moment. I knew I would arrive safely at my lodging place and that the students would be safely waiting there for me to arrive. I am not sure that night that I was wise, but I was determined to be harmless. In no way did I wish to endanger our Guatemalan hosts inside an already tense village. I had to be very alert and I had to be very quiet as I made my way home. What amazes me when I think about this story many years later is how very still inside my spirit was. I was not anxious about my life. When I heard the hymn, I knew it was not only being sung by and for the people inside the house; it was being sung for me as well. It was as if, inside my deep silence, I too was singing the hymn with them – a universal moment of deep inner stillness in which I was simply at home in the universe and in a sense, merged with the divine peace. I was, as were they, Christian in the truest sense of that word. We, in this divided land and time of military violence and humanitarian atrocities, were the people of Christ's peace. Nationality, culture, religious denomination, language differences, economic class, skin color, gender, etc., were all transcended in this moment where they and I were one.

Twentieth Rock

To summarize: we humans repeatedly metamorphose inside the chrysalis of our individual and communal spirituality. Seeking to become peace-makers and healers of the world's violence, we must turn to the wisdom of the world's spiritual teachings. But, and this is an important proviso, we must turn to them critically and analytically for they too, just as we do, carry the multiple viruses of our culture's proclivities for prejudice, conflict, violation and violence. It is not their ideologies and cultural forms [or ancient archetypes] we turn to in our search for healing. Rather, it is by means of their disciplined praxis; meditation, prayer, gratitude, living in community, twelve step meetings and teachings, scriptures, rites of passage celebrations, acts of concrete service to others, liturgy, etc. that we find our way into a spirituality that nurtures us, a spirituality, like an artesian well, that reminds us of our own needs for inner peace as we seek the peace of the external world; for inner healing as we seek the healing of the commons.

Ruth E. Krall

Nineteenth Letter

Personal Reflections

This disrespect [and that is the mild term]
for women is endemic in the clerical ranks.

Phyllis Zagano[533]

Introductory Comments

We began this correspondence when you asked me to read a book afterword in which you criticized women's absence as authors from the book's collected chapters. In the months since then we have roamed around the world in our long electronic letters to each other. The context of physical illness forms, in a sense, the brackets of these conversations. As each of us has needed to encounter the complex world of medical diagnosis, treatment, and issues of prognosis, we have continued to reflect on the issues which have most engaged us in our professional lives. While this redacted collection of these letters has been cast in my personal voice, they reflect your personal and professional voice in the background. Your letters elicited questions in my mind that seemed to need addressing in the commons. In addition, they shared your working hypotheses and conclusions.

The issue of women's subordinated position in the world affects every woman – whether or not she is privileged by virtue of having an education or disprivileged by living among the most abandoned of women in a refugee camp – surviving day by day (and in some situations hour by hour) as she cares for her family. The stress-and-trauma-filled narrative of being a female in a patriarchal and violent world pervades these letters. In particular, the narrative of sexual and gendered violence informs these written conversations. In the background, however, are our conversations about racism, gender orientation xenophobia, and various forms of prejudice based on sociological factors such as ethnicity or religion.

In this series of letters, our individual commitments to the peace of the world are visible; we began with women's experiences and with women's narratives of those experiences. Choosing to privilege women (and their children) as the focus of my life work of activism and scholarship has meant that my academic and activist work is not valued in the Mennonite patriarchy. But, as I near the end of my life, I would not change that focus or any of its different manifestations. Women's culturally diminished life in the patriarchy as lived everywhere around the world is a peace and justice issue. For women, it is also a religious and spiritual issue. Whether the abuse suffered by women is salary discrimination, exclusion from an insider status, shunning in her community, physical harassment, academic hazing by male peers, bullying bosses, domestic abuse by a spouse or parent, sexual violence, or their lived experiences of war, women and those for whom they are responsible, such as their children and the aged, suffer from their encounters with men's patriarchal prejudice towards them and men's enacted violence against them.

The aphorism about world religion and world spirituality – usually attributed to Mary Daly (*The world's religion is patriarchy and all of the world's religions are merely sects of the patriarchy*) is one that makes sense to me. As long as men (and their male-identified female acolytes), consciously or unconsciously, see women's presence and feminist analysis in the Academy as an irrelevant nuisance, then women will continue to be excluded from the conversations which involve them and from conversations where they can add valuable insights. Women's issues continue to be seen as irrelevant in doing the *real and necessary* work of nonviolence activism in the world: confronting the violence of others in matters of militarism, economics and criminal justice – in short the hard aspects of peace work. The presence of men's sexual violence inside the religious boundaries of any given community tends to be seen, therefore, as a soft, peripheral, and extraneous issue. Women's concerns about the sexual violation and gendered violence which encapsulates them and their children tend to be seen as irrelevant to the peace of the world.

Given that this male ignorance of and bias against women's sexual violence scholarship is omnipresent in the religious academy, it will continue to be, therefore, academic and activist women who raise these issues. And their voices, as inconsequential female ones, can be, and likely will be, denied credibility by their male colleagues. Thus, women's warnings about affinity abuse and sexual violations against women and their children *inside* the community of faith will continue to be ignored. Male led institutions such as the church will continue to pass resolutions and create programs while looking the other way when violations occur. Members of the religious hierarchy know that words are cheap while actions are costly. They will pontificate, therefore, but they will not act unless pressured to do so. They will collectively confess but never individually acknowledge and repent of their abusiveness towards women.

Ruth E. Krall

American feminist women's insistence that the personal is political and that the political is personal informs both my life and my scholarship. While I believe in activism against the political forms of violence which pervade life around the globe – in particular military and economic violation of others' lives or episodes of genocide and ethnic cleansing – I also believe we must address, individually and communally, the physical and sexual violence done by individuals who know each other and live inside of our religious communities.

This awareness of the need to address violence against women and their children is slowly spreading. In 2002, Nelson Mandela provided the Foreword to the World Health Organization's groundbreaking book about violence as the world's number one public health problem. He wrote:

> *Less visible [than warfare], but even more widespread, is the legacy of day-to-day individual suffering. It is the pain of children who are abused by the people who should protect them, women injured or humiliated by violent partners, elderly people maltreated by their caregivers, youths who are bullied by other youths, and people of all ages who inflict violence on themselves. That suffering – and there are many more examples that I could give - is a legacy that reproduces itself, as new generations learn from the violence of generations past, as victims learn from victimizers, and as the social conditions that nurture violence are allowed to continue.*[534]

The continuation of violence against women and their children creates a long, but usually unspoken, litany of issues. No one activist can address all of these issues. We each need to work in the corner of the universe of women we occupy. We do not need to think of ourselves as feminist clones. We each can address the suffering which presents itself to us in our various personal and professional worlds. Since we are not clones, our viewpoints will vary because our life experiences vary. We will not always agree. Yet we can continue to learn from each other. If our primary commitment is to end women's and children's suffering in the world, we will continuously seek out ways to support each other's work. We will continue to look for ways to make female lives healthier and safer. I hope that these humble letters of mine have lent you a sense of my support for the violence-confronting, conflict-transforming, and active peace-building work you do.

I want to conclude this series of letters with a much more personal form of address. This letter, therefore, is rooted much more in my life than it is rooted in your questions about my life and thought. This is the kind of letter I might write to one of my closest friends.

As you know, my life in the past twenty-four months has been held in a life and death balance I never foresaw happening to me at this time in my life. Waking in the middle of the night with the unnerving symptom of extreme hyperventilation,

I could not at first imagine what was wrong with my body. I had no language at all to explain this to myself other than *very threatening*. In the early morning hours, before going to the emergency room, I used the World Wide Web to get a working list of potential diagnoses. Some, such as heat exhaustion I could eliminate immediately. Others, not so easily!

After I entered America's emergency medical care system in March, 2014 the emergency room team eventually told me I had multiple blood clots in my lungs. I was immediately placed on complete bed rest while the hospital's in-patient medical care team began to medicate me and treat the symptoms of this life-threatening diagnosis. At the time I was too ill to be frightened. Only after my discharge from the hospital when I began to encounter my pervasive breathlessness, physical weakness, loss of physical and emotional balance, and nearly complete inability to do the simplest physical things in my ongoing and very ordinary life – only then did I begin to comprehend how ill and handicapped I really was. Swabbing a toilet, loading a dishwasher, or doing the laundry sent me scurrying back to bed or to a chair while I deliberately re-regulated my breathing and my pulse resumed its normal rhythmic beating. I lived with an oxymeter around my neck – and checked it frequently in abrupt episodes of breathless paranoia – needing to know if I was still really alive and, more importantly, healing.

Almost simultaneously with this event, you reached into my life with a request that I read and comment upon a book afterword that you had written. You had found me, you told me, through my *Enduring Space* blog and the issues which I raised there about the meaning(s) of the connection between John Howard Yoder's theology and his abusive behavior towards adult women.

This kind of synchronicity must be, I believe, honored. As I told you in a very early electronic letter, I had almost no energy for physical activity. But I could still think. The computer became my ally – allowing me to "talk" with my friends and guardian angel nephew when I physically had no extraneous breath that allowed for personal conversations. I picked up our initial electronic conversations because I was interested in what you were doing and thinking in your own personal and professional life. I prowled around the World Wide Web and discovered you were mid-career in active peace-making work as a feminist- Anabaptist-Mennonite woman, a rich career you had developed in the years since you exited your undergraduate and graduate classrooms. What I didn't anticipate, in advance of this first, and of necessity, somewhat quick search for your curriculum vitae was the almost immediately visible reality that we had so many concerns in common – now expressed generationally in quite different work environments.

For example, both of us are concerned with the traumatic aftermath of warfare; both of us are concerned with active advocacy on behalf of the world's peace; both of us are aware of the socio-cultural roots of advocacy work; both of us have encountered gender discrimination; both of us are interested in liturgy and ritual as forms of peace and healing work; both of us have maintained deeply personal ties with individuals of other world faiths; and both of us have concerns about the safety and welfare of women and their children. In addition, both of us have personally encountered Anabaptist Mennonite men's passive-aggressive chauvinism and active sexist hostility, perhaps even disdain, towards us and our work. Each of us has had, in our past, the experience of being betrayed by important friends, mentors, or supervisors - people we once trusted as elders and guides who subsequently betrayed us.

As we have picked up these conversations and deepened our awareness of each other's work through our personal self-revelations, I began – because it was all I had physical energy to do – to reply to your questions. Somewhere along the line you suggested keeping track of our back-and-forth dialogue, and somewhat later I decided to formalize some of my very roughly drawn and very informal electronic letters to you. This book of letters in a personal voice is a result of that decision. Somewhere along the line you suggested we might want to write a book together. Whether or not that will ever happen remains an unknown.

Whether or not you were aware of this as we wrote back and forth, you were extending a life-line of professional and personal courtesy and conversation to me that I desperately needed. Fearing my physical strength might never return, I needed to believe that my mind was not dead. Not able to vacuum my living room, I could at the very least listen to your ideas and concerns and think about them. This was better for my mental health than obsessing over the physical things I could no longer do. Somehow or other writing to you felt less like narcissistic self-preoccupation – something that was so easy to fall into when my body ached and my breathing was labored. Whether or not this is realistically true, it felt like I was still capable of making a contribution to the world's needs for peace advocacy and healing work.

I am still learning about my physical capabilities and limitations as I move through an extended rehabilitation process. Some days are much better days than others. My physical body – and consequently my emotional body – makes its protests known. My mood swings still distress me. But my breathing is stronger. Once again I can actually talk to people and walk at the same time without being overcome by breathlessness. I can now actually walk through my house without collapsing on the random chairs I had earlier placed everywhere. I no longer need naps every two or three hours. I have gradually resumed doing sexual violence advocacy and consultation work.

In these past twenty four months three of my personal friends have died. I pay attention to these inevitable deaths as my cohort group ages in place. I grieve my friends' absence from life and celebrate the life they actually lived and am comforted by the long years of close emotional ties with them. I know that I soon (and *soon* is a rubber- band like word in that it stretches but has a finite limit to that stretch) am likely to cross over – even as I now bargain every day with life herself for more time to finish a host of unfinished chores that include tasks ranging from the mundane or even silly ones to more intellectually challenging ones.

I cannot, therefore, promise you that we will ever write that book together. So, this book, Lisa, is my very personal gift to you in honor of the work you do and the wonderful adult person you have become. It is my way of saying *thank you* for being willing to read and respond to my words. It is a way to express gratitude for the work for peace and justice which you do in the world.

But, I won't say, *never.* When you finish the next several months of previously contracted work, we may then decide to work together. If my physical body continues to regain its strength and if my mind stays lucid and flexible, we may then decide it is time to see what we might co-create.

I am absolutely convinced that no human life is free of trauma and suffering. This means that as we seek to do our work in the world – the work of helping others find a way to peace and justice and healing – we must be deeply committed to the everyday work of our own healing.

When I retired, I read a lot of books about the developmental and spiritual tasks of aging.[535] As I read, I established an inner sense of what good aging looks like, what a healthy aging body/Self looks like. I set myself some goals – goals of involvement in the world and goals of adequate self-care. After years of eating on the run, I re-learned to cook for myself. Restaurant meals are now a treat, rather than a necessity.

Several words stood out for me: flexibility, resiliency, adaptability, active problem-solving, courage, hope for the future, determination, friendship, meaningful work, and now, in the wake of this most recent health-loss episode, I would add personal integrity and personal accountability to those who love us and watch over us.

I have never thought I would age gracefully. I am too impatient in my basic personality. This present episode of illness in my life has begun to teach me about being gracefully and thankfully dependent on others in ways I could not have foreseen. Instead of being impatient, for example, with the need to see medical care personnel on a regular basis, I have been so grateful to these individuals for their compassion and for their knowledgeable support.

We have talked on several occasions about gratitude as an enduring spiritual practice. I want to say that when my life recently got really rugged and demanding here in this great and beautiful American desert, I have found spaces for gratitude every day. Gratitude for breath – a celebration of one's own breath (and life) is so amazing. It opens the inner heart chakra to embrace others who, in so many different ways, are also suffering and struggling for life.

My determination to get my life back on course is evidenced by the presence of these very homely little letters. There is no new wisdom here. But I kept writing to you because it was the only thing that interested me other than my wounded but healing body. It was all that I had the physical strength to do. Reading your written work and your electronic letters, I kept finding things I wanted to say to you and to other men and women who are engaged in activism and advocacy on behalf of others' welfare.

In addition, your personal determination to make a difference by your own life work has inspired me. I am in awe of the work you do. It is such important work. Your life passion clearly involves international peace-building; my life passion has been making the world safer for women and their children. In the same way that war-making and rape go together, our concerns for the peace of the world and our concerns for the welfare and safety of women and their children go together.

Both of these unique sets of life-work passion have now intersected in these letters. Maybe in the course of these humble conversations we have begun to uncover more of what we individually know that we didn't previously know we knew. Maybe in the synchronicity of these conversations, born inside the chalice of my life-threatening illness and your sense of physical tiredness and potentially life-threatening diagnosis last summer, we have begun to unearth a different future for Anabaptist-Mennonite women than the one we inherited from our respective ancestors.

Suffering is rarely random. It usually has causality. But, as we learn to manage our personal stash of suffering, we can then begin to understand the shattering life suffering of others. More and more I am convinced that a too-perfect and a too-pure life is not the goal or the manifestation of our shared Anabaptist-Mennonite faith. More and more every day I am certain that the Jesus path takes us into the heart of others' suffering. We have to be willing to get our hands and minds inside the world's violent messes in order to begin to help others who are even more vulnerable than we are – others who are trapped by their encounters with encapsulating cruelty and violence – these very ordinary and very prevalent forms of human betrayal. Encountering other's stories and their suffering, we have, I think, a spiritual and moral obligation to stop, pay attention, and offer whatever help we can.

In the middle of these conversations, you, too, have encountered frightening physical symptoms that initially appeared to be life-threatening. Skirting the topic of imminent death, we began to talk about healing. Together, we mused about the spirit-healing messages of butterflies. You have talked about the healing nature of your garden. I have talked about the healing nature of a neighborhood swimming pool. Both of these are relatively solitary places where we can find the mystical powers of Spirit entering our lives. Mother Earth is a wonderful nurturing resource for regaining or refurbishing our damaged powers in the world.

Watching the cycle of flowers, for example, leads me to watch the cycle of birds and insects which depend on these beautiful flowers for nourishment and life itself. I have not had the energy this past fifteen months to keep my hummingbird feeders fresh and in-place. But the flowering vines that cover my water-harvesting tank draw them and when I catch a glimpse of them, I celebrate their feisty nature and iridescent beauty.

Only recently have I begun seeing the butterflies of summer here. Each time I see one, I remember they are a spiritual harbinger of metamorphosis. When I am alone in the pool, they often flit by and hover over my wet body. I am just awed by their beauty and by what they represent to me – a message from the spirit world that once again I am alive, mending my broken body, and would I please stop long enough to know this and trust it? I speak softly to them and they do not immediately fly away. It is as if they want me to notice them before they move on into being butterflies in their own world of flight, scent, and beauty.

When the life roads ahead get rough and filled with potholes – as they inevitably will – these moments and places where our inner spirit meets or intersects with the divine Spirit are the moments and places where we gather courage, hope, personal fortitude, a personal determination to make a difference, compassion, spiritual resiliency, flexibility, and integrity. Increasingly I have come to believe that the markers of a genuine spirituality – a compassionate, loving spirituality – are not the markers of scrupulosity, ostentatious piety, purity, rigid dogma, theological doctrines of exclusion, and institutional orthodoxy. They are, instead, the markers of orthopraxis – the lived faith we demonstrate, often without words, in our ordinary and daily lives within the commons.

Thank you for re-entering my life. I am grateful to you for these conversations. I am grateful for the work you do in the world. It is necessary work. I often close letters to my closest personal friends with the following words: *Thank you for putting up with me for all these years.* I would say the same to you about these past twenty months.

Whether or not your Mennonite male colleagues ever choose to recognize and publicly acknowledge your work as valuable, it is important for me to say this to you: your work is important, for it addresses the needs of some of the most vulnerable people in the world. In your scholarship and work at resolving international conflicts, your work directly and immediately benefits the women and children who, as victims of the world's war machine, are simply seen as collateral damage in the ongoing wars of the patriarchy with itself.

In my scholarship and activism, I address the needs of women and their children – those individuals who are most likely to be sexually violated by another set of patriarchal warriors – the men who live with them and interact with them as their social intimates. While mostly these men do not do their harm with hard weaponry, they, do harm, nevertheless. They use the body's most intimate parts as their weaponry. The damage both sets of warriors inflict upon the body/selves of individuals and the peace of the world is simply incomprehensible.

Ruth E. Krall

I conclude, therefore, that warfare and politically motivated economic efforts at domination are forms of violence that Mennonites should concern themselves with. I also conclude that gender-based sexual violation is another very common form of violence that Mennonites should also concern themselves about. If the Jesus path is one of peace-making, healing, and consoling the desolate and the devastated, then both forms of work are at the center of a pacifist Christianity in a Mennonite voice.

I will quote Phyllis Zagano from the end of her online *National Catholic Reporter* article.

> So long as women who might disagree are excised from the halls of power and so long as only submissive women walk on their polished floors, the church will be a mirror of the abuses elsewhere, not a beacon signaling refuge and respite.[536]

Both of us have, therefore, initiated conversations inside our denominational home about patriarchal misogyny and men's violation of women and children. In other situations we have initiated conversations about the incompatibility of sexual orientation xenophobia with the Jesus path. These conversations are not always comfortable or easy ones and may even, at times, seem to others to be a waste of our time. However, I am personally convinced that even when Mennonite men (and their female acolytes) ignore us or actively shun us, it is worth the effort to see if we can build bridges. If for no other reason that our shared Anabaptist-Mennonite history and theology seems to offer a resource to the violent world, it seems worth trying to create a common language.

For many years I have clung to an ancient Christian notion: God does not judge us by our successes. Rather we are judged by our faithfulness. So, our challenge as we do our work in the world is to seek to be faithful to the vocation which we have been given by divine providence. This means, as a side issue, that we strive for excellence in all that we do. It means, also, that we allow the results of our work to be judged by eternity rather than by the seconds of our individual lives.

As we exit this type of conversation, blessings, Lisa, blessings! May the divine face shine upon you and may SHE bring you healing and peace. As your physical body continues to heal from its surgical intervention, may you find your personal stash of hope and courage renewed and may you soar – as with eagles' wings....or with the grace and beauty of butterfly's wings.

Twentieth Letter

To The Next Generation of Pacifist Theologians[537]

Written by Dr. Lisa Schirch

Yoder, the radical follower of Jesus – the Jewish pacifist. Yoder, the brilliant and prolific theologian. Yoder, the awkward and sexually abusive man. Yoder, the man whom the church protected. This book paints a portrait of an exceptionally complicated, gifted, and troublesome man.

The talented male authors of the book are long on their contribution to the study of Yoder and his many contributions. Their careful scholarship brings out an important analysis of key themes in Yoder's many publications, particularly the fact that Yoder draws attention to Jesus as the primary source for Christian theologians as opposed to those who simply build on Nicene orthodoxy. It is a positive step forward that these male authors condemn Yoder's abuse in these chapters. The stated agenda of the book was to describe Yoder's methodology. But by virtue of their identities, the authors in this book cannot speak from the perspective of a woman, a problem addressed in this Afterword. A book in 2014 on any topic, but particularly a book on John Howard Yoder, requires an analysis from women scholars, including victims of Yoder's assaults, as well as from Latino, African, Asian, and Pacific theologians, from people of diverse sexual orientations, and from peacebuilding practitioners who draw inspiration from Yoder to translate pacifist theology into pragmatic real-world strategies.

I write this Afterword as a woman born and raised in the Mennonite Church. I have seen the negative effects of Yoder's assaults and the church's delayed response impact three generations of Mennonite women over the last thirty years in over a dozen Mennonite institutions. Some of Yoder's victims were his peers in his own generation. Some were his students in the next generation. Women in both of these generations who spoke about the assaults experienced significant backlash. In today's world, a third generation of women theologians continues to be marginalized for their critique of Yoder and the church. I am not aware of any female Yoder scholars, an important point that Weaver notes in the beginning of this book. Today's Bible and theology department in Mennonite institutions are predominantly male. In my opinion, Yoder's assault on women and the broader church's protection of Yoder at the expense of women's safety are important reasons why many talented Mennonite women pacifist theologians have left the Mennonite Church and have move on to other denominations.

Women's voices and analysis are essential to the conversation on Yoder's role in Christian theology. Future generations of theologians reading Yoder need to hear their voices. Mennonite women such as Ruth Krall and Carolyn Holderread Heggen Barbra Graber, Sara Wenger Shenk, Linda Gehman Peachey, Hanna Heinzekehr, Stephanie Krehbiel, Charletta Erb, and others write on sexual abuse and have made recommendations to the church on how to address Yoder's abuse. These women offer a fair acknowledgment of Yoder's contribution and his humanity. This Afterword summarizes some of the contributions of these women and includes information directly sourced from one of Yoder's victims.

I write this Afterword from the perspective of a peacebuilding practitioner. John Howard Yoder's theology positively impacted the field of peace3building. Peacebuilding requires a set of ethics and processes. As a pacifist, I concur with Yoder himself on the need to speak out against injustice and affirm the humanity of all people, even perpetrators. Yoder's abusive actions are a tragedy for the women victims, a tragedy for Yoder's family and a tragedy for Yoder's legacy and those who devoted their lives to being "Yoderian" scholars. There is still important peacebuilding work for the church to do in order to address the wounds from the past and recover the integrity of peace theology. This Afterword identifies a peacebuilding agenda for the church in doing justice, loving mercy, and working humbly. In 2014, the Mennonite Church is undergoing a "John Howard Yoder Discernment Group." In his message to Mennonite Church USA, conference moderator Ervin Stutzman listed the shared assumptions about Yoder's behavior.[538] These include the following:

- We know abuse happened
- We know there are victims–some known, some not known
- We know wounds remain unhealed
- We know that despite previous efforts by church leaders to stop the abuse and to enable healing, further work on the part of the church is being called for and is indeed needed
- We know that the truth will set us free.

The goals of the group are to listen and to contribute to the healing of all those impacted by Yoder's abusive actions and the church's response; to thank the women who have tenaciously worked to have the abuse, addressed; and to prepare a church wide process for lament, prevention of abuse, and healing for victims and offenders.

No one stands to gain from the ignoring or covering up what happened. We all need healing. The victims are not responsible for hurting Yoders' reputation by reporting on his assaults. And Mennonite women writers urging the church to address victim's wounds are not guilt for defaming Yoder's name. Yoder alone is responsible for the damage to his credibility. No one stands to gain financially or politically from knowing the truth. In contrast, everyone stands to heal and to recover integrity from acknowledging what happened, lamenting the harm caused to so many, and deciding, as men and women in the church, to move the pacifist agenda forward by ensuring that sexual abuse ends.

The goal of this Afterword is not to *de-Yoderize* peace theology by taking Yoder's contributions away. The goal is to deodorize peace theology–healing the sickening wounds of silence requires the light and oxygen of public acknowledgement and lament. Even Yoder's most ardent male supporters seem to agree that the soul of Yoder's pacifist, radical Christian theology depends on a critical analysis of Yoder's actions toward women and the church's equally appalling actions in protecting Yoder at the expense of the safety of his women students and women in the church. If theologians fail to understand fully the causes and consequences of Yoder's abuse and the church's long delays in justice, what hope is there for the future of pacifist theology? For the next generation of theologians reading this book, here six ideas to consider if the church wants to recover the integrity of pacifist theology from this tragedy.

1. *Yoder committed both sins of sexual immorality and acts of domination in sexual assaults.*

    Sexual immorality and sexual assaults are two different types of behavior and imply different types of harm. Evidence seems to suggest that Yoder had extramarital relationships with women who desired a relationship with Yoder and pursued his attention. At the very least, this was immoral sexual behavior. But at least some of these women were admiring students who came to Yoder to be mentored. Excerpts of their adoring letters can be found online. Scholarly research on sexual abuse details that people in positions of power may use that power to attract sexual attention. No relationship involving a differential of power (such as a professor and an admiring student) can be truly consensual.[539] But between fifty and a hundred other women theologians indicated to Mennonite leaders that they did not invite sexual advances from Yoder, yet he forcibly kissed them, groped their private parts, wrote them sexually explicit letters, seemed to stalk them on their way to their homes late at night and even physically jumped on them.[540]

These are acts of domination that tore at the dignity of brilliant and potentially powerful women Yoder deliberately chose to violate. Yoder's violence changed the lives of the se women.

New York Times writer Mark Oppenheimer's 2013 article on Yoder's sexual assaults asks the reaming critical question about Yoder's scholarship: "Can a bad person be a good theologian?"[541] At what point does our bad behavior overwhelm or negate our writings about doing good? In today's world, Yoder's actions would be legally identified as sexual harassment and sexual assault. It is appropriate then to speak of Yoder's crimes against women. In today's world, institutions are legally responsible for addressing sexual harassment and sexual assault. Thus church leaders who knew of Yoders actions but did not take aggressive actions would also be criminally liable in today's world.

Having new language and laws to identify Yoder and the church's actions offers us more insight into the seriousness of their actions. It is not anachronistic to name behavior as criminal just because the laws on sexual harassment have evolved. Slavery was always criminal even though slavery was technically legal for centuries. Naming an action as criminal helps the church recognize the seriousness of the situation and the need to take preemptive action to ensure the safety of women in the church. Despite the seriousness of Yoders actions, I am not aware of anyone asserting the need for any type of formal criminal justice process against Yoder or the church. No one suggests that Yoder's theology should be thrown out because of the abuse or that he did not make other positive contributions in his personal life.

Excuses for Yoder abound. Some blame the victims, suggesting they all wanted Yoder's sexual attention. Some downplay the harm from his "sexual experiments." Some blame his Asperger-like symptoms of social awkwardness. Yoder's followers are eager to move back to their main pursuit of discussing Yoder's peace theology. But to name Yoder's behaviors as "abuse" is more honest. Yoder was well aware about what he was doing to women, as he offered elaborate justifications for it in his final posthumous writings on punishment.[542]

In her book on Yoder abuse titled, *The Elephant in God's Living room: The Mennonite Church and John Howard Yoder – Collected Essays,* Ruth Krall asks critical questions about what shaped Yoders view of women and what went wrong in his life that led to his sexual assaults of women. Krall's book is by far the most helpful clinical and psychological analyst of what Yoder himself may have suffered of experienced that influenced his abusive actions. Krall and others note that Yoder had many normal, healthy and even pastoral social interactions and was not abusive in all aspects of his life. Krall writes,

"While occasionally his harassing actions may have been opportunistic ones, in most reported situations they appear to be pre-panned and methodically carried out. Potential victims were identified and they were groomed for acts of victimization."[543]

In the tradition of great pacifists who reach out to those causing harm, women writers like Ruth Krall have gone out of their way to affirm Yoder's humanity and to lament that the church failed not only the victims but also Yoder and his family by not stopping the abuse sooner. Future generations of pacifist theologians should not diminish or excuse the harm Yoder caused but should acknowledge and lament the tragic consequences of Yoder's immoral and sexually violent actions and the effect they had on women, his family, and the pacifist tradition.

2. *The church itself needs to take responsibility for the institutionalized patriarchal setting that contributed to Yoder's abuse. Yoder grew out of a patriarchal church and his writings as a white man reflect this privileged status.*

A toxic cocktail of patriarchy, sexual repression, and entitled leadership beyond reproach contributes to religious leaders around the world committing a high rate of sexual abuse. In a *Christian Century* article titled "Evangelicals 'Worse' than Catholics on Sexual Abuse," which quotes leading Christian voices working to stop such abuse, it is stated that "too many Protestant institutions have sacrificed souls in order to protect their institutions."[544] In the context, Yoder's abuse of his power as a professor was a symptom of a much wider problem.

Peacebuilding requires looking at root causes, not just symptoms of violence. Rather than blaming or diagnosing Yoder alone, a peacebuilding response to Yoder's abuse requires the church at large to examine the sickness of patriarchy. Yoder's abuse needs to be viewed in the context of the church's affirmation of patriarchy, where men are granted systematic entitlement to positions of power. Patriarchal systems limit women's access to education and positions of power and view women as second-class citizens

Given the pervasiveness of institutionalized patriarchy, it would be surprising if Yoder's writing did not reflect patriarchal beliefs. As indicative of his patriarchal beliefs, Stephanie Krehbiel cites Yoder's description of women in his most recent, posthumous book, *The End of Sacrifice,* which seems to have been written in response to women's call for accountability for his assaults. "More recently men as a class have come to be vulnerable in a new way, as compensation for pain suffered by women when that pain can be blamed upon the prior patriarchal tilt of society." In a footnote to this sentence, Yoder added,

There should be room, logically, for the objection that beneficent patri-
archal care, properly understood and benevolently exercised would not
be harmful; that was has hurt woman has been the violation, not the
implementation of proper fatherly caring. The excuse would however
not change the retaliatory dynamics, since the root of the power of the
punitive drive is located not merely in a mistake the stronger party
made but in the weaker party's anger at being weaker.[545]

Yoder suggests that women's anger at men is not necessarily due to men (such as he) having victimized women, but rather that women are angry because they are "weaker than" men. Yoder seems to see himself as an innocent symbolic scapegoat for women's anger at patriarchy.

Further, Yoder's earliest writing on the idea of "revolutionary subordination" did not resonate with many women, as discussed by Gerald Mast in chapter 8 of this volume ("Pacifism as a Way of Knowing"), Yoder identified patriarchy as a problem. But Yoder's writing is cryptic and a little too eager to emphasize women's subordination in biblical cultural context without providing a vision for equal relations between men and women today's church. Hannah Heinzekehr argues, "[Yoder's} theology seemed to veer dangerously close to setting up frameworks that would not just allow…abuse to happen, but make it seem honorable or noble"[546] Women should not suffer domestic violence or sexual assaults or view subordination of their identity as having redemptive power. In order to willfully subordinate, one must have a sense of agency and empowerment. One must feel entitled to respect in order to submit to disrespect. In this book, Weaver's and Mast's chapter "Extending John Howard Yoder's Theology" makes these points in its discussion of atonement theology.

South Africans only chose nonviolent resistance after a concerted movement of Black consciousness to unlearn the oppressive practice of teaching black South African children that they were less human than white South African children. In Latin America, Paulo Friere described the process of "conscienticization" as a necessary first step before impoverished Brazilians could start the revolutionary process of nonviolently questioning their oppressive government. In the women's liberation movement, developing a feminist consciousness of "women's power' is also a primary step.

As a woman and a peacebuilding practitioner who advocates non-violent resistance, I believe revolutionary subordination requires two conditions.

a) Suffering requires empowerment. Empowerment comes from self-awareness and a lucid power of analysis to identify that oppression is unjust and unnatural. Every human being deserves dignity. But not every person recognizes this human right in a world o social hierarchy and humiliation. Jesus critiqued the oppressive religious, social, and political powers of his day. He told downtrodden people like the Samaritan woman at the well that she was worthy of his respect and that she was a child of God. Only empowered people conscious of their right to dignity can make subordination revolutionary. Without empowerment, subordination may become internalize oppression where victims choose subordination because they cannot imagine that they deserve dignity.

b) Suffering must be a voluntary choice. In most cases, suffering is revolutionary only if there are other choices that do not require suffering. Jesus had a choice other than the cross. His choice to suffer made the subordination revolutionary. But many people do not have choices.

As a woman peacebuilding practitioner, there are times in my life when I willfully chose powerlessness and to believe in the strategy of revolutionary subordination. When I was living in Kabul, Afghanistan, to conduct research on Afghan perspectives on peacebuilding during the years 2009-2011, I chose to live in an unarmed guesthouse, knowing full well that most foreigners had armed guards and stayed in gated hotels. Choosing subordination and vulnerability made sense–not having armed guards sent an important message to both my Afghan colleagues and to any Taliban or insurgents watching my movements that I was not part of the foreign occupation. I also choose revolutionary subordination when I provide training on peacebuilding at U.S. military bases. I am often the only woman and the only civilian in a room full of military leaders in uniforms. I make a choice to enter a space where my audience often opposes and belittles my experience. I speak diplomatically but forcefully on the rights of civilians and the alternative to war even as I feel the silent and invisible poison darts coming at me as I speak.

In other contexts, I deliberately avoid subordination. While attending graduate school in Washington, DC, there were times when I would have to walk late at night, and I chose to carry hot pepper spray so that would be able to defend myself by nonlethal means, if necessary. When men in my church belittle my contributions, I confront the substance of their critique While I may be willing to choose to die or suffer for my beliefs in some situations, I will not willfully submit to humiliation and violence in a context where those in my own community deny my personal agency. Most girls around the world are taught to be submissive. Their subordination is not revolutionary, as it is not chosen. When women's subordination is force, it is violent.

People who have a critical mass of supporters in their homes and communities may develop an internal strength so that they can engage in the "revolutionary subordination" from a place of power and choice. Women tend to share their stories of sexual abuse and discrimination with each other, in order to become conscious of the systematic, impersonal denigration of our individual and collective voices. A feminist consciousness and a community of other women who share a gender analysis of the church enable me to engage critically but respectfully on issues of sexual abuse. Women in the church who lack such feminist support either stay quiet and subordinate, or they walk way from an oppressive church who "body politics" excludes and dismisses their voices.

Yoder, of course, was a white male, as are most of his followers. They operate in a patriarchal church that only recently has made important strides to include women. These patriarchal structures did not protect women in the church. Since Yoder assaulted many of his female students and rising church leaders, his action directly impacted a generation of women's leadership. The continuing absence of women in many centers of pacifist theology at Mennonite institutions today means that new generations of pacifist theologians may also not be informed by a gender or power analysis or take into consideration the privilege and entitlement that males enjoy. Even putting Yoder's behavior with women aside, new generations of pacifist theologians need to bring other lenses and voices to engage with Yoder's theological concepts, including "revolutionary subordination." The church at large, and pacifist theologian in particular, need to critique patriarch and embrace a wider set of ideas about pacifism and how it relates to people in different social positions.

3. *Christian pacifism is not dependent on the credibility or idolatry of Yoder.*

The outline of this Afterword came together as I was explaining to my fourteen-year-old daughter the three ways Yoder's life and work Impact my life. First, I told her that Yoder's theology influenced a generation of my mentors and colleagues at the Center for Justice and Recompilation at Eastern Mennonite University. Mennonites worked for peace before Yoder. But without Yoder, It might have taken much longer for the Mennonite Church to translate pacifist theology into institutionalized efforts in restorative justice and peacebuilding. I have spent most of my life attending or working for Mennonite institutions. I grew up in a church that often seemed to be as Yoder-centric as it was Jesus-centric. Countless people have come

Ruth E. Krall

to see Jesus as a "Jewish Pacifist" and have understood the political message in the Bible because of Yoder. I might not be working in the field of peacebuilding had it not been for Yoder's contributions to those who mentored me. But I came to devote my life to peacebuilding and pacifism without every having read Yoder. Other mentors and authors in the church– not Yoder–taught me to support peace and justice.

The two Mennonite professors who had the most impact on my understanding of pacifist theology were mental health clinician-theologian Ruth Krall[547] and musician Carol Ann Weaver, whose own academic training prepared them to bring a wider set of questions to teaching theology. These women steered me towards a reading list on feminist theology, liberation theology, and black theology. I read Mary Daly and Starhawk alongside Martin Luther King and Gandhi, two other powerful pacifist men from patriarchal contexts who faced allegations of sexual impropriety. From this broader theological perspective, Yoder's theses in *The Politics of Jesus* did not seem radical when I read them later in my life. The final chapter in this volume, Gerald Mast's "Sin and Failure in Anabaptist Theology" is an important effort to begin to have a dialogue between Yoder and theologians who self-identify as feminist, womanist, black or liberation theologians.

Second, I draw on Yoder's work to explain why it makes sense for me, a Mennonite, to be married to a Jew. My daughter identifies herself as both Jewish and Mennonite. Yoder's writing on Jesus as a Jewish pacifist and on the h Jewish-Christian schism, discussed in Weavers and Mast's and Weaver and Zimmerman's chapters will make important contributions to my children's ability to theologically justify their identity to the wider Christian church (if they ever care to do so).

Third, when other Mennonites denounced my work to educate the United States government and military about peacebuilding, Yoder's theology as well as his own work with the ROTC program at the University of Notre Dame helped me articulate a theological justification to the church for this practical engagement of the U.S. Military. Yoder's concept of speaking about religious ethics though secular terms or "middle axioms" gave me theological justification for talking to governments and military forces about human rights, violence against women, the structural causes of violence and how to build peace. I did not start to work with the military because of Yoder. Rather Yoder's writings helped me articulate the theological basis for my work to a conservative Christian audience who questioned reaching out to "the enemy."

As a peacebuilding practitioner, I recognize that all of us who work for peace are less than perfect. If we were to wait for a perfect messenger to speak on peace and justice, we would greatly hinder any progress towards improving the human condition. Yet the true measure of the quality of witness for peace is not what you say, but what you do. The inconsistencies in the lives of most peace and justice practitioners are far less dramatic than Yoder's

The real world application of pacifist theology in the fields of restorative justice and peacebuilding provide the next generation of theologians' with a much more compelling vision of pacifism. It is much easier to "see" a pacifist Jesus in the men and women who are running victim-offender reconciliation programs, facilitating dialogue between Muslims and Christians, advocating for social justice or training the Congolese military in how to respect women's rights. I would choose to admire the silent, humble generosity of a quiet peacebuilder long before I would applaud an articulate theologian who pushed women down and jumped on them.

Yoder has a place on our bookshelves, but not on a pedestal. The integrity of pacifist theology does not depend on Yoder. Idolatry of Yoder is wrong. First, it diminishes the voices of the victims he hurts. Second, it stumbles and contorts itself t o alight a theology of peace with the actions of an abusive man. Third, it pulls attention away from the many other pacifist voices whose lives and writings better illuminate the pacifist path. The authors of this book deserve to be read in their own right. They make important contributions to Christian pacifism. A new generation of Christian pacifists should be read not for their insights on Yoder, but for their own unique contributions.

4. *Pacifism and feminism require the same ethical commitments.*

"The world is crazy." My daughter shook her head as I told her of Yoder's assaults. Like most women around the world, I have a duty as a mother to prepare my daughter to live in a world where some people will devalue her humanity and underestimate her intellect. She needs to learn how to respond to the epidemic of men who assault women (approximately on in three women will be assaulted in their lifetime.)

There is no gap between pacifism and feminism. Ruth Krall taught me to ask a question: "Why is sexual violence and domestic violence tolerated by Mennonites when military violence is not tolerated? Both forms of violence share in the sinfulness of the human community. Both destroy human life and well-being. Neither represented a divine will for the human community."[548] So I explained to my daughter that as a Menomonie pacifies, feminist, peacebuilding practitioner, I care just as much about ending war in Afghanistan and Syria as I do about the safely of girls and women who suffer a shocking level of attack on their humanity. The link between public violence and private violence is evidenced in the rape of women in the mist

Ruth E. Krall

of war, in the alarming rates of domestic violence on military training bases, and in the level of sexual violence in the patriarchal church.

Unlike Yoder and many other Mennonite pacifist theologians, my life's work has been about connecting the public violence of war with the private violence of domestic violence and violence against women. Pacifism and feminism both recognize the dignity and humanity of all people while seeking to end the harm that come in any act of violence, domination, or subordination. Weaver's book *The Nonviolent Atonement is an* example of a male pacifist who embraces feminism. Mast also cites feminist and woman-ist writers in this book. But all too often, women alone are left to speak out on sexual violence or devote their careers to the difficult work of raising issues of sexual violence in the church.

Feminism is a call to a new relationship between men and women based on mutual respect. Feminism fosters opportunities for women's leader-ship and appreciation of women's contributions to society. Feminism is the radical notion that women are human beings. Feminism is not about hating men. Most feminists are married to men. Men can be feminists too. Feminism is inherently pacifist. There are no calls for women to take up arms against men or to punish men.

Feminism requires a commitment to stop sexual violence against women and men. Because there is so much violence in the world against women, many feminists are indeed angry and want to stop this selective violence. Feminism requires listening to women's unique perspectives, acknowledg-ing the differences in men's experiences and women's experiences without deeming one more valuable than the other.

Peacebuilding is a process of putting hand and feet on pacifism and femi-nism. Peacebuilding requires practical strategies of empowerment, building relationships that illustrate the dignity of every human being, and advocat-ing for just social relations. Peacebuilding requires that we view as equally damaging any form of harm done to children, women and men, to workers, to the environment, and to countries gripped by war.

When a country invades another country to secure its oil interests, that is violence. When a corporation exploits workers and destroys the environ-ment, that is violence. When a man pushes a woman down and gropers her in his office, that is violence too. When the church criticizes women for naming abuse committed by a powerful church leader, and when it demands harmony, silences women's voices, and protects a perpetrator, that too is violence. An engaged pacifist theology needs to be concerned about all these forms of violence.

Yet, to this day, there are two places where I am usually the only woman in the room: when I am training the military in peacebuilding and when

I am discussing pacifist theology. When it comes to security and theology, the men who hold powerful positions in the U.S. military and in the church's theological institutions often actively exclude women's voices and approaches. What is the explanation for this? Are women less intelligent? Less ambitions? Do we have fewer opportunities for higher education? Are many women just not interested in security and theology? Or do men actively exclude, overlook, or even denigrate women because it is easier to work with "their own kind" and it can be difficult to "fit in" a woman's perspective?

In my opinion, women are left out of discussions on security and theology because we have a different set of experiences that lead us to hold different opinions. In both settings, we define violence differently. Some men are uncomfortable with our auger and our perspectives. So we are left out of conferences, books, and collegial circles between academic peers. Because women's understandings of security and theology are so different, women also self-select not to put themselves in situations where they will be a minority voice. Women seek safer pastures in which to tend their intellectual sheep.

Future generations of pacifist theologians need to interrogate this pattern. Pacifist theologians need to engage directly with feminist writers. Pacifist theologians need to read and engage the community addressing sexual violence with the same intensity with which they address violence by the state. They need to study women's writings, advocate among men to stop violence against women, and illustrate with their lives their desire to empower women's leadership and to make space for women's voices.

5. *Yoder and the Church that loved him damaged a radical pacifist agenda and undermined the politics of Jesus.*

Yoder questioned the authority and self-interest of Jewish leaders in his day. Early Anabaptists shared this skepticism of church and state authorities. Like Jesus, they seemed to have no interest in creating or maintaining institutions. As part of the Anabaptist tradition, Yoder questions church and state authority with a pacifist ethic. Unlike other theologians who seem to have more interest in consolidating the power and control of the church over its followers than in following Jesus, Yoder asks Christians to question authority.

In the authority-questioning tradition of Jesus and the Anabaptists, pacific theologians should question the self-interest of the church in addressing sexual violence. Ruth Krall documents the Mennonite Church's delays in responding to Yoder's violence:

For more than twenty years denominational administrative personnel officers and chief executives managed allegations, rumors, and gossip about Yoder's behavior by secrecy and by facilitating geographical and professional work relocations. They chose, therefore, a preferential option to maintain Yoders" theological career as a spokesperson for a Mennonite theology of non-violence and cultural identity rather than a preferential option to provide safety to vulnerable women potentially in Yoder's grasp. Thus, denomination leaders, knowingly or unwittingly created a hostile religious climate in which Yoder's behavior could continue and proliferate. Victims and potential victims were left to fend for themselves. Ideology, intuitional authority and denomination leader power, therefore, trumped a visible living communal praxis of justice, accountability, individual healing and collective reconciliation.[549]

Women who did try to warn other women of Yoder's potential assaults were chastised for "gossiping" and disrupting the harmony of the church. When women later brought their stories-first privately and then publicly-to the attention of Mennonite leaders in the hope that they would stop Yoder's behavior, Yoder threatened a lawsuit against them and accused some of them of not being "sophisticated." Some people in the church accused them of making up the stories of seducing Yoder themselves, asking "Why didn't' they just say no?" (Reports suggest Yoder accepted "no' from some women, but harassed others for many months after they said no.) Some in the church accused the women of hurting Yoder's family and spreading false rumors. In other words, Yoder and the church punished the victims and the victims' supporters for speaking truth.[550]

Yoder is responsible for hurting his victims. Yoder, not his victims, is responsible for hurting his family. And Yoder, not his victims or their supporters, are responsible for hurting the pacifist agenda.

Krehbiel argues the church's response was "too little, too late, and more about institutional damage control than about justice or healing for Yoder's victims.[551] While the field of restorative justice drew theological inspiration from Yoder's writing,[552] there was nothing restorative about the church's process of addressing Yoder's abuse. Restorative justice is victim-centered. Church institutions offered forgiven to Yoder, not the victims. Restorative justice does not seek to punish. Rather, in restorative justice offenders acknowledge and take responsibility for the harm they have done to others. The church "punished" Yoder in a variety of ways, including banning him from attending church. But the victims were not in the center of the church's first attempts at addressing the abuse.

Some of the women who experienced Yoder's assaults wrote letters to him, first asking him to stop writing them inappropriate letters. Yoder did not stop. Some women also assert that they themselves wrote Yoder long letters detailing the pain the hurt his assaults caused in their lives. Reportedly, Yoder never felt remorse for his actions that caused this pain, nor did he apologize directly to these women.[553] As noted earlier, his professional writing after the church process laid out a complex justification for his behavior and seemed to blame women themselves for the pain they suffered.

The church's efforts to protect Yoder's family also seemed inept at best, if not a double victimization of their own suffering related to Yoder's actions. Yoder reportedly cooperated with church leaders in what may have been numerous painful meetings at the kitchen table, most likely led by well-meaning church leaders with little experience of knowledge of sexual abuse. Krall notes, "By not recognizing Yoder's suffering and by not recognizing the women's suffering their shared faith community failed in its collective spiritual task of bringing healing to them."[554]

The church has evolved in the last twenty years. There are new safeguards in place for women in the church. The Mennonite Church's process of discernment is a positive sigh that the church is taking responsibility for addressing the harms that Yoder and the church itself did to Yoder's victims. Future generations of pacifist theologians will need to continue to challenge institutions to use a moral compass and not their status, power, or financial interests to guide them through the thicket of sexual violence in the church.

It is ironic that Yoder, the radical theologian, advocated biblical teachings on justice and peace with his words but led the church away from Jesus' radial teachings with his actions. In this book, Zimmerman quotes Yoder regarding the split between Swiss Reformer Zwingli and the Anabaptists: "To place the unity of Zurich above the faithfulness of the church is not only to abandon the church: it is also the demonization of the state, for persecution becomes a theological necessity."[555] In the same way, to place the unity of the Mennonite Church above the faithfulness of the church is not only to abandon the church; it was the demonization of the church, since the required silencing of women's voices–a form of persecution–became a theological necessity.

Naming wrongdoing by Yoder and the institutional church is not out of lack of care for Yoder's legacy or the church. Rather, it illustrates that we do care about the pacifist agenda and the integrity of the church. Future generations of pacifist theologians can restore credibility to pacifism not by downplaying Yoder's action but by naming the abuses, lamenting the harm done to the victims and to Yoder's family, and working to end sexual abuse in the church.

Ruth E. Krall

6. *Moving forward requires all of us to do things differently.*

The magnitude of the impact of Yoder's abuse and the church's long delay in addressing it require action to make things right. Peacebuilding requires truth-telling, victim-centered restorative justice, new initiatives to prevent future sexual violence, and both lament and trauma healing for Yoder's victims, family and the church as whole. Krall argues that in order to move forward, we need first to collectively reflect.

> [It is in] acknowledgement of the factual truth of an abuser's fully embodied life that we and future generations begin to free ourselves and our communities to make different behavioral choices than he chose to make during his lifetime. Acknowledging the legacy of good he did in his lifetime frees us from the need to demonize him. Recognizing the legacy of harm he did to us and others frees us from idolatry. Once free, we can view his life as a precautionary tale that teaches us, and future generations, what not to do. In recognizing and speaking the factual truth of our lives, we individually and collectively free ourselves and future generations from the tyranny of his legacy of abuse. If we allow it do so, a perpetrator's abusive live and the harm he did to others can serve as a searchlight that reveals the fault lines in the communal realities we once shred with him. If we allow his life in all of its complexities, to teach us, we can examine the painful realties and fault lines of our own lives.[556]

Perhaps this book is a start on that journey. I laud the authors of this book for naming Yoder's actions as abusive and beginning to question the church that protected him. But there is more work to do.

Barbara Graber lays out the specific strategies for moving forward. These include the following. [557]

1) Anyone writing or speaking about Yoder should directly name Yoder's actions as "sexual assaults and abuse" rather than call it "inappropriate behavior" or other ambiguous terms relating to his social skills.

2) Journalists should acknowledge the harm Yoder did along with his accomplishments.

3) Church leaders should commit to doing justice for Yoder's victims and in every sexual abuse case.

4) Men should learn more about sexual violence against women and take steps to address it in their own communities.

5) Peace and justice educators should make clear that sexual violence is an issue of equal concern as war and public violence.

6) Victims should find ways to get support and voice their experiences so as to prevent violence against others in the future.

I would like to add one more to Graber's list. The widespread impact of Yoder's theology on global scholars and practitioners requires a broader set of voices from authors of diverse identities. My colleague Howard Zehr has made a commitment to question any invitation to speak on a panel that is made up entirely of white men. White men concerned about peace and justice should make a commitment to advocate for the inclusion of women's voices and men of other ethnic and racial backgrounds in their professional speaking and writing careers. Like all people, white men are not objective or neutral. We are all subjective. White men's perspectives are valid and real. But because of society's structures, white men's experiences are different from others. Some of us have institutional power and other do not. So a further strategy for addressing Yoder's impact is to make a commitment than any edited book, conference, or panel about Yoder will include the voices of women, including those named at the beginning of this chapter, who write critically on Yoder's negative impact on pacifist women in the church.

This Afterword is just the beginning of a map for future generations of pacifist theologians to bring together orthodoxy (right belief) with orthopraxy (right action). Addressing Yoder's violence in only a part of this peacebuilding process. Our larger task is to ensure that the radical message in some of Yoder's writings gets translated into radical acts of inclusion of other voices on pacifist theology so eloquently articulated in this book. Passing the pacifist torch requires that the church itself, and those leading pacifist theology, listen to the voices of those not in power.

Ruth E. Krall

Twenty-first Letter

Toward Mennonite Sexual Integrity[558]

Written by Dr. Lisa Schirch

The Mennonite church needs a conversation about sexual integrity, how people respect their own bodies and those of other people. Sexual abuse – and even sexual promiscuity – requires dehumanizing male and female bodies as objects to consume. We live in a consumption-based culture. As Anabaptists, we should interrogate our complicity with all forms of consumption.

A conversation about sexual integrity could help the Mennonite church find common ground that allows us to dialogue with each other more productively in both talking about sexual abuse and in discussing how to welcome all people, including those with same-sex sexuality into our churches.

Here are four things Mennonites should consider on sexuality integrity.

1. In too many Mennonite homes and congregations, sexual abuse has been passed on from generation to generation. We need to be careful not to only focus on specific perpetrators in Mennonite institutions, but also examine a broader pattern of abuse. Did our collective persecution and trauma feed into this cycle of abuse? Communities that experience persecution from outside forces – Like Mennonites did – often eventually take on abusive behaviors within their communities. Unheard trauma festers on, revealing itself in self-destructive behaviors. For example Indigenous communitas suffered genocidal violence in North America. Today sexual abuse and substance abuse plague Indigenous communities, replacing persecution by outside forces, an echo of their traumatic past. Indigenous leaders are now leading a historical healing process to address current sexual abuse and to heal the generational trauma. Mennonites desperately need to match our

public pacifism with reflection on our collective public and private traumas, and the violence in our midst.

2. A perverse theology of redemptive suffering paired with belief in male entitlement and female subservience still encourages too many victims of sexual abuse to simply bear the cross of sexual violence and stay silent. In too many Mennonite institutions there are continuing patterns of misogyny – a subtle but stern exclusion and silencing of women and the gifts and insights they have to offer. The secular culture of patriarchy has been mistakenly embraced as a religious belief. Mennonite theology cannot have an authentic pacifist voice that endorses domination and suffering of any kind. Suffering sexual violence is not redemptive.

3. Most Mennonites have never had the opportunity to consider their sexual orientation. Scientists do not yet know what percentage of the populations holds a same-sex sexual orientation. Most surveys show that 3-6 percent of people "self-identify" as having a same-sex orientation. But we can assume the actual number is much higher since anyone willing to identify themselves as gay, lesbian, bisexual, transgender or queer (GLBTQ) will without doubt suffer social punishment – both from seculars and religious homophobia. Researcher find that surveys guaranteeing anonymity result in much higher numbers of people – somewhere between 10-30 percent of the population – admitting to having had a same-sex attraction at some point in their life. All church leaders should remember that it is statistically probable that there are multiple people with a same-sex orientation in every church meeting.

   Some people gifted with same-sex sexuality choose to deny and closet their sexual identity. They stay single or marry some one of the opposite sex just because it seemed to be the only acceptable option in their community. New policies that welcome people with all sexual orientations may fundamentally devastate the very identity of those who have built every aspect of their lives on the need to repress their sexuality. It may call into question a lifetime of personal sacrifices. Those on all sides of the Mennonite Church USA discussions – especially progressives pushing for inclusion – should remember the pain of our brothers and sisters who prefer to remain in the closet rather than question their life choices in the context of new Biblical understandings about sexuality. Church leaders and advocates of LBGTQ inclusion should make it safe for new generations of Mennonites with same-sex sexuality to be welcomed fully in the church at the same time that we acknowledge the deeply personal, traumatic and life-altering impacts of opening closet doors for those who were forced into a closeted life.

4. The church's silencing of women victims of Mennonite leaders and their rejection of people with the same-sex sexuality must be seen within a larger context of closeting all aspects of sexuality Both are indications that sexuality continues to be taboo within many Mennonite communities.. Repressing sexuality and refusing to talk about it creates problems.

The churches repression of open discussions of sexuality and its recitation of simple rules about sex in marriage does not support sexual integrity. A review of Anabaptist family records shows us that in the early church, childbirth out of wedlock was widespread. Furthermore, some of the same leaders who chose to ignore and downplay sexual abuse happening in Mennonite institutions are now leading the charges against Mennonites who welcome membership of people with diverse sexual orientations. All things having to do with sex have been forced into a closet.

Children taught to know and understand their bodies and their sexuality are more likely to report sexual abuse and make healthy choices in their own lives, based on knowledge, no fear and ignorance. Empowering youth to learn how to live with sexual integrity requires teaching them to critique secular media and sexual violence that exploits people's bodies. The church can do better to support a theology of sexual integrity, including preparing to protect youth from sexual predators, educating both youth h and adults about patters of abuse and sexual violence, making it safe for victims to speak out, the biological and emotional dangers of sexual objectification, sexual promiscuity, and abusive sexuality and acknowledging the beauty of our bodies and the natural desire for non-exploitative human touch.

Afterword

Written by Dr. William D. Lindsey

If you've read the book for which these concluding comments are the afterword, you'll know already what I'm going to tell you, with one additional observation that may not have occurred to you. This is that what you've just read is a classic in the making, which will, I predict, one day be widely used by historians of American Christianity as a lens through which to look carefully at what was going on in American Christianity in the turbulent period in which this book was written. As a classic text (one characterized, as with other classics, by thick description), it manages to pursue a number of important tasks simultaneously. It's **first of all** a series of letters a masterful teacher writes to a former student who has reconnected with her down the road from their teacher-student days.

Like Ruth Krall, her former student Lisa Schirch has been propelled by Mennonite formation to a life of advocacy for non-violence. Ruth's peacemaking advocacy has taken the form of teaching and writing, living among and working on behalf of the poorest of the poor in Latin America, and, notably, seeking to hear and help women who have endured violence, including sexual violence, at the hands of their male significant others.

Lisa brings peacemaking into the lions' den as she works with the U.S. military. In their exchange of e-letters over a number of years, these two women with Mennonite roots, teacher and former student, reflect on what it means to live their commitment to non-violence as two generations of Mennonite-rooted women in the world today. They reflect, in particular, about what it means to commit themselves to lifting up women and children in the world at large and the Mennonite community in particular.

Second, this book is a sustained reflection on the recurring, endemic, deeply entrenched abuse of women and children by privileged males across religious and cultural boundaries. Ruth and Lisa agree that it's impossible to engage in the peacemaking task in the world at large without engaging sexual violence within their own Mennonite community, where such violence has often been ignored by the male leaders of the church as issues of war and peace form the overweening focus of those leaders' pacifist concern.

A primary contribution of this classic-in-the-making is that, though, it does not focus on affinity violence by entitled males against women and children in any *single* religious context. It recognizes that such violence occurs widely in the cultures (and religions) of the world, because assumptions about male privilege and female subordination permeate *many* if not most world cultures and religions. Ruth's case study of affinity violence by male spiritual guides in the Zen Buddhist tradition in the U.S. is one of the most important contributions of this book. This study broadens our discussion of sexual abuse of women and children by male religious leaders (and we imperatively *need* such broadening, if we're to understand the roots of such abuse and address them effectively everywhere they're found) from the Christian churches – the Catholic church, in particular – to the world religions in general.

Third, the book is at the same time a valuable chronicle of the sustained attempt of a group of courageous Mennonite women to call their church to accountability for its leaders' cover-up of the sexually predatory activities of the preeminent twentieth-century Mennonite theologian and theoretician of non-violence, John Howard Yoder. As Ruth[559] and Lisa [560]tell us repeatedly throughout the book, they share the conviction that their peacemaking work in contexts outside the church makes little sense unless it takes notice of and challenges sexual violence within the Mennonite community itself.

Both note the significant finding that it has been Mennonite *women* but not, in general, Mennonite *men*, who have wanted to confront Yoder's activities and legacy as a sexual predator with unsparing honesty. Both note the tendency of the Mennonite male establishment within the leadership structures of the church and in its academy to circle the wagons and defend Yoder. Both note the powerful defenders Yoder has also found among other male academics in churches and church-sponsored academies outside the Mennonite church.

This is historically important testimony. It's one of the reasons this book will, I suggest, one day be regarded as a premier text of American Christian history and thought in the early twentieth century.

Fourth, the book is a meditation about the spiritual foundations needed to sustain healthy advocacy work, and about the wisdom to carry out such arduous work without harming oneself in the process. Throughout the book, Ruth notes her conviction that the blinkered orthodoxy of her own Mennonite community or, indeed, any single religious tradition, cannot by itself offer the spiritual resources necessary to undergird creative, effective advocacy for non-violence in the contemporary world.

She testifies to the power she finds in various religious traditions of the world to provide spiritual foundations for her work. She notes the importance (an *epistemological* notation) of building inclusive, wide-ranging conversations as we engage in the task of seeking to heal a fragmented world. She points to the feminist roots of this drive to inclusivity in her own thought and that of others she admires. And Lisa adds her testimony to Ruth's here, noting that one of the important things she learned in Ruth's classroom was the obligation to consult spiritual traditions and welcome intellectual resources that transcend the resources available within a discrete religious tribe.[561]

Fifth (and finally), the book is a reflection on the connections between various *isms* including sexism, heterosexism, racism, classism, and affinity violence of all sorts. Both Ruth and Lisa note their bemusement that, while they were seeking to protect a leading theologian preying on women students and women in his pastoral and classroom care, the male leaders of the Mennonite church were engaging in what amounts to war against LGBT members of the church. They want to know *why* their church leaders have behaved in this perplexing way.

What connects the impulse of male leaders of various institutions to protect heterosexual men preying on women while they marginalize LGBT people and heap on them accusations of singular sexual sordidness? As Ruth says "if we *don't* ask such questions – if we don't look at what connects *ism* to *ism* – we cannot design effective intervention protocols "that may help bring about lasting, permanent, and positive change in how individuals and entire communities choose to encounter each other."[562]

I.

In the same way that war-making and rape go together, our concerns for the peace of the world and our concerns for the welfare and safety of women and their children go together.[563]

As I've just noted, this book consists of a series of letters in which a teacher-mentor who has been contacted by a former student imparts wisdom rooted in a life history full of rich experience. It reflects a back-forth discussion of two Mennonite women of different generations, both committed to peacemaking and addressing violence against women and children, about how to live their shared convictions in new contexts.[564] As Ruth says think of Rilke's *Letters to a Young Poet* or William Sloane Coffin's *Letters to a Young Doubter*.[565]

Here's Lisa on why Ruth has been a powerful influence on her thought and life:

> It [i.e., this book] is a gift to future generations, recording the
> rich and scholarly life of a Mennonite woman whose perspective
> is much wider than many of her male colleagues as she draws
> on a variety of religious traditions, psychological scholars, and

the natural world of creation, which is the most authentic voice of God.[566]

And:

> The two Mennonite professors who had the most impact on my understanding of pacifist theology were mental health clinician-theologian Ruth Krall and musician Carol Ann Weaver, whose own academic training prepared them to bring a wider set of questions to teaching theology. These women steered me towards a reading list on feminist theology, liberation theology, and black theology. I read Mary Daly and Starhawk alongside Martin Luther King and Gandhi, two other powerful pacifist men from patriarchal contexts who faced allegations of sexual impropriety. From this broader theological perspective, Yoder's theses in *The Politics of Jesus* did not seem radical when I read them later in my life . . . .

> Ruth Krall taught me to ask a question: "Why is sexual violence and domestic violence tolerated by Mennonites when military violence is not tolerated? Both forms of violence share in the sinfulness of the human community. Both destroy human life and well-being. Neither represented a divine will for the human community.[567]

As a series of letters reflecting a *real* dialogue of two activist scholars, rooted in their different life experiences as they pursue a shared goals of peacemaking, the book tends in the direction of soundings rather than linear, logical argument. This does not mean it lacks the latter. It is academically rigorous, written by fiercely intelligent women determined to dig to the roots of ideas while linking theoretical reflection to hard-won lived experience.

This determination accounts for the bond that has brought Ruth and Lisa together years after Ruth taught Lisa in the formal setting of the classroom. As Ruth notes, her e-correspondence with Lisa began when Lisa asked her to read an afterword she had written for a book criticizing the absence of women among the authors of essays gathered in the book. This initiated a conversation that "roamed around the world."[568]

As it happened, this dialogue began at a significant moment in Ruth's life: Lisa contacted Ruth just after she had been discharged from the hospital following a life-threatening illness that left her debilitated, unable to do physical or mental work.[569] Lisa's questions became a lifeline for Ruth, keeping her intellectual life alive and connecting her in a vital way to her life's work of combating violence:

Whether or not you were aware of this as we wrote back and forth, you were extending a life-line of professional and personal courtesy and conversation to me that I desperately needed. Fearing my physical strength might never return, I needed to believe that my mind was not dead. Not able to vacuum my living room, I could at the very least listen to your ideas and concerns and think about them. This was better for my mental health than obsessing over the physical things I could no longer do. Somehow or other writing to you felt less like narcissistic self-preoccupation – something that was so easy to fall into when my body ached and my breathing was labored. Whether or not this is realistically true, it felt like I was still capable of making a contribution to the world's needs for peace advocacy and healing work.[570]

And so a book was born: as Ruth explains, as she and Lisa swapped letters, Lisa suggested that Ruth keep track of these, and "[t]his book of letters in a personal voice is a result of that decision"[571] – a book that Ruth considers her tribute to Lisa for the wonderful person she has become, an expression of gratitude for Lisa's work on behalf of peace and justice.[572]

One other thing binds Ruth and Lisa together, they recognize as they reconnect via their e-letters:

> In addition, both of us have personally encountered Anabaptist Mennonite men's passive chauvinism and active sexist hostility, perhaps even disdain, towards us and our work. Each of us has had, in our past, the experience of being betrayed by important friends, mentors, or supervisors - people we once trusted as elders and guides who subsequently betrayed us.[573]

As Lisa notes, her own experience of being treated as an outsider to Mennonite men's conversations about pacifism has yielded a particular orientation in her work, in which pacifism and feminism link:

> Unlike Yoder and many other Mennonite pacifist theologians, my life's work has been about connecting the public violence of war with the private violence of domestic violence and violence against women. Pacifism and feminism both recognize the dignity and humanity of all people while seeking to end the harm that come in any act of violence, domination, or subordination.[574]

And this leads her to formulate a question (*question*: a key word recurring from one letter to another in the conversation captured in this book):

> [T]o this day, there are two places where I am usually the only woman in the room: when I am training the military in peace-building and when I am discussing pacifist theology. When it comes to security and theology, the men who hold powerful positions in the U.S. military and in the church's theological institutions often actively exclude women's voices and approaches. What is the explanation for this?[575]

II.

If, as Mary Daly has often asserted, the world's encompassing religion is patriarchy, then we must begin to seriously de-construct the presence of patriarchal thinking as one contributing factor to the sexual abuse scandal inside many world religions.[576]

As a sustained reflection on the recurring and deeply entrenched abuse of women and children by privileged males across religious and cultural boundaries which recognizes that such violence occurs widely in the cultures (and religions) of the world, this book is preoccupied with questions about the roots from which sexual violence arises in various cultures of the world:

> Until we begin to understand the supporting underground and largely invisible root structures for sexual violence, I don't believe we will be able to make progress in the human community towards eradicating this worldwide endemic problem. Until we understand the cultural soil in which these trees grow, we have little or no hope at making a lasting difference that changes the culture of violence to a culture of peace[577].

In Ruth's considered judgment, one place we **cannot** expect to find helpful analysis of those invisible root structures for sexual violence is in the bulk of theological and ethical work about peacemaking authored by males.[578] There, unfortunately, "traumatically hobbled individuals" who might provide first-hand testimony about the painful effects of cultural misogyny and exclusion generally are not to be heard: "There is apparently no place for the life-taught wisdom of sexually violated women and children in their theological and ethical anti-violence canon."[579] Ruth adds: "In these same male-authored academic writings, I have noted the striking absence of concern for hearing about any of Yoder's victims' experiences and perceptions."[580]

　　　　　　　　　　　　　　　　　　　　　　　　Ruth E. Krall

One of the reasons Ruth objects to this exclusion of the voices of those primarily affected by affinity violence within theological discussions peacemaking is that it violates a key canon of Mennonite belief – namely, that the proof of the validity of orthodox belief is orthopraxis, the *enactment* of what is stated as belief:

> When word and deed are separated (or when orthodoxy and orthopraxis are no longer held in tension), then there is a strong tendency for religious leaders to abuse the trust of their religious community and their spiritual followers or disciples.[581]

It is this dissonance, the disconnect of word from deed and orthodoxy from orthopraxis in the work of many religious leaders, that propels Ruth to look for the deeply hidden, largely invisible, roots of sexual violence in the various cultures and religions of the planet, as she notes in the following deeply probing statement of personal testimony:

> My personal hypothesis – based on my life journey to date – is that we begin to question our childhood's religious indoctrination when we experience deep moments of cognitive dissonance. We become disillusioned about our religious heritage when we encounter the reality that what we have been taught by our well-meaning elders and by our community are lies. The beginnings of our descent into the dark night of the soul are often complex and multi-faceted. We can encounter dogma and doctrines about the nature of truth that are clearly not about truth; we can have doubts about orthodoxies and customary pieties that have no reasonable response or answers for our doubts and life questions; we can find no meaningful reassurance and guidance for our lives when we directly encounter the issues of hypocrisy, dishonesty and untrustworthiness in the religious commons; we can encounter teachings about principled morality that religious leaders do not model; we can witness cruelty wearing the mask of helpfulness; we can observe hate being described as love; we can be disastrously betrayed by physically, sexually, or religiously abusive spiritual authorities and abruptly enter the enchanted forests of religious betrayal.[582]

Behind the gaping chasm between word and deed as many religious leaders deal with questions of violence against women and children, and behind the silence that excludes the voices of those directly affected by such violence from their religious conversations, Ruth spots **denial**, denial that, in the view of Laurie Ferguson, deserves careful attention in theological discussions of violence, since denial is always more than mere aporia or elision: it's there for a reason. As Presbyterian minister Laurie Ferguson maintains, *denial is always in the service of something.*[583]

Denial is, in short, an *institutional* mechanism designed to shield systems of abuse from careful inspection. As Ruth notes repeatedly throughout her letters,[584] she has learned from close study of the work of Roman Catholic Dominican priest Tom Doyle on the abuse crisis in the Catholic Church that institutions display predictable institutionalized patterns of response, denial included, to those seeking to ferret out sexual abuse of the vulnerable within their boundaries:

> Father Thomas Doyle has reminded all of us that these sexual abuse problems are not parasites or barnacles which have attacked the church or spiritual teaching centers from the outside. Instead, they are endemic structural realities – well-rooted and actively nurtured systemic realities inside our various world religions[585].

These patterns of systemic obfuscation are not exclusive either to the Roman Catholic Church or the Christian churches in general. As Ruth maintains – and this is a significant contribution of this study –

> When we look at world religions, including Eastern philosophies and guru-disciple communities, what we find is that they are no freer of these disturbing and disciple dis-enablement issues of spiritual teacher abusiveness than are Western theologies and their communities. The problems of religious leader abuse of their disciples and members of the laity are, therefore, endemic spirituality-disabling problems in human religious institutional structures and in the spirituality of human psyches.[586]

And, she goes on to add:

> The cultural forms (or archetypal patterns) of religious leader abuse are present in many, perhaps all, world religions. Thus, religious abuse of spiritual disciples and members of the laity by the priest, the guru, the minister, the imam, the rabbi, the shaman, or other spiritual leader is a regularly repeating pattern of organized religious life. These abusive violations represent repetitive disruptive patterns of authority initiated or enacted by an individual with systemic or structural power. They are received by an individual with less power. In religious communities this power or the human priest or minister, in most religious traditions, is

Ruth E. Krall

spiritually tied to the non-visible power of the divine. Thus, it can be named as an archetype in terms of the individual's unconscious *and* in terms of the community's collective unconscious.[587]

This is a point that Ruth demonstrates persuasively in her Seventeenth Letter through a close case study (citing the work of Natalie Goldberg and Ishmael Ford) of two situations of abuse of disciples and students by spiritual leaders inside the Soto Zen Sect of Buddhism in the United States – the case of Richard Baker Roshi of the San Francisco Soto Zen community, and of Jakal Dainin Katagiri of the Minnesota Soto Zen community.

And so she concludes: "While Christianity and Soto Sect Zen Buddhism have very different world-views, the structure of community responses to religious leader abuse inside a religious or spiritual community is very similar.[588]

III.

If the male Mennonite God and His – usually – male representatives did not protest the sexual violation of women and their children as evil, for example, then this patriarchal and parochial God and his teachings were not now and never could be good news for Mennonite women, for their Mennonite children[589].

Ruth's Seventh and Eighth Letters provide illuminating glimpses into why she has considered it imperative, along with other Mennonite women, to call the church to accountability for its male leaders' cover-up of the sexually predatory activities of John Howard Yoder. These two letters also cast important light on her claim shared by Lisa that peacemaking work outside the church makes little sense if it refuses to notice sexual violence within the Mennonite community.

As Ruth explains to Lisa in her Seventh Letter,

> My personal distrust of religious institutions qua institutions as bearers of spiritual idolatry and corruption began quite naively. It began when I first heard stories of sexualized violence and domestic violence done by Mennonite evangelists preaching the one and only true way to salvation; violence done by the denomination's Biblical scholars; violence done by Mennonite missionaries, preachers, and teachers of peace orthodoxies; violence done by Mennonite administrators of social welfare agencies and mission agencies; violence done by Mennonite therapists inside Mennonite hospitals and outpatient clinics; violence done by Mennonite teachers and administrators in academic settings.[590]

And so, as she adds, both as a clinician dealing with issues of sexual violence and as a teacher, she has repeatedly had to re-think her own understanding of pacifism as she has watched her Mennonite community seek to resolve interpersonal conflicts and issues of authority and violence with social and relational violence.[591]

As the epigraph to this section of the afterword notes, the cover-ups of sexual abuse by Mennonite leaders have led Ruth to question the integrity of Mennonite communal life and praxis, since, if the male Mennonite God and his male representatives did not protest the sexual violation of women and their children, then this patriarchal God and his message as conveyed by church leaders could not now or ever be good news for Mennonite women and their children.[592]

As Ruth also explains to Lisa, after having clung to pacifism for many years as her badge of Mennonite identity, in the middle of her academic career, wounded by ill health compounded with the pain of experiencing shunning from Mennonite leaders due to her commitment to feminism, she began actively to nurture a spirituality of healing that deliberately opened to the insights of wise teachers beyond the boundaries of the Mennonite world whose words *and* life made sense to her.[593]

And then as she adds in her subsequent letter,

> It has been the sustained – and to me – totally irrational hostility of some church leaders and some church academics to my very existence as an Anabaptist-Mennonite anti-violence scholar and peace studies activist which has so devastated my own inner spirit.
>
> Thinking that I belonged to this community of faith because of its values about active peace work in the world, over the years I slowly realized I was first de-valued and then eventually discounted and excluded because of my concerns for women's lives and women's healing; for children's lives and for their domestic safety. Over the course of many years, I first needed to realize and then secondly to acknowledge to myself that my voice and my work in sexual violence activism were not welcomed in the contemporary Anabaptist-Mennonite denominational commons. The reason seemed simple to me: rather than studying, at a distance, other people's addiction to violence, I was studying and critiquing affinity violence *inside* the community. In addition, in a religious denomination which, in the 20th century, oriented most of its peace witness theology to an ideology of redemptive suffering and non-resistance to evil, I was suggesting that there was no such thing as redemptive suffering in the lives of sexual violence survivors and that nonresistance was a blind alley when women and small children confronted abusive individuals – usually but

not always male – in their lives. Active resistance, non-lethal resistance, public protests, and utilization of police protection seemed to me to be a better way for victimized individuals to proceed.[594]

As Lisa informs us in her foreword to Ruth's book of letters, she and other Mennonite women share Ruth's conviction that it is impossible for the Mennonite community to be a credible witness to the path of non-violence unless it addresses violence within the community itself: "Seeking to understand a consistent Mennonite pacifism, we pay attention to her studies in sexual violence as a critical component of Mennonite peace studies."[595]

Bluntly stated, Ruth tells us, academic Mennonite men in general "do not see sexual violence as an important peace and justice issue"[596]. And so it has been Mennonite *women* like Ruth Krall and Lisa Schirch who have insisted that the leaders of their church and its institutions deal honestly with John Howard Yoder's legacy:

> For the most part, then, it has been knowledgeable Anabaptist-Mennonite women who have called for a re-analysis of Yoder's legacy of written work and his interwoven system of ethics, ecclesiology, and theology. It has mostly been concerned church women who have continued to remind Mennonite Church bureaucrats that they must be accountable to the community for their actions in hiding Yoder's behaviors from public awareness. For the most part it has been academic Mennonite women who have confronted the theological silence of the Mennonite Church's academic guilds regarding the need to study Yoder's work in a way that does not deny his lived-life. To my knowledge to date, the earliest academic written comments about Yoder's behavior as a theological or ethical issue are in Mennonite women's doctoral dissertations and master's theses.[597]

And, she continues:

> Your letter, this week, therefore tells me you have become a member of a growing group of Anabaptist-Mennonite women – a few of whom have kept insisting for more than thirty-five years that the John Howard Yoder-Mennonite Church story must be truthfully and factually addressed by the church *for the church to heal its own woundedness.* Our concern for Yoder's victims' healing and for the church's victims' healing has not been a vendetta against the church or against Yoder. It has never been an act of

lunacy. Our ongoing concern about this historical narrative and its ongoing socio-theological trajectory in the heart of the Anabaptist-Mennonite community of faith has been rooted in our clinical and socio-psychological-spiritual concerns for the healing of victimized women *and* for the socio-religious-theological wholeness of the institutional church. Our concern is now (as it has been for more than thirty-five years) to prevent future similar violations and victimizations inside the socio-cultural and theo-religious borders of Anabaptist-Mennonite communities.[598]

But as subsequent letters from Ruth to Lisa inform us, once that growing group of Mennonite women turned its attention to issues of sexual violence *within* the Mennonite community and to Yoder's legacy in particular, it encountered a "Mennonite militia" of academics and religious leaders "whose weaponry includes excommunication, employment termination, shunning, excluding, isolating, outright lying, money manipulation, character assassination, and demeaning back-stabbing gossip".[599] Ruth enumerates the traits and weapons of this militia in an amusing (and instructive) section of this letter defining and critiquing the "Mennonite phallacy".[600]

The Mennonite phallacy and its techniques of back-stabbing and character assassination is on full display in a 1994 document, *Tales from the Reptile House*, which has floated around for years now in a Mennonite underground, as Ruth notes in her Twelfth Letter. As she reports, the document was written by one N.W. Ann Onymous. It seeks to attack the credibility of women coming forward with allegations that Yoder sexually abused them by describing those women as alligators in a swamp.[601]

And so, Ruth concludes,

> This entire essay is, therefore, a very venomous – albeit very anonymous – assault on the characters and the truthful witness of abuse victims and abuse victim advocates. It is, therefore, also an assault on truth-telling. It is an assault on bearing faithful and truthful witness.[602]

As she also notes, the letter was circulated at a point in the 1990s at which certain "backdoor lobbyists" with considerable power in various academic and church institutions were working to have Yoder rehabilitated and restored to academic life as soon as possible. These included Southern Baptist Glenn Stassen, Methodist/Episcopal Stanley Hauerwas, and James William McClendon, who identified himself as a small case baptist.

Ruth writes,

Ruth E. Krall

Yoder's chief apologist Stanley Hauerwas led the evangelical infantry charge in an effort to restore Yoder as soon as possible. He preached a forgiveness sermon at Goshen College's April, 1992 commencement – in advance of the Church's formal announcements of its actions with Yoder – later revealed in the *Elkhart Truth's* June and July, 1992 series of articles about Yoder's sexual behaviors. In this sermon, there was little evidenced concern for the experiences of victims of violence and violation or, so it seemed to me when I re-listened to this sermon several years ago. There was little evidence of a theological or psychological awareness for a religious leader victimizer's need, in all reconciliation processes, to be accountable to his victims, as well as to his church. I heard no awareness that a Roman Catholic form of institutional absolution is totally inappropriate in an Anabaptist-Mennonite confession of faith and communally-embodied-polity. I no longer remember who first said to me that the Mennonite process with Yoder was essentially one of absolution rather than repentance and reconciliation. Whoever this individual was, I continue to hold the opinion that s/he was correct in this penetrating analysis of what went wrong in the Yoder discipline process.[603]

In the Twentieth and Twenty-First Letters in this collection, now written in Lisa's voice, there is a call for a conversation among a new generation of Mennonite pacifists about sexual integrity and the obligation of Mennonite pacifists to deal with intra-communitarian violence against women, children, and LGBT people as they combat violence in society at large, Lisa adds her testimony about Yoder to Ruth's:

> Yoder, of course, was a white male, as are most of his followers. They operate in a patriarchal church that only recently has made important strides to include women. These patriarchal structures did not protect women in the church. Since Yoder assaulted many of his female students and rising church leaders, his action directly impacted a generation of women's leadership. The continuing absence of women in many centers of pacifist theology at Mennonite institutions today means that new generations of pacifist theologians may also not be informed by a gender or power analysis or take into consideration the privilege and entitlement that males enjoy. Even putting Yoder's behavior with women aside, new generations of pacifist theologians need to bring other lenses and voices to engage with Yoder's theological concepts,

including "revolutionary subordination." The church at large, and pacifist theologians in particular, need to critique patriarchy and embrace a wider set of ideas about pacifism and how it relates to people in different social positions.[604]

Her participation in the struggle within the Mennonite community to see its leaders held accountable for their handling of Yoder's actions has led Ruth to a number of significant conclusions. First, as she states strongly in her Eighteenth Letter, she recognizes that,

> We have had, as a Mennonite people, almost no teaching over the centuries that these forms of domestic affinity violence and violations are as costly to the human personality and human community as the violence of the state.[605]

Watching the Mennonite militia collaborate with backdoor lobbyists to plaster over Yoder's predatory behavior has also taught Ruth something about the ability of religious bodies to rot from within: as she notes in her Thirteenth Letter,

> As a result of these letters between us, I have come to the conclusion that when a religious organization becomes more concerned about status, control, power, theological agreements, sociological unity, authority, behavioral purity, and orthodox words than about embodied and compassionate love of the neighbor, justice in situations of injustice, spontaneous acts of charity and helpfulness towards the vulnerable, and mutual compassion for each other's humanity in the face of great personal and social differences, it has already crumbled on the inside. What remains is the white-washed face of the tomb where dead religions now rest.[606]

Since she views rape as "the ultimate symbol and the penultimate weapon of patriarchal cultures,"[607] which walks hand in hand with its "cultural sibling," domestic violence, Ruth finds it impossible to pay serious attention to the Mennonite community's witness to non-violence when this witness prescinds from issues of domestic and sexual violence:

> While I have personally witnessed the Mennonite community of faith excommunicate young men who enrolled in military service, I have never witnessed the excommunication of individuals who have perpetrated rape, battery, incest, emotional abuse, etc., inside the Mennonite commons. I have never witnessed an abusive

Ruth E. Krall

spouse or parent publicly criticized or disciplined for the violence he or she has done inside the family. I have never witnessed excommunication of abusive and authoritarian institutional administrators. Until very recently, I have never heard sermons against abusive and corrupt church institutions.[608]

And so she has reached the following conclusion regarding the call to pacifism in the Mennonite community today:

> In my scholarship and activism, I address the needs of women and their children – those individuals who are most likely to be sexually violated by another set of patriarchal warriors – the men who live with them and interact with them as their social intimates. While mostly these men do not do their harm with hard weaponry, they, do harm, nevertheless. They use the body's most intimate parts as their weaponry. The damage both sets of warriors inflict upon the body/selves of individuals and the peace of the world is simply incomprehensible.

> I conclude, therefore, that warfare and politically motivated economic efforts at domination are forms of violence that Mennonites should concern themselves with. I also conclude that gender-based sexual violation is another very common form of violence that Mennonites should also concern themselves about. If the Jesus path is one of peace-making, healing, and consoling the desolate and the devastated, then both forms of work are at the center of a pacifist Christianity in a Mennonite voice.[609]

IV.

Complex topics such as sexual violence, therefore, need multiple voices. In particular, deliberately marginalized voices need to be invited to the table as full and equal participants in the conversations).[610]

As a meditation about the spiritual foundations needed to sustain healthy advocacy work, and about the valuable resources she finds in the various religious traditions of the world as she engages in this work, Ruth notes the imperative need for peacemakers to pay attention to the excluded or absent voice.[611] As she explains, authentic inclusion is different from tokenism.[612]

There is a theological warrant built here into the quest to be a peacemaker: you are not making peace and doing justice when you exclude. There's also a feminist warrant, since feminist commitments require those engaging in theoretical discussions to acknowledge the personal and the life situations from which theoretical analysis arises. Attached to this warrant is what might be called an *epistemological* imperative to bring as many voices into conversations about these issues as one may – and, in particular, the voices of those excluded by power-brokers:

> When people with something important to add to the conversation are deliberately excluded from conversations which deeply involve them, we can conclude that the orthodoxy cavalry has gathered its horses and has circled them continuously around religious institutions and religious academies. This orthodoxy cavalry does this to protect the calcified beliefs and dogma that allow some individuals to be excluded as less than fully human. It does this, I am increasingly convinced, because it is too lazy to search for and enable more complexity.[613]

As Ruth notes here, the very complexity of the issues under consideration demands a multiplicity of perspectives.[614] As she also notes,

> It is increasingly clear to me that consumers of academic scholarship are enablers of academic denial when they do not insist upon practices of inclusion and practices of disclosure by authors.[615]

As Ruth adds in her Fourth Letter (citing Elie Wiesel, Mary Gail Frawley-O'Dea, and Phillip Halle),[616] an extended meditation on the painful journey truth-tellers undertake, we can all too easily deceive ourselves about our motives as we search for the truth – and incorporating the perspectives of others helps to correct our solipsism and check our self-deception. As she explains in her Fifth Letter,[617] such correctives and the intellectual integrity they demand of us are particularly important today, given how new historical conditions reframe discussions of pacifism at this point in history.

A case in point: because patriarchal forms of violence are to be found all over the place, from culture to culture and religious body to religious body, a multiplicity of perspectives and voices is required if patriarchy is to be analyzed in any *productive* way that might result in effective dismantling of this system of thought and cultural organization:

> I personally believe we need as many languages and as many allies as we can find and muster because the more circumscribed and cliché-like the personal and professional languages we use to clarify cultural nuances in situations of violence and violation, the

Ruth E. Krall

less damage we do to the patriarchy; the less able we are in carrying out our Christian feminist task of dismantling the patriarchy and its oppressive orthodoxies for our sons' and daughters' futures.[618]

In her Seventh Letter, which is an articulation of the multi-faceted and powerful spiritual foundations on which she draws in her witness to the way of non-violence, Ruth insists that we need as many languages and allies as possible to pursue the work of non-violence, because the task before us is as broad as the task of forming the beloved community on earth:

> Our human task, as simple and as complex as any task, is to form the beloved community on earth. In my words, this is a community of resistance. In your words [this is directed to Lisa], this is a community of transformation. In Robin Meyer's words, it is a community of rebellion, subversion and defiance. In Tom Doyle's words, this is the people of God, the re-configured and non-abusive church.[619]

We also need wide representation at the table discussing peace and justice issues because, Ruth points out, "Everyone in the violence narrative has a history".[620] And given the difference between your history and mine, you may well see what I cannot see, with my own limited experience:

> No idea is perfect – no matter how brilliant its author. Every theological idea, for example, must be tested in the academic commons to see if it supports the patriarchy or if it supports the critique of the patriarchy. These ideas must also be tested to see if they express a preferential option for that which oppresses other human beings or if they express a preferential option for vulnerable, abused, and often discarded human beings. I distrust all forms of theological orthodoxy which are not grounded in an awakened, compassionate self-and-world orthopraxis.[621]

And so: "We need to make allies wherever and whenever we can. I think we need to be prepared for surprise when we see who shows up in our lives.[622]

In several fascinating passages, Ruth links the epistemological imperative for wide consultation to the importance of asking questions (a core term in the book, as I've noted), and refusing to settle for easy answers. As she explains in her Tenth Letter,

The value of questioning and doubting for one's own self as a way of determining the guiding principles and values of one's own life is one of the core values of my life. It is linked with a pantheon of heroes – men and women who have done or are still doing critical peace and justice work without resorting to obnoxious controlling piety or male hormone bullying to defend themselves. Unthinking and uncaring belief in the hairy verities and patriarchal entitlements of a religious culture is simply not acceptable to me as a way to live my life.[623]

As she adds in the subsequent letter, her strong emphasis on the importance of questioning and doubting arises out of her experience of being shaped from childhood forward in a religious tradition with such a heavy communitarian emphasis. In her view, this emphasis in Mennonite culture works against valuing the individual – something that poses a particular challenge for feminist Mennonites. In fact, it reflects and reinforces patriarchal assumptions about male entitlement within the community, Ruth proposes.[624]

Ruth's experience of struggling with this particular religious tradition and its patriarchal outlook has led her to ask the following important questions:

My personality is more comfortable with questions than with answers; I am not much interested in orthodoxy. I want to know how people live their lives. I want to know the actual stories of their lives – rather than the doctored stories they have created to survive in the patriarchy. Are they kind? Do they demonstrate compassion for others' suffering? Do they live with integrity? Are they tolerant of diversity or even celebratory in its midst? Is their spirit welcoming or rejecting? Are they competent in the work they do? Can they accept human diversity as the way life is? Are they curious about why people do what they do, or are they immediately judgmental and harshly critical? Can they live within conflict and not need to settle it immediately – but rather allow the conflict of ideas and opinions to ripen so that it can teach them flexibility, resiliency, and curiosity? Do they express curiosity about life, or do they already know everything there is to be known? Are they interested in truth or just ideology?[625]

Or, as she also puts the point, if the divine source of life so clearly celebrates diversity (look at the natural world and it's impossible to avoid reaching this conclusion, Ruth thinks), why does the Mennonite tradition insist that in order to be faithful to the Creator of such a diverse world, we must fit people into "narrow boxes of appropriate and inappropriate; faithful or unfaithful; prophetic or wrong-minded?"[626]

Ruth's critique of the heavy communitarian emphasis in Mennonite culture does not, it goes without saying, blind her to the significance of community – particularly for those engaged in the arduous work of peacemaking and justice-seeking. Her Fourteenth Letter is an extended reflection on the need of activists to find "enduring space" in which they may re-humanize themselves after they've expended too much of themselves in advocacy work[627]. Ruth's vision of such enduring space comprises supportive community as part of the process of self-care for activists – space in which one wounded healer may gather with another as the two seek healing together.[628] In such healing spaces, those engaging in peace-making advocacy may, Ruth proposes, turn from the "dangerous fire-breathing dragons roaming free in the commons" and begin dealing with their own internal dragons[629].

As Ruth notes, it's in part her awareness that advocates for non-violence must pay attention to their need for self-care that has caused her to turn with great respect to the various spiritual traditions of the world. Her Fourteenth Letter turns the scornful phrase "cafeteria-style spirituality" on its head, as she notes how much she has learned from a wide variety of religious and philosophical traditions.[630] As she explains in her subsequent letter,

> I have found Huston Smith's insistence upon the principle that all of the world's religious traditions contain repositories of human wisdom about the spiritual life to be helpful. I am not limited, therefore, to just one fountain of deep spirituality. I can drink from many wells. My own spirituality, therefore, is deeply influenced by the great contemplative spiritual traditions of the world.[631]

And so at this point in her life journey, Ruth has concluded that a worldview exclusively informed by Mennonite beliefs or Mennonite ideas – a worldview characterized by unrealistic notions about perfection – works against the ability of the peacemaker to get into the "world's violent messes," something he or she absolutely has to do in order to pursue the work of non-violence.[632] This brings Ruth to the following conclusion:

> My personal peace theology therefore is no longer Mennonite or even institutionally Christian. Having seen the damages to individuals and human communities, violence quite simply is not the path I wish to pursue. As healers, nurses and doctors are taught a quite simple maxim: *first, do no harm!* I no longer need my denominational church to teach me that physical war and economic war

is wrong. These forms of war harm precious and unique people. They destroy individual lives and they destroy entire communities. In addition, they spread the virus of violence.[633]

V.

I am puzzled about why sexual xenophobia occurs so frequently in proximity to sexism, racism, and to domestic violence against women and their children.[634]

Finally, this book is a reflection on the connections between various *isms* including sexism, heterosexism, racism, classism, and affinity violence of all sorts. In particular, it asks probing questions about the choice of Mennonite leaders dealing with the Yoder legacy to protect heterosexual men preying on women while conducting a kind of intra-ecclesial warfare against LGBT members of the church. As Ruth puts the point in her Third Letter, "the Mennonite Church's cover-up silence about religious leader sexual abuse of the laity and its aggressive denominational denunciations of homosexuality as a purity violation" are "discrete poisonous trees" with intertwined root systems.[635]

Ruth frames the exclusionary treatment accorded to LBGT people and their loving relationships by some communities of faith as a form of violence demanding the attention of those committed to pacifism:

> Today's (and yesterday's) institutional Christian churches often refuse to accept mutual, consenting, and loving sexual relationships between two same gender adults (refusing them a full participating membership and a spiritual blessing on their relationship) even as the church actively hides, and therefore both enables and implicitly blesses, repeated events and acts of sexual violence and sexual harassment done by its clergy and religious leaders . . .[636]

> We have, therefore, the spiritual-religious-theological irony that victims of clergy sexual violence and institutional clericalism, like their same gender compatriots in exile, are also force-marched out of their church. Their life situation is, therefore, remarkably similar to the fate of same gender partnered couples who have sought the institutional church's blessing on their relationship: continuous victimization and revictimization in the name of God and God's people.[637]

Ruth E. Krall

As a result, as Ruth sagely notes, any attempt to look at the phenomenon of clergy sexual abuse of the laity must carefully engage the way in which church leaders so frequently obfuscate, when it comes to covering up sexual abuse of the laity, by seeking to conflate homosexuality with sexual abuse by members of the clergy.[638] As she notes,

> [C]hurchly discussions in the last century and in the current century have so conflated the two phenomenons (same gender sexual desire and clergy sexual abuse of the laity – especially when this abuse involves same gender victims) in such ideologically dense ways that whenever the scandal of sexual abuse by Christian clergy surfaces into a public view, the issue of same gender sexual desire also surfaces into the public consciousness as well. It is as if these two unrelated experiential phenomenons are Siamese twins: one cannot appear without the other appearing as well.

> What is largely ignored in these convoluted discussions is that some and perhaps most clergy sexual violations of small children, adolescents, and vulnerable adults are male-female violations rather than male-male or female-female ones. Because of the single gender nature of the Roman Catholic priesthood, this Christian denomination provides us with an exception to the rule. Most acts of sexual abuse of the laity in Christendom and in other world religions represent, therefore, male-female abuse. To put it bluntly, male clergy abuse female victims.[639]

And:

> Let me state my thinking today as a clear hypothesis: the poisonous tree of xenophobic responses to homosexuality is a completely separate tree from the poisonous tree of clergy sexual abuse. Phenomenologically, therefore, these are two separate problems for institutional Christian churches and individual Christians to address.[640]

Ruth offers us an important caveat about why leaders of many churches engage in this particular kind of obfuscation now:

> Yet, as a woman I am suspicious of some of these theoretical approaches. My personal sense of the matter – an intuitive sense – is that issues of male dominance and male authoritarianism

are more determinative of clergy abuse than issues of gender or issues of homoeroticism. Issues of power, in my opinion, are much more prevalent than current discussions give credence. In part, I suppose, this is because so many of the voices in the debate about clergy sexual abuse and institutional clericalism are male voices. I am, it turns out, not the only skeptic.[641]

Adding to the problems confronting those trying to deal with this diversionary behavior among church leaders challenged to deal with issues of clergy sexual abuse, there is also, as she notes, the "institutionalized use of money as an analogy for corrupted power".[642]

The intertwining roots of the cover-up of sexual abuse by clergy and of hostility to LGBT people strike deep, then, into the soil of patriarchy itself: these roots are interpenetrated by "ideologies of male dominance and female subordination; of male superiority and female inferiority; of male authority and female obedience".[643] It is not in the least accidental, Ruth underscores, that what've learned about affinity violence targeting women and children has been discovered largely by feminists, who have done groundbreaking research in this area.[644]

It is, Ruth insists, to a great degree her own feminist commitments that have sensitized her both to the omnipresence of violence faced by women and their children, and to the connections between the *isms* that denigrate and target various minority groups for exclusion:

> The issue of women's subordinated position in the world affects every woman – whether or not she is privileged by virtue of having an education or disprivileged by living among the most abandoned of women in a refugee camp – surviving day by day as she cares for her family. The stress-and-trauma-filled narrative of being a female in a patriarchal and violent world pervades these letters. In particular, the narrative of sexual and gendered violence informs these written conversations. In the background, however, are our conversations about racism, gender orientation xenophobia, and various forms of prejudice based on sociological factors such as ethnicity or religion.[645]

Her feminist commitment has not, however, come without considerable cost within a religious academy that, as she tells us in the Sixteenth Letter, is much less eager to integrate women as full peers than is the secular academy.[646] This commitment is also devalued in her own Mennonite community and its academy):

Choosing to privilege women (and their children) as the focus of my life work of activism and scholarship has meant that my academic and activist work is not valued in the Mennonite patriarchy. But, as I near the end of my life, I would not change that focus or any of its different manifestations. Women's culturally diminished life in the patriarchy as lived everywhere around the world is a peace and justice issue. For women, it is also a religious and spiritual issue. Whether the abuse suffered by women is salary discrimination, exclusion from an insider status, physical harassment, academic hazing by male peers, or bullying bosses, sexual violence, or the lived experiences of war, women and those for whom they are responsible, such as their children and the aged, suffer from their encounters with men's patriarchal prejudice towards them and men's enacted violence against them.[647]

And so Ruth concludes with great eloquence:

As long as men (and their male-identified female acolytes), consciously or unconsciously, see women's presence and feminist analysis in the Academy as an irrelevant nuisance, then women will continue to be excluded from the conversations which involve them and from conversations where they can add valuable insights. Women's issues continue to be seen as irrelevant in doing the *real and necessary* work of nonviolence activism in the world: confronting the violence of others in matters of militarism, economics and criminal justice – in short the hard aspects of peace work. The presence of men's sexual violence inside the religious boundaries of any given community tends to be seen, therefore, as a soft, peripheral, and extraneous issue. Women's concerns about the sexual violation and gendered violence which encapsulates them and their children tend to be seen as irrelevant to the peace of the world.[648]

Have I said that I think the book you've just read will be a classic some day, not far down the road? I've practically reproduced the book in this too-lengthy afterword, in order to demonstrate to you how powerful and wide-ranging its arguments and intuitions are. If all the words of this verbose afterword convince you to re-read the book, then perhaps the afterword will have done its work!

Index to Appendices

Appendix A

Tales from the Reptile House

For Immediate Release
September 28, 1994

When we scan our church papers these days, the one single most important topic that meets our eye is allegations. There are allegations of inappropriate racial attitudes and allegations of sexual misconduct. There are allegations of financial irregularities and allegations of abuse of power and person. No matter what one does, says, or thinks nowadays, some will see it as "politically incorrect", and no matter what one's real intentions may have been, it can be re-interpreted as having been wrong, wrong, wrong.

It seems evident, therefore, that the most pressing item on our denomination's agenda is not the proposed merger between our two sister denominations as some would have us believe. Nor will it be the precise wording of our new Confession of Faith, or any other issues affecting the health, the education, the spiritual welfare of our beloved Mennonite brotherhood. (pardon us, *peoplehood*!) Rather, we desperately need a week-long study Conference on Allegations and we need it now!

With new allegations popping up all over, there obviously must be a myriad of alligators out there. The question is: who are these alligators? What do they look like? In what part of the Great North American Mennonite swamp do the alligators live? What do alligators feed on? Do they really savor white, male church leaders who are already on the endangered species list?

Do alligators float alone, or do they travel in packs, posing a far greater threat than we heretofore realized? We need to know. Is it true they lurk in the shade, avoiding the light of day as much as possible? Do they really stay nearly submerged, ready to take a bite out of the next unsuspecting passerby?

We can hardly wait to meet in Wichita in 1995 to gather around the central study themes: <u>Alligators in the Church.</u>

We envision the spacious halls of Century 11 filled to overflowing with folks wishing to meet and hear the most prominent live alligators among the Mennos. And, while we are dreaming: why not make this event a great big celebration? For, like the entertainment community has its annual award ceremonies - the Emmy, the Oscars, the Grammys – we Mennos could easily outdo all three combined.

Just imagine the excitement of seeing who will capture this year's "Lorney." (For your information: the Lorney was named after J. Loren Peachey, who edits a national wildlife magazine printed at Scottdale, PA). He also has successfully raised alligators as a hobby for years. The competition will be fierce. Will the winner be Jenny G. from Goshen who has singlehandedly nurtured a small school of the nippy reptiles? Or will it be ....Carolyn H. H. from Albuquerque? Could it be Carol G. from Scottdale (no relation to Jenny G., as far as we know) – the biggest, meanest alligator of them all? Will nominations from the floor be allowed? Will the winner's name and achievements be enshrined in Elkhart and in Goshen and in Newton in their new Alligator Halls of Fame?

Oh glory! We can see the Lorney Awards Ceremony reported by Jim Bishop not for one, but in two successive editions of his Virginia Ham columns. In fact, this may be Bishop's one chance at literary greatness. And imagine: the Board of Congregational Ministries - always short on funds – peddling alligator tee-shirts and ending their fiscal year with a hefty surplus. Judges for the first ever Lorney Awards Ceremony will most certainly come from Allegheny Conference, and not only because that Conference is listed first in The Mennonite Yearbook. The names of Stoltzfus and Sharp are frequently mentioned.

The Chinese have their year of the Dog and the Year of the Dragon (we never know which is which). But one thing is clear, for Mennos, this will be the year of the Alligators!

NOTE: Written and disseminated by N. W. Ann Onymous. N. W. for Name Withheld. Ann Onymous is a current best-selling author among the Mennonites. You may have seen her work in the Gossip Herald and in the Mennonite Distorter.

TRANSCRIBER'S NOTE: July 28, 2014: Transcribed from a photocopy of the original by Ruth E. Krall. A photocopy of the original is stored with my archival files in Goshen, IN and in Berkeley, CA.

Appendix B

National Violence against Women Survey

Report Authors, Patricia Tjaden and Nancy Thoennes

Physical Assault

51.9% of surveyed women; 66.4% of surveyed men reported being physically assaulted as a child by an adult caretaker and/or as an adult by any type of attacker.

An estimate 1.9 million women and 3.2 million men are assaulted annually in the US.

Rape

17.6 % of all women surveyed said they had been a victim of rape or attempted rape at some time in their lifetime.

(a)   21.6 % were younger than age 12 at the time of their first rape
(b)   32.4 % were between the ages of 12 and 17

Thus, more that half of the female rape victims identified in this survey were younger than the age of 18 when they first experienced attempted or completed rape.

Stalking

8 % of surveyed women and 2.2 of surveyed men reported being stalked at some time in their life

% of women reported being stalked in the previous 12 months
While 0.4% of men reported this

Approximately 1 million women and 371,000 men are stalked annually in the USA.

Ethnicity Issues

American Indian/Alaskan Native women report more violent victimization than do women/men of other racial backgrounds; they were more likely to have been raped and more likely to have been stalked.

Native American and Alaskan Native men were more likely to report they had been physically assaulted.

Hispanic women were significantly less likely to report being raped than non-Hispanic women.

Previous Violence as Minors

Women who reported that they were raped before age 18 were twice as likely to report subsequent victimization events

Women who reported being physically assaulted as a child by an adult caretaker were twice as likely to be physically assaulted as an adult

Women who reported being stalked before the age of 18 were seven times more likely to report being stalked as an adult

Domestic Violence

22.1% of surveyed women; 7.4% of surveyed men report that they were physically assaulted by a former or current spouse, cohabiting partner,

Ruth E. Krall

boyfriend or girlfriend or date at sometime in their lifetime.

1.3% of surveyed women and 0.9% of surveyed men reported such assaults in the previous twelve months

Approximately 1.3 million women and 835,000 men are physically assaulted by an intimate partner annually in the USA

Violence against women

Violence against women is primarily intimate partner violence. 64% of surveyed women who reported being raped, physically assaulted, and/ or stalked since age 18 were victimized by a current or former husband, cohabiting partner, boyfriend or date. 16.2 percent of surveyed men reported victimization by such a perpetrator.

Women are much more likely to be physically injured during rape and other assaults. The likelihood of physical injuries increases when their assailant is a current or former intimate. 35% required medical treatment after their most recent rape; 30.2 required medical treatment after a physical assault.

Survey Implications
- Violence against women is primarily intimate partner violence
- Violence against women should be classified as a major public health and criminal justice concern in the USA
- Violence against women is endemic
- Future research must pay demographic attention to demographic, social and environmental factors that may (1) account for the variation in victimization rates among women of different ethnic and racial backgrounds and (2) examine the link between victimization as a minor and victimization as an adult.

Note: June 14, 2015: Redaction of research survey findings by Ruth E. Krall, Ph.D. Report Authors: Patricia Tjaden and Nancy Thoennes. (November, 2000). National Institutes of Justice:. Retrieve full report from https://www.ncjrs.gov/ pdffiles1/nij/183781.pdf

Author Profiles

Ruth Elizabeth Krall

A Mennonite, Dr. Ruth Elizabeth Krall is a retired psychiatric-community mental health nurse and college professor. She is also a pastoral thealogian who has specialized in sexual violence studies. Her B.S.N. is from Goshen College in Indiana. Her M.S.N. is from the University of Cincinnati. Her Ph.D. is from The Southern California School of Theology at Claremont in Claremont, CA. She is Emerita Professor in Religion, Nursing and Psychology and Emerita Program Director of Peace, Justice and Conflict Studies at Goshen College, Goshen, IN. In retirement she continues to research and write about social issues, pacifism, and sexual violence. A cradle Mennonite, she is single. Dr. Krall was the convener and a founding member of the Anabaptist-Mennonite Chapter of SNAP (www.snapnetwork. com). More information about her work can be found on her webpage, www. enduringspace.com.

Dr. Krall is the author of

Krall, R. E. (2016) *Soul Betrayal: Religious and Spiritual Trauma.* Enduring Space. Retrieve from www.ruthkrall.com

Krall, R. E., (2014) *The Elephants in God's Living Room: Bearing the Unbearable*, vol. 4. *A Collection of Conversational Essays.* Enduring Space. Retrieve from www.ruthkrall.com

Krall, R. E., (2013) *The Elephants in God's Living Room: The Mennonite Church and John Howard Yoder*, vol. 3, *Collected essays.* Enduring Space. Retrieve from www. ruthkrall.com

Krall, R. E. (2013) *The Elephants in God's Living Room: Problems in Christian Faith: Clergy sexual abuse and clericalism in the American church.* Vol.2. A self-directed study guide. Enduring Space. Retrieve from www.ruthkrall.com

Krall, R. E. (2012). *The Elephants in God's Living Room: Clergy sexual abuse and institutional clericalism,* vol. 1. *Theoretical Issues.* Enduring Space. Retrieve from www.ruthkrall.com

Krall, R. E. (2006/2016). *Inanna's Way: A Personal Journey into the Underworld.* Enduring Space. Retrieve from www.ruthkrall.com

Holsopple, M. Y., Krall, R.E., and Pittman, S. W. (2004). *Building Peace: Overcoming Violence in Communities.* Geneva, Switzerland: World Council of Churches Publications.

Krall, R. E., Kraybill, D. and Eby, J. W. (1991). Dean's Workshop: *Community and Diversity – Can We Have Both?* Goshen, IN: Goshen College Office of the Dean of the Faculty.

William D. Lindsey

Dr. William (Bill) Lindsey is a Roman Catholic theologian and socio-theological blogger at www.bilgrimage.com where he writes about the interplay of belief and culture.

His B.A. in English is from Loyola, New Orleans. His M.A. in English is from Tulane University in New Orleans. His M.A. and Ph.D. in theology are from University of St. Michael's College, Toronto School of Theology.

A non-closeted gay man, he has been partnered for more than 44 years and, thanks to social changes in American law, is now married. He is a victim's advocate for SNAP.

Dr. Lindsey is the author of the following books:

Lindsey, W. D. with Mark Silk (2004). *Religion and Public Life in the Southern Crossroads Region: The Showdown States,* Walnut Creek, CA: Alta Mira.

Lindsey, W. D. (1997). *Shailer Mathews' Lives of Jesus: The Search for a Theological Foundation for the Social Gospel.* Albany, NY: State University of New York Press.

Lindsey, W. D. (1991). *Singing in a Strange Land: Playing and Acting with the Poor.* Kansas City, MO: Sheed and Ward.

Lisa Schirch

Dr. Lisa Schirch is the North American Research Director for the Toda Institute for Global Peace and Policy Research (Japan), Senior Policy Director with the Alliance for Peacebuilding (Washington, D.C.), and Research Professor at the Center for Justice and Peacebuilding at Eastern Mennonite University (Harrisonburg, VA).

She holds a BA in Political Science and International Relations, University of Waterloo, Waterloo, Canada; A MS and PhD from the Institute for Conflict Analysis and Resolution, George Mason University, Washington, DC.

A cradle Mennonite, she is married and the mother of two children.

She is a founding member of the Anabaptist-Mennonite Chapter of SNAP.

Dr. Schirch is the author of the following books:

Schirch, L. (2015).*Local Ownership in Security: Case Studies of Peacebuilding Approaches,* The Hague, The Netherlands: Global Partnership for the Prevention of Armed Conflict. The Hague, The Netherlands: Global Partnership for the Prevention of Armed Conflict.

Schirch, L. (2015). *Handbook for Human Security: A Civil-Military-Police Curriculum,* The Hague, The Netherlands: Global Partnership for the Prevention of Armed Conflict.

Schirch, L. (2014). *Conflict Assessment and Peacebuilding Planning: Toward a Participatory Approach to Human Security.* Boulder, CO: Lynn Reinner Publishers.

Schirch, L. (2007). *The Little Book of Dialogue for Difficult Subjects: A Practical Hands-on Guide.* Intercourse, PA: Good Books.

Schirch, L. (2006). *Civilian Peacekeeping: Preventing Violence and Making Space for Democracy.* Uppsala, Sweden: Life Peace Institute

Schirch, L. (2005). *The Little Book of Strategic Peacemaking: A Vision and Framework for Peace with Justice.* Intercourse, PA: Good Books.

Schirch, L. (2004). *Ritual and Symbol in Peacemaking.* Boulder, CO: *Kumarian Press*

Schirch, L (2004). *Women in Peacebuilding: A Resource and Training Manua*l. Harrisonburg, VA: Eastern Mennonite University.

Acknowledgments and Appreciation

Appreciation is expressed to Professor Lisa Schirch for her willingness to have our personal electronic correspondence transformed into these informal letter-essays and for her willingness to read these letter-essays as they evolved during a historical time period in both of our lives when we needed to deal with serious, acute physical illnesses.

Appreciation is expressed to Father Thomas P. Doyle for his willingness to read and to comment upon several of these letters. In addition I am very grateful for the work he does in the world to address the wounds of sexual violation caused by his denomination's priests and their institutional supervisors.

Appreciation is expressed to Blogger Dr. William (Bill) Lindsey for his willingness to read and comment upon these letters. His copy editing has clarified and corrected with style and grace. His blog, **Bilgrimage** can be found at http://bilgrimage.blogspot.com/

Appreciation is expressed to Ellen Swanson for her careful and critical reading of these letters. She helped to find many of the tiny misspellings that bedevil every author.

Appreciation is expressed to Carolyn Holderread Heggen for unearthing *Tales from the Reptile House* from her files at my request. I have known for years about this so-called anonymous bit of scurrilous writing but over the course of many moves, had lost my personal copy. For more than twenty five years Carolyn and I have shared a common cause – that of alerting Mennonite communities to the presence of rape, incest, sexual harassment, and domestic violence inside our shared community of faith.

Appreciation is expressed to WIPF and Stock for their permission to reproduce Dr. Schirch's chapter *To the Next Generation of Pacifist Theologians.* It first appeared in *John Howard Yoder: Radical Theologian* (2014) edited by J. Denny Weaver and Earl Zimmerman.

Appreciation is expressed to the *Mennonite World Review* Editors for their permission to reproduce Dr. Schirch's essay, *Toward Mennonite Sexual Integrity.* It first appeared in the May 25, 2015 issue.

Appreciation is expressed to the professional editors at Friesen Press for their help in creating a *real book.*

Authors' Note to Readers: Resource items found on the World Wide Web can be exceedingly ephemeral as addresses change or items are removed. As of June 10, 2016, all World Wide Web URL addresses were current. If an address does not open, try typing in the full title. Usually, the file can be found.

Endnotes

Foreword

1   Schirch, L. Afterword: To the Next Generation of Pacifist Theologians in J. Denny Weaver, (Ed). John Howard Yoder: Radical Theologian. Eugene, OR: Wipf and Stock, Pp. 377- 395 [reprinted in this collection of letters with the permission of Wipf and Stock, pp. 295-311.

2   Krall, R. E. (2012, 2013, and 2014). The Elephants in God's Living Room, vols. 1, 2, and 4. Enduring Space, www.ruthkrall.com. Most especially, I wanted permission to quote material from vol. 3 and its case study analysis of John Howard Yoder's sexual abuse of women during his long and productive academic career at the Associated Mennonite Biblical Seminaries in Elkhart, IN and at the University of Notre Dame in South Bend, IN.

3   Second Letter , p. 49

4   Seventh Letter, p. 97

5   Thirteenth Letter, p. 187

6   Thirteenth Letter, p. 187

7   Eighteenth Letter, p. 269

8   Eleventh Letter, p. 152

9   Fourteenth Letter, p. 194

10   Eighteenth Letter, p. 274

11   Second Letter, p. 49

12   Eighteenth Letter, p. 278

13   Nineteenth Letter, p. 293

Introduction

14   Schirch, L. (2014). Afterword: Schirch, Lisa: To the Next Generation of Pacifist Theologians (Pp. 377- 395) in Weaver, J. D., (Ed.). John Howard Yoder: Radical Theologian. Eugene, OR: WIPF/Stock [Re-published here

with the kind permission of Wipf and Stock]. This Afterword can be found on pages 295-310 in this book.

15   It is important to note that Dr. Schirch has been consulted about this project of essay-letters and has given her permission to proceed with publishing her comments and my responses to them.

16   Rilke, R. (1914/2014). Letters to a Young Poet. New York, NY: Penguin.

17   Coffin, W. S. (2005). Letters to a Young Doubter. Louisville, KY: Westminster/ John Knox.

18   June, 2014: Describing women as "the most beautiful **thing** (emphasis mine) God has made," Pope Francis in his first interview with a woman journalist since taking the papal throne, joked about women being taken from men's rib. To add further insult to injury, when he was asked about appointing a woman to head an influential Vatican department, he joked that "priests often end up under the sway of their housekeepers." Retrieve this news report from http://www.theguardian.com/world/2014/jun/29/pope-francis-woman-from-rib-avoids-pledge-reform-catholic-church

19   Lindsey, W. (May 31, 2014): there is a discussion of the cult of masculinity. Retrieve from
      http://bilgrimage.blogspot.com/2014/05/andrew-ohehir-on-how-elliot-rodger-is.html
      Lindsey, W. (June 2, 2014): there is a discussion of female objectification and gender discrimination. Retrieve from
      http://bilgrimage.blogspot.com/2014/06/rebecca-solnit-on-struggle-to-name.html
      Lindsey, W. (June 3, 2014): there is a discussion of men, guns, god and violence against women, Retrieve from
      http://bilgrimage.blogspot.com/2014/06/ta-nehisi-coatess-case-for-reparations.html#more
      Lindsey, W. (June 3, 2014): there is a discussion of racism and sexism and the media's talking heads' collective denial about the roots of misogyny. Retrieve from
      http://bilgrimage.blogspot.com/2014/06/ta-nehisi-coatess-case-for-reparations.html
      Lindsey, W. (June 6, 2014): there is a discussion of misogyny and gender/ Maya Angelou's death. Retrieve from
      http://bilgrimage.blogspot.com/2014/06/end-of-week-news-roundup-venus-mars.html
      Lindsey, W. (June 7, 2014): there is a discussion of testosterone and the construction of male identity. Retrieve from
      http://bilgrimage.blogspot.com/2014/06/andrew-sullivan-et-al-on-testosterone.html

Lindsey, W. (June 7, 2014): there is a discussion of the papal encyclical Humanae Vitae and women's subordination in Catholic theology. Retrieve from

http://bilgrimage.blogspot.com/2014/06/patricia-miller-on-why-paul-vi-kept-ban.html

Lindsey, W. (June 7, 2014): there is a discussion of the social construction of masculinity. Retrieve from

http://bilgrimage.blogspot.com/2014/06/theres-doctor-em-steve-says-and-giftie.html#disqus_thread

Lindsey, W. (June 10, 2014): there is a discussion of male identity, guns and homophobia. Retrieve from

http://bilgrimage.blogspot.com/2014/06/testosterone-castration-american.html#disqus_thread

First Letter
Introducing the Johari Window

20   Source of Diagram: The Career Life Institute: Retrieve from: https://encrypted-tbn2.gstatic.com/images?q=tbn:ANd9GcSUvstK1tei3dsITlqCLl4P7UZECJakMADVKnWr9P-jQeoGZoC98Q

21   Synergy can be defined as the interaction of two or more organizations, substances, or other agents to produce a common effect greater than the sum of their individual effects. Two or more agents working together, therefore, can achieve something greater than the sum of its parts. Synergy usually arises when two or more people with unique yet complementary skills and abilities cooperate

22   COPD: Chronic obstructive pulmonary disease

23   PTSD: Post-traumatic stress disorder

24   For a quick look at some of this theory, see http://semantics.uchicago.edu/kennedy/classes/sum07/myths/myths4-gender.pdf

25   Falcon, Rafael and Christine (June 2, 2014). Electronic correspondence with author.

26   For more military jargon about the progression of military situational indicators, see http://www.urbandictionary.com/define.php?term=SNAFU

27   See http://dictionary.reference.com/browse/rootlet

28   See https://www.google.com/webhp?sourceid=chrome-instant&rlz=1C1LENN_enUS458US458&ion=1&espv=2&ie=UTF-8#q=define%20taproot

29   See http://www.cropsreview.com/plant-root-system.html

Second Letter
The Writer's Voice and Patriarchy

30   President's Task Force on Crime. See https://www.ncjrs.gov/ovc_archives/reports/impact/welcome.html

31   This issue surfaces I think whenever a woman is the first woman to break the cultural sexist barrier, commonly called the glass ceiling, for example, the first woman admitted to a college of medicine or the first woman executive of a Fortune 500 company, the first woman member of Congress or the first woman president of an Ivy League University. For these women to be successful, they must navigate strong cross-current streams which include the omnipresent cultural beliefs that (1) they are somehow unnatural or unfeminine women; (2) they can't possibly succeed; (3) they must speak the dominant language of their culture; and (4) they must avoid introducing irrelevant issues such as women's concerns into their professional work. In my observations and life experience, such women have needed strong male mentors and supportive male colleagues in their life history – men who believed in their work, men who protected them while they learned their skills, and most importantly, men who did not insist upon sexual access as the price of their mentoring and friendship. Some early studies of these ground-breaking women indicated that many had a strong and mentoring father or father-figure in early childhood and adolescence, a male parent or parent-like-figure who both protected them from harm and who was an active part of their daily experience of respectful parenting. Whenever I read this research, I think of one woman I knew in my mid-forties. She was the no-nonsense chair of a prestigious academic clinical sciences program. Her father was in the construction business and from early childhood into late adolescence, he took her up on the roof with him and taught her construction skills. She never became a contractor, but she did absorb the more subtle lessons of competency, personal mastery, leadership, self-confidence, etc. I learned about the important role her father played in her life's development one summer when she decided to re-roof her home. She not only knew how to do this work, she did it efficiently, with gusto, self-confidence, and pride in her work.

32   Del Martin and Phyllis Lyons, San Francisco, were journalists, community organizers, and lecturers on these topics before most straight women acknowledged these forms of violence were problems inside the feminist community of women. For more information about Martin and Lyons, see http://en.wikipedia.org/wiki/Del_Martin_and_Phyllis_Lyon.

33   World Health Organization (2002a). World Report on Violence and Health. Geneva, Switzerland; World Health Organization (2002b). Summary: World Report on Violence and Health. Geneva, Switzerland.

34   WHO Summary Report, p. 1.

35   Doyle, T. P. (October 19, 2014). Address to New Perspectives in Faith (College Mennonite Church, Goshen, IN). The Once, Now, and Future Church.
      Retrieve from http://www.newperspectivesgoshen.org/pages/wp-content/uploads/TomDoyle-Part1.mp3

36   http://en.wikipedia.org/wiki/H%C3%A9lder_C%C3%A2mara

37   Another young Mennonite woman has entered this greater Mennonite conversation about the absence of concern for the victims' voices. See her blog, http://survivorsawakenthechurch.com/2014/08/22/theology-schmeology-what-about-christianity/

38   Hallie, P. (1997). In the Eye of the Hurricane: Tales of good and evil; help and harm. Middletown, CT: Wesleyan University Press. Hallie writes: The victimizer does not feel the blows, the victim feels them. Do not ask the sword about wounds, look to the person on whose flesh the sword falls. Victimizers can be blinded by simple insensitivity, by a great cause, by a great hatred, or by a hundred self-serving "reasons." Victims too can be desensitized but usually they are the best witnesses to their pain. They feel it in their flesh and their deepest humiliations and horrors (p. 71). Somewhat later he reminds his readers: The points of view of victims and beneficiaries [to other's helpfulness] are vital to an understanding evil and good (ibid.).

39   Krehbiel, S. (February 11, 2014). The Woody Allen Problem: How do we read pacifist theologian (and sexual abuser) John Howard Yoder? Retrieve from http://www.religiondispatches.org/archive/culture/7544/the_woody_allen_problem__how_do_we_read_pacifist_theologian__and_sexual_abuser__john_howard_yoder/

40   See Waltner Gossen, R. (January 5, 2015). Peaceful Theology: Violent Acts; Abuse of Women by Mennonite's Leading Theologian Had Far-reaching Consequences; Institutions Slow Response Allowed Harm to Continue. Mennonite World Review online. Retrieve from
      http://mennoworld.org/2015/01/05/peaceful-theology-violent-acts/; See also Waltner Gossen (August 6, 2016). Women's Bodies, Sexual Ethics: Women Challenge John Howard Yoder.. Our Stories Untold. Retrieve from http://www.ourstoriesuntold.com/mennonite-bodies-sexual-ethics-women-challenge-john-howard-yoder/
      See also Waltner Gossen, R. (January 5, 2015). The Failure to Bind and Loose: Responses to Yoder's Sexual Abuse. Our Stories Untold. Retrieve from http://www.ourstoriesuntold.com/2015/01/05/the-failure-to-bind-and-loose-responses-to-yoders-sexual-abuse/

41   For further documentation about Yoder's sexual misbehaviors and vio-
      lence against women, see Waltner Gossen, R. January 2, 2015). Defanging
      the Beast: Mennonite Responses to John Howard Yoder's Sexual Abuse (pp.
      7-80). Mennonite Quarterly Review 89 (1)

42   Schrag, P. (March 23, 1992). Bethel cancels invitation to Yoder after receiv-
      ing protest letters. Mennonite Reporter.

43   Signed Statement of Eight Women (1992). Presented to Mennonite Church
      denominational institution executives at Prairie Street Mennonite Church
      in Elkhart, IN.

44   See the Twelfth Letter (pp. 155-173) for a submitted essay to the editor of one
      of the Mennonite Church's official publications. Doing a word play game,
      the anonymous author defamed women who were known to have pre-
      sented allegations to the church about John Howard Yoder's sexual miscon-
      duct by naming them alligators. To its credit, the Mennonite Church press
      never published this essay.

45   See Darla Shumm's master's thesis (1992). Nonviolence Reconsidered:
      Mennonites, patriarchy and violence, Berkeley, CA: Pacific School of
      Religion. See Carol Penner's doctoral dissertation (2000). Mennonite
      Silences and Feminist Voices: Mennonite peace theology and violence
      against women. Toronto, ON: University of St. Michael's College.

46   For information about this service see; (1) https://www.ambs.edu/
      news-events/documents/March22-Afternoon.pdf; (2) https://www.
      ambs.edu/news-events/documents/March22-Apology-and-Confession_
      SaraWengerShenk.pdf (3) https://www.youtube.com/watch?v=MBmtzylxX-
      M; (4) Richard Kauffman opinion piece, http://mennoworld.org/2015/03/02/
      opinion/opinion-mistakes-regrets-lessons/; (5) Michelle Sokoll/The
      Elkhart Truth http://mennoworld.org/2015/03/02/opinion/opinion-mis-
      takes-regrets-lessons/; (6) Rich Preheim/The Mennonite http://menno-
      world.org/2015/03/02/opinion/opinion-mistakes-regrets-lessons/; (7) Rich
      Preheim/Mennonite World Review http://mennoworld.org/2015/03/02/
      opinion/opinion-mistakes-regrets-lessons/

47   See Peter Dula (2014). Psychology, Ecclesiology and Yoder's Violence in
      Mennonite Life # 68. Retrieve from http://archive.bethelks.edu/ml/issue/
      vol-68/article/psychology-ecclesiology-and-yoders-violence/.

48   As I wrote this letter in the late summer of 2014, a multiple author article
      was published in the August 4, 2014 edition of Christian Century Magazine:
      Cramer, D., Howell, J., Martens, P. and Tran, J. Theology and Misconduct:
      the Case of John Howard Yoder. Christian Century Online 13 (17). Retrieve
      from http://www.christiancentury.org/article/2014-07/theology-and-mis-
      conduct. See also Cramer, D. Howell, J. Martens, P. and Tran, J. (July 7, 2014).
      Scandalizing Yoder. The Other Journal.com; An Intersection of Theology

and Culture. Retrieve from · http://theotherjournal.com/2014/07/07/scan-dalizing-john-howard-yoder/

49   Nation, M. T. with Marva Dawn. (September 23, 2013). On Contextualizing Two Failures of John Howard Yoder. EMU Anabaptist Nation. Retrieve from http://emu.edu/now/anabaptist-nation/2013/09/23/on-contextualiz-ing-two-failures-of-john-howard-yoder/

50   For an example of this principle in action see Melinda Berry's (2014) essay Avoiding Avoidance: Why I Assigned Body Politics this Spring, in Mennonite Life, # 68, Retrieve from http://archive.bethelks.edu/ml/issue/vol-68/article/avoiding-avoidance-why-i-assigned-body-politics-th/

51   1 in 5 women and 1 in 71 men in the United States have been raped at some time in their lives; 1 in 2 women and 1 in 5 men have experienced other forms of sexual violence victimization in their lifetime (e.g. made to pen-etrate someone, sexual coercion, unwanted sexual contact and sexual ex-periences). Victimization often occurs for the first time before the age of 25 (42% of female victims report being raped before the age of 18 and 37% report being raped between the ages of 18 and 25). United States: Center for Disease Control and Prevention.

52   PJCS: Short-hand for Peace, Justice and Conflict Studies.

53   One strong temptation (for the first woman who does this or does that inside the academic world) is to see herself as somehow ontologically, even narcissistically, unique and special. Another temptation is to become more male-identified than the genetic males with whom she competes. I have long been convinced that both of these solutions for women are patriarchal traps. The solution to this problem, in my opinion, is to make a personal commitment to get the door open as wide as possible and as soon as pos-sible so that other women can enter professions and jobs where they have been excluded solely because of their gender. This means mentoring and actively helping other women so that they too can succeed inside the male establishment. It means working to change the ground rules which are used to exclude any person from any culturally-despised minority. Only this en-during and life-long commitment makes a real change in patriarchal cul-tures. Male-identification and its concomitant female gender self-hate or self-disdain by women, are therefore, traps for every professional woman in the male-identified Academy. When American medicine, for example, began to be pressured by American feminists to admit more women to medical schools across the nation, the first quotas were that no more than 10% or 33% of a class could be women. As these pioneering women entered the medical academy and then began to practice medicine, it soon became evident that more and more extremely well-qualified women were apply-ing to medical schools for admission. I am certain that some schools still

have informal quotas to maintain a male-female ratio but most schools abandoned this formal quota system by the end of the 20th century. Women physicians are now accepted as equal in competence to male physicians in most of the medical sub-specialties. No longer is a woman physician limited to women's health, obstetrics, gynecology, family practice, or pediatrics as her choice of a specialty. What is perhaps of even greater importance as a marker of social change is that male and female patients now utilize and are satisfied with the services offered by both male and female physicians.

54   For two examples of previously untold stories, see (1) Anonymous Mennobitch (March 28, 2015). An Open Letter to AMBS re: the service of lament. Our Stories Untold. Retrieve from http://www.ourstoriesuntold.com/open-letter-re-ambs-service-lament/; (2) Detweiler, S. (January 9, 2015). John Howard Yoder: My Untold Story after 36 years of silence. Retrieve from http://www.ourstoriesuntold.com/stories/john-howard-yoder-my-untold-story-after-36-years-of-silence-by-sharon-detweiler/

55   In using the word integrity, I include its nuances of meaning: honest and morally upright; decency; fairness; truthfulness; moral uprightness; trustworthiness.

56   See http://www.brainyquote.com/quotes/authors/e/elie_wiesel.html

57   For a conversation about this issue of particularity and inclusiveness see the 1979 correspondence between American poet Audre Lorde and American, Roman Catholic theologian and philosopher Mary Daly. Retrieve from
       http://www.historyisaweapon.com/defcon1/lordeopenlettertomarydaly.html

58   We rarely think about religious or spiritual extortion as a factor in denominational decisions. However, when some individuals or groups of individuals, with access to denominational authority, controlling power and money, threaten: If this game of power and control does not yield me as the absolute and clear winner, I am taking my marbles and going home, this threat functions as a piety-disguised form of extortion. Congregational threats to exit the denomination if decisions are not made one-way most certainly function that way in the administrative decisions of today's Mennonite Church vis-à-vis members of disdained minorities who seek to be heard; who seek to be included in the decisions about community membership and religious or spiritual life that affect them. The denominational power to excommunicate and to exclude others from our human presence is rarely, perhaps never, a spiritually mature power. When decisions to exclude others are implemented, these decisions reveal more about the spiritual and psychological immaturity of the person(s) or institutions doing the excluding than they do about the spiritual wholeness of those who are being excluded.

59   In 1992, Pope John Paul the Second reversed the church's teaching about Galileo's heresy and admitted that Galileo had been correct. Since then a statue of Galileo has been installed inside the Vatican's inner courtyard. One wonders when Teilhard de Chardin (1891-1995) and his work will be similarly vindicated. One wonders if the contemporary work of Leonardo Boff, Mary Daly, Tom Doyle, Matthew Fox, Hans Kung, or Elizabeth Johnson will ever be reclaimed by the future Catholic Church. How many centuries will it take before the contemporary contributions of these individuals to their communal life of faith can and will be acknowledged?

60   See (a) Burgess, A. W. and Holmstrom, L. L. (1979). Adaptive Strategies in Recovery from Rape (pp. 1278-1282). American Journal of Psychiatry (136); (b) Burgess, A. W. and Holmstrom, L. L. (1974). Rape: Victims of Crisis. Brandy Games Publishing; (c) Holmstrom, L. L. and Burgess, A. W. (1983). The Victim of Rape: Institutional Reactions. Los Angeles, CA: Transaction Publishing; (d) Koss, M. and Oros, C. J. (1982). Sexual Experiences Survey: A Research Instrument Investigating Sexual Aggression and Victimization (pp. 645-654). Journal of Consulting and Clinical Psychology 50 (3); (e) Russell, D. E. H. (1984). The Politics of Rape. New York, NY: Stein and Day; and (f) Warshaw, R. (1984). I Never Called it Rape. New York, NY: Harper and Row.

61   For a good clinical discussion of the need for trauma victims to re-create accurate historical narratives about the violence which they have experienced, see Mendelsohn, M., Herman, J. L., Schatzoa, E., Coco, M., Kallivayalii, D., and Levitan, J. (2011). The Trauma Recovery Group: A Guide for Practitioners. New York, NY: Guilford Press.

62   Two powerful personal narratives can illustrate this. One is Katz, J. H. (1984). No Fairy Godmothers, No Magic Wands: The healing process after rape. Saratoga, CA: R & E Publishers. The second is Krapf, N. (2014). Catholic Boy Blues: A poet's journey of healing. Nashville, TN: Greystone Publishing.

63   See Von Bragt, T. (1660). The Martyr's Mirror (The Bloody Theater). Contemporary Herald Press Print and Kindle editions are both available on-line.

64   The word patriarchy comes from the Greek word patriarckhes and literally translated it means the rule of the fathers. For a useful definition of the multiple ways that this word has been used historically and currently, see Wikipedia online: http://en.wikipedia.org/wiki/Patriarchy. I am using the term patriarchy to describe the organization of human cultures and social systems in which men are in positions of authority and power while women and children are located in positions of subordination to men. According to Starhawk (1981), the organization of patriarchal cultures is organized in a pyramidal model with relatively few individuals in social positions

of power-over. See Starhawk Truth or Dare: Encounters with power, authority and mystery. San Francisco, CA: Harper and Row. Today's Roman Catholic Church provides us with a good model of a patriarchal organization. The male pope heads a world-wide religious organization led by other men. Other Christian Churches are more or less equivalently patriarchal. In recent generations we have seen some churches in the worldwide Christian movement begin to abandon the patriarchy as a God-given model for organizing human cultures and institutions. However, the presence of a woman leader (such as the United Kingdom's Queen Elizabeth the Second or former United Sates Secretary of State Hillary Clinton) – in positions of genuine leadership and social power do not necessarily provide examples of a non-patriarchal commons.

Third Letter
Speaking Truth about Sexual Violence

65   Jordan, M. D. (2003). Telling Truths in Church: Scandal, Flesh and Christian Speech. Boston, MA: Beacon, p. 35.

66   Krehbiel, S. (July 24, 2014). Naming Violation: Sexualized Violence and LBGTQ Justice. Our Stories Untold. Retrieve from http://www.ourstoriesuntold.com/tag/stephanie-krehbiel/; Krehbiel, S. (March 20, 2014). Why Heterosexism and Sexualized Violence Are Linked, Part One. Our Stories Untold. Retrieve from http://www.ourstoriesuntold.com/2014/03/20/why-heterosexism-and-sexualized-violence-are-linked-part-i/; Krehbiel, S. (March 21, 2014). Why Heterosexism and Sexualized Violence Are Linked, Part Two. Our Stories Untold. Retrieve from http://www.ourstoriesuntold.com/category/free/our-stories-untold-blog/

67   http://bilgrimage.blogspot.com/

68   Krall, R. E. (1990). Rape's Power to Dismember Women's Lives: Personal realities and cultural forms. Claremont, CA: Southern California School of Theology at Claremont. See also Krall, R. E. 1992). Christian Ideology, Rape and Women's Post-rape Journeys (pp. 76-92) in Yoder, E. G. (Ed.). Occasional Papers # 16: Peace Theology and Violence against Women, Elkhart, IN: AMBS/Institute of Mennonite Studies.

69   I have been deeply influenced by the radical voice of lesbian women inside the second wave of American feminism. For example: Daly, M. (1978). Gyn/Ecology. Boston, MA: Beacon; Lorde, A. (2007). Sister Outsider: Essays and speeches. Crossing Press Feminist Series; Rich, A. (1995). On Lies, Secrets and Silence: Selected prose, 1966-1978. New York, NY. W. W. Norton.

70   A meme can be defined as an element of culture or an organized system of behavior which is transmitted from one individual to another by non-genetic means – usually, therefore, by rites of cultural initiation.

71   Jordan, M. D., op.cit.

72   Boston Globe Investigative Staff. (2002). Betrayal: The crisis in the Catholic Church. Boston, MA: Little, Brown and Co. See also Breslin, J. (20-04). The Church that Forgot Christ, New York, NY: Free Press. See also, the 2016 Academy Award winner, the movie, Spotlight.

73   Jordan, op cit, p. 6

74   Jordon, Ibid, p. 1

75   Ibid, p. 5

76   Ibid, p. 6

77   Ibid.

78   Ibid, p.7

79   Ibid.

80   Ibid, p. 8

81   Ibid.

82   Ibid.

83   Ibid, (p. 9)

84   Ibid.

85   Schirch, L. (March 23, 2015). Toward Mennonite Sexual Integrity. Mennonite World Review, (pp. 311-313 in this book). Retrieve essay from http://mennoworld.org/2015/03/23/the-world-together/toward-mennonite-sexual-integrity/

86   See Dr. Schirch's Afterword in this book as Letter # 20, p. 296 ff.

87   Jordan, op.cit, p.11

88   Ibid.

89   Ibid. p. 12

90   Ibid.

91   Ibid.

92   Krall, R. E. (1992). op.cit; Krall, R. E. (1990), op. cit.

93   Psalm 139:13

94   Schirch, L. op. cit.

95   Schirch, ibid (pp. 1-2)

96   Ibid, p. 2

97   Jordan, op.cit, p.12

98   Ibid, p. 13

99   Ibid.

100   Ibid.

101   Ibid.

102   Ibid, p. 14

103   Ibid, p. 15

104   Ibid, p. 16

105   Ibid, pp. 16-17

106   Ibid, p. 17

107   Ibid, p. 18

108   Ibid, p. 19

109   Jordan references Christian ethicist Beverly Harrison's essay, "The Power of Anger in the Work of Love" in Harrison, B. (1986). Making the Connections: Essays in Feminist Social Ethics. Boston, MA: Beacon Press.

110   Jordan, op.cit, pp. 19-20

111   Ibid, pp. 20-21

112   Ibid, p. 22

113   Ibid.

114   Ibid, p. 24

115   Ibid, pp. 24-25

116   Ibid, p. 26

117   Here Jordan is referencing a body of work by Simone Weil

118   Doyle, T. P. (October 19, 2014). Address to New Perspectives in Faith, College Mennonite Church, Goshen, IN: The Once, Now, and Future Church. Retrieve from http://www.newperspectivesgoshen.org/pages/2014/11/09/audio-thomas-doyle-october-19-2014/

119   Doyle, ibid.

120   Lindsey, W. (November 5, 2014). Electronic correspondence with author.

121   Ibid.

122   Doyle, T. P., Sipe, A. W. R., and Wall, P. J. (2006). Sex, Priests and Secret Codes: The Catholic Church's 2000-year Paper Trail of Sexual Abuse, Los Angeles, CA: Volt.

123   Doyle, October 19, 2014, op. cit.

124   Jordan, Op. cit., pp. 34-35

125   Ibid., p. 35

126   Two documentaries by Etoile Productions, Susa A. and John J. Michalczyk, Producers, Boston, MA explore ongoing issues in the lives of sexual abuse survivors and their helpers or advocates. These are: Who Takes Away the Sins: Witnesses to Clergy Abuse (2013) and A Matter of Conscience: Confronting Clergy Abuse (2015).

127   Doyle, op. cit.

Ruth E. Krall

Fourth Letter
Living in the Hurricane's Eye, Part One

128   Kornfield, J. (2002). The Art of Forgiveness, Lovingkindness, and Peace. New York, NY: Bantam, p. 141.

129   Moyers, B. (1988). Facing Evil: A PBS Documentary. (Filmed at the Chicago School for the Humanities Lectures held at Saledo, Texas). Retrieve information http://www.shoppbs.org/product/index.jsp?productId=11252196

130   To hear Angelou recite this poem, retrieve from https://www.poeticous. com/maya-angelou/the-mask-1?locale=en or from
http://billmoyers.com/episode/full-show-maya-angelou-on-facing-evil/

131   A recent (2013) film, Twelve Years a Slave, serves as a contemporary reminder of slavery's brutality for those who were enslaved.

132   For comparative racial statistics on incarceration, see the NAACP fact sheet at http://www.naacp.org/pages/criminal-justice-fact-sheet

133   The United States has had a series of racially-inflamed murders. One happened on Wednesday, June 17, 2015 in Charlestown, South Carolina when a man armed with a gun attacked members of a prayer meeting at Emmanuel AME Church. On Friday, June 19, 2015 family members of those who were murdered addressed the judge and the murderer. See http://www.nytimes. com/2015/06/20/us/charleston-shooting-dylann-storm-roof.html?_r=0

134   For Freeman's comments, see http://marquee.blogs.cnn.com/2013/10/24/ why-morgan-freeman-wont-be-seeing-12-years-a-slave/

135   Haillie, P. (19970. In the Eye of the Hurricane: Tales of Good and Evil, Help and Harm. Middletown, CT: Wesleyan University Press, p. 3.

136   Elie Wiesel quoted in Frawley-O'Dea (February 23, 2012). Perversion of Power: When Mourning Never Comes. Naples, FL: Address to Voice of the Faithful. Retrieve by typing in the full title of her address on a search engine. This is needed because some URL addresses do not seem to work for retrieval.

137   Henry, G. (undated) The Life and Work of Wiesel: Story and Silence: Transcendence in the work of Elie Wiesel. Retrieve from http://www.pbs. org/eliewiesel/life/henry.html

138   Ibid.

139   Frawley-O'Dea, M. G., op. cit.

140   For a daily update on clergy sexual abuse allegations and trials worldwide, see http://www.bishop-accountability.org/AbuseTracker/

141   Frawley-O'Dea, p. 1.

142   Ibid, pp. 3-4.

143   Cathexis is defined as the concentration of emotional energy on one particular person, object, or idea. In depth psychology this is used in clinical

diagnoses to refer to an unhealthy degree of focused energy. We may casually talk about this as an unrealistic or obsessive preoccupation with a person or with an idea.

144   Frawley-O'Dea, op. cit, p. 9.

145   Ibid, p. 10.

146   For a good description and discussion of betrayal trauma, the reader is referred to Freyd, J. J. (1996). Betrayal Trauma: The legacy of forgetting childhood abuse. Cambridge, MA: Harvard University Press.

147   Frawley-O'Dea, op. cit. p. 3.

148   Ibid, p. 6.

149   Ibid.

150   Ibid.

151   Ibid, p. 5.

152   Ibid, pp. 18-19

153   Herman, J. L. (1997). Trauma and Recovery: the aftermath of violence-from domestic abuse to political terror. New York, NY: Basic Books.

154   Herman, J. L. (1997). Trauma and Recovery: the aftermath of violence from domestic abuse to political terror. New York, NY: Basic Books. See also Kreisler, H. (September 21, 2000). The Case of Trauma and Recovery: Conversations with Judith Herman, M. D. Berkeley, CA. Institute of International Studies of the University of California at Berkeley. This is an interview in four parts and each part can be retrieved from the worldwide web.

- Part One: Background - Retrieve from: http://globetrotter.berkeley.edu/people/Herman/herman-con1.html
- Part Two: Seeing Face to Face – Retrieve from http://globetrotter.berkeley.edu/people/Herman/herman-con2.html
- Part Three: Post-traumatic Stress Disorder – Retrieve from
- http://globetrotter.berkeley.edu/people/Herman/herman-con3.html \
- Part Four: Lessons Learned – Retrieve from http://globetrotter.berkeley.edu/people/Herman/herman-con4.html

155   Eastern Mennonite University, Harrisonburg, VA

156   Schirch, L. (June 29, 2014) Electronic Correspondence

157   Hallie, P. (1994). Lest Innocent Blood Be Shed: The Story of the village of Le Chambon and how goodness happened there. New York, NY: Harper Perennial.

158   Retrieve information about Nhat Han's role during the Vietnamese-American War from Wikipedia: https://en.wikipedia.org/wiki/Th%C3%ADch_Nh%E1%BA%A5t_H%E1%BA%A1nh

159   For information, see http://www.womeninworldhistory.com/contemporary-07.html

160   Kiser, J. (2003). The Monks of Tiburine: Faith, Love and Terror in Algeria. New York, NY: St. Martins/Griffin

161   Allen, J. (2008). Desmond Tutu: Rabble-Rouser for Peace. Chicago, IL: Chicago Review Press.

162   Meyerding, J. (1984). We Are All Part of One Another: A Barbara Deming Reader, Philadelphia, PA: New Society.

163   Esquivel, J. (1982). (1994). Threatened with Resurrection: Prayers and poems from an exiled Guatemalan. Elgin, IL: Brethren Press.

164   Forest, J. (1991). Living with Wisdom: A Life of Thomas Merton, Maryknoll, NY: Orbis.

165   For information about Hamer, see http://www.biography.com/people/fannie-lou-hamer-205625

166   McCoy, J. A. (2015). A Still and Quiet Conscience: The Archbishop who challenged a pope, a president and a church. Maryknoll, NY: Orbis

167   To see Bishop Gumbleton's farewell to his congregation, see http://www.metrotelvc.com/gumbleton/videos.php; to read his National Catholic Reporter Peace Pulpit Column, see http://ncronline.org/search/site/BHishop%20Gumbleton

168   For information about Dr. King, see http://www.thekingcenter.org/about-dr-king

169   Thomas, C. A. (2004). At Hell's Gate: A soldier's journey from war to peace. Boston, MA: Shambala. See also Glassman, B. (2013). Bearing Witness: A Zen Master's lessons in making peace. New York, NY: Blue Rider Press/Penguin/Random House.

170   For more about Blaine's work and story, see http://ncronline.org/news/accountability/thanks-ncr-my-crisis-became-cause

171   Kaiser, R. (2015). Whistle: Tom Doyle's Steadfast Witness for Victims of Clerical Sexual Abuse. Thiensville, WI: Caritas.

172   There is a new (2014) documentary in which Roman Catholic whistleblowers discuss the pathway they took to becoming activists It provides us with a very good discussion of resistance by lay, ordained and religious whistleblowers inside the Roman Catholic Church, see A Matter of Conscience: Confronting Clergy Abuse (2013) produced by Susan A. and John J. Michalczyk. Boston, MA: Etoile Productions.

173   2014, Ibid. In this documentary, a wide variety of whistleblowers and activist discuss the moments of discovery in their lives and their subsequent actions in light of what they learned about sexually abusive clergy inside the Roman Catholic Church. They talk candidly about denominational push-backs.

174   For a Christian discussion of the "powers" see this series of books by Walter Wink

1) Wink, W. (1992). Engaging the Powers: Discernment and resistance in a world of domination. Minneapolis, MN: Fortress;

2) Wink, W. (1984). Naming the Powers: The language of power in the New

3) Testament. Philadelphia, PA: Fortress.

4) Wink, W. (1988). The Powers that Be: Theology for a new millennium. New York, NY: Doubleday.

5) Wink, W. (1985). Unmasking the Powers: The invisible forces that

6) determine human existence. Philadelphia, PA: Fortress.

175   Krall, R. E. (2014). The Elephants in God's Living Room, Volume Four, Bearing the Unbearable: A collection of essays. Enduring Space Publications. See www.ruthkrall.com

176   Hallie, P. (1997). Frontispiece (p. vi). In the Eye of the Hurricane: Tales of good and evil, help, and harm. Middleton, CT: Wesleyan University Press.

177   Hallie, P. (1994). Lest Innocent Blood Be Shed: The story of the village of Le Chambon and how goodness happened there. New York, NY: Harper Perennial.

178   Hammerstein, O. (1958). Lyrics for the musical South Pacific were composed by Richard Rodgers. For the complete lyrics to the song "You've got to be carefully taught," see http://www.stlyrics.com/lyrics/southpacific/youvegottobecarefullytaught.htm

179   For an excellent discussion of enemy-making, see Keen, S. (2006). Faces of the Enemy: Three Slide Lectures, San Rafael, CA: Sam Keen Productions. See also Keen, S. (1991). Faces of the Enemy: Reflections of the hostile imagination. New York, NY: Harper and Row.

180   For a discussion of crucifixion imagery that is pertinent to these paragraphs see Carroll, J. (2001). Constantine's Sword. Boston, MA: Houghton Mifflin.

181   Lanzmann, C. (1985). Shoah, Parts one, two, three, four, and five. For more information, see http://en.wikipedia.org/wiki/Shoah_%28film%29

182   Many months after this chapter was completed, I purchased Bernie Glassman's 1998 book, Bearing Witness: A Zen Masters' Lessons in Making Peace. New York, NY: Bell Tower. It begins at the gates of Auschwitz-Bierkenau and is a reflection of collective responsibility. I highly recommend this set of reflections by a Jewish Zen Master.

183   Carroll, J. (2001). Constantine's Sword. Boston, MA: Houghton Mifflin. See also Oren Jacoby, (September 16, 2008). Director, Constantine's Sword: No War is Holy. DVD/First Run Features.

184   Brock, R. N. and Parker, R. (2009). Saving Paradise: How Christianity Traded Love of this World for Crucifixion and Empire. Boston, MA: Beacon Press.

185   Cohan, S. (2001). States of Denial: Knowing about Suffering and Atrocities. Cambridge, UK: Polity.

186   Hallie, (1997), op. cit. p. 48

187   Kornfield, J. (2002). The Art of Forgiveness, Lovingkindness, and Peace. New York, NY: Bantam: To make peace we cannot ignore war, racism, violence, greed, the injustice and suffering of the world. They must be confronted with courage and compassion. Unless we seek justice, peace will fail. Yet in whatever we do we must not let war, violence, and fear take over our own heart p. 141.

Sixth Letter
Living in the Eye of the Hurricane, Part Three

188   Nepo, M. (2000). The Book of Awakening: Having the life you want by being present to the life you have. Berkeley, CA: Conari Press, pp. 155-156.

Seventh Letter
Living in the Hurricane's Eye, Part Four

189   Meyers, R. (2015). Spiritual Defiance: Building a Beloved Community of Resistance. New Haven, CT: Yale University Press, p. 42. Emphasis in the words quoted is his.

190   Ibid, pp. 42-4 3. Meyers highlights various dictionary definitions for the word resistance: to withstand, to oppose, to work against; to refuse to cooperate with; to argue or work against; to keep from yielding; to keep from being affected by. He repeats Camus' warning that resistance is not revolution and that we should be wary of joining revolutions because they substitute one ideology for another.

191   Wink, W. (1992). Engaging the Powers: Discernment and resistance in a world of domination. Minneapolis, MN: Fortress.

192   Jeremiah 20:9 (ESV). Reading Jeremiah 20 is to find the prophet in deep spiritual and emotional pain at the work he feels he must do. He curses his birth and the day he was born. Then in Jeremiah 21, without apology he delivers his message of the destruction which awaits the city because of its moral decay, its economic corruption and its idolatries.

193   Ezekiel 34: 1-3; 10 (NIV).

194   When Mennonites identify themselves as a plain people they are talking about religious dress and an appearance that immediately identifies them as cultural outsiders in much the same way a nun's habit does.

195   Clericalism: An institutional clergy structure and practice that protects the clergy and church institutions at the expense of the laity.

196   Mathew 18:20: For where two or three of you gather in my name, I am there in their midst.

197   Gossen, R. W. (2015). (January 2, 2014). Defanging the Beast: Mennonite Responses to John Howard Yoder's Sexual Abuse. Mennonite Quarterly Review (89).

198   Global Anabaptist Mennonite Encyclopedia Online. Retrieve from http://gameo.org/index.php?title=Denck,_Hans_%28ca._1500-1527%29

199   Fox, M. (2011). Christian Mystics: 365 Readings and Meditations. Novato, CA: New World Library; Fox, M. (2003). Digital Recording: Radical Prayer: Love in Action. Boulder, CO: Sounds True; Fox, M. (2004). One River, Many Wells. Los Angeles, CA: Jeremy Tarcher; Fox, M. (2016). A Way to God: Thomas Merton's Creation Spirituality Journey. Novato, CA: New World Books.

200   Smith, H. (2010). Tales of Wonder: Chasing the Divine: An Autobiography. New York, NY: HarperOne

201   In proximity to my biological father's death in 1963, in an example of mystical reading, I found Will Oursler's book about Fulton Oursler's death and the spiritual journey of doubt. In his meditations on his father's death and its meaning for an adult son, the book comforted me in ways I still have no words for. I carried that book with me everywhere and it has been read multiple times. Underlined in multiple colors from these many readings, it sits on my book shelf today. The book comforted my intense grief at my father's premature death and it gave me mytho-poetic language about the spiritual path of doubt as a valid one. Oursler, Will (1960). The Road to Faith. New York, NY: Holt, Rinehart and Winston

202   After my Claremont graduate school years as I continued to read, I discovered Buddhist spiritual teachers who also wrote about peace activism such as Thich Nhat Hanh and Jack Kornfield. I read about the activism of Gandhi through the lens of his personal Hindu spirituality. I read the sermons, lectures, and books of Martin Luther King, Jr., William Sloane Coffin, Paul Tillich and Frederick Buechner. I read the Berrigan Brothers. I read and re-read Mary Daly, Adrienne Rich, Carol Christ, Lauren Artress, Rita Nakashima Brock, Rebecca Parker, Angeles Arrien, Mary Catherine Bateson, Judith Plaskow, Muriel Rukeyser, Nelle Morton, Dorothee Soelle, Audre Lorde, and Starhawk. Feminist analysis and feminist thealogy continued to inform my female spirituality. In addition, I read and later met in a conference setting Paulo Friere. I read Gustavo Gutierrez and later heard him speak on a North American tour, I read black and womanist theology from North America; I read post-colonial theology from Africa. I read Latin

American theologians in a Roman Catholic voice and in a Protestant voice; in a male voice and in a female voice.

In some ways, perhaps, reading traditional and Métis Native American voices such as Anne Cameron, Brooke Medicine Eagle, Black Elk, Fools Crow, Sun Bear and Rolling Thunder provided the mystical core to the inner spirituality that was emerging. Amerindian spiritual understanding of the inter-penetration of all as oneness and of all as connectedness began to be my personal way of understanding the social world and its relationship to my inner world.

Mystical Christian teachings began to come alive again. Coming to understand that the medicine wheel teachings not only exist in the outer world but that they live in the inner world as well began to change me in ways that are very hard to describe. Later, when I met the Christian labyrinth traditions, it was easy for me to overlay them in my personal spiritual practice. Neither needed to exclude the other; both, in fact, enriched each other.

As a healer, I read and re-read the works of Rachel Naomi Remen. I read Carl Hammerschlag, Emmett E. Miller, Herbert Benson, Ken Pelletier, David Bressler, Judith Herman, Peter Levine, Andy Weil, James Gordon, Martin Rossman, Jeanne Achterberg, Frank Lawliss, Jean Shinoda Bolen, Bessel van der Kolk, and others in the emerging psycho-neuro-immunology movement; in the body-mind movement, and in the ongoing trauma research movement. I attended conferences and pursued certification programs. The clear overlap of body, soul, spirit and mind grew increasingly clear to me. While we could separate them intellectually, our experiences of them were of unity. Healing spirits and healing bodies were in some way or another correlated to one another. The person we are and the work we do in the world are also in some way or another correlated to each other. While wellness and wholeness are not exactly the same reality, they too are deeply correlated with each other. We can be ill and whole: that is a certainty. We will all die. That too is certain. But our spirit can be whole and well – even in moments of emotional despair and deep grief.

203 Meyers, R. (2013). The Third Lyman-Beecher Lecture, Yale University. Undone: Faith as Resistance to Empire. Retrieve from
     https://www.youtube.com/watch?v=6oPl4zp5ePE&index=6&list=PLbQl NmUy3n7Yzm9pO4gO1BnZFAr14j5Ng

204 Proverbs 23: 7 Paraphrase.

205 Luke 10:25-37 (NSRV).

206 For a contemporary exegesis and application of the gospels' teaching that the poor will always be with you, see the blogger Patheos. Retrieve   from   http://www.patheos.com/blogs/slacktivist/2014/12/10/

ignorant-christians-need-to-stfu-about-the-poor-you-will-always-have-with-you-until-they-can-be-bothered-to-understand-what-jesus-actually-said/

207   Matthew 20:16; Matthew 19:30; Mark 10: 31; Luke 13: 30

208   SNAP: The Survivors Network of those Abused by Priests. See www.snap-network.org

209   Road to Recovery; See http://www.road-to-recovery.org/

210   Catholic Whistleblowers. See http://www.catholicwhistleblowers.com/

211   Tutu, D. (2011). God is Not a Christian and other Provocations. New York, NY: Harper One.

212   Esquivel, J. (1982). (1994). Threatened with Resurrection: Prayers and Poems from an Exiled Guatemalan. Elgin, IL: Brethren Prcss.

213   Kaiser, R. B. (June, 2015). Whistle: Tom Doyle's Steadfast Witness for Victims of Clerical Sexual Abuse.

214   Thomas, C. A. (2004). At Hell's Gate: A soldier's journey from war to peace. Boston, MA: Shambala.

215   http://www.cpt.org/

216   http://www.pinkmenno.org/

217   http://peacewalktucson.org/

218   http://bilgrimage.blogspot.com/

219   Halder, R. (June 5, 2012). Our Stories Untold Blog. http://www.ourstoriesuntold.com/about/

220   Meyers, R. (2015). Spiritual Defiance: Building a Beloved Community of Resistance (The Yale Lyman-Beecher Lectures). New Haven, CT: Yale University Press.

221   Meyers, R. (2013). The Third Lyman-Beecher Lecture, Yale University. Undone: Faith as Resistance to Empire. Retrieve from
https://www.youtube.com/watch?v=6oPI4zp5ePE&index=6&list=PLbQl NmUy3n7Yzm9pO4gO1BnZFAr14j5Ng

Eighth Letter
Living in the Hurricane's Eye, Part Five

222   Kabat-Zinn, J. (2005). Wherever You Go, There You Are: Mindfulness Meditation in Everyday Life. New York, NY: Hatchette Books.

223   Roof, N. (1994). The Impact of War on Humanitarian Service Providers: A Workbook on Secondary Traumatic Stress and Burnout: Symptoms, Management, Prevention. Cambridge, MA: Harvard Medical School of Psychology and Social Change.

224 While the word blame can be used to demonstrate accountability as in I have myself to blame, it generally carries the linguistic nuance of judging, finding fault, criticizing, and censuring.

225 Miller, E. E. (1997). Deep Healing: The Essentials of Mind/Body Healing. Carlsbad, CA: Hay House.

226 https://www.youtube.com/watch?v=OSsPfbup0ac

227 Roof, N. (1994). The Impact of War on Humanitarian Service Providers: A Workbook on Secondary Traumatic Stress and Burnout: Symptoms, Management, Prevention. Cambridge, MA: Harvard Medical School of Psychology and Social Change.

228 Gugenbuhl-Craig, A. (1991). (J. R. Haule, Trans.). Power in the Helping Professions. Woodstock, CT: Spring Publications.

229 Meyers, R. (2015). Spiritual Defiance: Building a Beloved Community of Resistance. New Haven, CT: Yale University Press.

230 Herman, J. L. (1997). Trauma and Recovery: the aftermath of violence-from domestic abuse to political terror. New York, NY: Basic Books.

231 See also Conversations with History: Institute of International Studies, UC Berkeley (September 21, 2000). Interview with Judith Lewis Herman. Retrieve from www.globetrotter.berkeley.edu/people/herman/

232 LeShan, L. (1994). Cancer as a Turning Point: A Handbook for People with Cancer, their Families, and Health Professionals. New York, NY: Plume/ Penguin; Sounds True (2000). Cancer as a Turning Point: From Surviving to Thriving. Boulder, CO: Sounds True.

233 PJCS: Peace, Justice and Conflict Studies

234 See Krall, R. E. (Spring, 1996). Anger and an Anabaptist Feminist Hermeneutic (pp. 145-163), Conrad Grebel Review 14(2).

235 Erikson, E. H. (1969). Gandhi's Truth: On the Origins of Militant Nonviolence, New York, NY: W. W. Norton.

236 Matthew 23:27

237 For more information about Meyer's lecture, see, http://www.salon.com/2015/04/25/faith_must_fight_capitalism_forget_theological_purity_%E2%80%94_the_church_needs_a_revolutionary_spirit/; to listen to Meyers lecture, retrieve it from https://www.youtube.com/watch?v=60P14zp5ePE&index=6&list=PLbQINmUy3n7Yzm9pO4gO1BnZFAr14j5Ng

238 One of the common insider aphorisms which you and I have both heard and refer to is this: Mennonites gathered in communities such as the large colonies in Pennsylvania, Ohio, Virginia and Indiana (to mention just a few) reek like horse manure because of the way we Mennonite people inside these dense ethnic enclaves or faith communities treat other Mennonite people. In addition, also in play with this aphorism is an implicit commentary about the way Mennonites play the games of institutional power

politics. Mennonite friends of mine who comment on this aphorism often spontaneously remark that when Mennonites live outside the communal Mennonite setting, they often live good and decent lives of genuine service to others without the need to demonize their faith sisters and brothers in the pursuit of denominational political power. Unlike our faith contemporaries in the Roman Catholic tradition of spiritual, theological, and practical activism, we Anabaptist-Mennonites have not studied the toxic realities of institutional clericalism – that social virus of professional ministry and institutional management which seeks to protect the power and authority and control of the few over the lives of the many.

This failure to understand the corporate political nature of religious institutions needs to be addressed at multiple levels. In particular, I believe, our seminaries need to help young ministers in training to confront and then to grapple with their desire for control and power over other people – in the name of doing God's work in the world. This means, of course, that seminary faculty and church administrators must also struggle to understand this authoritarian shadow of religious life in their own individual lives and in their corporate lives as well.

Ninth Letter
Uncovering the Roots of Sexual Violence

239   For additional information about Dr. Schirch and her work see
http://www.emu.edu/personnel/people/show/schirchl

240   In his lecture to the New Perspectives in Faith Group at College Mennonite Church on October 19, 2014, Father Thomas Doyle reminded his audience that talking about sexual violence inside the community of Christian faith is scary. I think that is also a factor in the Mennonite Church's discomfort with my scholarship over the years. I have wanted to talk about things inside my community of faith that apparently nobody else wanted to talk about. To listen to Father Doyle's lecture, retrieve from
http://www.newperspectivesgoshen.org/pages/category/transcripts/

241   Here are some postings which I found to be quite useful to my own questioning about the relationships between these separate rootlets of the violence tree. For further discussions it will be useful to have easy access to these informed blog discussions led by Bill Lindsey, a gay male Roman Catholic theologian who grew up Baptist.

a)   May 31, 2014 there was a discussion of the cult of masculinity
http://bilgrimage.blogspot.com/2014/05/andrew-ohehir-on-how-elliot-rodger-is.html

b) June 2, 2014 there was a discussion of female objectification and gender discrimination
http://bilgrimage.blogspot.com/2014/06/rebecca-solnit-on-struggle-to-name.html

c) June 3, 2014 there was a discussion of men, guns, God and violence against women
http://bilgrimage.blogspot.com/2014/06/ta-nehisi-coatess-case-for-reparations.html#more

d) June 3, 2014 there was a discussion of racism and sexism and the media's talking heads' collective denial about the roots of misogyny
http://bilgrimage.blogspot.com/2014/06/ta-nehisi-coatess-case-for-reparations.html

e) June 6, 2014 there was a discussion of misogyny and gender/Maya Angelou's death
http://bilgrimage.blogspot.com/2014/06/end-of-week-news-roundup-venus-mars.html

f) June 7, 2014 there was a discussion of testosterone and the construction of male identity
http://bilgrimage.blogspot.com/2014/06/andrew-sullivan-et-al-on-testosterone.html

g) June 7, 2014 there was a discussion of the papal encyclical Humanae Vitae and women's subordination in Catholic theology
http://bilgrimage.blogspot.com/2014/06/patricia-miller-on-why-paul-vi-kept-ban.html

h) June 7, 2014 there was a discussion of the social construction of masculinity
http://bilgrimage.blogspot.com/2014/06/theres-doctor-em-steve-says-and-giftie.html#disqus_thread

i) June 10, 2014 there was a discussion of male identity, guns and homophobia
http://bilgrimage.blogspot.com/2014/06/testosterone-castration-american.html#disqus_thread

242 Brownmiller, S. (1975). Against Our Will: Men, women, and rape. New York, NY: Simon and Schuster; Davis, A. (1983). Women, Race and Class. New York, NY: Vintage Books; Lorentzen, L. A. and Turpin, J. Eds. (1998). The Women and War Reader. New York, NY: University Press.

243 Doyle, T., Sipe, A. W. R., and Wall, P. J. (2006). Sex, Priests and Secret Codes: The Catholic Church's 2000-year Paper Trail of Sexual Abuse, Los Angeles, CA: Volt.

244 Frawley-O'Dea, M. G. (February 23, 2012). Perversion of Power: When Mourning Never Comes. Naples, FL: A lecture to Voice of the Faithful, p.

12. Retrieve by typing in the full title of her address because some URL addresses do not seem to work.

245   Frawley-O'Dea, ibid, p. 12-13.

246   Ibid, p. 14.

247   For a theological-pastoral discussion of the issues raised by Frawley-O'Dea, see Meyers, R. (2015). Spiritual Defiance: Building a Beloved Community of Resistance, Chapter Four, Undone: Faith as Resistance to Empire, pp. 81-124. New Haven, CT: Yale University Press.

248   For commentary, see http://www.thecatholictelegraph.com/pope-francis-priests-should-be-shepherds-living-with-the-smell-of-the-sheep/13439

249   Thealogian Elisabeth Schussler Fiorenza coined the word kyriarchy to define a social system or an interlocking set of social systems built around domination, oppression and submission. The word is an intersectional extension of the patriarchy beyond gender. Inside the kyriarchy an individual might be privileged in some aspects of her or his life and oppressed in others.

250   For the prophet Ezekiel's commentary on corrupt shepherds and sheep, see Ezekiel 34.

251   Lerner, M. J. and Simons, C. H. (1958). Observers Reactions to the innocent Victim: Compassion or Rejection? Journal of Personality and Social Psychology 4(2), 203-210: Lerner, M. (1980). The Belief in a Just World: A fundamental delusion. Philadelphia, PA: Springer.

252   Love, B. J. and Cott, N. F. (2006). Feminists Who Changed the Face of America: 1963-1976. Chicago, IL: University of Illinois Press.

253   For a much more complete discussion of the emergence of the anti-rape and anti-domestic violence movement in the United States, see my 1990 dissertation. Krall, R. E. (1990). Rape's Power to Dismember Women's Lives: Personal realities and cultural forms. Claremont, CA: Southern California School of Theology at Claremont

254   Doyle, T. P. (October 19, 2014). The Once, Now, and Future Church. Goshen, IN: Lecture to New Perspectives on Faith, College Mennonite Church. Retrieve from http://www.newperspectivesgoshen.org/pages/category/transcripts/

255   Fortune, M. M. (1983a). Sexual Abuse Prevention. New York, NY: Pilgrim; Fortune, M. M. (1983b). Sexual Violence: The unmentionable sin, New York, NY: Pilgrim.

256   SNAP: Survivors Network of Those Abused by Priests. For more information see http://www.snapnetwork.org/

257   Road to Recovery. For more information, see http://www.road-to-recovery.org/

258   Catholic Whistleblowers, For more information see http://www.catholic-whistleblowers.com/

259 Labacqz, K and Barton, R. G. (1991). Sex in the Parish. Louisville, KY: Westminster/John Knox.

260 Our Stories Untold. For more information, see http://www.ourstoriesuntold.com/

261 Anabaptist-Mennonite Chapter of SNAP. For more information, see http://www.snapnetwork.org/mennonite

262 Mennonite Central Committee: We Will Speak Out. For more information, see http://mcc.org/learn/more/we-will-speak-out; See also http://www.wewillspeakout.org/pledge/

263 Robert Finn, Roman Catholic Bishop of the Kansas City-St. Joseph's Diocese, was convicted on October 14, 2011 of the misdemeanor crime of failure to report a priest suspected of child abuse; In Philadelphia, Monsignor William Linn, former Secretary for the Clergy in the Philadelphia Diocese, was convicted of child endangerment in June, 2012. On June 15, 2015, Archbishop Nienstedt's resignation and Auxiliary Bishop Piche's resignation were accepted by Pope Francis ten days after civil prosecutors in Minneapolis-St. Paul filed criminal charges against the archdiocese "for its failure to protect children."

264 For Protestant as well as Roman Catholic authors, see Frawley-O'Dea, M. G. and Goldner, Eds. (2007). Predatory Priests, Silenced Victims: The sexual abuse crisis and the Catholic Church. New York, NY: The Analytic Press.

265 For two very different approaches, see the following
a) The Presbyterian Church:
http://boz.religionnews.com/2014/06/20/denomination-confronts-child-sexual-abuse-positive-step-forward/
b) Conservative Fundamentalist-Evangelical Colleges
http://ringoffireradio.com/2014/06/why-are-christian-fundamentalist-universities-crucifying-rape-victims/

266 Blow, C. M. (June 1, 2014). Yes, All Men. International New York Times – The Opinion Pages. Retrieve from http://www.nytimes.com/2014/06/02/opinion/blow-yes-all-men.html?hp&rref=opinion&_r=0

267 For more information, see Krall, R. E. (2013). The Elephants in God's Living Room: Volume Three: The Mennonite Church and John Howard Yoder. Retrieve from Enduring Space at www.ruthkrall.com.

268 Frawley-O'Dea, op. cit. p 14.

269 For a discussion of the patriarchy and feminist consciousness, two books are particularly helpful. They are (1) Lerner, G. (1993a). The Creation of Feminist Consciousness. New York, NY: Oxford; (2) Lerner, G. (1993b). The Creation of Patriarchy. New York, NY: Oxford. In addition, three of Mary Daly's books address the patriarchal roots of violence. These are (1) Daly, M. (1973). Beyond God the Father. Boston, MA: Beacon; (2) Daly, M. (1968).

The Church and the Second Sex: With a new feminist post Christian introduction by the author. New York, NY: Harper Colophon; (3). Daly, M. (1978). Gyn/Ecology. Boston, MA: Beacon. Finally, an early book by Simone de Beauvoir is a useful addition as Western scholars have constructed a working knowledge of the patriarchy: de Beauvoir, S. (1974). The Second Sex. New York, NY: Vintage-Random House.

Tenth Letter
Encountering Social Nastiness Inside Church Doors

270   Mathew 10:16

271   For a discussion of anywhere but here as a prey-predator reality, see my chapter "Anywhere but here" (pp. 30-50) in Krall, R. E. (2014). The Elephants in God's Living Room, v.4, Bearing the Unbearable, A Collection of Conversational Essays.

272   For a discussion of Mennonite politics about lbgtq inclusion inside the boundaries of the Mennonite Church – USA, see Stephanie Krehbiel's doctoral dissertation. Krehbiel, S. (2015). Pacifist Battlegrounds: Violence, Community, and the Struggle for LBGTQ Justice in the Mennonite Church – USA. Lawrence, KS: University of Kansas.

273   (July 2015) Q/A Krehbiel on the LBGBTQ inclusion movement in MC USA. The Mennonite Online. Retrieve from https://themennonite.org/opinion/qa-krehbiel-on-the-lgbtq-inclusion-movement/

274   For further information about Pink Menno and its activism work at the Kansas City Mennonite Church 2015 House of Delegates meeting, see http://www.ourstoriesuntold.com/pink-menno-diversity/

275   On Thanksgiving Day, 2014, the troubling news from and about racial tensions in Ferguson, MO is sobering to any concerned citizen who cares about full equality for every individual citizen and for every peace-maker who cares about social justice for the most oppressed members of our society. See http://www.cbsnews.com/ferguson-missouri-police-shooting-protests/. Violence erupted in Baltimore, MD. Charlestown, SC followed soon followed.

276   As I write this in August, 2016, Clinton has just been confirmed as the Democratic Party's candidate for the American Presidency.

277   Bolen, J. S. (1999). The Millionth Circle: How to change ourselves and the world. Berkeley, CA: Conari; Bolen, J. S. (2005). Urgent Message from Mother: Gather the women and save the world. Boston, MA: Conari.

278   Minor, R. N. (2007). When Religion is an Addiction. St. Louis, MO: Humanity

Eleventh Letter
The Mennonite Phallacy

279   Nouwen, H. J. M. (1972). The Wounded Healer: Ministry in Contemporary Society. Garden City, NY: Doubleday and Company.

280   Gergen, K. (1991/2000). The Saturated Self: The Dilemmas of Identity in Contemporary Life. New York, NY: Basic Books

Twelfth Letter
Tales from the Reptile House

281   Jacobs is from the Turtle clan of the Cayuga Nation. He is the Keeper of the Circle, Sandy-Saulteaux Spiritual Center Beausejour, Manitoba, Canada. Quoted to me by Dr. Carolyn Heggen in electronic correspondence on July 30, 2014.

282   N. W. [name withheld] Ann Onymous. (September 28, 1994). Tales from the Reptile House. Manuscript/correspondence. See Appendix A for a newly-transcribed copy of this 1994 document. Somewhere in the early spring of 2014, I asked Dr. Carolyn Heggen if she had a copy of "Tales" in her files. She did and kindly made a photocopy for me. Her copy came to her from someone inside the Mennonite Publishing House editorial offices in Scottdale, PA and carried a date stamp. Mine, if I recall, had been given to me by some no-longer remembered colleague at Goshen College. But since that particular memory is very vague, perhaps my now-lost copy also originated in Scottdalem PA where, in that era, several of my relatives lived: some worked for the Mennonite publishing industry; all attended local Mennonite churches in that vicinity.

283   Hauerwas, S. (2010). Hannah's Child: A theologian's memoir (pp. 242-247). Grand Rapids, MI: William B. Erdmann's. See also a somewhat earlier set of correspondence: Stoltzfus, V. (Winter, 1991). Correspondence with James Lapp, J. R. Burkholder, Arlene Mark and Marlin Miller in which the emphasis is on the church's urgent need for John's theology. This letter was written in the context of the rumors about John's behavior which was already hobbling the church's use of him as its dominant theologian. The Believer's Church conference on the Goshen College campus in the 1991-1992 academic calendar year was yet another attempt by the church to re-furbish John's tarnished image in Michiana and beyond.

284   Schrag, P. (March 23, 1992). Bethel cancels invitation to Yoder after receiving protest letters (p. 3). Mennonite Reporter 22 (6).

285   Hauerwas (2010), op. cit.

286   Price, T. (July 16, 1992). Teachings Tested: Forgiveness, reconciliation in discipline, The Elkhart Truth, B-1 ff.

287   On June 26, 1992, the John Howard Yoder Task Force issued a formal report to Prairie Street Mennonite Church elders and laity and Indiana-Michigan Conference that John has acknowledged the truth of the charges and has expressed deep regret for the hurt his actions have caused for the women. John has recognized the deep rifts in integrity and trust which have developed between himself and the church and its institutions. Furthermore, John has agreed to yield to the will of the church regarding standards of conduct between men and women. He has committed himself to begin no new sexually intimate relationships, and has since acted to cut off ongoing relationships which violate church standards.

       At the same time, the task force has sensed in John a high degree of rationalization and a denial of the problems associated with his sexual misconduct. We have strongly recommended that John participate in therapy to work thoroughly with the issues involved and that he meet periodically with an accountability group to be assisted and monitored as he works at change. He has agreed to these two recommendations.

       Indiana-Michigan Conference, after consultation with Ohio Conference (the original holder of Yoder's ordination credentials) suspended his ordination credentials – putting them on hold for the duration of the formal denominational disciplinary process which lasted until December, 1995.

288   Hauerwas, S. (April, 1992). Why Truthfulness Requires Forgiveness: A Commencement Address for Graduates of the Church of the Second Chance, Goshen, IN: Goshen College. ITS Media Collection and Mennonite Church Archives.

289   Ibid.

290   In 2015, John Howard Yoder's friend and chief apologist, Stanley Hauerwas told Soli Solgado, reporter for the June 22, 2015 National Catholic Reporter Online that he learned about Yoder's sexual misdeeds in early 1992 from Yoder's sister Mary Ellen Yoder Meyer and her husband Al Meyer at Bethel College after he replaced John Howard Yoder [disinvited keynote speaker] at a Bethel College symposium on Nonviolence in America. Hauerwas told NCR that I didn't, quite frankly, understand the extent of it at the time nor did I think it was happening at Notre Dame. I probably didn't take it as seriously as I should have....It was just absurd; I just assumed it wasn't happening [at Notre Dame]. I know people think that is engaged in some kind of cover-up. I just don't know if that's true or not.

291   Price, T. (July 16, 1992). Teachings Tested: Forgiveness, reconciliation in discipline, The Elkhart Truth, B-1 ff.

292   Price, Ibid. See also Hauerwas, S. (op.cit, April, 1992).

293   Price, T. (July 16, 1994, B-1/B-5). The church task force's initiative in working with John to solve the problem and John's humbling himself to participate in the process that the task force sets out is a remarkable witness to the very themes of the church as an alternative community, peace-making, reconciliation, Christian discipleship, and servanthood that his writings have taught so many of us, said Glen Stassen, professor of Christian ethics at Southern Baptist Theological Seminary.

294   See Rachel Waltner Gossen's review of various Yoder-Mennonite Church encounters in the following resources: (1) Waltner-Gossen, R. (January 2, 2015). Defanging the Beast: Mennonite Responses to John Howard Yoder's Sexual Abuse (pp. 7-80). Mennonite Quarterly Review 89 (1); (2) Waltner Goossen, R. (January 5, 2015). The Failure to Bind and Loose: Responses to Yoder's Sexual Abuse. Our Stories Untold.

295   For an extended discussion of the Yoder-Mennonite Church confrontations, see Mennonite historian's major essay: Gossen, R. W. (January 2, 2015). Defanging the Beast: Mennonite Responses to John Howard Yoder's Sexual Abuse. Mennonite Quarterly Review (89).

296   (1) We admitted we were powerless over alcohol – that our lives had become unmanageable; (2) Came to believe that a power greater than ourselves could restore us to sobriety; (3) Made a decision to turn our will and our lives over to the care of God as we understood him; (4) Made a searching and fearless moral inventory of ourselves; (5) Admitted to God, and to another human being the exact nature of our wrongs; (6) Were entirely ready to have God remove all these defects of character; (7) Humbly asked Him to remove our shortcomings; (8) Made a list of all persons we had harmed, and became willing to make amends to them all; (9) Made direct amends to such people whenever possible, except when to do so would injure them or others; (10) Continued to take a personal inventory and when we were wrong, promptly admit it; (11) Sought through prayer and meditation to improve our conscious contact with God as we understand him, praying for knowledge of his will for us and the power to carry it out; (12) Having had a spiritual awakening as the result of these steps, we tried to carry this message to alcoholics and to practice these principles in all our affairs. For more information see http://en.wikipedia.org/wiki/Twelve-step_program

297   Gossen, R. W. (January 2, 2015). The Failure to Bind and Loose: Responses to Yoder's Sexual Abuse. The Mennonite online. Retrieve from

      https://themennonite.org/feature/failure-bind-loose-responses-john-howard-yoders-sexual-abuse/

      See also http://www.ourstoriesuntold.com/2015/01/05/the-failure-to-bind-and-loose-responses-to-yoders-sexual-abuse/; Waltner Gossen, R. (January 5, 2015). Peaceful Theology: Violent Acts; Abuse of Women by Mennonite's Leading Theologian Had Far-reaching Consequences; Institutions Slow Response Allowed Harm to Continue. Mennonite World Review online. See also: http://mennoworld.org/2015/01/05/peaceful-theology-violent-acts/

298 See Linda Gehman Peachey's essay (January, 2015). Naming the Pain/ Seeking the Light: The Mennonite Church's Response to Sexual Abuse (pp. 111-128), Mennonite Quarterly Review 89 (1).

299 Doyle, T. P. (2013), Retrieve from http://vimeo.com/60664365

300 The Rev. Laurie J. Ferguson is a fourth generation Presbyterian pastor and served her denomination as a member of six separate regional subcommittees composed of clergy and members of the laity for whom the task was to investigate clergy sexual abuse. Her summary of learnings is entitled "A Protestant Approach to Clergy Sexual Abuse" (pp. 189-194) and is found in an edited collection of essays by Frawley-O'Dea, M.G. and Goldner, V. (2007). Predatory Priests - Silenced Victims: The Sexual Abuse Crisis and the Catholic Church. New York, NY: The Analytic Press/Lawrence Erlbaum Associates.

301 Ferguson, L. J. (2007), p. 191.

302 Ferguson, L. (ibid, pp. 101-102).

303 See Matthew 19: 13-14; Matthew 5:3; Matthew 5:10

304 (1) Pew Research Center. (2015) Religious Landscape Study. Retrieve from http://www.pewforum.org/religious-landscape-study/;

(2) Pew Research Center. (2015). America's Changing Religious Landscape. Retrieve from: http://www.pewforum.org/2015/05/12/americas-changing-religious-landscape/

305 A wide variety of Roman Catholic authors note the statistics and the claim is frequently made that 30 million previously Catholic adults now claim former or non-practicing or non-believing Roman Catholic as their religious identity.

306 For an example, see Sharon Detweiler's personal story (January 8, 2015), John Howard Yoder: My Untold Story After 36 Years of Silence on the blog Our Stories Untold. Retrieve from http://www.ourstoriesuntold.com/stories/john-howard-yoder-my-untold-story-after-36-years-of-silence-by-sharon-detweiler/

307 Doyle, T. P. (2011). Sexual Abuse by Catholic Clergy: The spiritual damage (pp. 171-182) in T. Plant and K. McChesney (Eds.) Sexual Abuse in the Catholic Church: A decade of crisis, 2002-2012. Santa Barbara, CA: Praeger.

308 SNAP. What to do when your minister/priest is accused of abuse. Retrieve from http://www.snapnetwork.org/what_to_do_when_your_priest_is_accused_of_abuse

309 Cohan, S. (2002). Chapter Ten: Acknowledgment Now (pp. 249-277) in States of Denial: Knowing about Atrocities and Suffering. Cambridge, UK: Polity.

310 For example see Attorney Glenn Friesen's article, The Church Discipline of John Howard Yoder (May 1, 2014) on Mark Nation's Eastern Mennonite University web page EMU Anabaptist Nation. Retrieve from http://emu.edu/now/anabaptist-nation/2014/05/01/the-church-discipline-of-john-howard-yoder-2/

311 This essay was written in the summer of 2014. Since that time multiple articles have been published in the nation's religious press about the Yoder-Mennonite Church narrative. A primary resource is Mennonite historian Rachel Waltner Gossen's long article (January 2, 2015). Defanging the Beast: Mennonite Responses to John Howard Yoder's Sexual Abuse (pp. 7-80). Mennonite Quarterly Review 89 (1).

312 See Tim Huber's report, Oregon school, conference facing 5.5 million lawsuit. Mennonite World Review (p. 1). May 5, 2015. Retrieve from http://mennoworld.org/2015/03/05/news/oregon-school-conference-facing-5-5-million-lawsuit/

313 Released in November, 2015, the American movie Spotlight documents issues of sexual abuse and institutional cover-ups as it tells the true story of the Boston Globe's investigations of the Boston Diocese and its cover-up of sexually abusive clergy.

314 See, for example, a series of articles about domestic and sexual violence inside Amish and Mennonite communities of Lancaster County in Pa. The series (authored by Espenshade and Alexander) ran from July 12 – 16, 2004 and were posted online by the Intelligencer Journal on August 4, 2004. This series has now apparently been deleted from its web address and is no longer available online. It is likely hard copies can be obtained from the newspaper.

315 A good resource for the serious scholar or for the citizen who wishes to be informed is Kathy Shaw's blog, Abuse Tracker (http://www.bishop-accountability.org/AbuseTracker/). Shaw's blog is hosted by Bishop Accountability's web presence (http://www.bishop-accountability.org/).

316 Price, T. (June 29, 1992) Theologian cited in sex inquiry (B-1ff). The Elkhart Truth: Citing a Prairie Street Mennonite Church investigation into multiple charges of sexual misconduct, Price writes: The charges brought by the women are accurate, and John has violated sexual boundaries," according to a task force at Prairie Street Mennonite Church, at which Yoder is a member. "John has acknowledged the truth of the charges and has expressed deep regret for the hurt his actions have caused for the women. In order to provide readers with easy access to Tom Prices' series of articles, I

have placed them in the appendices section of this manuscript where they can be retrieved.

317   Price, T. (June 29, 1992, ibid.)

318   Juhnke, J. C. (June 1, 2014). News Analysis: The Decision to Disinvite John Howard Yoder to Speak: An Interview with James Juhnke, former history professor at Bethel College. Includes editor's note by Gordon Houser. The Mennonite.

319   Krall, R. E. (2012). The Elephants in God's Living Room: Clergy Sexual Abuse and Clericalism, v.1, Theoretical Issues. Enduring Space Publications. Retrieve from www.ruthkrall.com.

320   See Tom Price Elkhart Truth articles (1992) in the Appendix section of this manuscript.

321   As of January 2, 2015, this situation of institutional silence and denial has changed with the publication of Waltner Gossen's article, Defanging the Beast: Mennonite Responses to John Howard Yoder's Sexual Abuse (pp. 7-80). Mennonite Quarterly Review 89 (1).

322   An example of this intellectual turn-of-phrase usage can be found in Zimmerman, E. (2007). Preaching the Politics of Jesus: The origin and significance of John Howard Yoder's social ethics (with a foreword by John Paul Lederach). Telford, PA: Cascadia. He writes: Later in Yoder's life various women accused him of strange and unwanted patterns of sexual language and behavior. These allegations led to a church disciplinary process (p. 64, footnote 37).

323   Krall, R. E. (2012). The Elephants in God's Living Room: Clergy Sexual Abuse and Clericalism, v.1, Theoretical Issues. Enduring Space Publications. Retrieve from www.ruthkrall.com.

324   Heggen, C. H. (June 1, 2014). Opinion: Misconceptions and Victim Blaming in Yoder Coverage.. The Mennonite. See:
      http://www.themennonite.org/issues/17-7/articles/Misconceptions_and_victim_blaming_in_Yoder_coverage?utm_source=TMail+June+30&utm_campaign=TMail+June+30&utm_medium=email

325   For the Discernment Group's press release see http://mennoworld.org/2014/06/30/mc-usa-group-reports-more-evidence-of-abuse/ See also the January 2, 2015 edition of the Mennonite Quarterly Review which examines the Mennonite Church-John Howard Yoder encounters in depth.

326   Heggen, C. (June 1, 2014, ibid.)

327   Heggen, C. (Ibid.)

328   Heggen, C. (Ibid.)

329   For a complete transcribed copy of this anonymous essay, see Appendix A, (pp. 338-340.

330 Doyle, T. P. (2010). Clergy Sexual Abuse in the Catholic Church: Reflections, 1984-2010. http://www.awrsipe.com/Doyle/2010/2010-08-27-reflections. htm

331 Baker, T. (October 10, 2014). Why Are Young People Leaving the Church in Such Numbers: In this discouraging book the future looks bad for just about every flavor of Catholic. From, Global Pulse review of Emerging Adults: In, Out, and Gone from the Church (2014) by Christian Smith, Kyle Longest, Jonathan Hill, and Karl Christofferson. New York, NY: Oxford University Press. Retrieve from http://www.globalpulsemagazine.com/news/why-are-young-people-leaving-the-church-in-such-numbers/163

332 They Scandalized My Name. To retrieve Kathleen Battle and Jessye Norman in performance, retrieve from https://www.youtube.com/ watch?v=S6EOXT6_inw; to hear Paul Robeson's version, retrieve from
    https://www.youtube.com/watch?v=zoXouw9RzUo; for a copy of the lyrics, see http://www.lyrics007.com/Paul%20Robeson%20Lyrics/ Scandalize%20My%20Name%20Lyrics.html

333 In June, 2015, an accused priest filed suit. For information, see http:// www.stltoday.com/news/local/govt-and-politics/federal-lawsuit-filed-by-st-louis-priest-cleared-of-child/article_b13a09e4-e683-56ad-a5b6-0ff-5bacbd667.html. See also http://stlouis.cbslocal.com/2015/06/26/priest-sues-accuser-after-sex-abuse-charges-dropped/; See also http://www. snapnetwork.org/mo_statement_by_david_clohessy_director_of_snap

334 Doyle, T. P. (2013). Address to SNAP in Dublin. Retrieve from http://vimeo. com/67774835

335 Doyle, T. P. (August, 2014). Address to SNAP: Where We've Been and Where We Are Going: How Survivors Have Changed History. Retrieve from http:// www.awrsipe.com/Doyle/2014/Where%20We%20Have%20Been%20 and%20Where%20We're%20Going%20-%20Aug.%2011,%202014.pdf

336 Pew Forum on Religion and Public Life: Pew Religious Landscape Research (2007). While nearly 1 in 3 Americans (31%) were raised in the Catholic faith, today fewer than 1 in 4 (24%) describe themselves as Catholic. Those figures would have been even more pronounced were it not for the off-set-ting impact of immigration. http://religions.pewforum.org/reports. A wide variety of commentators over the past few years have also looked at statis-tics about the declining number of Catholics who participate in the sacra-ments of (1) the weekly mass and (2) the rite of reconciliation-confession. Some authors conclude that if this group were a denomination, former and

alienated Roman Catholics would be the second largest denomination in the United States.

337   In the interval between when this letter was first written (2014) and its copy-edited revisions in place (2016), the Mennonite Historical Society published an issue of the Mennonite Quarterly Review (89/1) devoted exclusively to the dual legacy of Mennonite theologian and ethicist John Howard Yoder. On March 22, 2015, the Associated Mennonite Biblical Seminaries hosted a worship service of confession and lament. Information about this service can be retrieved at several locations: (1) The Elkhart Truth (March 22, 2015). Retrieve from http://www.elkharttruth.com/living/faith/2015/03/22/Anabaptist-Mennonite-Biblical-Seminary.html; (2) The Mennonite (March 23, 2015). Retrieve from http://www.elkharttruth.com/living/faith/2015/03/22/Anabaptist-Mennonite-Biblical-Seminary.html; (3) The Mennonite World Review (March 23, 2015). Retrieve from http://mennoworld.org/2015/03/23/news/ambs-on-abuse-we-failed-you/; (4) AMBS post documents from Reunion, Listening, Confessing. Retrieve from

https://www.ambs.edu/news-events/reunion-listening-confessing.cfm; Also can be retrieved from https://www.youtube.com/watch?v=MBmtzylxX-M

338   Fox, M. (2011). The Pope's War: Why Ratzinger's secret crusade has imperiled the church and how it can be saved. New York, NY: SterlingEthos

339   Kornfield, J. (2008). The Art of Forgiveness, Lovingkindness and Peace. New York, NY: Bantam.

340   White, W. F. (1986). Incest in the Organizational Family: The Ecology of Burn-out in Closed Systems. Cincinnati, OH: Lighthouse Training Institute. Quoted in Wells, K., Earle, R. E., and Earle, M. R. (2011). Outpatient and Inpatient Intensive Treatment Models (pp. 65-820 in Thoburn, J., Baker, R., and Maso, M. D. (Eds). Clergy Sexual Misconduct: A Systems Approach to Prevention, Intervention and Oversight. Carefree, AZ: Gentle Path Press, p. 80.

341   Wells, K., Earle, R. E., and Earle, M. R. (2011). Outpatient and Inpatient Intensive Treatment Models (pp. 65-820 in Thoburn, J., Baker, R., and Maso, M. D. (Eds.). Clergy Sexual Misconduct: A Systems Approach to Prevention, Intervention and Oversight. Carefree, AZ: Gentle Path Press, pp. 79- 80.

342   Wells, Earle and Earle, ibid.

343   Kramer, J. and Alstad, D. (1993). The Guru Papers: Masks of authoritarian power. Berkeley, CA: Frog Ltd.

344   No man is an island, entire of itself, every man is a piece of the continent, a part of the main; if a clod be washed out to sea, Europe is the less, as well as if a premonitory were, as well as any manner of thy friends of thine own were; any man's death diminishes me, because I am involved in mankind.

345 I am most aware of professional or administrative bullying inside the religious academy but I know it goes on in other denominational institutions as well. The literature about institutional bullying is vast. To begin to research this topic, students can start here: http://bulliedacademics.blogspot.com/2008/09/what-is-corporateinstitutional-bullying.html

346 Kelman, Herbert C. and Hamilton, V. L. (1989). Crimes of Obedience, New Haven, CT: Yale University Press.

347 The bystander effect or bystander apathy is a social phenomenon described by social psychologists vis-à-vis cases in which individuals do not respond with helpfulness to victims when other people are present. They simply do not respond and look the other way. The proximity of help is inversely related to the number of bystanders. For additional information see https://www.psychologytoday.com/basics/bystander-effect; For a comprehensive look at bystander research, see Cohen, S. States of Denial: Knowing about Atrocities and Suffering. Cambridge, UK: Polity, pp. 140-167.

348 https://www.google.com/webhp?sourceid=chrome-instant&ion=1&espv=2&ie=UTF-8#q=define%20hypocrisy

349 http://www.merriam-webster.com/dictionary/hypocrisy

350 http://www.merriam-webster.com/dictionary/hypocrisy

351 http://dictionary.reference.com/browse/hypocrite

352 http://www.livescience.com/23479-tikal-mayan-civilization.html

353 http://www.livescience.com/23262-chichen-itza.html

354 http://www.livescience.com/22869-machu-picchu.html

355 http://science.nationalgeographic.com/science/archaeology/teotihuacan-/

356 For example, see the Pew Surveys on American religious life. http://religions.pewforum.org/reports

Fourteenth Letter
Managing Our Wounds

357 The African-American spiritual, They Scandalized My Name, provides us with a penetrating commentary about character assassination and betrayal. To see the lyrics, retrieve from: http://www.lyrics007.com/Paul%20Robeson%20Lyrics/Scandalize%20My%20Name%20Lyrics.html

358 Van Der Kolk, B. (2014). The Body Keeps the Score: Brain, Mind and Body in the Healing of Trauma. New York, NY: Viking Press.

359 Information about Dr. Van Der Kolk can be retrieved here. http://www.traumacenter.org/

360 Van Der Kolk, B. A., McFarlane, A. C., and Weisaeth, L. (Eds.). (1996). Traumatic Stress: The effects of overwhelming experiences on mind, body and society. New York, NY: Guilford Press.

361 From the Enduring Space Homepage: www.ruthkrall.com.

362 Mindfulness involves paying attention to our inner thoughts, feelings, bodily sensations, and to the outer world of our surroundings. It involves acceptance – a form of non-judgmental consciousness. Mindfulness, as a spiritual practice, involves living in the present moment – rather than obsessively re-hashing the past or anxiously worrying about the future. I think of it as a form of is-ness rather than should-ness or should not-ness. That what is, therefore, is what it is. In dealing with life, learning to deal with what is rather than illusory and wishful fantasies about what should be is a learned skill. My introduction to meditation and mindfulness training came as a result of a physical illness and my strong desire to return to health.

363 Nouwen, H. J. M. (1972). The Wounded Healer: Ministry in contemporary society. Garden City, NY: Doubleday and Company.

364 http://www.physlink.com/Education/AskExperts/ae401.cfm

365 Cohan, S. (2002). States of Denial: Knowing about Atrocities and Suffering. Cambridge, UK: Polity.

366 Miller, E. E. (1997). Deep Healing: The essentials of mind/body healing. Carlsbad, CA: Hay House

367 Lemle, M. (2003). Ram Dass: Fierce Grace. Zeitgeist Video.

368 Morton, N. Claremont, CA, ca, 1983 or 1984, personal conversations

369 Bateson, M. C. (1989). Composing a Life. New York, NY: Grove.

370 Here I am differentiating between the small s/self of ego from the large S/Self which encompasses the embodied spirit as well as the mind.

371 Wesselman, H. (2003). My Journey to the Sacred Garden: A guide to traveling in the spiritual realms. Carlsbad, CA; Hay House Press, p. 29.

372 Van der Kolk, B. A. (2014). The Body Keeps the Score: Brian, Mind, and Body in the Healing of Trauma. New York, NY: Viking.

Fifteenth Letter
Weaving Parachutes

373 William Safford (1993). Robert Bly (Ed.). "Any Time" The Darkness around Us Is Deep: Selected Poems of William Safford. New York, NY: Harper Perennial, 1993, 10.

374 Crimes of Obedience: For an in-depth analysis of crimes which are linked to human obedience in various governing systems such as the military in ambiguous combat situations or large industrial corporations where financial

profit is more essential than human rights, see the social psychology analysis of Herbert C. Kelman and V. Lee Hamilton (1989). Crimes of Obedience, New Haven, CT: Yale University Press. In this book they provide diagnostic insights into social science's questions about why people who would ordinarily be compassionate individuals become insensitive to and abusive of the rights of others to be treated humanely and with justice. For an examination of criminal malfeasance and misconduct by religious leaders and clergy, see the collected works of sociologist Anson Shupe: (1995). In the Name of all that's Holy: A theology of clergy malfeasance. Westport, CT: Yale University Press; (2008) Rogue Clerics: The social problem of clergy deviance. Brunswick, NJ: Transaction; (2007) Spoils of the Kingdom: Clergy misconduct and religious community. Chicago, IL: University of Illinois Press; (1998). Wolves within the Fold: Religious leadership and abuses of power. Brunswick, NJ: Rutgers University Press; with Stacey, W. A., and Darnell, S. E. (Eds.). (2000). Bad Pastors: Clergy misconduct in America. New York, NY: New York University Press.

375   Clergy Malfeasance: The exploitation and abuse of a religious group's followers by trusted elites and leaders of their religion.

376   Clericalism: An institutional clergy structure and practice that protects the clergy and church institutions at the expense of the laity.

377   Doyle, T. P. (2013). Address to SNAP in Dublin. Retrieve from http://vimeo.com/67774835.

378   Kramer, J. and Alstad, D. (1993). The Guru Papers: Masks of authoritarian power. Berkeley, CA: Frog Ltd.

379   Doyle, T. P. (May 20, 2010): Introduction to Cumulative Bibliography – More Reflections on the Journey. Father Doyle (July 20, 2014, electronic correspondence) has generously given his permission for this set of paragraphs to be used in their entirety in this letter. For more information about Father Doyle and the work he has done in victims' advocacy work, see D'Antonio, M. (2013). Mortal Sins: Sex, crime, and the era of Catholic scandal. New York, NY: Thomas Dunne Books/St. Martin's Press. See also, Kaiser, R. B. (2015) Whistle: Tom Doyle's Steadfast Witness for Victims of Clerical Sexual Abuse. Thiensville, WI. Caritas. For more information about the early unfolding of the sexual abuse scandal in the contemporary American Catholic Church, see Jason Berry (1992). Lead Us Not into Temptation: Catholic priests and the sexual abuse of children. New York, NY: Doubleday. For a discussion of the costs of whistle-blowing, see the 2015 documentary, A Matter of Conscience: Witnesses to Clergy Abuse. Boston, MA: Etoile Productions.

380   Roig-Franzia, M. (September 20, 2011). Despite Investigating Catholic Scandals, Author Jason Berry Keeps the Faith. The Washington Post. Retrieve from http://www.washingtonpost.com/lifestyle/style/

despite-investigating-catholic-scandals-author-jason-berry-keeps-the-faith/2011/09/20/glQA4tkYjK_story.html

381   Roig-Franzia, Ibid.

382   Doyle, T. P. (2013, op.cit).

383   Christ, C. (1995). Diving Deep and Surfacing: Women writers on spiritual quest. Boston, MA: Beacon.

384   Smith, H. (2010). Tales of Wonder: Chasing the Divine/An autobiography. New York, NY: HarperOne.

385   Fox, M. (2000). One River: Many Wells: Wisdom emerging from global faiths. New York, NY: Jeremy P. Tarcher.

386   Oursler, W. (1960). The Road to Faith. New York, NY: Holt, Rinehart and Winston.

387   Meyer, R. (2010). Saving Jesus from the Church: How to stop worshipping Christ and start following Jesus. New York, NY: Harper; Meyer, R. (2015). Spiritual Defiance: Building a beloved community of resistance (The Yale Lyman Beecher Lectures). New Haven, CT: Yale University Press.

388   Wiesel, E. See http://en.wikiquote.org/wiki/Elie_Wiesel

389   Roig-Franzia, op. cit.

390   I am indebted to Father Doyle for his exegetical gloss of Mathew 18:5 "to cause one of the little ones who believe in me to stumble... little ones of any age."

Sixteenth Letter
Markers of the Christian Patriarchy

391   For a discussion of the inter-relatedness of the various patriarchal isms, see http://bilgrimage.blogspot.com/2014/11/a-reader-writes-in-history-this-sort-of.html#disqus_thread

392   For example, see the following authors: (1) de Beauvoir, S. (1974). The Second Sex. New York, NY: Vintage-Random House; (2) Daly, M. (1973). Beyond God the Father. Boston, MA: Beacon and (1978). Gyn/Ecology. Boston, MA: Beacon; (3) Janeway, E. (1981). Powers of the Weak. New York, NY: Morrow Quill Paperbacks; (4) Lerner, G. (1993b). The Creation of Patriarchy. New York, NY: Oxford; and (5) Starhawk. (1981). Truth or Dare: Encounters with power, authority and mystery. San Francisco, CA: Harper and Row.

393   I am indebted to Roman Catholic theologian William Lindsey for drawing my attention to hooks' work. See his blog, Bilgrimage, November 16, 2015 for an important discussion of hooks' work and its implications in the aftermath of ISIS terrorist bombings in France on November 13, 2015. Retrieve from http://bilgrimage.blogspot.com/2015/11/bell-hooks-on-worship-of-death-as.html

394   Ibid., pp. 192-193.

395   In Genesis 1:27 we are told that God created human beings in the divine image – male and female were created in the image of God.

In Genesis 2:21- 23 we are told that God did major surgery – removing a rib from Adam's side. From Adam's rib God then created woman. When he took the woman to Adam's side, Adam said, This is now bone of my bone, flesh of my flesh and she shall be called woman because she was taken out of man.

396   For an exegesis of this point of view, see http://www.bible.ca/marriage/submission-independent-of-culture.htm

397   This ancient creation story mythology is told in the Enuma Elish. See https://www.knowingthebible.net/yahweh-the-leviathan-and-sea

398   Genesis 2: 15

399   Genesis 3: 2

400   See Wikipedia for a brief introduction to this ancient Talmudic story http://en.wikipedia.org/wiki/Lilith

401   Plaskow, J. (1992). The Coming of Lilith. Retrieve from Jewish Women Archive: Sharing Stories, Inspiring Change at http://jwa.org/media/coming-of-lilith-by-judith-plaskow

402   For a beginning introduction to a discussion of gender complementarity discussions as a form of socially dysfunctional binary essentialism, see http://bilgrimage.blogspot.com/2014/11/a-reader-writes-in-history-this-sort-of.html#disqus_thread; see also the online gay, lesbian, bi-sexual, transgender, and queer culture encyclopedia for a good discussion of the patriarchy. http://www.glbtq.com/social-sciences/patriarchy.html

403   www.LBGTQ.com, Ibid.

404   Johnson, E. A. (2007). Quest for the Living God: Mapping Frontiers in the Theology of God. New York, NY: Continuum, p. 14.

405   Meyers, R. (2015). Undone: Faith and Resistance to Orthodoxy (Chapter two, pp. 41-80) in Spiritual Defiance: Building a Beloved Community of Resistance. New Haven, CT: Yale University Press.

406   For information about the patriarchal structures of the Christian Church after Constantine, see https://en.wikipedia.org/wiki/Pentarchy

407   Denzley, N. (2007) Chapter Seven: Pope Demasius, Ear Tickler (pp. 176-204) in The Bone Gatherers: The lost worlds of early Christian women, Boston, MA: Beacon Press.

408   For information about Dr. Blackwell, see http://www.nlm.nih.gov/changingthefaceofmedicine/physicians/biography_35.html

409   For more information about the Rev. Dr. Pauli Murray see http://www.biography.com/people/pauli-murray-214111#synopsis

410   For information about Dr. Mary Daly's work and life, see

http://religiondispatches.org/beyond-radical-mary-daly-feminist-theologian-changed-worlds/

411 http://www.history.com/this-day-in-history/woman-suffrage-amendment-ratified

412 http://www.equalrightsamendment.org/overview.htm

413 See Dr. Candace Pert's account about this form of male plagiarism in the laboratories which did the basic research about the structures and role of neuropeptides in the human body. I have heard Pert speak in professional conferences on numerous occasions and she is very soft-spoken. She is, however, very determined that her intellectual and research work about the role of the neuropeptides in emotional responses not be stolen from her: Pert, C. B. (1997). Molecules of Emotion: Why you feel the way you feel. New York, NY: Scribners.

414 Contemporary apologists for the theology of John Howard Yoder often refer to themselves and are also referred to by others as Yoderians.

415 Retrieve from www.ruthkrall.com

416 Weaver, J. D. (Ed.) (2014). John Howard Yoder: Radical Theologian. Eugene, OR: Wipf and Stock.

417 Starhawk. op.cit.

418 For one research protocol and findings see http://listeningandspokenlanguage.org/uploadedFiles/Connect/Meetings/2014_Convention/Its%20Not%20Fine.%20Its%20Not%20Ok.research.pdf

419 See, for example, http://www.npr.org/blogs/health/2014/05/15/312737124/medicine-needs-more-research-on-female-animals-nih-says

420 For historical statements about women and their essential nature see http://www.shc.edu/theolibrary/resources/women.htm

421 For Knox's diatribe against queen mothers as regents for their daughters or for queens as actual rulers, see http://en.wikipedia.org/wiki/The_First_Blast_of_the_Trumpet_Against_the_Monstruous_Regiment_of_Women

422 When using a search engine with the phrase crackdown on American nuns, many articles and essays pop up for review. For one example among many, see http://blog.seattlepi.com/seattlepolitics/2014/05/05/vatican-tightens-crackdown-on-u-s-nuns-sartain-to-have-active-role/

423 See Emily's List: http://www.emilyslist.org/

424 As this essay is being copy-edited, ten-year-old rape allegations have re-surfaced about comedian Bill Cosby. For a timeline of these accusations, see http://www.vulture.com/2014/09/timeline-of-the-abuse-charges-against-cosby.html; See also http://www.nytimes.com/2014/11/21/upshot/bill-cosbys-sudden-fall-explained-sociologically.html?emc=eta1&_r=1&abt=0002&abg=1

425 http://journalistsresource.org/studies/society/public-health/sexual-as-sault-rape-us-college-campuses-research-roundup#; http://www.nytimes.com/2014/07/31/us/college-sexual-assault-bill-in-senate.html?_r=0; http://www.nytimes.com/2014/04/29/us/tougher-battle-on-sex-assault-on-cam-pus-urged.html

426 See http://www.womensmediacenter.com/feature/entry/date-rape-revis-ited; for an extended report of Koss's research findings, see Warshaw, R. (1984). I Never Called it Rape. New York, NY: Harper and Row.

427 For example, see this essay on Wikipedia http://en.wikipedia.org/wiki/William_Kennedy_Smith

Seventeenth Letter
Case Study: A disciple of the Buddha does not misuse sexuality

428 Third Precept

429 Comforti, M. (January 23, 2015). Winter Dream Conference Presentation: Dreams, Archetypes and the Complex: The Songs of Angels and the Howls of Demons. Tucson, AZ: Westward Look Wyndham Grand Resort and Spa.

430 Some recent books in this genre include physician Herbert Benson's 1997 book, Timeless Healing: The Power of Biology and Belief. New York, NY: Scribners; Psychologist Jon Kabat-Zinn (2013). Full Catastrophe Living: Using the Wisdom of Your Body and Mind to Face Stress, Pain and Illness. New York, NY: Bantam Books; Physician Martin Rossman (2000). Guided Imagery for Self-Healing, Novato, CA: HJKramer/New World; and Psychiatrist Bessel Van Der Kolk: (2014) The Body Knows the Score: Brain, Mind and Body in the Healing of Trauma. New York, NY: Viking.

431 See chapter three, Speaking Truth about Sexual Violence in Church, in which I do a close reading of Jordan's 2003 book, Telling Truths in Church: Scandal, Flesh and Christian Speech. Boston, MA: Beacon.

432 For example, see http://www.pbs.org/wgbh/pages/frontline/religion/se-crets-of-the-vatican/tom-doyle-vatican-is-the-worlds-last-absolute-mon-archy/

433 For an extended discussion of narcissism as a predominant feature of cler-ical culture, see Doyle, T. P. (Spring, 2013). Address to SNAP in Dublin re-garding clericalism and clerical narcissism. Retrieve fromhttp://vimeo.com/67774835

434 For a brief summary of official Roman Catholic teachings about same sex orien-tation, see, http://www.catholicnewsagency.com/resources/life-and-family/homosexuality/what-the-church-teaches-about-homosexual-inclinations/

435   Clericalism: An institutional clergy structure and practice that protects the clergy and church institutions at the expense of the laity.

436   Smith, H. (1958/1986). The Illustrated World's Religions: A Guide to our Wisdom Traditions. New York, NY: HarperOne.

437   I am referring here to Gandhi's teachings regarding Satygraha (holding on to truth or truth force) and his modeling of active non-violent resistance in the face of Britain's colonial political and structural oppression in India.

438   See Krall, R. E. (2012) The Elephants in God's Living Room, vol. one: Clergy Sexual Abuse and Clericalism, Theoretical Issues; (2013) The Elephants in God's Living Room, vol. three: The Mennonite Church and John Howard Yoder, Collected Essays; (2014) The Elephants in God's Living Room, vol. four: Bearing the Unbearable, Collected Essays, at Enduring Space Publications at www.ruthkrall.com

439   Guggenbuhl-Craig, A. (1991). (J. R. Haule, Trans.). Power in the Helping Professions. Woodstock, CT: Spring Publications.

440   Krall, R. E. (1990). Rape's Power to Dismember Women's Lives: Personal realities and cultural forms. Claremont, CA: Southern California School of Theology at Claremont.

441   Phelan, Taitaku Pat, Teaching and Receiving the Precepts, Part Six: A Disciple of the Buddha does not Misuse Sexuality, Retrieved from http://www.chzc.org/pat13.htm

442   Nhat Hanh, T. (1987). Interbeing, Berkeley, CA; Parallax, p. 6.

443   Ibid, p. 8.

444   Phelan, op.cit, p. 1

445   Ibid.

446   Ibid, pp. 1-2

447   Ibid, p. 2.

448   Ibid.

449   Ford, J. I. (2006). Zen Master Who: A Guide to the People and Stories of Zen, New York, NY: Wisdom Publications.

450   Ibid, p. 120

451   Downing, M. (2001). Shoes outside the Door: Desire, devotion and excess at San Francisco Zen Center, Washington, DC: Counterpoint.

452   Ford, op. cit.

453   In Zen Buddhism, dharma transmission is a custom in which an individual is established as a successor in an unbroken lineage of Zen teachers and disciples; this is a spiritual "bloodline" theoretically traced back to the Buddha himself. For further information see http://en.wikipedia.org/wiki/Dharma_transmission

454   Wikipedia, http://en.wikipedia.org/wiki/Zentatsu_Richard_Baker

455   Ibid, Wikipedia

456 Ford, op. cit, pp. 124-135

457 Schneider, S. (Winter, 1994). The Long Learning Curve: An interview with Richard Baker Roshi. Tricycle: The Buddhist Review. For an additional interview, with Goldberg about Katagiri's death, see Goldberg, N. (September, 2004). When the candle is blown out: On the Death of Katagiri Roshi, Shambala Sun: Buddhism, Culture, Meditation, Life, Retrieve from http://www.lionsroar.com/when-the-candle-is-blown-out-on-the-death-of-katagiri-roshi/

458 Goldberg, N. (2004). The Great Failure: A bartender, a monk and my unlikely path to truth. Boulder, CO: Sounds True.

459 Ford, op. cit.

460 On July 7, 1937, the Marco Polo Bridge Incident led to a declaration of war between Japan and China; on September 1, 1939, German invaded Poland. For more discussion about the starting date of World War Two, see http://www.historynet.com/world-war-ii

461 Goldberg, op cit.

462 Roshi is Japanese Zen terminology for old teacher. It carries a connotation of the venerable master. In Soto Sect Zen, the Roshi is a Zen master who has received the seal of his enlightenment from his own teacher and, in turn, he transmits this seal to his disciples or Dharma heirs.

463 JHY is short-hand language among many Mennonites for John Howard Yoder.

464 Lisa Schirch (November 16, 2014). Electronic correspondence with author.

465 Fortune, M. (August 25, 2014). The Message of the Messenger: A Question of Legacy. Faith/Trust Institute. See http://www.faithtrustinstitute.org/blog/marie-fortune/203

466 Ibid.

467 Krall, R. E. (2013). The Elephants in God's Living Room, vol. 3. The Mennonite Church and John Howard Yoder: Collected Essays. Retrieve from http://ruthkrall.com/downloadable-books/volume-three-the-mennonite-church-and-john-howard-yoder-collected-essays/

468 CBC News, Windsor, Canada: A CBC Q and A with Buddhist Rob Hogendoorn, who investigates abuse in Buddhism. Retrieve fromhttp://www.cbc.ca/news/canada/windsor/a-cbc-q-a-with-buddhist-rob-hogendoorn-who-investigates-abuse-in-buddhism-1.3718010

469 Goldberg, op cit, p. 2

470 Goldberg, ibid.

471 Goldberg, ibid., p. 3.

472 Goldberg, N, (2006) What Failure Can Teach Us: Interview with Lisa Scheldner, Beliefnet. Retrieved from http://www.beliefnet.com/Faiths/Buddhism/2005/02/What-Failure-Can-Teach-Us.aspx

473 Goldberg, 2004b, op. cit, p. 101.

474 Goldberg, ibid. p. 102

475 Goldberg, ibid. p. 107

476 Goldberg, ibid. p. 112

477 Goldberg, ibid. p. 136

478 Goldberg, ibid. p. 110)

479 Goldberg, ibid. p. 136

480   Goldberg, N, 2006, op. cit., Beliefnet.

481 Kramer, J. and Alstad, D. 1993). The Guru Papers: Masks of Authoritarian Power. Berkeley, CA: Frog Ltd.

482 Kramer and Alstad, ibid., p. 92

483 Goldberg, (2004), op. cit. p. p. 93

484 Ibid., p. 93

485 Ibid., P. 93

486 Goldberg, N. (2004a). Audio-book, The Great Failure: A Bartender, A Monk and My Unlikely Path to Truth, Boulder, CO: Sounds True.

487 Goldberg, 2004, op. cit., p. 115

488 Kramer and Alstad, op. cit., pp. 95-96

489 Iyre, P. (1992). The Lady and the Monk: Four Seasons of Life in Kyoto. New York, NY: Vintage

490 Kramer, J. and Alstad, D. op. cit, p. 90.

491 Doyle, T. (October 19, 2014). College Mennonite Church, New Perspectives on Faith presentation: http://www.newperspectivesgoshen.org/pages/wp-content/uploads/TomDoyle-Part1.mp3; Doyle, T. (October 20, 2014). Anabaptist-Mennonite Biblical Seminary Presentation: http://anabaptist.dreamhosters.com/podcasts/guest-presentations/?p=archive&cat=guest_speaker

492 Fortune, op. cit.

Eighteenth Letter
Resurrection Morning

493 Fitzgerald, R. T. (April 6, 2015), See http://bilgrimage.blogspot.com/2015/04/easter-monday-collage-they-wanted-to.html#disqus_thread.

494 Esquivel, J. (1994). Threatened with Resurrection: Prayers and Poems from an Exiled Guatemalan [trans, Ann Woehrle], Elgin, IL. Brethren Press.

495 Quoted by Jeff Gundy (2002), The Christian Century (November 6-19, 2002), pp. 20-27. Retrieve from:
     http://www.religion-online.org/showarticle.asp?title=2625

496   Toews, M. (2014). All My Puny Sorrows, San Francisco, CA; McSweeneys, p. 22.

497   Van Braght, T. M. (1660/1938). The Martyrs Mirror (The Bloody Theater). Scottdale, PA: Herald Press.

498   Kornfield, Jack, The Art of Forgiveness, Lovingkindness, and Peace,
New York, Bantam, 2002, p. 28.

499   See Matthew 23: 23 - 26. Woe to you teachers of the law and Pharisees, you hypocrites. You give a tithe of your spices: mint, dill, and cumin. But you have neglected the more important matters of the law – justice, mercy, and faithfulness. You should have practiced the latter without neglecting the former. You blind guides. You strain at a gnat but swallow a camel. Woe to you teachers of the law and Pharisees, you hypocrites. You clean the outside of the cup and dish, but inside they are full of greed and self-indulgence. First, clean the inside of the cup and dish and then the outside also will be clean.

500   See Loren Johns article about the Mennonite Church and Homosexuality for a discussion of the institutional church's response to lbgtq individuals. Retrieve from http://ljohns.ambs.edu/H&MC.htm.

501   In July, 2015 the Mennonite House of Delegates in its biennial convention in Kansas City approved two resolutions – somewhat contradictory ones – in a hope to keep the Mennonite Church USA together. For more information see http://mennoworld.org/2015/07/03/news/delegates-approve-for-bearance-uphold-membership-guidelines/

502   Herman, J. L. (May 16, 2013). Interview with Judith Herman (pp. 130- 151) in Caruth, C. (2014). Listening to Trauma: Conversations with leaders in the Theory and Treatment of Catastrophic Experience. Baltimore, MD: John Hopkins Press, p. 149.

503   There is a new documentary, A Matter of Conscience: Confronting Clergy Abuse, Boston, MA: Etoile Productions USA. In this documentary a wide variety of Roman Catholic religious leaders discuss whistle-blowing in the context of clergy sexual abuse of children. The experienced phenomenon of shunning is described by several individuals as the consequence of their actions.

504   Psalm 85:10.

505   Romans 7:18 -20.

506   John 4: 4 – 42.

507   Matthew 23:23.

508   See Roman Catholic priest and author Henri Nouwen's discussion of the priest-minister as a wounded healer. Nouwen, H. J. M. (1972). The Wounded Healer: Ministry in contemporary society. Garden City, NY: Doubleday and Company.

509   Muller, W. (1993). The Spiritual Advantages of a Painful Childhood. New York, NY: Simon and Schuster Touchstone.

510   Lamont, A. quoted in Meyers, R. Spiritual Defiance: Building a beloved community of resistance. New Haven, CT: Yale University Press, p. 43.

511   Wesselman, H. (2012). The Journey to the Sacred Garden: A Guide to Traveling in the Spiritual Realms. Carlsbad, CA: Hay House Publications.

512   Brother David Steindl-Rast. See http://www.gratefulness.org/brotherdavid/

513   Nhat Hanh, T. Retrieve from http://www.wisdomcommons.org/author/Thich%20Nhat%20Hanh.

514   John 3: 5.

515   The Mennonite Central Committee (Akron, PA) is the relief and service arm of the Mennonite Church. For information, see http://mcc.org/; Mennonite Disaster Service repairs and builds homes in the United States and in Canada in the wake of natural disasters such as Superstorm Sandy or Hurricane Katrina. For information, see http://www.mds.mennonite.net/home/.

516   Emma Sommers Richards was the first woman ordained in the Mennonite Church in 1973 and with her husband Joe served as co-pastor of Lombard Mennonite Church until 1991. For more information about Richards, see her obituary at http://www.yoderculpfuneralhome.com/memsol.cgi?user_id=1393755

      See also http://en.wikipedia.org/wiki/Emma_Richards_(minister).

517   Zimbardo, P. G. (2008). The Lucifer Effect: Understanding how good people turn evil. New York, NY: Random House Trade Paperbacks.

518   (A) Keen, S. (1991). Faces of the Enemy: Reflections of the Hostile Imagination. San Francisco, CA: Harper and Row; (B) Keen, S. (2006). Faces of the Enemy: Three Slide Lectures, San Rafael, CA: Sam Keen Productions.

519   Roof, N. (1994). The Impact of War on Humanitarian Service Providers: A Workbook on Secondary Traumatic Stress and Burnout: Symptoms, management, prevention. Cambridge, MA: Harvard Medical School of Psychology and Social Change.

520   Kelman, H. C. and Hamilton, V. L. (1989). Crimes of Obedience, New Haven, CT: Yale University Press.

521   (A) Grossman, D. (1995). On Killing: the psychological cost of learning to kill in war and society, Boston, MA: Little, Brown and Company; (B) Roof, N. (1994). The Impact of War on Humanitarian Service Providers: A Workbook on Secondary Traumatic Stress and Burnout: Symptoms, management, prevention. Cambridge, MA: Harvard Medical School of Psychology and Social Change; (C) Van Der Kolk, B. (2014). The Body Keeps the Score: Brain, Mind, and Body in the healing of Trauma. New York, NY: Viking Press.

522   An on-line dictionary defines vendettas in two ways: the first definition includes blood feuds and vengeance-seeking behavior; the second is defined as a prolonged bitter quarrel with a campaign against someone or some group. This is very strong language to describe a cradle member of the Mennonite community just for speaking out against sexual violence inside the Mennonite commons. As I write, I wonder who, in sociological reality, has the vendetta: me or those who claim I am a vendetta seeking person.

523   In a similar style, a professional colleague in my congregation suggested to my employer that I should be disciplined and fired as unfaithful – just before the final vote on my academic tenure was to be taken by the college's rank and tenure committee. Neither he nor senior college administrators talked with me about this recommendation. Warned about this letter at the time by a friendly mid-level college administrator, I later found a copy of it in my permanent personnel files as I exited the college in retirement. I strongly came to suspect that these kinds of professional push-backs against my work happened in situations where sexual violence and sexual misconduct were being covered over and hidden by abusive and abusing individuals and institutions. In this case, I could not prove or disprove this hypothesis but it does remain my hypothesis. In this particular situation, therefore, I believe that my accuser was an individual guilty of abusiveness. Otherwise, he would not have sought so aggressively to dislodge me from my place of employment in the Mennonite Church.

524   The Psalmist asks, how shall we sing God's song in a foreign land?

525   To hear Kathleen Battle and Jessye Norman sing this in concert, retrieve from https://www.youtube.com/watch?v=S6EOXT6_inw; To read the lyrics, retrieve from http://www.lyricsfreak.com/p/paul+robeson/scandalize+my+name_20172208.html

526   For more information, see http://peacewalktucson.org/.

527   For example, the blog of Roman Catholic theologian William Lindsey has a world-wide following of informed and passionate Christians who advocate for full-inclusion, justice, mercy and compassionate charity. See http://bilgrimage.blogspot.com/.

528   I am indebted to the author of this essay for his concept of weaponizing Jesus which I have adapted to weaponizing Christianity. See http://www.salon.com/2015/05/13/wingnuts_have_weaponized_jesus_how_the_religious_right_hijacked_christianity/.

529   See the May 12, 2015 report of the Pew Research Center. Retrieve from http://www.pewforum.org/2015/05/12/americas-changing-religious-landscape/. For analysis of this report, see: http://www.religionnews.com/2015/05/12/christians-lose-ground-nones-soar-new-portrait-u-s-religion/.

530   Glassman, B. (1998). Bearing Witness: A Zen Master's Lessons in Making Peace. New York, NY: Bell Tower Books. Glassman begins this book outside the gates of Auschwitz. A group of people have gathered to learn from Auschwitz what it can teach them – and us – about making peace. Jew, Christian, and Muslim as well as agnostics and atheists have gathered to mourn and to bear witness to the murdered dead.

531   Quoted in Toews, M. (2014). All My Puny Sorrows. San Francisco, CA; McSweeney's.

532   See Matthew 10: 16; one modern day translation (The Message Bible) is perhaps even clearer to twenty-first century urban minds. Stay alert. This is hazardous work I am assigning you. You're going to be like sheep running through a wolf pack. For a wide variety of additional translations, see http://www.biblestudytools.com/matthew/10-16-compare.html.

Nineteenth Letter
Personal Reflections

533   Zagano, P. (October 22, 2014). Bad News around the World. National Catholic Reporter Online. Retrieve from http://ncronline.org/blogs/just-catholic/baad-news-around-world

534   Mandela, N. (2002). Foreword (p. v.) Summary, World Report on Violence and Health, Geneva, Switzerland: World Health Organization.

535   Here is a sampling of the books I read – and sometimes re-read. Anderson, J. W. (2005). A Walk on the Beach: Tales of Wisdom from an Unconventional Woman. New York, NY: Broadway Books; Anderson, J. W. (2000). A Year by the Sea. New York, NY: Broadway Books; Bateson, M. C. (2001). Composing a Life. New York, NY: Grove Press; Bateson, M. C. (2011). Composing a Further Life: The Age of Active Wisdom. New York, NY: Viking; Bolen, J. S. (2004). Crossing to Avalon: A Woman's Midlife Quest for the Sacred Feminine. San Francisco, CA: Harper/San Francisco; Bolen, J. S. (2014). Goddesses in Older Women: Archetypes in Women over Fifty. New York, NY: Harper; Erikson, E. and J. M. (1998). The Life Cycle Completed. New York, NY: W. W. Norton; Erikson, E. and J. M. (1994). Vital Involvement in Old Age. New York, NY: W. W. Norton; Erikson, J. M. (1991). Wisdom and the Senses: the Way of Creativity; New York, NY: W. W. Norton; Hillman, J. (1997). The Soul's Code in Search of Character and Calling New York, NY: Grand Central Publishing; Hillman, J. (2000). The Force of Character and a Lasting Life. New York, NY: Ballantine Books.

536   Zagano, pp. Cit.

Twentieth Letter
To the Next Generation of Pacifist Theologians

537 This letter was first published as an Afterword in Weaver, J. D. and Zimmerman, Earl, (Eds.) (2014). John Howard Yoder: Radical Theologian. Eugene, OR: Wipf and Stock. Reprinted here by permission of Wipf and Stock.

538 See Stutzman, E. September 23, 2014. Discernment Group and Sexual Abuse in the Church. Retrieve from http://mennoniteusa.org/menno-snapshots/john-howard-yoder-discernment-group-2/

539 See, for example, Heggen, Sexual Abuse in Christian Homes and Churches, Scottdale, PA: Herald, 1993.

540 Krall, The Elephants in God's Living Room, vol. 3, p. 370. Retrieve from www.ruthkrall.com.

541 Oppenheimer, M. (October 11, 2013). A Theologian's Influence and Stained Past Live on. New York Times, p. A13. Retrieve from http://www.nytimes.com/2013/10/12/us/john-howard-yoders-dark-past-and-influence-lives-on-for-mennonites.html?_r=0

542 Yoder, J. H. Chapter 5: With and Beyond Girard. Manuscript.

543 Krall, Elephants in God's Living Room, vol. 3, p. 14.

544 Allen, B. (October 10, 2014). Evangelicals 'Worse' than Protestants on Sex Abuse, Christian Century online, p. 16. Retrieve from http://www.christian-century.org/article/2013-10/evangelicals-worse-catholics-sexual-abuse

545 Yoder, "Chapter 5: With and Beyond Girard," italics added. An adaptation of this quote can also be found in Yoder, "You Have It Coming," 183. However, in the published version, the editor, John C. Nugent, removed the three italicized words in Yoder's original text.

546 Heinzekehr, H. (August 9, 2013). Can Subordination Ever Be Revolutionary?" Reflections on John Howard Yoder. The Femonite Blog. Retrieve from http://www.femonite.com/2013/08/09/can-subordination-ever-be-revolutionary-reflections-on-john-howard-yoder/

547 Dr. Krall holds an MS in psychiatric-community mental health nursing and a doctorate in theology and personality. In addition, she taught peace studies at Goshen College for eighteen years.

548 Krall, Elephants in Gods Living Room, vol. p. 3, 20.

549 Ibid. pp. 10-11.

550 This information comes from an e-mail exchange with one of the women who experienced aggressive sexual behavior from Yoder.

551 Krehbiel, S. February 11, 2014. The Woody Allen Problem. Religious Dispatches. Retrieve from http://religiondispatches.org/the-woody-allen-problem-how-do-we-read-pacifist-theologian-and-sexual-abuser-john-howard-yoder/

552 See Zehr, Changing Lenses.

553 Krall, Elephants in God's Living Room, vol.3, 109.

554 Ibid., 150.

555 See chapter 2, "Sixteenth—Century Anabaptist Roots."

556 Krall, Elephants in God's Living Room, vol. 3, 61.

557 Graber, "What's to Be Done?" Barbara Graber is a retired professor of theater at Eastern Mennonite University and Associate Editor of Our Stories Untold (www.ourstoriesuntold.com).

558 This article first appeared in the Mennonite World Review (May 23, 2015). It is included here with the permission of the editor.

Afterword

559 Krall, Eighteenth Letter, p. 280

560 Schirch, e.g., Foreword and Twentieth Letter, p. 295

561 Schirch, Foreword, pp. 12-15

562 Krall, Introduction, p. 22

563 Krall, Nineteenth Letter, 292.

564 Ruth to Lisa, ibid., p. 291.

565 Krall, Introduction, p. 17

566 Schirch, Foreword, p. 16

567 Schirch, Twentieth Letter, p. 304.

568 Krall, Nineteenth Letter, p. 286

569 Krall, ibid., p. 288

570 Krall, Nineteenth Letter, p. 290.

571 Krall, ibid., pp. 289-290

572 Krall, ibid., p. 290)

573 Krall, ibid., p. 289.

574 Schirch, Twentieth Letter, 304.

575 Schirch, ibid., p. 305.

576 Krall, Nineteenth Letter, p. 287.

577 Krall, First Letter, p. 33.

578 Krall, Second Letter, p. 34.

579 Ibid.

580 Ibid.

581 Krall, Fifteenth Letter, p. 206.

582 Ibid. p. 210

583 Ferguson, Twelfth Letter, p.159.

584 Krall, Twelfth Letter, p. 159.

585 Krall, Seventeenth Letter, p. 252.

586   Ibid., pp. 233-253.

587   Ibid., p. 236.

588   Ibid., p. 252.

589   Krall, Seventh Letter, p. 100.

590   Ibid., p 95.

591   Ibid.

592   Ibid., p. 101.

593   Ibid., p. 103.

594   Krall, Eighth Letter, p. 124.

595   Schirch, Foreword.

596   Krall, Second Letter, p. 36.

597   Ibid., p. 36.

598   Krall, Ninth Letter, p. 138.

599   Krall, Eleventh Letter, p. 149.

600   Ibid, pp. 147-154.

601   Krall, Twelfth Letter, pp. 155-173.

602   Ibid., p. 172.

603   Ibid., p. 156

604   Schirch, Twentieth Letter, p. 302.

605   Krall, Eighteenth Letter, p. 274.

606   Krall, Thirteenth Letter, p. 186.

607   Krall, Sixteenth Letter, pp. 231-232.

608   Krall, Eighteenth Letter, p. 275.

609   Krall, Nineteenth Letter, p. 293.

610   Krall, Second Letter, p. 42.

611   Ibid., pp. 39f.

612   Ibid., pp. 40f.

613   Krall, Third Letter, pp. 41-42.

614   Ibid., p. 42.

615   Ibid., p. 44.

616   Krall, Fourth Letter, pp. 70-78.

617   Krall, Fifth Letter, pp. 79-88.

618   Krall. Seventh Letter, p. 91.

619   Ibid., p. 109)

620   Krall, Eighth Letter, p. 113.

621   Ibid., p. 125.

622   Krall, Ninth Letter, p. 132.

623   Krall, Tenth Letter, p. 144.

624   Krall, Eleventh Letter, p. 147.

625   Ibid., p. 151.

626   Ibid.

627   Krall, Fourteenth Letter, p. 188.

628   fIbid., p.191.

629   Krall, Eighteenth Letter, p. 270.

630   Krall, Fourteenth Letter, pp. 292-203.

631   Krall, Fifteenth Letter, p. 211; and see Seventeenth Letter, p. 234.

632   Krall, Nineteenth Letter, p. 292.

633   Krall, Eighteenth Letter, P. 280)

634   Krall, Introduction, p. 23.

635   Krall, Third Letter, p. 51.

636   Ibid., p. 51.

637   Ibid., p. 52.

638   Krall, ibid., p. 57.

639   Ibid., p. 59.

640   Ibid., p. 67.

641   Ibid., p. 64.

642   Ibid., p. 52.

643   Krall, Ninth Letter, p. 134.

644   Ibid., p. 137.

645   Krall, Nineteenth Letter, p. 286.

646   Krall, Sixteenth Letter, p. 226.

647   Ibid., p. 286.

648   Ibid., 287

CPSIA information can be obtained
at www.ICGtesting.com
Printed in the USA
FSOW03n0203040717
35838FS